Two week loan

Please return on or before the last
date stamped below.
Charges are made for late return.

IS 239/0799

INFORMATION SERVICES PO BOX 430, CARDIFF CF10 3XT

Beyond Welfare Capitalism

Beyond Welfare Capitalism

Issues, Actors and Forces in Societal Change

Ulf Himmelstrand
Göran Ahrne
Leif Lundberg
Lars Lundberg

Institute of Sociology,
Uppsala University, Sweden

HEINEMANN · LONDON

Heinemann Educational Books Ltd
22 Bedford Square, London WC1B 3HH

LONDON EDINBURGH MELBOURNE AUCKLAND
HONG KONG SINGAPORE KUALA LUMPUR NEW DELHI
IBADAN NAIROBI JOHANNESBURG
EXETER (NH) KINGSTON PORT OF SPAIN

British Library Cataloguing in Publication Data
Himmelstrand, Ulf
    Beyond welfare capitalism.
    1. Social history — 1970
    2. Communism and society
    I. Title

309.1   HN17.5

ISBN 0-435-82405-8

Typeset by The Castlefield Press of Northampton
in 10/12pt Journal Roman, and printed in Great Britain
by Biddles of Guildford Ltd.

Contents

Acknowledgements   x

Preface   xii

PART I: **CAPITALISM, DEMOCRACY and CLASS STRUGGLE:**
              A ROAD TO SOCIALISM? By Ulf Himmelstrand   1

Chapter 1.   *Capitalism, State and Socialism*   3
              Socialism — A Word Tainted or Diffuse   5
              The Capitalist State and Social Democracy   6
              The Art of Defining Socialism   10

Chapter 2.   *Socialism and Social Liberalism Compared*   17

Chapter 3.   *The Conditions and Likelihood of a Socialist*
              Transformation of Swedish Society   23

PART II: **SETTING THE STAGE FOR SOCIETAL CHANGE.**
              By Ulf Himmelstrand and Lars Lundberg   33

Chapter 4.   *Some Theoretical and Political Issues*   35
              Issue-Formation in Capitalist Societies: Human
              Predicaments and Political Culture   35
              On the Status of Marxian Notions of Contradiction
              in Marxism and Sociology   37
              Capitalism: Separation and Commodification of
              Labour and Capital   40

The Distinction between Basic and Extended
Contradictions   43
A Basic Definitional Contradiction: Capital
versus Labour   44
The Increasing Contradiction between Forces and
Relations of Production   46

Chapter 5.   *Empirical Indicators of the Social Character of*
Productive Forces, and the Private Character of
Social Relations of Production   51
Interdependence — Horizontal and Vertical   52
Social Vulnerability   56
Micro-aspects of Capitalist Relations of Production   58
Capitalist Property Relations   60
Capitalist Work Relations   64

Chapter 6.   *Changes in the Market Structures of Capitalism*   69
The Self-Destruction of Competitive Markets:
Monopolization and Trade Cycles   69
Summary   82

Chapter 7.   *Changes in the Incentive Patterns of Capitalism*   83

Chapter 8.   *An Introduction to the Extended Contradictions*
of Capitalism   89

Chapter 9.   *The Social Character and Private Production of*
Negative Externalities   93
Pollution in Capitalist and So-called
Socialist Countries   93
Unemployment and its Effects   98
Occupational Accidents and Diseases   104
Summary   106

Chapter 10. *The Interventionist State and the Contradictions*
of Capitalism   110
The Quandary of Mature Welfare Capitalism   126

Chapter 11. *Resolving the Contradictions of Capitalism:*
Options and Constraints   130

PART III: **ACTORS ON THE STAGE: LABOUR AND CAPITAL.** By Göran Ahrne, Leif Lundberg and Ulf Himmelstrand   139

Chapter 12. *Social Structures, Actors and Predicaments*   141
    The Notion of Predicament   145
    Struggling Actors and Dimensions of
    Class Struggle and Power   149
    An Outline of Part III   152

Chapter 13. *The Delimitation and Organization of the Working Class*   155
    Numerical Strength: Three Approaches to
    Defining the Working Class   155
    The Extended Working Class: Some Empirical Data   158
    The Organizational Strength of the Extended
    Working Class   162

Chapter 14. *The Social Consciousness of the Extended Working Class*   167
    Social Consciousness in an Affluent Society   168
    Working Class Identity   180
    Some Correlates of Working Class Consciousness   182
    A Summary   185

Chapter 15. *The Political Strength of the Extended Working Class*   187
    The Electoral Bases of Parties Competing for the
    Vote of the Extended Working Class   187
    The Responsiveness of Political Parties and
    Types of Political Mobilization   190
    Piecemeal and Structural Issues:
    The Performance of Political Parties, and Two
    Processes of Electoral Mobilization   196
    A Look into the Future   203
    The Future of Working Class Power: Vulnerabilities   205

Chapter 16. *The Strength of Capital: Systemic, Political and Ideological Aspects*   210
    On Definitions of Power   210
    Is the Systemic Power of Capitalists Decreasing?   211
    Political and Ideological Sources of Strength
    and Weakness of Capital   218

Chapter 17. *Subjective Aspects of Relationships between*
            Capital, Labour and State   245
            Labour Law and Management   226
            Assessment of the Actual Influence of Capital
            and Labour within Enterprises   229
            Assessments of the Ideal Distribution of
            Influence between Capital and Labour   234
            The Potentially Political Nature of Questions
            on Working-life and Business Enterprise   239

Chapter 18. *Images of the Future and Subjective Sources*
            of Weakness   245
            Capitalist Power — A Hollow Strength?   251

PART IV: ACTION ON THE STAGE. By Ulf Himmelstrand   255

Chapter 19. *Wage-earners' Funds*   257
            The Art of Street-crossing   258
            Wage-earners' Funds: Why and What?   261
            Comparisons between Profit-sharing and Savings
            Schemes in Sweden and some other Countries   268

Chapter 20. *Some Objections to Wage-earners' Funds*   273
            What Kind of Innovations do we Need?   285

Chapter 21. *Wage-earners' Funds and the Contradictions of*
            Mature Capitalism   289
            Wage-earners' Funds and the Contradiction
            between Capital and Labour   289
            Wage-earners' Funds and the Contradiction
            between Forces and Relations of Production   291
            Wage-earners' Funds and Market
            Self-destruction   295
            Wage-earners' Funds and the Destruction of
            Incentive Structures   297
            Wage-earners' Funds and Negative Externalities   299
            Wage-earners' Funds and the Contradictory Nature
            of the Capitalist Welfare State   299
            Summary and Conclusions   300

Chapter 22. *Beyond Wage-earners' Funds and Economic Democracy*   308

APPENDIX I: **Selected Tables**   316

APPENDIX II: **Methods of Sampling and Statistical Analysis**   319

Notes   324

References   346

Subject and Author Index   359

Acknowledgements

Without a sizable research grant from the Bank of Sweden Tercentenary Foundation this book would not have materialized. We are grateful to the Board of the Foundation, composed as it is largely of MPs from different political parties, for their trust in our ability to carry out serious scientific work, in spite of the fact that we made it quite explicit from the very beginning that our research would be carried out not from an elevated 'value-free' standpoint, but from the perspective of the labour movement.

A most essential part of the labour within our project has been carried out by our project secretary Lola Billås. She has allowed us to exploit her unfailing secretarial and administrative abilities far beyond what we and the Tercentenary Foundation were able to pay for her labour power.

Peter Ekegren and Mai Männik, two graduate students, not only rendered important bibliographic services to our project, but also made useful comments on earlier drafts of our manuscript. We are also grateful for the frank and uninhibited comments of dozens of doctoral students working on other projects, among whom we spent four years of this project, and for all the valuable help and assistance our project received from many of them.

No organization or other sponsor asked us to launch the work which resulted in this book. In that sense our work is purely autonomous and academic. On the other hand the very conception of the project, and its later revisions, were mainly prompted not by the conceptual frameworks and methodological predilections of the academic community, but by what we thought we saw happening in an increasingly deadlocked society struggling at great costs to overcome difficulties which seemed to be part and parcel of the very structure of our advanced welfare capitalism.

Many of our original hunches and later insights we obtained in meetings with trade unionists from LO and TCO, the two main Swedish trade union confederations, and with political party activists and intellectuals, as well as officials in various branches of public administration. In particular we would like to thank Rudolf Meidner, LO, Berndt Öhman, Secretary of the Government Commission on Wage-earners Funds, and Jan Lindhagen and Sven Ove Hansson, the Swedish Social Democratic Party, for reading and commenting on various parts of our manuscript. C.H. Hermansson, former Chairman of the Communist Party and a well-known commentator, took the trouble to write a long and useful commentary on Part II of our draft in spite of his involvement at that time in the overtures of the 1979 election campaign.

Thousands of employees and hundreds of company board members, employers as well as trade-union representatives, have answered our questionnaires, and helped us to assess some of the subjective aspects of current conflicts between labour and capital.

This is a book which uses Sweden as an illustration of a more general predicament, with many variations in other mature capitalist societies. Because of our main concern with the more general attributes of this predicament we have found it necessary to neglect more detailed historical, cultural and social background information on Sweden in this book. Therefore we are happy to acknowledge the existence of a number of other books and publications which may better serve the reader with a special interest in the Swedish case, for instance:

Samuelsson, K. (1968), *From Great Power to Welfare State*, London: Allen and Unwin.

Tomasson, F. (1970), *Sweden: Prototype of Modern Society*, New York: Random House. (A somewhat outdated and structural-functionalist account but rich in descriptive material).

Heclo, H. (1974), *Modern Social Politics in Britain and Sweden*, New Haven: Yale University Press.

Korpi, W. (1978), *The Working Class in Welfare Capitalism*, London: Routledge and Kegan Paul.

Wilson, D. (1979), *The Welfare State in Sweden*, London: Heinemann.

Finally our thanks go to Betty Low. Without her pedantic care about the grammar and intelligibility of our English, this book would certainly have been much less readable.

ULF HIMMELSTRAND
GÖRAN AHRNE
LEIF LUNDBERG
LARS LUNDBERG
JUNE 1980

Preface

A book such as this addresses itself to many readers — to colleagues in the same field of research, to students, to political activists of all ages, to opinion leaders and commentators, to trade unionists, to politicians and even to businessmen with a taste for new perspectives or for intelligence in the camp of a suspected foe.

But a book whose title refers to something 'beyond' the present situation naturally addresses itself particularly to those who will live most of their lives in that 'beyond', to the young who hopefully will contribute actively to shape that future rather than to allow blind and rolling master processes of unguided history to run their course.

Youth today is said to be indifferent to 'economic factors' and about the conduct of 'politics', 'business', 'social democracy' and 'trade union bosses'. This attitude would seem to imply a doubt about the possibility of attaining a more meaningful social and personal life by struggling for better material conditions. Spiritual, emotional, artistic or sensuous experiences are seen as autonomous domains which can be cultivated in the areas of private or group life without concern for economics, politics, trade unions and the like. A German sociologist, Ronald Ingelhardt (1971) has spoken about the 'silent revolution' of post-industrial attitudes among younger people who are more concerned with warm social relationships than with social relations of production, and more involved in the full development of their personalities or their personal tastes than in the development of labour, capital and state. Yet our book deals with everything which the so-called post-industrial attitude of youth is said to hold in contempt. If that is so, let us look more closely at what this contempt, real or imagined, is all about.

This is a book about the problems that a mature capitalist economy creates for itself, for the extended working class, and for the state. It is a book on how the demands of working class movements and the state interventions that emerge in response to those problems of capitalism, create further problems for capitalism, and thereby also in a vicious circle for labour and state. In the following, this circular process will be called capitalist problem-generation; a great deal of this book, and in particular Part II, will deal with processes of problem-generation within mature capitalism. Certainly not everything in the relationship between capital, labour and state has been vicious and circular. Caution, pragmatic wisdom and restraint have kept this circular problem-solving as well as problem-generating process within acceptable limits, thus maintaining the legitimacy of the system.

But in the 1970s the vicious elements of this circular process have become more and more difficult to contain within the framework of democratic and egalitarian values, and thus also within the limits of legitimacy (Wolfe, 1977). The hawks have taken command over the business community, and to some extent over political life, not only in Sweden (which is treated as an illustration of mature capitalism in this book), but even more so in some other capitalist countries. Whatever elements of collaboration that existed between capital and labour — and in social democratic Sweden they were rather extensive if not quite as comprehensive as some new leftists imagined — have been seriously disrupted. The state has increasingly overstepped the limits of so-called market forces in its interventions into the economy.

The political parties in the centre of the political spectrum in Sweden and elsewhere have failed to acknowledge the inconsistencies of the system itself, and thus limited themselves to sermons about the blessings of a 'mixed economy', and to limited and piecemeal palliative measures. However, the leaders of the business community and of the labour movement increasingly have addressed themselves to the systemic inconsistencies of our societies, and to the vicious circle of problem-generation which is now becoming more clearly visible. Capital and labour, being the main actors on the stage of our economic system, obviously see these systemic problems more clearly than others. But the systemic solutions voiced by their most vocal proponents would seem to be quite different.

The proponents of capital call for a return to a more consistent market economy, less political meddling in business, cut-backs in public welfare spending, and a more disciplined workforce. Labour on the other hand has called for entirely new actors on the economic scene. Let labour in; let labour with its broader and more socially relevant repertory of interests take significant control over capital to reduce and eventually remove the destructive and costly contradictions between labour and capital.

Who will win this struggle between system-reversal and system-transcendence — labour or capital? In this book we have tried to assess changes in the relative strength of these two actors on the stage. We have indicated that only the 'scratch test' of political and economic praxis will tell who is the stronger. For the final result of that test we must wait yet for some time, in Sweden and elsewhere, even though we can already now assess who maintains or increases, and who loses strength in Sweden.

Finally we discuss and evaluate some proposals emanating from the Swedish labour movement aiming at a successive change in our economic system towards what is called 'economic democracy'. Our evaluation of these proposals is not undertaken from an ideological standpoint. We are not primarily interested in whether or not these proposals approximate some idealized model of socialism. Our main question is rather whether or not these proposals address themselves in a comprehensive and reasonably realistic fashion to the vicious circle of capitalist problem-generation. This could be considered a scientific rather than an ideological evaluation, if we accept assessments of the *comprehensiveness* and *relevance* of given proposals in relation to the problems at hand as scientific criteria of evaluation. In laboratories and academic research centres this is by no means an accepted and self-evident criterion. The experimental method itself often implies that the researcher concentrates in a piecemeal fashion on the effects of one or a few variables while randomizing or matching other variables which are considered less relevant for the purpose of the experiment. In this setting comprehensiveness is a sin rather than a virtue. But to apply this research strategy of limited focus, justified as it may be in the laboratory, to scientific evaluations of political proposals outside the laboratory would, in our view, be a great mistake. In real life practical proposals cannot be implemented after randomizing or matching problematic aspects of reality which one would prefer not to touch.

This was an outline of our book. But does our message touch the hearts of our readers? Does it ignite the fire of curiosity and involvement in searching for even better knowledge about our predicament? Does it inspire a search for ways to break out of the contradictions and constraints which lock us into a quandary? Can an account of 'economic factors' and the need for 'new social relationships of production' appeal to those who are concerned about spiritual values, warmer social relationships, the full development of human personalities and personal tastes, and to those who have learnt to feel nothing but contempt for bureaucracy and 'haggling politicians', 'business mentality' and 'trade union bosses'?

But why, we may ask, is it at all important to impress young readers with the urgency of the problems of contemporary capitalism and the unfulfilled promises of democratic socialism 'beyond welfare capitalism'? Are not the values of youthful 'counter-culture' and 'alternative life-styles' a sufficient basis for building a more humane future less be-laboured by crass economic interests and alienated production and consumption? Or if these values are insufficient, as they may be, why be concerned? Is not pluralism of values a healthy thing?

For the last few years I have been supervising a doctoral student involved in a study of so-called counter-culture or alternative life-styles (Jonsson, 1978). In the course of her research I have come to know and respect the young members of a farmers' commune included in her project. Some of them have a very explicit philosophy. They wish to retrace the history of material production back to the point in history where it all went wrong, where social relations of production started to become fetters upon the development of productive forces, to quote Karl Marx. They are not dogmatically against technological develop-ment, but believe that technology should develop in accordance not only with human needs in a limited sense, but also with long-term interests of human development and survival rather than in the short-term interests of profit and consumerism. Technology should never be allowed to develop in such a manner that warm and humane social relationships are sacrificed. Others in this commune rather believe that they are building a sanctuary of survival not only for themselves and their children in a world of self-destruction but also a model for human survival.

You may share these beliefs or not. But they are taken seriously by those involved in this commune, and they should be taken seriously by us. These beliefs shape their daily lives, and their daily lives provide experiences which further articulate these beliefs. They express their philosophy by participating in demonstrations against the use of poisonous defoliants, the development of nuclear power, the destruc-tion of old but renewable urban living quarters, etc.

I have provided this thumb-nail sketch of communes practising alternative life-styles because I want to make perfectly clear that the concern I have expressed for the 'attitudes of youth', real or alleged, do not relate to those who try to practise alternative life-styles in the manner briefly indicated above. My concern is rather with *privatized* opinions expressing contempt of modern technology, bureaucracy, politics in a diffuse and generalized manner outside such communes, and without any foundation in their praxis. In this outside world such a distrust and contempt for dominant aspects of contemporary society, particularly in their more fashionable and superficial forms, serves only one function, in my opinion, namely to pacify the only forces which can effectively challenge contemporary society at large, namely broad-based collective forces of change operating within the system, and experiencing the contradictions of the system in their daily working lives. Anti-system attitudes in their privatized and fashionable forms serve only to weaken the forces which possibly may be able to oppose and change the direction of our contemporary history at the cross-road where we find ourselves.

In the 1979 election campaign in Sweden not only bourgeois news-papers but also 'neutral' television gave a lot of coverage to interviews with young voters who expressed their disenchantment with politics and politicians. This cultivation of contempt was paralleled by the reiteration in newspaper articles of some of the main theses of a report from the so-called Trilateral Commission, financed by David Rockefeller, pointing out the dangers of too much politics and the 'excesses of political democracy' (see below, p. 113). In Germany *Bild-Zeitung,* the well-known Springer magazine, waged the same kind of campaign some time ago.

Young people often tend to be radical. If their disenchantment with politics and contemporary society is effectively reinforced, they are unlikely to vote, and the conservative forces are strengthened, relatively speaking. Conservative youth and elders vote regardless of their contempt for politics, because their politics is to get rid of politics, and to give free enterprise a free ride to wealth.

The privatized expressions of 'counter-culture', and capitalist 'free enterprise' in holy pluralist matrimony! In strict scientific terms this is still only a hypothesis. But even hypotheses can generate concern. This book is partly an expression of that concern, and an attempt to docu-ment through empirical research and theoretical analysis how our so-called welfare capitalism generates problems which have called for solutions that often further aggravate the situation. Medication some-times has effects as serious as the illness treated. Whereas our concern and fears about the effects of privatized counter-cultural values are based on unconfirmed hypotheses, our diagnosis of the contradictions of welfare capitalism will certainly not remain unsubstantiated.

Those of us who do not have the right convictions or experiences to join counter-cultural communes, but make our existence as best we can in this world rather than theirs, cannot do them a better service than to explore what this world is like, and to struggle to make it better

on the basis of the knowledge we acquire. It is not enough to understand the world, we must also change it. But first we must understand
it a little better than we do. Contempt and disenchantment should not
be allowed to block curiosity and research on what is held in contempt.

The Marxian theoretical tradition is basic to our attempts to understand
what mature capitalism is about and to our efforts to come to terms
with the question what we can expect beyond welfare capitalism.
'Orthodox' Marxists — and there are many orthodoxies around the
world — may find that we are lacking in faithfulness to the old master.
This is unavoidable if we wish to use Marx mainly as a theoretical guide
to empirical research. Some of the finer distinctions in Marxian theory
must be neglected in the search for empirical data; and where Marx is
vague and inconclusive, we must take responsibility for more precise
interpretations which make Marxian concepts amenable to empirical
research.

On the other hand many Western sociologists who have remained
largely uninfluenced by the Marxian tradition could quite justifiably
maintain that we are too orthodox in our Marxian approach. Why not
pay more attention to non-Marxian innovations in modern sociological
theory, and what about the contributions of the anti-Marxist *nouveaux
philosophes* in France? Why should we stick so rigidly to the theoretical
framework of historical materialism when new fertile ideas abound
which sometimes have taken advantage of the Marxist renaissance but
understood its limitations, and dare to go beyond it?

To us the answer is simple. No one can go *beyond* the *limitations* of
a given theoretical tradition unless some of us first have been allowed to
make a full use of the perspectives, conceptions and methods suggested
by that tradition — up to its limits. New 'innovative' and 'fertile' ideas
in the social sciences are bound to become arbitrary and inspirational
unless they have a foundation in a systematic analysis based on penetrating and reasonably complete studies undertaken within social
science frameworks already available. The Marxian theoretical tradition — in spite of its so-called renaissance — has not yet had a chance
to unfold its full potential in a scholarly fashion, and on an empirical
basis, with reference to contemporary societies.

Our 'heresies' will certainly become obvious to the Marxist reader
when he reads this book. Our 'orthodoxy' is very simply this. We think
that there is an unfinished task of Marxist scholarship and empirical
study, and we wish to contribute to it as far as we can. We are doing
this without in any way concealing that some other 'innovative' and

'fertile' ideas — even some of those stemming from the *nouveaux philosophes* — seem to us not only thought-provoking but positively exciting. However, such ideas stand a better chance of surviving and becoming a part of a living intellectual heritage if they are articulated on safer ground than that provided by singular but disconnected insights, or by thinkers who cannot even distinguish between Marxian theory and the ideological praxis of Eastern European countries.

Why then Marxism? In the Marxist tradition there are questions asked which do not appear in any other social science tradition; and most of these questions are asked from a perspective — the working class perspective — which until recently has been virtually non-existent in the predominant strain of academic sociology in the West. The capitalist perspective has dominated economics, and the managerial, administrative or integrationist perspectives have dominated sociology.

But does the working class perspective necessarily call for a Marxian or Marxist theory rather than something else? Why not choose non-Marxist theories of conflict, which also recognize class conflict but in a more sophisticated and intellectually satisfying fashion than does the rugged and primitive notion of struggle between classes which is so pervasive in Marxian writings?

Hopefully this book will answer these questions.

Ulf Himmelstrand
Cavtat, 6 October 1979

Postscript: For various reasons a rather long time elapsed between the writing of this book, the reading of the page proofs in July 1980, and the final printing in June 1981. We are grateful to Heinemann for the opportunity to add a postscript on some recent events at the end of chapter 19 just before the book was printed.

PART I

Capitalism, Democracy and Class Struggle: A Road to Socialism?

by Ulf Himmelstrand

1 Capitalism, State and Socialism

Without exception those countries that today call themselves socialist have become so through a process of violent conflict, internal or external, or both. The aftermath of war made it possible not only for the Soviet Union to emerge, but also brought about a 'socialist transformation' of Eastern Europe after the Second World War. Communist China and Vietnam emerged in wars against external and internal forces. This seems to be the only common background characteristic of these countries rather than any particular level of development of the productive forces within a 'mature' capitalist system, as understood by Marx in his conception of historical materialism. No highly industrialized society in the West exhibits a social and economic order which could be called socialist.

Two alternative conclusions can be drawn on the basis of these observations. First a socialist transformation of modern capitalist societies is neither inevitable nor particularly likely. Capitalism provokes and stimulates socialist forces of change mainly in 'peripheral' (from the Western point of view) and underdeveloped territories. Second the seeds of socialism certainly grow in the womb of modern capitalist societies; but in the recent past few of these societies have been experiencing structural contradictions so intense and unchecked that they have been ripe for a profound socialist transformation of their social and economic orders. Sooner or later they will become ripe for socialism, however.[1]

The first type of conclusion is not only politically uninspiring to a true socialist but also less challenging from the point of view of sociological analysis. As a sociologist I will therefore explore the second standpoint, and proceed to discuss the meaning, shape and likelihood of a socialist transformation in a highly developed capitalist society. Such a discussion, in the ideal case, should be pursued with a comparative approach, and with full information on relevant historical and contemporary aspects of the countries involved in the comparison.

But what is ideal in principle is often not feasible in practice due to difficulties in collecting or assembling relevant and comparable historical and contemporary data from many countries. These difficulties were demonstrated in Harold Wilensky's (1975) pioneering but much criticized effort to compare the welfare effects of various political regimes in a great number of countries.[2] Cross-national statistical studies such as Wilensky's tend to become particularly shallow in their coverage of dynamic or dialectical processes of a historical nature. Therefore, in our attempt to inquire into processes which may contribute to make capitalist societies 'ripe for socialism' I find virtue in necessity; theoretically and methodologically it would seem better first to concentrate on studying in some depth the conditions of *one* country rather than scattering our resources on a rather shallow cross-national analysis. However, cross-national comparisons will also be utilized where they are feasible and contribute to our analysis.

Marx and Engels, in their pioneering effort at developing a historical theory of capitalism, to a considerable extent utilized their observations from one country — England — the first nation in the world to undergo extensive industrialization.

Sweden, being one of the most advanced capitalist countries of today, with an experience of forty-four years of social democratic labour rule, now succeeded by a few years of bourgeois government, would seem to be particularly suited for theoretically and empirically exploring whether social democracy is just another way of refining welfare capitalism, or actually paves the road to socialism. The significance of this question concerning the historical role of labour reformism is certainly not restricted to Sweden alone. Social democratic parties with somewhat different outlooks are found in government, or in significant opposition, not only in the Nordic countries but also in Austria, the Federal Republic of Germany, United Kingdom and France. With the advent of so-called Eurocommunism rejecting the notions of proletarian revolution and dictatorship — in Italy, France and Spain — a new branch of labour reformism has emerged. In the USA social democratic forces are much weaker, but are beginning to form an important caucus within the Democratic Party.[3] The problems of labour reformism in either refining welfare capitalism or paving the road to socialism would thus seem to be of a virtually universal importance in the more or less advanced capitalist societies of today. This is a main rationale for writing this book. Another rationale is our conviction that theoretical and empirical research has more to contribute in resolving these problems than abstruse and non-empirical theorizing, or sheer ideologizing about the nature of late capitalism and the meaning of socialism. Therefore, this book should not be considered simply as a study of some challenging aspects of Swedish welfare capitalism. It is mainly intended as a contribution to the debate and research about labour reformism today and tomorrow.

In the USA Sweden is often believed to be a socialist country.[4] The Social Democratic Party which until 1976 had ruled Sweden for forty-four years does indeed nurture some socialist ideas as far as future developments of Sweden are concerned; but so far social democrats have been constrained to administer our capitalist economy. This means 94 per cent of production in the manufacturing industry is privately owned (Företagen, 1974). Private gross investments (housing excluded) is 57 per cent, and private machine investments 78 per cent. Private enterprise employs about 44 per cent of all gainfully employed (Företagen, 1975). Swedish exports, which constitute about 25 per cent of GNP and which therefore must be considered a crucial element for the welfare of the country, derive almost completely from private enterprise.

Sweden is certainly not a very typical capitalist country – no other capitalist country has had a labour party rule for forty-four years – but it is precisely this fact that makes Sweden a crucial case in exploring the theme 'beyond welfare capitalism', just as England was a crucial case in studying the historical processes beyond feudalism and early capitalism. After necessary amendments and qualifications our 'case study' of Sweden at the cross-road of welfare capitalism and democratic socialism should be of some interest in the international debate about the present predicament and future prospects of a democratic reformist socialism, and in suggesting research methods relevant for the study of these problems – methods which hopefully will be applied in more full-fledged cross-national studies in the future.[5]

Socialism – A Word Tainted or Diffuse

To discuss the prospects of socialism without beginning from a reasonably precise definition of socialism could be quite misleading. The fact that there are alternative conceptions of socialism does not make the need for a definition less urgent.

A central and controversial concept in explicating the notion of socialism relates to the function of the *state*. In Swedish political lore socialism is often believed to imply a nationalization of industry, that is a take-over of industry by the state. The Swedish word for this is *socialisering* – socialization.[6]

From this terminological vantage point Swedish social democracy has been criticized both from the left and the right. The left have criticized social democracy for not being socialist since, after more than forty years in government, they have failed to nationalize (socialize) any significant portion of Swedish industry. The right, on the other hand, is picking ceaselessly on every suggested piecemeal nationalization and speaks, in such contexts, about the impending threat of socialism, pointing a warning finger to the East. The Soviet system is used as an evil enigma, and a true representation of modern socialism (Jolin, 1974).

It is probably true to say that broad segments of the Swedish public, including parts of the working class, have been educated about the meaning of socialism not by the social democrats but by conservatives and liberals through their majority control of the mass media. The social democratic leadership, knowing fully well that socialism has become a bad word, not the least among strategically important voters in the middle strata, have thus been reluctant to use this word in their election campaigns. Instead of applying a head-on offensive to re-educate these strategically important segments of the electorate about the meaning of socialism in Sweden, as distinct from Eastern Europe, the social democratic leadership has taken a rather defensive approach in rebutting conservative allegations of creeping socialism.[7]

Fortunately, the renaissance of Marxian and Marxist thought during the past ten years provides us with sharper conceptual tools with which to cut into the confusing verbiage of anti-socialist as well as defensive social democratic rhetoric. I am thinking particularly of the present Marxist discussion concerning the capitalist state, and of the state under socialism. Social scientists as well as politicians have something to learn from this discussion. I expect this discussion to help in this chapter to clarify further the meaning of socialism, as a prelude to our inquiry concerning the likelihood of a socialist transformation of Swedish society.

The Capitalist State and Social Democracy

It seems useful here to distinguish a *pluralist* liberal approach, and two Marxist approaches to the capitalist state, an *instrumentalist* and a *structuralist* one. (Esping-Andersen, Friedland and Wright, 1976, pp. 186f). In the *pluralist* perspective the state is seen as a neutral aggregating mechanism allocated a legitimate monopoly of coercive power, and responding to the competing demands and interests of groups acting on a political market of electoral and non-electoral political action. Just as on any other market some groups win the contest, at least temporarily. They are thus able to make more effective use of the state for their purposes, but the principle of neutrality of the state is still maintained. Competing groups are never completely excluded from access to the state as long as they attract a sufficient number of voters; and by increasing their number they can themselves acquire increasing control of the state machinery. They maintain a foothold in the state in some proportion to their electoral strength.

A main difference between the pluralist model and the other two approaches is the main importance pluralists attach to the political decision-making process while they neglect the decisions, the growth processes and the structural constraints imposed on society as a whole by the economy at large. Pluralists rather emphasize the 'monopoly of coercive power' of the state, and its central position as an aggregating mechanism. The state is seen as the main controlling agent in society, and this even when the state decides to refrain from certain decisions to allow the 'invisible hand' of the market to regulate economic and social development.

The pluralist model of the state is basically a processing model. It must be supplemented by a model of the structural cleavages in society which produce the issues that are processed. To my mind Stein Rokkan has accomplished the most elaborate and satisfactory attempt to view societal issue production and political processing within a pluralist perspective. Still this attempt falls short of a number of scientific requirements (Lipset and Rokkan (eds.), 1967 Chapter 1 and Rokkan, 1970).

Clearly, it does not offer any full-fledged theoretical analysis of the *generation* of structural cleavages, and their translation into political issues. It mainly provides a useful taxonomic framework and a descriptive historical account of the relationships involved. This in its turn made it difficult for Stein Rokkan to discover some important hidden implications of the issues recorded in his historical panorama.

To *describe* in historical retrospect the changes in the content of politics as reflecting changes in 'cleavage structures' is one thing; to explain the dialectics, or dynamics, of present and prospective changes is another matter. Historically given categories of political action must certainly be understood in such a prospective approach, but a grasp of the unfolding and construction of new categories of action is equally necessary. In this the approach of Rokkan, and other less sophisticated pluralist political scientists, is insufficient.

The *instrumentalist* approach (for instance Miliband, 1969) attaches much less importance to the state than to the economy. The main locus of power in capitalist society is the capitalist class which uses the state as an instrument to further its purposes and to reproduce itself. The determining factor is the class input and control of policy formation effected through bourgeois or 'embourgeoisied' political parties, and through recruitment of bourgeois elements into all crucial segments of state administration. If the 'class input' is changed through class struggle, the capitalist state can be transformed into a socialist state; it is just a matter of take-over. The state is thus maintained; but by emancipating it from, and in the process destroying monopoly capital, and replacing it by a collective societal ownership of the means of production, a socialist society is created. Among Scandinavian Marxists this is called the STAMOCAP approach, from 'state' and 'monopoly capital' (Björkman and Fleming, 1974).

Marxist instrumentalists do differ in their views of the needed suddenness of this take-over. But even though some instrumentalists seem to accept a somewhat more gradual development toward socialism, all these instrumentalists agree that socialism requires a complete destruction of the capitalist system and the capitalist class. The more revolutionary instrumentalists assert that the 'shell' of capitalism requires a sudden and total destruction.

The *structuralist* Marxist approach does not emphasize the political role of class input into state policy-making as much as the *systemic* requirements inherent in the *structure* of capitalism. There are certain things which a capitalist economy, and a capitalist class, cannot by themselves carry out, and which they must leave to the state. Infrastructural investments, social welfare policies, the management of business cycles and negative externalities within a capitalist system are essential for the social existence of capital, but must be left to an interventionist state because capital cannot itself accomplish these tasks. This is the essence of the analysis of *economic* structuralists such as Altvater (1973), and to some extent Mandel (1975). Among Scandinavian Marxists this is called the STINCAP approach, from 'state intervention' and 'capitalism' (Björkman and Fleming, 1974).

Political structuralists such as Althusser (1971) and Poulantzas (1973) rather emphasize the incapacity of the bourgeoisie of achieving class unity in the same fashion as the working class, as a result of the structure of capitalist competition. State power is thus needed to organize the bourgeoisie and to accomplish the domination needed to reproduce capitalism.

In both types of structuralism, the economic and the political, the state is thus 'residually defined by the functions capital units cannot perform' (Esping-Andersen et al., 1976, p. 189). The state is not simply an instrument of the capitalist class but a partly autonomous machinery operating under the systemic requirements and structural constraints of the capitalist order. No strings are needed to make the capitalist state carry out this task. Even a social democratic government voted to power by the working class under capitalism is bound to act to maintain the system and reproduce capitalism, according to this view.

Among the systemic requirements and structural constraints operating on such a social democratic government, we also notice the pressure to win a majority again in the next election, and the risks of losing votes if the existing capitalist order is not effectively managed. Only when the contradictions of capitalism become very clearly visible to all significant voters, can we expect any sizeable portion of the electorate to take the leap, and the risks of temporary economic set-backs, to support a party explicitly stating that they are on the way to abolish the capitalist system.

Structuralists unlike instrumentalists do not generally have a clear-cut notion about the course of a transformation of capitalism into socialism. This is partly because structuralists, unlike some instrumentalists, have seen their task as mainly analytic and intellectual rather than political. The views of at least some instrumentalists have been an integral part of a party political strategy as much or more than an intellectual effort to understand the operation of the capitalist state (Björkman and Fleming, 1974, pp. 5f and 19f). It is therefore difficult to say whether structuralists have the same or a different conception of socialism as most instrumentalists. Structuralism leaves the question open. But as we will see later on structuralism at least lends itself to analytic deductions pointing toward the possibility of more decentralized, non-etatist types of socialism. Such a conception is more difficult to deduce from instrumentalist premises.

Instrumentalism and structuralism can thus be compared only as intellectual endeavours, not as political formulas because structuralism has no explicitly stated political formula to offer. Such a comparison was made by Esping-Andersen et al. (1976, p. 109f):

> Thus, an overemphasis on 'structure' or 'systemic logic' will tend to view class originated inputs and demands as 'passive' responses to stimuli born out of the structure. On the other hand, the class instrumentalist perspective will tend to be somewhat situational and voluntaristic since it does not relate present class action to the historically determined constraints of the system. The instrumentalist view of the state stresses the *political input* into the state and the importance of the unequal class distribution of

power. The structuralist view of the state stresses the *political output* of state activity by which capitalist domination is reproduced and the cohesion of the social formation assured.

Neither approach contains a theory of the mechanisms that link political inputs and systemic constraints to the outputs of state activity. . . .

A fourth perspective is possible which focuses on state structure as an object of class struggle. The capitalist class attempts to create state structures which channel working class political activity in ways that do not threaten capitalist political dominance and object interests. Working class challenge makes the success of such attempts problematic. A political class struggle perspective on the state tries to locate the state within the dialectical relationship between class dominance and systemic constraints.

For space reasons I cannot here summarize the highly innovative attempt made by Esping-Andersen et al. to integrate the instrumentalist and structuralist approaches within the framework of a class struggle approach which locates the state, in a dialectical manner, between the class struggle for control of state policy, and the effects not only of state policy but also of state structure on class struggle. They take a highly historical approach with due consideration both to structural universals and to the historical specificities of concrete cases — among them the case of Sweden (Esping-Andersen, p. 210ff.). This case is discussed very briefly, and in a manner which is somewhat outdated because of changes which have taken place within Swedish social democracy, and the Swedish trade union movement, in recent years. But as far as it goes their analysis is highly adequate. In concluding this section on the meaning of socialism I am taking an approach coming rather close to their 'fourth perspective', I believe. The state is seen partly as an object and arena of political class struggle, and not only as an instrument of class interest.[8]

The Art of Defining Socialism

After our analytic exposition of various ways of viewing the capitalist state, let us finally try ourselves in the art of definition. Socialism, I claim, is not the same as the nationalization of industry. Socialism can be defined in terms of the exclusive control which workers, as members of the working class, exert over the means and surplus of production.

To make such a preliminary definition more precise all the important terms in the definition — 'workers', 'members of the working class', 'exert control', 'exclusive control', and 'means and surplus of production' — must be made more precise first. And this in such a manner that probing questions are not left unanswered.

Are white collar employees 'workers' and 'members of the working class'? Does 'exclusive control' of workers mean that non-working consumers such as numerous pensioners, invalids and unemployed should have no influence over production? How in practice should control be 'exerted'? Through public ownership and the control of representative political bodies, or through workers self-management locally? Should science and technology be included among the 'means of production'?

In the process of such definitional explication it is of course possible to reintroduce the state either as a tool through which the 'workers' after a socialist transformation 'exert control' over the means of production, or alternatively only as a tool for taking over such control in an initial phase whereafter the state is allowed to 'wither away'.

Increasingly I am becoming dissatisfied with such definitional exercises. They often become very academic — and not only when undertaken in academic settings. Usually some classic formula is adopted as a definitional paradigm within which the kind of probing questions mentioned above are answered in a manner no less idealistic than that characteristic of bourgeois ideologists, that is with no or little reference to the concrete problems faced in a concrete historical situation.[9] Most of the definitions thus emerging tend to be phrased, more or less dogmatically, in terms of a *problem-solution* labelled socialism without explicitly taking into account the *nature of the problem* to be solved, in its more or less unique historical and national setting. But to my mind no profound analysis of the meaning of socialism can be undertaken without spelling out both the structural universals and the historical specificities of the problems to which socialism can be seen as a solution in the context of a particular society or set of societies. Therefore a historical and theoretical exploration of the *problems* of modern capitalism, as manifested in particular societies, should precede any definitional explication of the concept and reality of modern socialism.

Societal problems can be specified in two different ways. One way is to list concrete complaints and demands in an atomistic manner. From such a catalogue of problems one can derive a list of specific policies and decisions required to tackle these problems. But in actual policy-making such piecemeal decisions must be made with due consideration for available resources and for the balance between different piecemeal decisions in terms of interrelated effects, and in terms of the allocation of resources required. Such a balance sheet of resources, decisions and effects require some kind of understanding of society, at least as an aggregate. This piecemeal conception of societal problems, with or without attempts to assess aggregate effects, is the most common approach of politicians and political ideologies in liberal democracies under conditions of capitalism.

Another way of specifying societal problems is to take your point of departure in a holistic conception of society and its contradictions, and from there proceed to derive and identify the concrete problems emerging as a result of these contradictions. This manner of proceeding comes closer to a socialist conception of society and societal change.[10]

The basic problem of contemporary capitalism is the fact that its industrial forces of production become *increasingly societal*, while the decision-making machinery implied by capitalist relations of production exclude consistent and effective considerations of the wide-ranging societal aspects of production.

What is then implied by expressions such as 'the increasingly societal character of productive forces'? Here it is not sufficient to *read* Marx; his concepts must be explicated and expanded to take account of the complexities of the current situation of mature capitalism. Industry depends increasingly on society and state for infrastructural, productive, regulative and planning *inputs*, while managing its own internal investments in a manner conditioned by narrow and often short-term speculative and often socially improductive anticipations, and single-unit profitability. *Outcomes* of industry such as variations in productivity and related employment levels, and in the production of so-called negative externalities (environmental effects both inside and outside industry) also increasingly imply wide-ranging consequences for society as a whole. The resource-accumulating, decision-making and resource-allocating processes within capitalism do not match this increasingly societal character of productive forces. This is the basic problem of modern capitalism.[11]

Socialism should be defined in terms of these structural problems and the solutions needed. Such a definition, formulated in the first instance on a rather high level of deductive abstraction, could run like this:

> Socialism implies a remodelling of the resource accumulation, decision-making and resource allocating processes implied by capitalist relations of production to make them compatible with the increasingly societal character of the productive forces in advanced, highly industrialized nations.

However, it might be argued that this kind of definition is too broad because it may allow for the inclusion of a profoundly reformed 'social capitalism' under the label of socialism. On definitional grounds I do not find this argument very convincing. Capitalism cannot possibly be reformed to fulfil the requirements of our abstract definition of socialism; it would then no longer be capitalism as we know it. But in order to make our definition even more restrictive, we could add a further requirement. As Maurice Godelier has pointed out (see note 11) the term 'contradiction' in Marx's *Capital* has two meanings – one referring to the *increasing* contradiction between two structures – the forces and relations of production – as capitalism develops and matures, and another notion of contradiction which *constitutes* capitalism at any level of development, namely the contradiction between capital and labour. We could thus amplify our definition of socialism by making explicit the requirement that *changes in the social relations of production must be brought to a point where the contradiction between capital and labour is eliminated.*

Any knowledgeable reader will recognize that the abstract definition of socialism just given flows directly from the basic tenets of Marxian historical materialism. It is not a new or remarkably original definition. What is remarkable, however, is that socialism rarely is defined in this deductive manner from the premises of capitalist problem-generation, but rather in terms of more or less idealistically or dogmatically formulated problem solutions.

The abstract definition suggested is phrased in terms of the structural universals of contemporary capitalism. To make it workable in specific historical settings, it must be further elaborated in terms of the historical specificities of each case. What is meant concretely with the expression 'compatibility with the increasingly societal character of the productive forces' should be spelt out in detail with reference to *the specific ways in which productive forces are becoming increasingly societal in a given society.*

For instance, we may find that in a particular society a great deal of industry is concentrated not in large and industrially diversified urban agglomerations, but dispersed in smaller communities each dominated by one particular industry. To a considerable extent this is the case in Sweden. If such an industry is mismanaged, or laid down for reasons of greater profitability of other branches of the same company elsewhere, then the social costs and consequences are highly concentrated on the particular community dominated by that industry. Because of the dominant position of one industry in that community, unemployed workers settled in their own homes could not easily find alternative jobs on the spot. The societal consequences implied by this pattern of productive forces thus, in the first instance, are highly localized. In such a case a transformation of the relations of production to match this particular societal character of the productive forces would seem to require a great deal of local workers' self-management, and also an involvement of local political decision-making bodies.

If large diversified industrial settings were dominant and labour mobility rather extensive local workers' self-management might still be useful for some purposes. But other changes in production relations might be seen as even more important.

To take another example, the societal consequences of the capitalist mode of production in a nation like the USA may imply the generation of *urban* problems which are even more destructive of human dignity than industrial problems. The crisis of the City of New York is a case in point. New York industries may find conditions more profitable, for instance, in neighbouring New Jersey, while utilizing many of the facilities of New York. Inter-state or inter-city capitalist competition thus creates unemployment, a weakening tax base and a fiscal crisis in New York. Changes in social relations of production required under such circumstances may primarily involve profound changes in inter-city, inter-state and federal relationships (cf. the discussion in Esping-Andersen et al., 1976, pp. 194ff), while such changes may be less urgent in a small country such as Sweden where legislation already to a considerable extent addresses itself to such problems.

Consider a third example. If, in a country with a multilingual federal structure, the state was weak, fragmented and corrupted by, say, the dominant language group, or perhaps becomes strong and repressive to counteract divisive tendencies among different linguistic regions, then it would be very difficult to match the increasingly societal character of productive forces with state ownership, and state management of industry even if the economy otherwise would seem to require a lot of state regulation. Perhaps Yugoslavia could be analysed in such terms.

Examples are numerous. My point is this: apart from the consensus which is attainable among socialists, or students of socialism, in terms of the highly abstract kind of definition of socialism suggested above, we cannot expect consensus with regard to concrete forms of socialism, as they develop or are being practised in different societies.

Concrete definitions of the kind of socialism adequate to a particular country must be explicated in terms of the *specific* ways in which productive forces are becoming more societal in that country, but also in terms of the *specific* changes of productive relations and super-structure which are historically feasible, and reasonably free of a historical heritage of corruption, graft and mismanagement.

If our knowledge is incomplete with regard to these specific ways of development of forces and relations of production, the class structure and the superstructure of a given country, one obvious consequence follows from our argument. The type of socialism adequate to that country *cannot be formulated without a great deal of empirical research into the historical specificities of the forces and relations of production, the class structure and the superstructure* of that country.

This does not imply, however, an elitist role for social scientists in prescribing the content and direction of socialist praxis. But debates and policy formation in unions, socialist parties and organizations might profit from using the findings of social scientists on the historical specificities of capitalism and state in the countries concerned.

In a sense it would therefore be premature to suggest any more concrete design for the coming of socialism in a capitalist country until (i) significant research findings on the historical specificities of capitalism and state in that country have been presented, and (ii) until such findings have been debated within the labour movement of that country. This is the line we will follow. A sketch of what Swedish socialism could be like will hopefully emerge toward the end of this book, once we have presented our research findings, and some of the proposals presently being debated in the Swedish labour movement. Already now, however, we can certainly say that the image of Swedish socialism which is emerging is very different from Eastern European state socialism. If any references are made at all to foreign models of socialism in the internal debate of the Swedish labour movement, it is rather the Yugo-slav system of workers' self-management which attracts attention. But the Swedish preference for such a system springs from historical ex-periences and preconditions very different from those of Yugoslavia.

Yugoslavian preferences for decentralized, anti-etatist workers' self-management seem to have sprung from a reaction against Soviet influence, and the repressive Stalinist state, and from the experience of local mobilization, first against the Nazi invaders of the Second World War, and then against economic underdevelopment.[12] Sweden, on the other hand, has a rather long and relatively positive experience of political democracy and of a strong reformist labour movement reaping the benefits of capitalist economic growth; but it has also experienced a more problematical trend toward a centralization of capitalist wealth, and the growth of a redistributive and palliative welfare state increasingly exposed to capitalist demands and a fiscal crisis. Therefore it would seem rather safe to predict that Swedish socialism will be much more decentralistic than the Eastern European model, as an extension of Swedish experiences with political democracy and a relatively decentralized commodity market, but also as a reaction against centralized capitalist power, and some of the more bureaucratic aspects of welfare state administration. On the other hand, Swedish socialists will accept more of state-redistributive and planning measures than the Yugoslavs do at present.

At this point I will not venture any predictions or proposals beyond these rather sketchy indications of what Swedish socialism might look like in the future. But whatever the look of future Swedish socialism, we must remember that the road to that socialism takes off not from a situation of underdevelopment, internal or external repression, and internal or external warfare but from mature capitalism, relative affluence, political democracy and the class struggle of a reformist labour movement — a hitherto historically unique starting-point for a socialist transformation of any society.

In Sweden as elsewhere socialism requires that exclusive private or corporate company control over the means of production is reduced, and finally eliminated. This should be done not necessarily or even primarily by nationalizations, but by the introduction of a genuine decentralized and federated economic democracy involving consumers as well as workers control — a control over planning, co-ordination, exchange, so-called negative externalities, and redistributions between productive units as well as between production and consumption. Such changes in social relations of production, to take account of the highly societal nature of modern industrial production, marketing and externalities, will have inevitable effects on the structure and content of the consumer market but does not necessarily imply a complete elimination of the commodity market mechanisms of 'exit' — to use Albert Hirschman's (1970) fertile concept. But 'voice' — another Hirschman concept — will certainly become more important than now in determining the content of the market within a socialist order. On this point it is important to distinguish commodity, service, labour and capital markets. From a socialist point of view, and with specific reference to Sweden, it would seem most urgent to reduce the role of market mechanisms with regard to capital and labour. Such developments have already been initiated.

2 Socialism and Social Liberalism Compared

On closer inspection of modern liberalism as represented in Sweden[1] we find certain notions which roughly, but far from completely, correspond to Marx's notion of contradictions between the forces and relations of production under capitalism. Progressive liberals are also aware of what Marxists call the increasingly societal character of the productive forces, as contrasted with 'private' decision-making in directing production, and using the surplus of production.

Progressive liberal economists make an important distinction between business economics which emphasizes only *private* costs and benefits, and a broader concept of economics which includes *social* or *societal* costs and benefits. These liberal economists are also aware of the fact that divergences often exist between private and social costs and benefits; no longer is an 'invisible hand' assumed to bring about an automatic harmony between private and social economies. The divergence between private and social economies might be conceived as corresponding at least partially to the notion of contradictions between the increasingly societal character of productive forces and the private character of production relations in Marxian theory.

This liberal admission of recurrent divergences between private and social or societal economies is found not only in liberal economic theory, however, but also in bourgeois praxis — and even more in bourgeois rhetoric. Many industrial leaders and managers acknowledge their social responsibility for environmental problems, problems of employment in communities dominated by one industry, the marginalization of older workers even before pensionable age, and other equally visible manifestations of the divergence between private and social costs and benefits. Sometimes this is acknowledged not only in the rhetoric of public relations officers but also in practical terms. Business leaders also make demands for state intervention to improve the conditions of entrepreneurial and industrial activities.

But this adjustment of some capitalists to what Marxists call the increasingly societal character of productive forces does not eliminate the basic contradiction of the system. In some cases the actual effects of this contradiction are attenuated by such adjustments; in other cases when such adjustments are made only in terms of public relations oratory such effects are only masked. Whatever the case, the demands for profitability of individual firms remain fundamental within the 'mixed economies' of the Western world. The various support given by the business community to bourgeois parties in Sweden, and probably also elsewhere, give unequivocal evidence to the fact that business leaders prefer to give higher priority to demands of profitability than to prompted adjustments to act responsibly in terms of societal costs and benefits. If such conservative forces gain sufficiently many votes in political elections – as they have done in the 1976 and 1979 general elections in Sweden – this will probably lead to an intensification of the contradictions between forces and relations of production; business criteria will manifest themselves in a more naked and brutal manner. This is indeed what has happened in Sweden after the defeat of social democrats in the 1976 general election – even though the defeat represented slightly less than 1 per cent of the electoral vote. The Swedish Employers' Confederation (SAF), during the process of centralized collective bargaining with the trade union movement in the spring of 1977 took a very harsh and rigid stand not only with regard to salary increases – but specifically with regard to issues on which the Parliament rather recently has legislated, and which thus fell outside the traditionally accepted range of bargaining issues. Among other things SAF demanded restrictions on the current legislated system of income-substitution benefits during illness and legislated working and vacation time.

The political and trade union branches of the labour movement naturally claim that this new militant attitude of the SAF is a result of the new bourgeois government which has come to power. I will not in this context discuss the scientific validity of this claim. Nor will I here discuss the validity of social democratic allegations that the new bourgeois government has embarked on a new political approach – in practice if not always in political rhetoric – which is clearly antagonistic to the interests of wage earners, blue-collar and white-collar. In this context it is more immediately relevant to note that progressive liberals in the bourgeois government still seem to *acknowledge* the divergences between private and social economies indicated above.

If progressive liberals acknowledge such divergences between private and social economies just as socialists acknowledge contradictions between forces and relations of production, which are then the differences between progressive social liberalism and socialism?

Whereas the liberal notion of divergent interests flowing from private and social economies is an analytical concept on a rather high level of abstraction disregarding the concrete structural context of the individual firm as well as the national economy as a whole, the Marxist notion of contradiction is firmly based in an analysis of the increasingly societal nature of productive forces and the lack of compatible changes in relations of production.

Secondly, the divergence of interests figuring in the heads of liberal economists remains a theoretical construct which can be applied intermittently *only by decision-makers in government* if they are bright and well educated enough to understand what the problem is all about. The structural contradictions in Marxist parlance is not only a theoretical construct, however, but also a reality impinging upon and implying the exploitation of *those who have nothing to sell but their labour*, and who in their leisure time sometimes suffer from such negative externalities of capitalist production as air and water pollution, premature physical debilitation, insufficient public facilities, etc.

Thirdly, the idealistic character of progressive liberal notions is evident not only in the significance attached to the awareness of the problem of political decision-makers in government, as just indicated, but also in the neglect of the *structural constraints* which operate within capitalism, and which make it practically impossible to reduce significantly, and much less to eliminate the contradictions between private and social economies which are an integral part of the modern capitalist system, without changing that system.

Fourthly, the formation of *social classes* who act out societal contradictions on arenas of strike activity, political action, etc. is an element missing in the liberal notion of divergences between private and social economies.

Thus, the differences between social-liberal and socialist conceptions of 'divergences' or 'contradictions' of private and social economies can be summarized in Table 2.1. In this figure I have extended our conceptual arena to comprehend not only problems and problem-generating *structures* but also problem-generating and problem-solving *actors*. This is consistent with a Marxian approach which cannot satisfy itself only with an abstract analysis of interest-specific oppositions. From this figure it is obvious, furthermore, that *social liberalism — at least in its Swedish form — provides access only to one type of actor, the interventionist state*, democratically ruled as it may be, to take

Table 2.1: Some differences and similarities between socialist and
social—liberal approaches to basic problems of capitalism
in the Swedish context

		Socialist approach	*Social—liberal approach*
1	Level of Abstraction	Both abstract and more concrete	Abstract
2	Problem-generating structures and responsible actors	Contradictions between forces and relations of capitalist production; responsibility attributed to the capitalist class	Divergences between private and social costs and benefits; no particular actor responsible
3	Problem-solving actors	Working class organizations, with the support of labour party dominated government, attempting to establish workers control over capital accumulation and investment	More socially responsible capitalists; decision-makers in government; state intervention to solve problems not solved by the capitalist order itself*
4	Structural constraints	Requirement of structural reproduction of the capitalist economic order as a result of the systemic logic of capitalism	Constraints — if at all recognized — are seen as fiscal and political rather than structural
5	Foes or opponents	Big business leadership and spokesmen of etatist, bureaucratic tendencies in government	Central government bureaucracies and (sometimes) socially unresponsive big business leadership
6	Overall evaluation of comprehensiveness and consistency of the two approaches	More comprehensive both in terms of levels of abstraction, structures and actors; consistent across 1—5	Less comprehensive — certain types of structures and actors missing; 1—3 consistent but 5, and to some extent 4, inconsistent with 1—3

*Note: The single individual and the virtues of individualism which traditionally have occupied such an important place in liberalism, and still do (at least in contexts of political oratory), have been left out in this figure. The figure deals exclusively with approaches to *problems generated within capitalism which cannot be solved by individuals*. If the virtues of individualism were introduced in this figure this would further accentuate the internal inconsistency of the social—liberal approach.

responsibility for creating and maintaining infrastructural conditions for capitalist enterprises, for removing market imperfections, for neutralizing or counteracting negative externalities such as environmental problems etc. This is part of the internal inconsistency of social liberalism. Social liberalism also maintains a critical stand to the state and the action of central government bureaucracies. At the same time the most progressive social liberals express criticism of big business leadership as well. Other social liberals are less stringent in their criticism of private enterprise. All in all, however, the political arena represented in social—liberal thought is a relatively empty arena except for a few signs indicating abstracted interests; the only major actor beside private enterprise is the interventionist state, often despised and hidden in the background to satisfy old liberal anti-state sentiments but still allocated if not credited the awesome and sometimes dirty job of tackling the problems of capitalism.

Socialism as understood in Table 2.1 is here defined not in etatist terms but in a way which implies a crucial place for workers control and self-management. Furthermore this table clarifies the fact that socialism is more comprehensive and concrete than social liberalism not only in its conception of problem-generating contradictions but also in its conception of relevant actors. The organized working class does not at all appear on the political arena depicted by Swedish social liberals — even though the existence as *social facts* of working class organizations must be acknowledged even by these liberals. However, what is significant in the social—liberal perspective is that social liberals cannot mobilize this 'social fact', nor seem particularly interested in even theoretically considering the possibility of a liberal mobilization of this class because class action cannot be accommodated within the individualist theoretical framework of liberalism.

If I am right in assuming that the socialist conception of problem-generating structures and contradictions as well as its conception of problem-solving actors is more comprehensive, consistent and accurate in describing a given capitalist society than the corresponding social—liberal conception, then socialism must be seen as more *relevant* than social liberalism as a way of tackling the problems of capitalism, and of creating a more consistent and humane societal order. This concluding statement is ventured here not as a political but as a scientific statement amenable to refutation and falsification. The method of refutation to be used implies a scrutiny of socialist and social—liberal conceptions of problem-generating structures and problem-solving actors followed by a comparison of these conceptions with valid empirical findings concerning such structures and actors, and concluded with an analytical inquiry of the degree to which the problem-solutions of socialism and social liberalism respectively *address themselves* to the problems, the structural preconditions and the available actors documented in the previous empirical study.

This claim concerning the refutability and thus the scientific status of my statement regarding socialism as being *more relevant* than social—liberalism in tackling the problems and making use of the problem-solving resources of a modern capitalist society such as Sweden should not be misinterpreted as a belief in so-called scientific socialism, however. My claim concerns only, and nothing but, the *greater relevance* of socialism. Scientific socialism as expounded by some Marxist and Marxist—Leninist authors goes much further.[2] It claims to be a scientific theory not simply about the greater relevance of socialism but primarily about the historical inevitability of socialist transformations of capitalist societies. Many of the deterministic assumptions, the analogies with universal laws of the natural sciences, and the specific historical predictions contained in this line of socialist thought seem to me highly questionable. Personally I take a much more cautious, hypothetical, empirical and even, somewhat pragmatic approach to the questions involved in considering the likelihood of socialist transformations of modern capitalist societies like Sweden.

3 The Conditions and Likelihood of a Socialist Transformation of Swedish Society

Before we attempt to assess, in a pragmatic and empirical way, the likelihood of a socialist transformation of Swedish society, I will try to explore to what extent some current theoretical analyses of a Marxist nature address themselves to this kind of question.

Several Marxist authors, and some Weberians who seem to have borrowed some analytical tools of Marxism, have analysed the implications and consequences of relationships between the welfare state, ruled by reformist social democratic or liberal governments, and contemporary capitalism; some of these authors have also considered the changing position of the working class and the likelihood of socialist transformations in these so-called mixed economies. Anthony Giddens (1973, pp. 285f) provides an example:

> The working class or the political organizations which represented it, had to struggle to secure full incorporation within the polity of the modern nation-state; the result of this incorporation, however, has not been to weaken, but to stabilize, or complete, the institutional mediation of power in the capitalist order. *Social democracy, in other words, is the normal form taken by the systematic political inclusion of the working class within capitalist society.*

Another less known author (Stevenson, 1974), from a much less sophisticated New Left standpoint, writes more specifically on Sweden which he describes as

> a monopoly capitalist society which exhibits the problems inherent in such a system, even after over forty years of social democratic government. . . . social democratic governments must operate within capitalist parameters. In short, no significant alteration of the society will occur. . . . The state continues to preserve and reproduce the social relations essential to and functional for the capitalist class. Swedish social democracy is so confined and so preserves.

From such an interpretation of Swedish society many Marxist commentators have drawn the conclusion that Swedish social democracy, by facilitating the further development of capitalism in Sweden, has made a genuine socialist development in this country less, rather than more, likely. But since this conclusion is completely undialectical, even a non-Marxist political scientist like Herbert Tingsten could arrive at the same conclusion in his analysis of the ideological development of the Swedish social democratic party (1967, pp. 343—4).

If the social democrats and the bourgeois parties, that is virtually the whole people, forcefully embark upon 'supporting and stimulating' the prevailing (=capitalist) system, it would seem unlikely to collapse.

From a more genuine Marxist standpoint it would seem possible, however, to argue that Swedish social democracy by helping capitalism to develop and mature, in fact (if not always in a conscious and deliberate manner) has brought Swedish society closer to a socialist transformation. If Marx's predictions about the 'bursting asunder' of capitalist social relations of production should be borne out in any highly industrialized nation, this would be in Sweden, according to this view. Historical materialism implies that socialism springs from the internal contradictions of capitalism; and from this follows that a socialist transformation of a capitalist society becomes more likely the more highly developed its capitalist structure.[1] Admittedly, this highly dialectical and rather orthodox interpretation is rather unusual among Marxists commenting on contemporary Sweden. Nevertheless it does deserve closer scrutiny. Even those who reject the rather deterministic prognostications about socialist transformations of capitalist societies propounded by some Marxists could possibly find, in this dialectical interpretation of the socialist potential of capitalist Sweden, a basis for a theoretically and empirically meaningful analysis of the Swedish situation.

Obviously this line of argument does not imply that social democratic reform programmes as such in a step-wise fashion come closer to the realization of socialist ideals. It only implies that Swedish social democracy, by being part and parcel of modern capitalist development, dialectically has contributed to bring Sweden closer to a socialist transformation of society. Thus, it is quite possible to take the same view as Giddens and others, while still maintaining that the development of the productive forces in capitalist Sweden has been so much more far reaching under social democratic rule that this has amplified the contradiction between the productive forces and the dominant relations of production to the point of a real socialist transformation —

to stick to this vague but fertile Marxian conception. But it is not only this increasing contradiction but also the fact that the material conditions for the emergence of new social relations of production have had a chance to mature within the existing society which, according to this particular Marxist interpretation, makes Sweden closer to a real socialist transformation than any other advanced capitalist society.[2] Does that mean that we now simply have to wait for the 'fetters' of existing relations or production in Sweden to 'burst asunder' – perhaps with some little revolutionary aid?[3]

Marxist imagery of the impending socialist transformation of society makes reference to both violence and drama. This does not seem to fit particularly well with a common image of Sweden as an orderly and relatively stable society where crises certainly occur but are managed rather smoothly and efficiently.

Naturally this seemingly flexible stability at one time caused considerable concern among part of the far left in Sweden. Therefore where crises were absent they had to be provoked; where they were just emerging they had to be amplified and polarized, according to this view. Even though this occurred with much less abandon and force in Sweden than for instance in Germany and France, small groups of Swedish intellectuals-turned-workers, and even smaller numbers of workers on the extreme left certainly did try their own style of crisis management some years ago, creating or enlarging crises locally in order to polarize class conflict and thus provoking suppressive reactions which could give rise to further escalation of the process. But these attempts were insignificant in Sweden.

Had this extreme-leftist type of crisis management been somewhat more effective, it would, even less than the regular social democratic or social–liberal types of crisis management now so common in modern capitalist states, have changed the basic processes of capitalist society. In contrast to the crisis management undertaken by the political establishments in capitalist democracies, the extreme-leftist type is likely to strengthen repressive forces even where they are weak without in any way adding even corresponding strength to the collective forces of the working class. A transformation of society is thereby delayed rather than enhanced, it would seem. Western Germany provides several illustrations of this point.

Marx's advice to analyse a specific society thoroughly and scientifically before drawing any conclusions about the emergent forces of societal transformation should here be taken quite seriously. For a country like Sweden two considerations seem particularly important in rethinking the issue of societal praxis in societal change.

Firstly, we must consider the fact that in Sweden for some time the voter support for working class parties (social democrats and communists) has tended to be strongest at the peak of business cycles rather than in recessions or periods of economic crises.[4] Strike activity, an indicator less objectionable to the conventional revolutionary than voting statistics, shows similar fluctuations (Korpi, 1972). In periods of economic crises workers would seem more likely to be concerned with matters of individual consumption and welfare, and less free to acknowledge and collectively respond to issues of class and structural change. But the bargaining power of the business community, on the other hand, tends to be stronger in crisis situations than at the peak of business cycles. Thus the relative collective strength of labour versus capital would seem to be less in favour of labour than of capital in periods of economic crises, and more favourable when business is flourishing. This conclusion that peaks of business cycles are more favourable in the praxis of socialist transformation than periods of crises is sufficiently unorthodox to require further discussion but due to space limitations such a discussion cannot be undertaken here.[5]

Secondly, it must be considered an oversimplification bordering on factual inaccuracy to consider the Swedish social democratic party exclusively as a tool of capitalist development. Certainly the fierce opposition from the bourgeois parties which social democrats have experienced all through their history of governmental responsibility is not a sufficient criterion of independence from the interests of capitalist development which have been the basic source of bourgeois party ideology. Such opposition can be explained at least partly by the inherent logic of electoral competition. Nor can bourgeois support for social democratic policies, once they acquire the force of law, be interpreted unquestionably as an indication of affinity between social democratic policies and the interests of capital. There are perfectly good tactical reasons for bourgeois parties who for very long were placed outside government by electoral failure but who wished to attain – and now to retain – the majority required for taking or maintaining governmental powers not to challenge the demonstrated wishes of voters who have supported social democracy.

But in addition there are perfectly good *theoretical* reasons for rejecting the crude instrumentalism implicit in viewing social democratic governments simply as tools of capitalist development rather than as arenas for contradictory class interests, where the moves of each side often are problematic and non-conclusive in a way which allows a slow but sustained movement toward a victory of labour over capital — or vice versa of course (see pp. 7–9).

Decisive *empirical* criteria for rejecting the simplistic notion of social democracy simply as a tool of capitalist development can be identified only by scrutinizing the *content* and *effects* of social democratic policies — including those policies for which social democrats have failed to get, or not dared to seek support in situations of delicate parliamentary balance. A detailed scrutiny of this kind falls outside the scope of this paper, however.[6] But a few critical facts regarding such policies should still be mentioned.

Even though the most visible part of the 'historical mission' of Swedish social democracy up till now may seem to have consisted in bringing the Swedish capitalist order to fruition and to bring about 'social reforms without socialism',[7] any closer inspection would also reveal the following. Several of the reforms instituted by the social democratic government in recent years concerning the work environment and the relative power of labour and capital in that setting would seem to promise significant changes in relations of production in a socialist direction — much more important than any nationalization of industries as far as Sweden is concerned.

In a following chapter we will discuss these recent legislative reforms in more detail, and also interpret their underlying forces and possible consequences in their proper macro-sociological context. Here we only need to emphasize that such legislation not only reflects the relative strength of capital and labour in a structural sense, but also the strength of more or less articulate demands for such reforms from below, and the responsiveness of labour parties and trade unions to such demands. As we will show, the legislated reforms mentioned above were speeded up in response to various pressures from below in spite of the fact that the parliamentary majority of the Social Democratic Party, and its government position at that time was weaker than before.

But a socialist praxis adequate to Swedish conditions must be based not only on factual considerations of the relative strength of capital and labour in different phases of business cycles or on considerations of the responsiveness of Swedish labour parties to pressures from below demanding changes in the institutionalized power structure of the capitalist economic order. In addition there are *ideological* considerations related both to the meaning of democracy and the meaning of socialism.

In a country like Sweden more profound structural changes of society in the direction of, say, a humanist type of socialism must be democratic in the sense of receiving majority support at the polls within the existing system of liberal democracy — however incomplete this system may be from the point of view of controlling economic decisions basic to the development of Swedish society.

This means that the main problem-solving actor in the historically specific socialist scenario we are considering — namely the working class of Sweden — not only must be sufficiently large, conscious and well organized in terms of union activity but also be in a position to translate its consciousness into a majority support for a responsive labour party. Here a number of empirical questions emerge:

(1) How numerous and well organized is the Swedish working class?
(2) How conscious is it of its class position?
(3) If the Swedish working class is sufficiently conscious of the pressing problems of capitalism, is there a labour party sufficiently powerful and sufficiently responsive to organized demands for structural changes of the capitalist order, thus enabling the working class to translate its consciousness into adequate electoral support for such a party?
(4) What is the strength of bourgeois parties and the capitalist class, in neutralizing or resisting these pressures from below and the legislation that may be proposed by labour parties to bring about structural changes of Swedish society in a socialist direction?

Answering these questions with empirical research would render a *cross-sectional descriptive snapshot* of the position of class struggle in a country at a certain point in time. Such an empirical study could be extended along the time dimension toward the past by exploring trends, cycles and other fluctuations. But conclusions about possible future outcomes can be drawn only if such descriptive empirical studies are guided by theoretical considerations concerning the *social processes* that influence (i) the numerical and organizational strength of the working class, (ii) the consciousness of the working class concerning the contradictions of capitalism, (iii) the strength of labour parties and their responsiveness to organized demands for structural changes of the capitalist order, and (iv) the strength of bourgeois and capitalist opposition to a socialist transformation of capitalist society. Theoretical conjectures about such critical processes can also be empirically tested in a number of cases whereas in other cases the slow and partly hidden nature of such processes may prevent access to relevant empirical data.

The questions raised in the last two paragraphs indicate some of the main topics of this book: the actual *state of affairs* of, and the *social processes* affecting the strength of the forces involved in class struggle in late capitalism, and the responsiveness of political parties and the state apparatus to the pressures implicit in this struggle.

However, it is not enough to assess and analyse various aspects of the strength of actors involved. The stage is set for class action by largely impersonal forces of an economic nature. These economic processes both generate the contradictions of capitalism which appear on the stage as the subject matter of struggle, and determine the options and constraints within which this struggle takes place. These contradictions and constraints are the main problems of the actors involved. Therefore Part II of this book will be devoted entirely to explicating the notion of contradictions and constraints of late capitalism. However, we will not be satisfied to deal with this matter only in theoretical terms. We will also make an attempt to find empirical indicators of at least some aspects of the contradictions found within the present capitalist order. Once the stage is set in this manner we proceed to Part III where we will theoretically discuss and empirically illuminate various aspects of the definition and strength of actors involved in class struggle. Part IV will then consider some problem solutions suggested in Swedish political and legislative debate for the problems of late capitalism. Do the problem solutions actually fit the problem? Are the problem solutions suggested realistic both in the sense that they can mobilize a majority support in elections, and contribute to resolve the contradictions of capitalism without at the same time generating counter forces sufficiently strong to neutralize or reverse the transformation of the capitalist order intended? And to what extent can we rightly say that the problem solutions now contemplated by the Swedish labour movement are significant steps on the road to socialism? Here again emerges the tricky problem of how to define democratic socialism as distinct from what is called socialism in Eastern Europe.

But is socialism in one country at all possible unless it isolates itself from the surrounding capitalist world — at least in the initial phases of socialist transformation? Countries like Sweden are largely dependent on their export market in a predominantly capitalist world order, and this inevitably introduces various constraints on a development toward democratic socialism. This problem will be touched upon in all of the chapters to follow, but particularly in Parts II and IV. Here I am content to quote from a paper by Ernest Mandel with whom I essentially agree on this point:

> We start from the noticeable *fact* that at this stage, state structures, repressive structures and political power are still essentially

'national'. As it is much easier and much more likely (at least in medium-term range) to decisively modify relationship of forces on a national than on an international scale; as it is much more likely that the working class can eliminate the obstacle of a 'national' repressive apparatus than a European-wide one, then, obviously, it is in the interest of socialism, to postpone as much as possible the emergence of a European-wide centralized bourgeois state power. The conquest of power is *still* possible on a national scale. Relationships of forces between the classes develop unevenly on an European scale. To profit from any favourable change of these relationships in a single country so as to bring the weight of 'national' workers power to bear on an international scale, is then obviously the more efficient solution, rather than wait till relations will become favourable simultaneously in six or nine or twelve countries, which might take a very long time indeed.

However, one thing is to notice the possibility of a *conquest of power* on a national scale, by the working class. Something entirely different is to visualize the building of a socialist society (and economy) in an isolated Western European country (be it large or small). This last proposition is completely utopian. Under the present conditions of internationalization of the productive forces, it would entail strong economic regression, and would become a political failure after not too long a transition period. This should not be hidden from the workers, both for reasons of socialist morality and of political realism (it does not pay to lie). . . .

Internationalist consciousness — which does not arise 'automatically' inside the working class out of the internationalization of the productive forces — must be consciously sponsored and stimulated by socialist forces inside the organized labour movement. This is indispensable not only for principled reasons, and to combat the growing danger of xenophobia and racialism inside the European working class, which develops side by side with economic slowdown and unemployment. It is especially indispensable to prevent the internationalization of production to profit essentially capital, and to modify the social relations of forces at the expense of the workers. This has undoubtedly been the case till now, as the bourgeoisie meets much less obstacles to internationalize its operations than do the workers to internationalize their struggles. International wage negotiations for the same multinational corporation; European-wide labor struggles and strikes; strict solidarity with immigrant workers and the struggle to equalize their rights with those of the 'indigenous' workers, are key conditions for bringing about that international consciousness.

Any 'national' breakthrough to socialism, i.e. any victorious socialist revolution in a single European country, will immediately meet an international challenge by capital, which will take the form, in a first stage, of capital evasion, 'investment strike', financial blockade, interruption of international credit, diversion of trade, etc. The victorious socialist movement can meet that challenge only through a conscious effort at obtaining solidarity on a European-wide scale from the working class. It must address itself to the unions, the mass parties, and the workers and toiling masses directly, of all the other countries. It must ask them constantly whether they accept to be accomplices in an enterprise of 'destabilization' intended to punish the workers of one country for the 'crime' of initiating the realization of the programme of the workers of all European countries. . . . Capitalists of all European countries should know that any attempt to go on a collision course with the victorious socialist revolution will introduce the same collision right into their own country. But the precondition for the success of such a strategy is the realization of political and social conditions in the 'breakthrough' country, which are really 'revolutionary', really attractive for the mass of the European workers: radical reduction of work-time, real workers self-management, unlimited democracy, etc.

(Mandel, 1977, pp. 12-14)

The strategy outlined by Mandel then does not presuppose that all or most advanced industrialized nations become 'ripe for socialism' at the same time. One or a few countries could take the lead. This is another justification for our attempt to focus attention predominantly on the likelihood of a socialist transformation in one country. But we must be aware of the fact that such a transformation in one country is unlikely to be completely successful in the long run unless it receives support from working class organizations in other countries.

PART II

Setting the Stage for Societal Change

by Ulf Himmelstrand and
Lars Lundberg

4 Some Theoretical and Political Issues

Issue-Formation in Capitalist Societies: Human Predicaments and Political Culture

This part of our book concentrates on the objective circumstances which may influence the definition of issues and opinions in subjective consciousness, and for consequent political action. However, we do not claim that the issues and opinions which actually can be observed as most salient on the political arena always reflect the objective circumstances which constitute current and widespread human predicaments. On the contrary. Political culture is a most powerful source of issue and opinion-formation — often more powerful than widely shared human predicaments. If political culture reflects the past rather than the present, and the interests of social classes which in the past attained the dominant position which they still maintain, then we may find that crucial and wide-ranging issues which seem to emerge from a careful evaluation of current objective circumstances in mature capitalism in fact do not appear at all as issues in the mainstream of current political debate and action. Their salience may be very low indeed. This is an empirical question, however. In Part III of this book we will report some empirical data illuminating whether people's subjective consciousness at all reflects the kind of objective circumstances on which we will focus our attention here in Part II.

The prevailing political culture and its dominant ideological themes, as inherited from the historical past and cultivated by various political organizations, define various political goals conveyed to the citizenry from above through processes of mass-communication and political socialization. This is one source of political issues. But the history and current manifestations of political culture are just one aspect of the history from which issues arise. There is also a history of human predicaments which generate issues from below rather than from above, through direct experience or personal empathy about difficult and trying conditions offering few or very taxing paths of escape. The study of human predicaments as a source of political issues is a rather neglected field of study among political sociologists and political scientists. Research on the formation of political issues and opinions has focused attention mainly on the citizen as a recipient of messages through agents of political socialization or channels of political communication. The fact that we can point to some recent exceptions to this dominant approach — for instance in Ronald Ingelhardt's (1971) studies of the typical industrial versus post-industrial attitudes springing from generationally different economic and social predicaments — does not gainsay our assertion that there is a general neglect of issues arising from objective human predicaments rather than from subjective political culture. This neglect may have received some backing from empirical findings on the absence of significant correlations between subjective and objective welfare indicators (Allardt, 1976, p. 237).[1]

But what do we mean by 'objective circumstances'? And what about our allusions to 'the history of human predicaments'? For reasons of space, the historical depth of our following study is rather limited. We are more concerned with 'theoretical depth'. The choice of objective circumstances should be guided by theoretical considerations. Our theoretical framework is mainly historical—materialist, and focuses on notions of contradictions within the capitalist mode of production.

For a long time in the West this Marxist framework was relegated to arenas of ideological debate and political agitation far removed from academic use and scrutiny except as a target of critical attacks which claimed to be scientific, but often were of a disguised political nature. The ways in which the academic community has defined its object of knowledge in the social sciences could perhaps also be seen as reflecting the relative influence of culture and common human predicaments. Academic and bourgeois political culture would seem to have screened off social scientists not only from close and importunate knowledge of the collective predicaments of labourers struggling to improve their situation, but also from an understanding of the intellectual heritage of Marx. Only during the last fifteen years has Marxism gained a foothold — and still quite a precarious one — as an admissible analytic paradigm in some parts of the Western academic community. Therefore we will start our exposition of the contradictions of capitalism with a brief exposé of the status of some crucial Marxian notions within academic Marxist and sociological circles.

In the chapters following hereafter our 'theoretical depth' should not be judged in relation to Marxist treatises which devote most of their space to a theoretical explication and a development of Marxist theory.

Our aim instead is to carry out a theoretically guided empirical case analysis of mature capitalism, its basic and extended contradictions, the actors involved in these contradictions and their action. Our theoretical analysis will therefore only be brought forward to a point where we can formulate guidelines for our empirical analysis. But on many points our empirical aspirations must be tempered by the limited availability of relevant secondary sources, and by the unavoidable limitations imposed on primary research. Marxist empirical studies of contemporary societies are only in their beginning.

On the Status of Marxian Notions of Contradiction in Marxism and Sociology

William H. Shaw (1978, p. 1) asserts that historical materialism as conceived by Karl Marx has been insufficiently analysed conceptually and not properly evaluated as a guide to an empirically based understanding of history. Be this as it may. Our own attempts to survey various interpretations of the basic concepts of contradictions between forces and relations of production in Marxian theory have not rendered very substantial results. We have been struck not only by the lack of theoretical perseverance in tracking down the multi-dimensional nature of this pivotal concept which Marx himself left rather unexplicated (Shaw, 1978, p. 8), but primarily by the lack of thorough empirical studies of the various conceptual dimensions involved.

While this is a disappointing result of our search for explications of this concept in Marxist literature, it is less surprising that conventional US textbooks in their presentations of Marx and Marxist thought until recently have tended to exhibit rather acrimonious distortions or a silent neglect of the complexities of historical materialism. To confirm this impression we need not go back to the times when thousands of sociology students all over the world were treated with Pitirim Sorokin's (1928) crude presentation of Marx as a 'monistic' and economistic figure in the history of social thought. Sociological books in general use a great deal later (Coser and Rosenberg, 1957, pp 187f and 369–76) presented a few pages of the least analytical and theoretically fertile, and the most political and timeworn pages to be found in the writings of Marx as selections from Marx's collected writings.[2] Up till quite recently, simplified accounts of the Marxian terminology of class and class struggle, taken out of their structural and historical context conveyed an image of a rather primitive type of conflict theory to innocent sociology students. An older generation of American sociologists, who certainly had read Marx in original, and not only Sorokin, seem to have become so completely cut off from the Marxist theoretical tradition as a result of their disenchantment with Soviet communism and the experience of the Cold War that they failed to criticize the distortions and simplifications of Marxism peddled on the markets of US sociology textbooks. Agreeing or disagreeing with Marxist theory is not the issue here, however. No honest and scientifically reasonable disagreement with Marxian theory can and should be based on obvious distortions and stultifying simplifications of Marxist fundamentals.

Even a respected sociological scholar like Robert Nisbet (1966, p. 202) failed to recognize what is fundamental and what is derived in the Marxian theoretical tradition. Says Nisbet: 'Social class is the very basis of Marxian sociology . . .' and yet 'a clear, analytical conception of social class is not easy to derive from a reading of Marx'. On the other hand: 'for Marx what man does economically is the single most important and determining thing about his life. The type of work he performs, his position in the larger system of production in society, and the differential rewards he receives for his work — these are the essential elements on which a sociology of class must be built.'

Obviously this is a very inconsistent rendering of Marx. Social class cannot at the same time be 'the very basis of Marxian sociology' *and* a notion that 'must be built' on 'the single most important and determining thing', namely 'what man does economically'. The simple truth is that the first statement by Nisbet is problematic while the latter quotation comes closer to the truth — even though Nisbet's notion of 'differential rewards' is a psychologistic distortion of what Marx meant when he spoke of the capitalist appropriation of the surplus value of labour. Social class thus is a derived concept — derived from the much more fundamental notions of production and appropriation of surplus value, that is the difference between the full use value of the labour power from which capital is benefiting, and the value at which labour power is bought.[3] However, the fact that social class is a secondary concept when considered in a context of theoretical derivation, does not imply that social class is a secondary concept in the understanding of historical processes. There it is a central concept.

In his more political and less theoretical writings — from which Western sociologists prefer to take most of their quotations, perhaps to make Marx look all the more primitive — the notions of class and class struggle naturally are more salient. In his more analytical work, however, it would be much more correct to say, with Nisbet, that it is difficult to find 'a clear, analytical conception of social class'. In such analytical contexts Marx's theoretically fertile notion of contradictions between forces and relations of production is much more fundamental.

It is certainly true that Marx could have been much more explicit also about the meaning of his fundamental concepts of contradictions between forces and relations of production. But these concepts which have been so neglected in conventional textbook presentations of Marx constitute the centrepiece of historical materialism, and therefore appear in sufficiently many contexts in his writings to help unfold their implicit meaning to careful readers.

But if the concepts of forces and relations of production are the centrepiece of historical materialism why do they not occupy a more prominent place in *Capital*? We do not find the terms 'productive forces' and 'relations of production' in a single rubric of *Capital*. But this is because the argument in *Capital* moves on a level of more concrete analysis in comparison with Marx's earlier, more synoptic presentations of historical materialism (Dahlqvist, 1978, p. 519f). In *Capital* Marx writes about the 'labour process' as the specific form of productive forces under capitalism, and about the 'capital relationship', or capital as a specific economic form, rather than about the relations of production as a general concept. Productive forces and production relations are more general concepts applicable not only to capitalist but also to other modes of production. When applied to capitalism, the notion of emerging contradictions between forces and relations appears as a contradiction between the economic *form* of capital and its *content*, the labour process.

When forces and relations of production are treated as analytically separate concepts this must be done with full cognizance of the fact that these concepts refer to two different interdependent and increasingly contradictory attributes of one *unit*, a particular mode of production. No 'unity of opposites' would emerge unless the contradiction between the labour process and its capitalist form, that is between forces and relations of production, were part of one self-reproducing unit (Therborn, 1976, p. 397).

However, as our purpose is to look for guidance in empirically grasping the central terms of historical materialism, and to use the empirical indicators so identified for a descriptive study of the contradictions emerging in a specific country at a particular time, we will not in this chapter make any attempt to discuss the kind of mutual relationship assumed to exist between forces and relations of production at the conceptual level represented in Marx's *Capital*, nor their relationships in processes with greater historical depth than those explored here.

The renaissance of Marxist thought which has occurred recently among quite a number of sociologists (in the English-speaking world with the help of men such as Bottomore, Plamenatz and others), should make it unnecessary to lecture most of our readers about the basic tenets of historical materialism. Those readers who have been living for too long under an anti-Marxist theoretical hegemony, and who are victims of the ignorance thus generated, must look elsewhere for a more thorough presentation of historical materialism.[4]

Capitalism: Separation and Commodification of Labour and Capital

Basic to the understanding of the contradictions and constraints of capitalism is an understanding of the capitalist mode of production itself. What is capitalism?

Capitalism is often equated with the 'market economy', that is with an economy where the relationships between demand and competitive supply determine the prices and quantities of the goods produced. In the not so ideal case price competition may be supplemented or replaced by competition in advertisement and similar techniques for manipulating demand, but consumer demand, manipulated or not, remains the driving force in this conception of the market economy — and of capitalism.

However, there are markets not only for consumer commodities and services but also for so-called factors of production: labour, capital, land and raw materials. With the vanishing importance of fortune which was only inherited, not bought or sold, and with the advent of capital markets for the selling and buying of shares and bonds — that is making capital into a commodity in the form of financial capital — modern capitalism made its breakthrough more than a century ago. Historically speaking the transformation of labour into a commodity is even more basic to capitalism than the process for financial capital. Labour as a commodity had certainly existed earlier in slave economies. But with capitalism this assumed a new form: the worker is 'free' to sell his labour power, to withdraw it and to sell it to somebody else at his own 'discretion' within the framework of the demand—supply relationships on the labour market.

Through the development of the trade union movement and collective bargaining — and much later in some countries such as Sweden through the introduction of legislation which makes the firing of workers more difficult and thus less sensitive to market forces — rather far-reaching limitations have been placed on competitive market processes with respect to labour. Workers do not to the same extent compete with each other in selling their labour power. What is most distinctive in relatively developed but pre-monopolistic systems of capitalism is thus a combination of competitive commodity and capital markets, and increasing restrictions on the labour market as just indicated. Where oligopolistic and monopolistic features of capitalism emerge, market forces are increasingly constrained even in commodity markets.

Is it then still possible to conceive of capitalism as a market economy? Later on we will return to some of the illusions of this conception. Here we will be satisfied to point out the lack of social context and the mystifying nature of the idealized marked model where human beings are seen only in their capacities as economic or economizing men without any references to their *unequal positions in structures of use and 'exchange' of labour power.*

With regard to such inequalities Marxists introduce further structural criteria in their conception of capitalism: the capitalist's *possession* and *control* of the means and surplus value of production, and the fact that non-possessing workers in a capitalist system are economically *compelled* to sell their labour power at its exchange rather than its use value in order to survive. The difference between the use value of labour power and the exchange value at which labour power is bought provides the *surplus value* appropriated by capitalists. These criteria also define the class structure of capitalist society, according to the Marxist view.

Taking off from an observation made already by Marx that *possession* of capital and *control* of capital became separated with the emergence of joint stock companies, Ralf Dahrendorf (1959) in his watered-down 'neo-Marxism' minimizes the importance of property and possession, and emphasizes the significance of authority and control.[5] This interpretation is not justified. Managerial authority of command and control accrues from the property rights of shareholders who have delegated control to management, usually through an elected board of directors. It is only the holders of small shares who experience loss of control of their property. The big capitalists in fact have extended their control much beyond their own possession of capital. Where share-holding is scattered among many small shareholders, the larger shareholders can control the elected board of directors even if their shares represent only a minority of total shares. More significant than the separation of possession and control of capital in late capitalism is the fact that capital increasingly must share its control if not its legal possession of property with the state. Through legislation and concession the modern capitalist state limits the uses which capital can make of its property, of labour power and even of the consumer market — but until recently to the benefit of total capital, even if not to each single capitalist.

Max Weber, often pitted against Marx, in fact comes much closer to Marxist conceptions of capitalism and class than does Dahrendorf.

> It is the most elemental economic fact that the way in which the disposition over material property is distributed among a plurality of people, meeting competitively in the market for the purpose of exchange, in itself creates specific life chances. . . . This mode of distribution gives to the propertied a monopoly on the possibility of transferring property from the sphere of use as a 'fortune', to the sphere of 'capital goods', that is, it gives them the entrepreneurial function and all chances to share directly or indirectly in returns on capital. All this holds true within the area in which pure market conditions prevail. 'Property' and 'lack of property' are, therefore, the basic categories of all class situations.
>
> (1948, p. 181f)

This passage from Weber, immediately following his well-known definition of class, usually remains unquoted in non-Marxist and anti-Marxist sociological texts.

To summarize our discussion so far, capitalism can be defined as a mode of production where there is a class of private or corporate owners, *possessing* and *controlling* (with or without delegation of authority) the means and surplus of production, employing, firstly, 'free labour' compelled to sell its labour power on a more or less competitive labour market and, secondly, employing the results of previous surplus labour in the form of capital, more or less subjected to the forces of a competitive capital market, for the production of goods or services sold on a more or less *competitive consumer market*.

Different levels and types of capitalism can be defined by specifying the 'more-or-less' clauses in this definition. The contradiction between 'property' and 'lack of property', that is between capital and labour, constitutes the *genus proximum* of such definitions; the 'more-or-less' clauses indicate the *differentia specificae* which by their combinations define different types of capitalism, and corresponding class structures.

In specifying different types of capitalism, a number of taxonomical problems emerge which will not concern us here. For instance, if capital becomes highly centralized, in effect destroying the competitive capital market, this logically implies a destruction of competitive consumer markets as well. But if consumer market competition is reduced to insignificance in some specific monopolized context, we can still speak of capitalism — monopoly capitalism. If consumer market competitiveness were a necessary even if not a sufficient criterion, then monopoly capitalism would be a self-contradictory concept. Furthermore, it is in the nature of the innovative and competitive processes even of non-monopolistic capitalism that an innovation introduced by one particular company monopolizes the market at first until various competitors have adopted the innovation, by purchasing the patent if necessary. However, even if we must avoid self-contradictory concepts in contexts of definition, we must accept that our object of definition itself may become fraught with contradictions as a result of historical processes.

The Distinction between Basic and Extended Contradictions

Basic and extended contradictions of capitalism can be distinguished by the fact that some contradictions are *implicit* in the definition of capitalism given earlier, or follow from processes assumed to pertain to some of the elements *implied* by this definition, whereas other contradictions pertain to the relationship between capitalism and other modes of production such as feudalism or socialism, or between capitalism and other elements of the social formation dominated by capitalism.

In this sense the contradiction between capital and labour, and the increasing contradiction between forces and relations of production are *basic* to capitalism. The conflict between capitals on competitive markets and the resultant growth of oligopoly and monopoly, which are a result of processes of capital accumulation and concentration, also implies various *basic* contradictions, as do also the crisis-generating characteristics of capitalist markets.

Among *extended* contradictions we include not only conflicts with non-capitalist modes of production but also contradictions arising with agents or effects which were not originally part of the capitalist scheme but which have emerged in the process of capitalist development, provoked or demanded by it without being designed by the capitalist class itself. The emergence of *labour collectives* — for instance in the form of trade unions opposing the exploitation of workers — has introduced 'market imperfections' on the labour market which contradict a pure capitalist mode of production. The emergence of the *interventionist state* is often seen as an extension or instrument of capitalism (see Chapter 1), but in opposition to this crude instrumentalism one could maintain that the state in a Western democracy rarely is completely permeated by capitalist interests. It also to some degree responds to other interests, or operates according to processes other than those characteristic of the capitalist mode of production, and thus may come in opposition with capital, at least in a partial way. Similarly we can speak of so-called *negative externalities* — various negative non-market effects of capitalist production such as air and water pollution — as giving rise to extended contradictions.

A Basic Definitional Contradiction: Capital versus Labour

The contradiction between capital and labour is part of the definition of capitalism; it constitutes capitalism at any level of its development. The profit of the capitalist class derives from the labour of the working class, according to the Marxist view, and from the fact that labour power is bought at its exchange value whereas the capitalist reaps the benefit of its full use value. This contradiction is 'original in the sense that it is present from the beginning and goes on being present until the system disappears' (Godelier, 1972a, p. 78).

What has just been said may seem to imply that this particular kind of internal contradiction of capitalism is interesting mainly in a definitional context, not in the context of a historical analysis because the contradiction of capital and labour is a necessary and in that sense constant element in the history of capitalism.

However, when we consider the historical *manifestations* of this contradiction on the level of class action in politics and union struggle there are a number of processes that affect the intensity of manifest conflict:

1. Collective labour which has arisen within the extended structures of collective work and social communication generated by capitalism itself, has increased the exchange value of labour power. Trade unions, by reducing competition between labourers on the labour market, have contributed to raising the price of collective labour power above the level that would be obtained in a fully individualistic and competitive labour market. Thus, where trade unions have been efficient in collective bargaining, this has helped to reduce the intensity of the conflict between capital and labour without, of course, having removed this contradiction. In a long-term perspective, however, this would seem to increase the intensity of conflict. The strength of trade unions in collective bargaining reduces the profit of capital, and forces capital to find less labour-intensive methods of production through automation and robotization, as indicated below in point (4), and this again increases the potential for intense conflict.

It is in this sense that the contradiction of capital and labour is constant under capitalism. Wherever the *manifestations* of this contradiction seem to become less intense, for instance through accommodations to the pressures of well-organized labour, other manifestations of this contradiction emerge which again make the conflict between capital and labour more intense. The contradiction between capital and labour is relatively constant in a structural sense, but the conflicts and class struggle between labour and capital may vary in intensity due to the shifting pressures and accommodations at the frontiers of this struggle. Our main conclusion under this point is that the strength of pressures from well organized labour — particularly during the postwar decades of prolonged economic growth — reduced the intensity of the conflict between capital and labour, at least temporarily.

2. As everyone knows modern capitalism does not imply that the working class produces while the middle strata and the capitalist class consumes. With the advent of mass consumption society the price of labour is no longer only a matter of cost to capitalists but also a factor in consumer demand. The political acceptability of Keynesian theory (which in some respects resembles the much older Marxian theory of relative underconsumption as a cause of economic crises) has served to improve the situation of the working class. The cost of reproducing labour is no longer the only consideration in this context; the reproduction of consumer demand is as important — or at least has been so until recently when the new phenomenon of stagflation has called for new theoretical and political approaches. This implies that the intensity of the conflict between capital and labour was somewhat reduced during the era of Keynesian economic policies.

3. Another process which has served to decrease the intensity of the conflict between capital and labour is the unprecedented rate of economic growth during the postwar years up into the 1960s. This economic growth together with the Keynesian realization of the importance of well paid workers for mass consumption, and the strength of trade unions, has contributed to improve significantly the living standards of workers in Sweden not only absolutely but until about the early 1950s also in relative terms (Bentzel, 1953). Even a Marxist critic of Swedish social democracy such as Mats Dahlqvist (1975) admits that the rate of exploitation between capital and labour was weakened during this period up to a point where a class collaboration seemed beneficial to both parties.

4. However, more recently three processes have again contributed to increase the intensity of the contradiction between capital and labour: the re-emergence of the *tendential fall of the profit rate* (Wibe, 1978, p. 14f, Gillman, 1969 and Mage, 1963), a decreasing labour intensity and an increase of capital intensive *automation* and *robotization* in industry (Noble, 1977), and finally the process of *stagflation* (H. Wachtel and P. Adelsheim, 1978). For more technical accounts of these processes we must refer the reader to the relevant literature. Here the most significant aspect of these processes is that they imply increasing unemployment rates and a partial marginalization of labour.

Unemployment figures have been increasing in most parts of the capitalist industrialized world (see Table 4.1); no similar trend can be found in centrally planned socialist countries. The comparability of unemployment statistics from different countries can often be questioned, but trends for each country are quite clear. Sweden would seem to be an exception, but this is largely a result of the policy of the Swedish government to design more far-reaching special programmes for labour not absorbed by the regular open labour market (see p. 102). Even though unemployment is primarily an expression of the basic contradiction between capital and labour, we have chosen to discuss this matter in more detail later on under the rubric of extended contradictions. The main reason for this is the fact that unemployment and marginalization of labour generate various 'external' human and social costs for which we have no other comprehensive indicators than unemployment and labour marginalization.

Here it is enough to underline that the threats of unemployment, and the increasing concern with labour costs implied by the processes mentioned above again tends to increase the intensity of the conflict between capital and labour, and bring about a resurgence of class struggle.

The Increasing Contradiction between Forces and Relations of Production

While the contradiction between capital and labour is internal to the structure of capitalism as a whole, the contradiction between forces and relations of production is a contradiction *between two structures* which are both part of the capitalist mode of production (Godelier, 1972a, p. 79):

> Now, the paradox is that this contradiction, which is fundamental, since it has to account for the evolution of capitalism and for the

Table 4.1: Percentages of unemployed in some industrialized capitalist countries

Country	1962	1963	1964	1965	1966	1967	1968	1969	1970	1971	1972	1973	1974	1975	1976
Sweden	1.5	1.7	1.6	1.2	1.6	2.1	2.2	1.9	1.5	2.5	2.7	2.5	2.0	1.6	1.6
USA	5.5	5.7	5.2	4.5	3.8	3.8	3.6	3.5	4.9	5.9	5.6	4.9	5.6	8.5	7.7
Canada	5.9	5.5	4.7	3.9	3.6	4.1	4.8	4.7	5.9	6.4	6.3	5.6	5.4	6.9	7.1
United Kingdom	2.0	2.4	1.8	1.5	1.5	2.3	2.5	2.4	2.6	3.5	3.8	2.7	2.6	4.1	5.8
Fed. Republic of Germany	0.7	0.8	0.7	0.6	0.7	2.1	1.5	0.9	0.7	0.8	1.1	1.2	2.6	4.7	4.6
Italy	3.0	2.5	2.7	3.6	3.9	3.5	3.5	3.4	3.2	3.2	3.7	3.5	2.9	3.3	3.7
Netherlands	0.7	0.1	0.6	0.7	1.0	2.0	1.9	1.4	1.1	1.6	2.7	2.7	3.6	5.2	5.5
Belgium	3.3	2.7	2.2	2.4	2.7	3.7	4.5	3.6	2.9	2.9	3.4	3.6	4.0	6.7	8.6
Japan	0.9	0.9	0.8	0.8	0.9	1.2	1.2	1.1	1.2	1.2	1.4	1.3	1.4	1.9	2.0

Source: United Nations: Statistical Yearbook, 1971 and 1977.

necessity of its disappearance, is not *'original'*, in the sense that it did not exist in the system at its beginning. It appears 'at a certain stage', at a 'certain stage of maturity' of the system. And this stage is that of large-scale industry, that is, a certain stage of development of the productive forces. . . . In the beginning, on the contrary, far from contradicting the development of the productive forces, capitalist production relations stimulated them and caused them to progress impetuously, from the organization of the manufactories until the appearance of machine-production and large-scale industry.[6]

In the writings of Marx we find two ways of expressing the meaning of the contradiction between forces and relations of production, one more general and metaphorical and one more analytic and specific, which furthermore seem to relate to quite different phases of development of a given mode of production:

At a certain stage of development, the material productive forces of society come into conflict with the existing relations of production. . . . From forms of development of the productive forces these relations turn into their fetters. Then begins an era of social revolution.

(Marx, 1971b, p. 5)

And furthermore, in another context:

Hand in hand with this centralization, or this expropriation of many capitalists by few, develop, on an ever-extending scale, the co-operative form of the labour process, the conscious technical application of science, the methodical cultivation of the soil, the transformation of the instruments of labour into instruments of labour only usable in common, the economizing of all means of production by their use as the means of production of combined, socialized labour, the entanglement of all peoples in the net of the world-market. . . . Centralization of the means of production and socialization of labour at last reach a point where they become incompatible with their capitalist integument.

(Marx, 1976, p. 929)

The second quotation from Marx implies that the productive forces of capitalism, through an increasing division of labour, co-operation, and interdependence, take on an increasingly *social* character, while the social relations of production under capitalism — that is the 'capitalist integument' — remain essentially private in character. Forces and relations of production become incompatible.

Whereas the second quotation deals specifically with the emerging contradictions of the capitalist order, the first quotation is more general. It could be applied not only to capitalism, but also to other modes of production such as feudalism. Here we will completely neglect the question whether this claim to historical generality is empirically valid or not. Several writers — including some Marxists — have expressed doubts about the validity of the first quotation with regard to the transition from feudalism to capitalism.[7] In the present context, however, it is more pertinent to ask whether the first quotation, *when applied specifically to the capitalist mode of production*, refers to the same phase of historical development as the second quotation which specifically concerns the dialectics of capitalism. It would seem not.

In the writings of Marx, the metaphor of 'fettered' forces of production appears, repeatedly, in contexts where a new economic order is seen in the process of being born, against the obstacles being placed in its way by the old order, as a prelude to 'social revolution'.[8]

Once the first strains of bourgeois capitalism began to grow, by the introduction of wage labour into factories and commercial agriculture, and by the transformation or potential transformation of 'fortune' into capital, but still within a predominantly feudal and petty bourgeois society, the 'fetters' of this old order were being felt, according to the orthodox Marxist interpretation. The new order required an extension of free rather than bonded labour, free, financial capital rather than fixed fortune, and also required an increasing number of free consumers on expanding markets. All these extensions were not only restricted but resisted by the old order which thus prevented the further development of productive forces in emerging capitalism. A social revolution was needed for a breakthrough, and it came into being, most forcefully in France.

Similarly, when we apply this metaphor of 'fettered' forces of production in exploring the transformation of mature capitalism into socialism, this would seem to require that socialism has started to grow already in the 'womb' of capitalism, and is being forcefully resisted by this capitalist order. Marx himself had no access to empirical examples of this transformation which he could scientifically analyse. Several writers (Cutler, Hindess, Hirst and Hussain, 1977, and W. Shaw, 1978) have shown that Marx's speculative accounts of this transformation leave a lot to be desired in terms of conceptual clarity and unambiguity. These conceptual problems will not be discussed here but later under the heading of *extended* contradictions. It should be obvious by now that the metaphor of 'fettered' forces of production is applicable mainly in that context, and not in the context of what I have called the *basic* contradictions of capitalism, since the 'fetters' placed upon the development of productive forces are said to appear only when two *different* economic orders — established feudalism and emerging capitalism, or similarly capitalism and emerging socialism — are clashing in the *terminal* phase of each economic order.

The notion of contradiction indicated by the second of our two quotations from Marx, however, would seem to imply a growing contradiction *within* capitalism already in an earlier phase of capitalism, visible even during the lifetime of Marx himself, as a precursor to later extended contradictions. Since our main concern in this context is basic rather than extended contradictions, we will here attempt to explore and explicate only the meaning of contradictions as indicated in the second quotation: the contradiction between the increasingly social character of productive forces in mature capitalism, and the private character of its social relations of production. But our main task is to consider the kind of empirical indicators needed to establish scientifically the unfolding of this basic type of contradiction.

5 Empirical Indicators of the Social Character of Productive Forces, and the Private Character of Social Relations of Production

An increasing interdependence of different economic activities and units is obviously related to the growing size of single and interrelated productive units and their markets. The individual shoemaker or baker in social formations dominated by pre-capitalist modes of production did not involve more than an extremely limited sector of society in his undertakings. He used little or no labour power in addition to his own, and supplied his products only to a limited local market. The larger the size of productive units and markets, the more societal are the productive forces involved. But it is the interdependency of these growing units, and the dependency of an increasing sector of society as a whole on these units rather than their size alone which generates the contradictions between increasingly social productive forces and the private relations of production under capitalism. Another aspect of this process is the increasing vulnerability of capitalist society. When one or a few crucial economic units in a highly interdependent economic system are struck by crises, the effects may reverberate through the system as a whole, while the decisions made in the headquarters of private firms take account of a much more limited range of effects. In the following we will therefore concentrate on indicators of interdependency and vulnerability. Size of economic units enters our discussion mainly as an aspect of interdependency and vulnerability.

The increasing interdependence and dependency between economic units and functions are incontrovertible facts of life in mature capitalism. Empirical corroborations of these facts are hardly needed. But it would be interesting to look at empirical indicators monitoring the growth of interdependence and dependency *over time* — and a few indicators of this nature will now be presented for Sweden. The purpose is not primarily descriptive, however. Even readers with a special interest in Sweden are unlikely to find our figures and tables particularly exciting; they only depict what most readers already know or expect.

Our main point is rather to teach a lesson. We aim to demonstrate that the basic notions of Marx's theory of history can be empirically tested.

Interdependence — Horizontal and Vertical

First we will introduce a few simple indicators which can be picked from any annual of national statistics, and which deal with the inter-dependence created by a nationwide division of labour (SOU, 1976:4, p. 29). To begin with we will neglect the vertical or hierarchical dimension of such a division of labour.

If we look at the proportion working in various branches of the economy from 1870 to 1970, we find 72 per cent working in agriculture and subsidiary activities in 1870, and only 6 per cent in 1975. Still the 6 per cent in agriculture in 1975 could produce commodities covering most of the basic household needs in Sweden.[1] Thus nearly all Swedish households today *depend* on the work of the 6 per cent in agriculture. In 1870 most of the population could produce for their own subsistence, and did not to any greater extent depend on others in this respect.

Until 1965 the increasing division of labour in Swedish society is indicated by the growth of the manual/non-manual workforce employed in industry and mining from 15 per cent in 1870 to 44 per cent in 1965. However, after 1965 the percentage employed in industry and mining decreased from 44 to 34 per cent in 1978 — a sign of increasing industrial productivity; more could be produced by fewer men.

The growth of interdependence within this division of labour is indicated by the growth of transportation and commerce. In 1870 only 5 per cent of the workforce were found in this sector; in 1975 as much as 21 per cent were involved. The volume of transport has grown about 1.3 times the growth of the Gross National Product in recent years, due to the geographical expansion of distribution networks (SOU, 1966:69, p. 70). Distribution costs in 1920 were estimated to about 5-10 per cent of commodity costs; the percentage in 1970 has been estimated to between 50-60 per cent (Sarv, 1973, p. 9). The relative independence of the primary producers which dominated the economy in 1870 obviously is a thing of the past; productive forces have become increasingly societal to an extent which requires an expansion of non-productive activities not only in transport and distribution, but also in the public and private service sector. In 1870 and 1900 this sector accounted only for 7 to 8 per cent of the workforce. Between 1930 and 1970 this was the fastest growing sector of all, increasing its proportion of the workforce from 16 to 31 per cent.

It is doubtful, however, whether this increase in the public and private service sector can be interpreted only as a reflection of the increasing needs for co-ordination, administration and related competence within an increasingly interdependent economy. Particularly in the public sector the increasing workforce also reflects more indirect effects of this increasing interdependency — side-effects causing social damage which calls for public welfare services. To this 'socialization of reproduction' we will return later on. This is an aspect of the increasingly social character of reproduction which should be treated under the heading of extended effects.

So far we have emphasized mainly the non-vertical aspects of increasing interdependence — even though the growth of the public sector alludes to a vertical dimension. The basic vertical dimension in Marx's account of the increasingly social character of productive forces, however, refers to the increasing concentration and centralization of the means of production — that is the increasing size of individual capitals and firms, and the smaller number of capitalist decision-makers at the top of the industrial establishment. However, another relevant vertical dimension of interdependence concerns the relationship between larger firms and smaller sub-contractors involved in component or part production.

Unfortunately we have not found any time-series data on the historical development of sub-contracting, but its importance in the Swedish economy today has been demonstrated by several studies (Fredriksson-Lindmark, 1976, and SIND PM, 1975:4). About 25 per cent of the production in the toolmaking industry is based on sub-contracting. Firms in which more than half of their production is sub-contracted also exhibit greater variation in their turnover in relation to the business-cycle; sub-contracting thus seems to imply greater sensitivity to such fluctuations in business activity. Thus the social impact of larger firms can be underestimated if we count only their own employees. For instance, Volvo employs about 40 000 people in Sweden. If we include the employees of sub-contracted smaller firms, the figure is about 70 000 (Lindholm and Norstedt, 1977, p. 7).

With respect to the increasing concentration and centralization of the means of production, we will have more to say on this matter in a later section on the 'self-destruction of competitive markets'. Here we will only refer to figures on concentration of employees and sales in big business, on centralization of the means of production and the means of distribution under the control of a decreasing number of big companies, and the incidence of industrial mergers. We will not discuss in detail the differences between the notions of concentration and centralization. The term concentration refers to the process of *individual* capital accumulation whereas centralization involves not only the competitive *reduction* of many individual capitals by the formation of oligopolies, duopolies and monopolies, but also the *combination* of individual capitals into joint stock companies, and of such companies into groups of companies, cartels or investment companies. Whereas concentration is a quantitative incremental process, centralization at some point introduces a qualitative, not just a quantitative, change. But even though the processes of concentration and centralization are analytically different, they are in fact closely related in a causal sense, and they both increase the average size of productive units. In the relevant literature we have very frequently found that centralization of capital is called concentration. In such cases we have not corrected that terminology but maintained the terminology used by the authors to which we refer.

In 1903 about 5 per cent of workers in industry in Sweden were employed in units with more than 1000 employees. In 1930 and 1973 the corresponding figures were about 11 and 21 per cent, respectively (Wibe, 1976). In 1975 more than one-third of the workforce, the public sector excluded, was employed in a small fraction of all Swedish companies, more precisely 255 concerns with more than 500 employees each. The twelve largest business companies accounted for 45 per cent of the total stock value at the Swedish Stock Exchange (SOU, 1979:9, p. 134f).

In 1912 the ten largest companies in Sweden accounted for about 9 per cent of total industrial employment, whereas in 1936, 1963 and 1972, respectively, the figures were 16, 18 and 20 per cent. Obviously this trend toward concentration was most pronounced between 1912 and 1936 when many of the largest export-oriented companies in Sweden emerged. If we include employees abroad (about 250 000 in 1972) this tendency is even more pronounced. In 1972 30 per cent of all industrial employees were found in the ten largest companies. The fifty largest companies, according to the same criterion, accounted for 50 per cent of total industrial employment at home and abroad — and these fifty companies constituted only a small fraction of all the 40 000 companies involved in this calculation.

Industrial mergers have increased at a very fast rate since 1955 when forty-six mergers occurred. In 1969 there were already 221 mergers, according to Rydén (1971) whose figures, however, are based only on press releases and annual company reports, and thus may underestimate the real figures somewhat. Since 1970 the National Swedish Price and Cartel Office have been reporting more accurate figures. From 1970 to 1975 industrial mergers have increased from 328 to 828.

Industrial mergers in Sweden have been most common between companies competing on the same market, and thus imply monopolistic or horizontal integration. About 80 per cent of all industrial mergers between 1946 and 1969 were of this type (Rydén, 1971, p. 64). Vertical integration (incorporation of sub-contractors, distributors, raw material producers, etc.) and diversification (incorporation of new types of products and markets) through mergers were less common in Sweden before 1969, but may have become more frequent since then. However, there are mechanisms for bringing about vertical integration and diversification other than industrial mergers. Through investment companies, which we will discuss in more detail later on, and through bank financing a pyramidal conglomerate can be created which in fact contributes to vertical integration or diversification in spite of the fact that no formal merger has taken place. At the top of such a pyramid of interlocking companies partly owned by an investment company and by each other there is a small group of capitalists who have only a minority of shares but a majority of votes in the investment company and can therefore effectively control the whole structure without a formal merger. In Sweden the Wallenberg group of companies illustrates this pyramidal structure (Hermansson, 1971 and Lundh, 1973).[2] This kind of structure can be described in terms of the basic principle of finance capital as Hilferding (1973) understood it, that is to control a maximum of production and capital accumulation with a strategically selected minimum of shares.

We will now make some international comparisons on the concentration and centralization of industrial production, and thus also on some aspects of economic dependency and interdependence.

Unfortunately it is difficult to find recent international comparisons of capital centralization or concentration. Joe S. Bain (1966, pp. 48f) reports a study of industrial concentration in eight countries in the 1950s. Concentration was measured in terms of the proportion of employment of the twenty largest plants in each industrial branch, expressed as an index of the concentration in the United States. Sweden exhibited the highest concentration — about two times as great as the figure for the United States. If you look at the number of plants in each branch, which is responsible for at least 50 per cent of employment, a very similar picture is obtained (Bain, 1966, p. 52f). Bain attributes a 'significantly high degree of plant concentration' to branches where fifteen or fewer plants account for 50 per cent of employment. In the United States this was the case in four out of twenty-four investigated branches, in Great Britain six out of twenty-three, in France six out of twenty-two, in Japan seven out of twenty-two and in Italy eight out of twenty-three. The number of branches investigated vary depending on access to data. In Sweden as many as fifteen out of twenty-two branches fell into the category 'significantly high degree of plant concentration'.

Results very similar to those obtained by Bain have been reported in a more recent but also more limited study by Pryor (1972). Pryor makes use of another measure of concentration, namely the proportion of 'shipments' accounted for by the four largest firms in each branch. In Table 5.1 we again find that Swedish industry is the most concentrated, comparatively speaking, closely followed by Canadian, Swiss and Belgian industry. Pryor points out that industrial concentration seems to be inversely proportional to the size of the domestic market. In countries with a small domestic market only the largest and most concentrated industrial firms have been able to survive competition on the export market.

Another way to assess the centralization of capital in Sweden in comparison with other countries is to look at the development of industrial mergers. Rydén (1971), whom we have quoted above, has found that the development of mergers has increased rapidly during the 1960s in all Western countries. Depending on the access to statistical materials more precise comparisons can only be made between Sweden and the USA, and for these countries the frequency of industrial mergers was about the same.

Such statistics on the growth of interdependence and dependency do not exhaust the connotations of the concept of the increasingly social character of the productive forces under capitalist relations of production, however. It would also seem necessary to look at some more general system characteristics involved.

A common way to indicate the problematic of the interdependence and dependency patterns of 'advanced industrial societies' is to point out the *vulnerability* of these societies.

Social Vulnerability

The meaning of vulnerability could be explicated thus. *If* a major industry in a country goes bankrupt, or *if* the main transportation system breaks down because of a prolonged strike or a sudden fuel

Table 5.1: Four-firm concentration ratios as a ratio of United States concentration ratio for twelve countries in the beginning of the 1960s

Country	Ratio of concentration compared with concentration in the United States (= 1.0)
Belgium	1.46
Canada	1.52
France	0.90
West Germany	0.98
Italy	0.97
Japan	1.05
Netherlands	1.17
SWEDEN	1.58
Switzerland	1.49
United Kingdom	1.04
Yugoslavia	1.50

Source: Pryor, F.L.: An International Comparison of Concentration Ratios. *The Review of Economics and Statistics*, Vol. LIV, 1972, pp. 130-40.

Note: Except for Canada and Great Britain where data on concentration refer to 1948 and 1951 respectively, all the data in the table are from the period 1961 to 1965.

crisis, the whole system is seriously shattered. Another example which illuminates the close relationship between degree of centralization of production and system vulnerability relates to nuclear power. At present about 25 per cent of electricity generated in Sweden is derived from nuclear power plants. *If* the original government programme for adding six further plants to the six already in operation is endorsed by the parliament — which was quite likely after the referendum on nuclear power in the spring of 1980 — then Sweden will become even more dependent on nuclear power. Probably about 60 per cent of electricity generated will then come from nuclear power plants. The vulnerability of such a system of electricity generation to serious accidents and public pressure will be a great deal larger than the vulnerability of a less centralized and more diversified system of power generation. *If* a nuclear reactor is hit by a serious accident, and public pressure mounts for closing down all similar reactors, then the whole society is shattered.

Just as the interdependence between different units and functions of the system makes for positive multiplier effects in periods of growth and progress, we encounter *negative* multiplier effects when major units and functions are struck by crises or serious accidents. The difference between this way of conceiving system vulnerability in terms of negative multiplier effects, and the Marxist conception of contradictions between the highly social character of productive forces and the private character of capitalist relations of production, can be indicated by referring to the italicized *ifs* in the previous paragraph. In the Marxist conception of the capitalist system the crisis element is not an extraneous factor which, *if* it is introduced, shatters the system. Crisis-generation is seen as intrinsic. The capitalist system is not only highly vulnerable because of its high degree of concentration, centralization and interdependence all of which make it possible to shatter it with only a few blows; it also itself produces these blows, and often in such a manner that the threat is left invisible until the moment it strikes. Causes of crises are left unchecked, and crisis problems accumulate because the logic of capitalist economic decision-making exclusively or predominantly takes account of *private* costs and *private* benefits, while increasing *social* interdependence and dependency, and the *social* costs entailed thereby, are neglected within capitalist relations of production.

Micro-aspects of Capitalist Relations of Production

As we now proceed from our discussion of the increasingly social character of productive *forces* under capitalism to an exploration of empirical aspects of capitalist *relations* of production, we prefer to start our exploration in a rather unorthodox manner, with reference to decision-making processes on the level of the single business firm. In Marxist literature capitalist relations of production are otherwise usually treated in terms of property rights, more precisely in terms of the private ownership of the means of production, and the private appropriation of the surplus value of production which is characteristic of capitalist societies as a whole. We hope that our unorthodox manner of presentation will make it easier for readers less familiar with Marxist thought to see how the private character of the capitalist relations of production becomes incompatible with the increasingly social character of productive forces. This incompatibility will be discussed here in terms of *the relative range of social effects and managerial responsibility under capitalism*.

In mature capitalism *the range of self-defined business responsibility* in business decisions is much smaller than *the range of actual effects* of business decisions because actual effects extend far beyond the area within which business decision-makers are prepared to shoulder responsibility for such effects. The extended social effects of business decisions are simply not part of the arena of 'proper' business decisions which concentrate on matters of capital accumulation, profitability and productivity.

If all or most of these extended effects were predominantly beneficial for those affected, as supposed in the doctrine of the 'invisible hand', this discrepancy between the range of business responsibility and the range of social effects would not be a matter of concern. But today even liberal economists have doubts about the invisible hand; the discrepancy between areas of business responsibility and effects of business decisions then become a matter of great concern.[3]

The methodology of empirical exploration needed to establish the extension of the area of actual negative effects beyond the area of proper responsibility in business decisions could be developed at both micro and macro levels. Micro-data on how business leaders themselves define their area of responsibility and influence in contrast to the proper responsibilities and influence of, say, trade unions and the state, could be assembled by ordinary survey techniques. Such data will be presented in Part III.

Critical incidents such as *transgressions* of the limits of areas of self-defined business responsibility could also be studied. Such incidents may occur, for instance, at the limits placed by capital on business-controlled medical surveys and care of workers. A company doctor who is told that he will be fired if he pursues further his programme of medically surveying and preventing health hazards inflicted on employees at work, obviously has transgressed such a limit of the area of self-defined managerial responsibility. To the best of our knowledge there is no study of such critical incidents, and our own resources have not been sufficient to carry out anything of the sort.[4] This kind of study has been mentioned mainly to indicate the methodological possibilities of empirically investigating some aspects of the problematic of contradictions of forces and relations of production even at this micro level.

Much more difficult, at least in some cases, is to establish the *causality* of effects of business decisions presumably extending beyond the area of 'proper' business responsibility of a given firm or investment company.

However, a discussion of these methodological issues does not belong here; they will be considered under 'negative externalities'. In the present context we start from the assumption that 'external effects' have increased greatly as a consequence of the interdependence and dependency characteristic of advanced industrial societies, and we here only wish to emphasize the more limited range of the area of self-defined capitalist responsibility in that setting.

On the macro level these limitations of private entrepreneurial responsibility are indicated by the fact that the state is increasingly assuming responsibilities which obviously private capital cannot handle. Again this brings us closer to what we call 'extended' contradictions which will be discussed in more detail later on. But before we proceed to do so we must occupy ourselves at some length with an explication of the more orthodox concept of capitalist relations of production in terms of property rights. Our introductory remarks on the limits of managerial responsibility, as they appear on the micro level of single firms, are insufficient in spelling out the meaning of capitalist relations of production in Marxist thought. The concept of property rights is fundamental in Marxist analyses of the social relations of production under capitalism. What creates one of the basic contradictions of mature capitalism is the fact that property rights, and the decision-making power associated with them, remain private and restricted under capitalism, while productive forces are becoming more and more social in character.

Capitalist Property Relations

On the whole it would seem much easier to establish empirically the existing social relations of production than the increasingly social character of productive forces. To establish whether the means of production are a matter of private property, or state property, or are controlled more directly by associated labour, and in what proportions and industrial combinations this is the case would seem simple enough.

The matter is a little more complicated, however. Among other writers William Shaw (1978, pp. 42-7) has shown that the meaning of property in Marxian thought is far from exhausted by interpreting it as a legal concept. A peasant may be only a 'phantom' or 'nominal' owner of his means of production 'since by means of credit, mortgages, and taxation, the usurers, lawyers, banks, and state gained control over it. . . . the peasant, then, no longer enjoys "real" ownership since he is deprived — because of his weak and exploited economic position — of the *de facto* fruits of his property.' Similarly it would seem possible to conceive of capitalist property relations in the legal sense as somewhat divorced from the production relations which they represent.

Following the suggestions made by Swedish social democratic

theoreticians (such as Ernst Wigforss and Östen Undén), Gunnar Adler-Karlsson (1967a, Chapter 3) has reminded us that property, far from being an indivisible unit, can be divided into a relatively large number of *functions* relating to the rights to decide on the uses of various factors of production, the rights to decide on the distribution of wages, profits, etc., and the rights to decide on overall harmonization with regard to business cycles, concentration of economic power, relationships between economic and non-economic values, etc.

Two countries which formally speaking exhibit the same percentage of private ownership in industry may still, as a result of differences in company and labour legislation, and in the strength of labour unions and labour parties, turn out to have very different profiles in terms of the rights of various groups to control some of the economic *functions* which originally constituted private property. The state or labour unions may have acquired the legal rights to control or at least significantly influence some of the functions mentioned by Gunnar Adler-Karlsson.

As a consequence of this functionalist analysis of property Gunnar Adler-Karlsson maintains that it is possible to attain what he calls a 'functional socialism' through union and legislative action by transferring the control of most functions originally implied by private property rights into the hands of state and labour, while this property still in a formal sense remains private.

Let us look at our capitalists just as we look at our kings, says Adler-Karlsson. Sweden is still a monarchy, formally speaking, but the many functions once connected with royal power have successively been removed from the sphere of influence of the king. Similarly, we can maintain private industrial property in a formal sense — and Adler-Karlsson suggests some tactical and economic reasons for doing this[5] — while in fact removing the control of economic functions more or less completely from the hands of capitalists, a process which is already under way in most capitalist countries, according to Adler-Karlsson.

Because of its rather ahistorical and idealistic character we find Adler-Karlsson's argument about the *transition* to functional socialism far from convincing. However, his discussion of the divisibility of private ownership into a number of economic functions, the control of which can be distributed differently even while retaining private property in a formal sense, should still be taken seriously in any empirical study of the social relations of production. The conceptual tools suggested by Adler-Karlsson in this context are necessary but not sufficient, in our view. At the end of Chapter 17 we have in fact included a section on company and labour law in action which takes off from notions similar to those of Gunnar Adler-Karlsson (see p. 226). In the present chapter, however, we will content ourselves with having indicated some of the methodological complexities related to an empirical study of social relations of production in the sense of property rights — complexities such as those mentioned by Adler-Karlsson — without getting involved in a more substantive discussion of the matter.[6] We will satisfy ourselves and hopefully our readers by presenting only some rather conventional statistics on the distribution of ownership of different kinds of industrial capital in Sweden. In a later section we will discuss the role of state intervention in taking control over certain functions of capital (see p. 110).

Of a total 1.8 million employed by private and public firms in 1974, 93.4 per cent were employed in private companies, 2.2 per cent by local authorities and only 4.4 per cent in firms owned by the state. Apart from communication and transport the only other branch of the Swedish economy dominated by state ownership was mining where 68 per cent of all employees were employed in state-owned mines. Even here, however, the dominance of state ownership is a rather recent phenomenon; the large iron mines in northern Sweden were nationalized as late as in the mid 1950s. To conceive of this nationalization of the iron mines as a step toward socialism is scarcely justified. The outbreak of a prolonged wildcat strike at these mines in 1969 was partly a reaction against the tough attitude of management as they tried to implement the advice given by an American consultant firm (Dahlström et al., 1971).

Table 5.2 contains some comparative international data on extent of nationalization of industry in some European countries.

Table 5.2: **State enterprise in some European countries 1976.**
Millions employed, share of employment and investments

Country	Millions employed in the state enterprise sector	Proportion of total	
		Employment	Investments
Belgium	0.3	7	14
The Netherlands	0.3	7	19
Great Britain	2.0	9	19
Federal Republic of Germany	1.9	10	19
France	1.6	11	26
Italy	1.3	15	34
Sweden	0.3	7	11

Source: SOU 1978:85, p. 161.

The countries included in this table use somewhat different definitions of state enterprise. The share of state enterprises is probably under-estimated in some cases, especially for France and Germany, where the statistical definition is very strict, and where the state owns minority shares in quite a large number of firms. These figures are from 1976, the year when the social democrats were defeated in the general elections and a three-party bourgeois coalition took over the Swedish government. Since 1976 state ownership of industry, paradoxically, has expanded considerably in Sweden. Through a merger Swedish Steel AB was formed, with 50 per cent of the shares owned by the state. The state has also taken over almost all shipbuilding. Altogether these two ventures added 18 000 and 22 000 employees respectively to the state enterprise sector. The state has also extended its involvement in textile and computer industries. Still, more than 90 per cent of all employed in private and public firms work in the private sector.

As regards the *structure of private ownership* there is a clear trend away from personal ownership to institutional ownership by so-called investment companies, that is companies who do not themselves produce any commodities or services but buy shares in profitable companies doing so (Vem äger Sverige, 1968, p. 88; Meidner, 1978, p. 36; Frydén, 1977, p. 44). In the mid 1970s 40 per cent of all the firms registered on the capital market were estimated to have an investment company as the largest owner, and ownership by investment companies is expanding. It would seem reasonable to assume that this trend contributes to increasing the mobility of capital in the interest of profitability and economic growth but to the neglect of social considerations. In the case of personal ownership the owner is likely to have a personal involvement in the production of his company, and to keep his capital in the company as long as possible, while institutional owners such as investment companies can be expected to use their greater freedom of action by moving capital to where it renders maximum gain. The firms which are deserted by capital in this way are often still profitable, but less profitable than other firms which attract the capital of investment companies. As a result we obtain a greater destruction of capital, and a greater social cost than would have been the case with more committed personal, private ownership or, say, with workers self-management. The increasing importance of investment companies would thus seem to increase the contradiction between the increasingly social character of productive forces and capitalist relations of production.

In conclusion we feel justified to say that relations of production in Sweden are still overwhelmingly capitalist in character. State intervention or even state ownership in Sweden, where it is increasing, does not essentially change the most crucial elements in capitalist relations of production: the appropriation of surplus out of the labourers in the interest of capital accumulation, and the private sales and purchase of the shares or other units of capital for the benefit of capitalist rather than social interests. Social interests *which happen not to coincide with capital interests* are satisfied only indirectly and often rudimentarily, if at all, through state welfare redistributions (see below).

However, we must admit that this is a rather limited analysis because of the existence not only of 'nominal' or 'functionally restricted' private property as indicated by Shaw and Adler-Karlsson (see above), but also of the possibility of interpreting relations of production not only in terms of *ownership* relations but also in terms of *work* relations, as suggested by Shaw (1978, p. 28f). Unfortunately, Shaw's discussion of this matter remains at a very high level of abstraction — no doubt because Marx's own references to this thorny problem were scattered and abstract — and therefore we have been unable to derive much guidance for our empirical work from Shaw's suggestions on this point.

Capitalist Work Relations

A particularly thorny problem in this context is the fact that work organization was included among the *productive forces* rather than among the *social relations of production* by Marx himself. What is then the difference between *work organization* as a productive force, and Shaw's *work relations* as an aspect of the relations of production? The answer must be sought with full cognizance of the whole theory of historical materialism rather than through a search for Marxian quotations which superficially seem relevant. In this spirit it would seem most adequate to define *work organization as a productive force* in terms of man—nature, man—machine and man—man relationships of immediate relevance to the productive process itself, while defining *work relations as social relations of production* in terms of the relevance of such relations for capital accumulation and the appropriation of surplus value. In fact the concrete relationships involved could be the 'same' in both cases, denotatively speaking, but then quite different aspects or attributes of these relationships would refer to productive forces and relations of production respectively.

On this point I have found a discussion by the Swedish sociologist Torsten Björkman (1978, p. 17f) on 'Seven Frontiers of Capital Accumulation' quite illuminating. His discussion helps us to explicate the empirical meaning of the concept 'work relations' which Shaw has extracted through his close reading of Marx on relations of production. Björkman has pointed out that the *method* of capital accumulation has a greater effect on work relations and work environment generally than the rate of accumulation.

The *first method of capital accumulation* is to keep the price of labour as low as possible per unit of work. Low wages — kept as close as possible to the level needed for the reproduction of labour only — were characteristic of early capitalism. However, this particular method of capital accumulation can also be combined with increasing wages if productivity per work unit can be increased. An increasing division of labour contributes to increased productivity as Adam Smith explained already in 1776 in his classical example of pin-production. Fifty years later Charles Babbage pointed out that an increasing division of labour contributes to increasing productivity and capital accumulation mainly because the division of labour makes it possible to buy exactly the quantity of skill and muscular power needed for each single operation in the division of labour whereas a lack of such a division of labour makes it necessary to employ a person who has sufficient skills and muscular power to carry out even the most complicated and most demanding tasks included in the total work. Babbage emphasized, for instance, that it is profitable to remove the manual elements in mental work and to allocate them to less skilled and less paid workers in the division of labour. Babbage's principle thus presupposes wage differentials.

We can thus conclude that this first method of capital accumulation brings about work relations characterized by wage differentials related to different skill levels within an increasing division of labour.

If we move for a moment from early capitalism to late capitalism where in a country such as Sweden wage differentials have been narrowed through trade union action (Meidner, 1978, and Löner, priser, skatter, 1976) — for instance by substituting less differentiated monthly salaries for differentiated piece-rate payments — this would seem to counteract the first method of capital accumulation mentioned. But this method is still at work even under these relatively inhospitable conditions. Under these conditions this particular method operates by creating a greater demand for more productive labour power; low-performing workers become less attractive from the point of view of capital in this setting. They are likely to be fired; or if that is made difficult by legislation, management will be extra careful not to hire such low-performing labour. As a result we obtain not wage differentials but differentials between an elite of workers, and a category of second-class workers who tend to be unemployed for long periods, or employed in segregated, government sponsored workshops for second or third-class workers. This segregation of different categories of workers is another instance of work relations which in some cases of late capitalism result from the *first method of capital accumulation*. Table 9.3 on p. 100 presents some data on this trend of segregated work. In that section we will also present some statistics on the increasing number of 'unemployables' who are given premature pensions by the state due to the lack of suitable employment.

Because we are using Björkman's discussion here mainly to illustrate how the Marx–Shaw concept of work relations could be tackled empirically, we will not dwell equally on all the other methods of capital accumulation mentioned by Björkman. The *second method of capital accumulation* — increasing the length of working-time — would seem to be of less interest than some of the other methods mentioned.

The *third method of capital accumulation* is to minimize what Marx called the 'porosity' of the working day (*Capital*, Vol. I, p. 534) that is time for resting, for waiting, for walking between different stations at work, for making unnecessarily time-consuming movements of work, and generally to increase the intensity and speed of work. Taylor's methods of 'scientific management' were specifically geared to solve these problems. Through measurement of time and method of work (MTM) management acquires a monopoly of detailed knowledge on the productive process. All planning is removed from workers, and vested into a special planning section. Management's monopoly of knowledge and planning is used for a detailed programming and control of the production process; the worker only goes through the movements already programmed. Furthermore, to control and to increase the intensity of work, the assembly line was introduced. The work relations implied by this method of capital accumulation involves deskilling, routinization and complete loss of workers control over the work situation.

The methods of capital accumulation mentioned so far all imply a rationalization of so-called *variable* capital, that is of the use of labour. Such methods would seem particularly relevant for the empirical definition of work relations as a specific aspect of social relations of production. Björkman also mentions four methods of capital accumulation which imply a rationalization of *constant* capital such as buildings and space for industrial plants, industrial machinery etc.

Attempts to save space, to increase the intensity of machine-use, to speed up the flow of products in work, to decrease the vulnerability of the productive process to external disturbances all have various implications for work relations such as congestion, noise, continuous production with shift-work, functional sectionalization of production, etc. – and at least some of these work relations involve human and social costs which are not considered in a pure capitalist calculus.

In all fairness, however, the last mentioned frontier of capital accumulation – decreasing the vulnerability of production processes to external disturbances – implies arrangements which may improve work relations from the workers' point of view. For instance, in response to the 'external disturbance' of worker absenteeism, workers may be trained and required to carry out quite different tasks at work, to enable each worker flexibility to replace absent workers. Apart from being a method of capital accumulation this also implies a certain degree of job rotation and 'job enrichment' which could be conceived as being in the interest of labour as well as capital (Björkman, 1978, p. 27). However, the ultimate solution to the problem of production vulnerability is total automation – 'the unmanned factory'. Such designs may not influence work relations as much as unemployment levels.

On the whole the work relations defined by most of the various methods of capital accumulation discussed by Björkman do logically imply a neglect for human and social costs which hurt the worker and his class. Logically it also follows that in plants where such neglect is less pronounced this must be due to the operation of some other process contradicting the laws of capital accumulation, for instance trade union activities or effective labour legislation.

Therefore we can conclude our discussion of the two aspects of social relations of production – property relations and work relations – by saying that we have virtually no empirical evidence falsifying the assertion that social relations of production remain private in character, in contrast to the increasingly social character of productive forces which we have documented earlier.

The two empirical trends just mentioned, relating to the lack of change in production relations and the changing character of productive forces, also corroborate the Marxist assertion that the contradiction between forces and relations of production is becoming more pronounced in contemporary capitalist development.

However, it should be explained that our empirical operationalization of this concept of contradictions does not exhaust the theoretical implications of the concept — just as the mercury column in a thermo-meter only serves as a convenient empirical indicator without exhausting the theoretical implications of the notion of temperature. Just as a thermodynamic theory of molecular motion is required to make use of the concept of temperature in explanations of processes of heating and cooling, we need to understand the meaning of contradictions between forces and relations of production on a theoretical level in order to explain the place of such contradictions in processes of social repro-duction and change. In our earlier discussion we have touched upon two different but related theoretical implications of this concept of contradiction:

1. The notion of capitalism as a *form of decision-making* exhibiting an increasing discrepancy between the limited range of considerations basic to business decisions, and the increasing range of social effects of such decisions — a discrepancy which generates poor and even disastrous decisions from the point of view of society as a whole, and particularly from the perspective of the labouring classes which make up the majority of mature capitalist societies.

2. The notion of capitalism as an *economic form* which — because of its restricted focus on profit and capital accumulation — fails to adjust to the development of productive forces, and which thus increasingly becomes a 'fetter' upon these productive forces.

The former notion concerns a basic contradiction within the mature capitalist system as a whole. The second notion concerns a contradic-tion which acts as a constraint on the transformation of this capitalist system — a constraint which, however, may be 'burst asunder' as a result of the mobilization of the labouring classes and its allies in res-ponse to the effects of the first type of contradiction.

This is the theory. Later on we will return to the question concern-ing the likelihood of this theory being borne out by the facts of social practice. But first we must deal with some remaining theoretical and empirical tasks.

6 Changes in the Market Structures of Capitalism

While our discussion so far has concentrated on relative changes in various human, organizational, economic and social aspects of the *productive* apparatus of capitalism, we will now turn to changes in the structure of *markets*, and to changing *incentive patterns* under capitalism. However, when we distinguish productive forces and market forces this does not imply that these forces can be treated as completely separate and unrelated. Productive forces and market forces are closely intertwined; they are different aspects of the same master processes of capitalist development. For instance, the centralization of capital which we have discussed earlier as one aspect of the increasingly social character of productive forces, also implies certain changes in the structure of markets. The same master process appears with several aspects because of the particular arena of change from which we choose to view the given process.

The Self-Destruction of Competitive Markets: Monopolization and Trade Cycles

The mechanisms of supply and demand of the competitive market, based not only on the sale of goods and services but also on the making of labour and financial capital into commodities, was an essential element of the social relations of production in early capitalism. Economists claim that these market mechanisms ensure an *optimal allocation of resources* in the economy, and that the consumer is sovereign in determining the direction of the economy to his own benefit through effective consumer demand, as long as the conditions of free competition are fulfilled on the market. Consumer demand generates profits, capital follows profit, labour follows capital, and the use of capital and labour in production eventually produces not only the goods and services most in demand but also the wage (price of labour) which is needed to pur chase these on the market. This is a circle of cumulative causation which provides not only benefits to all but also an economic growth not attained by any other economic system, according to the dominant Western school of economics. There is no better way to ensure optimal allocation of scarce resources, and the satisfaction of consumer demand, than to allow market mechanisms to work it all out — with some marginal state interventions in times of crisis.

The neoclassical market model is abstract and unhistorical. As long as we stay within this unhistorical framework it is difficult not to be convinced by its abstract logic. Difficulties appear only when we descend from this abstract, non-historical level of analysis to the real world and history of enterprise, labour and consumption.

Historically we find that approximately free competition gives way successively to oligopolistic, duopolistic and monopolistic structures. Prices determined by supply and demand relationships are increasingly replaced by the 'price leadership' of perfect oligopolies and the fixed prices of monopolies. Producers increasingly must design their production without the information obtained from competitive markets, and on the basis of long-term considerations of research and development; they then create, rather than respond to, consumer demand, through advertising and other types of sales promotion.

However, it is interesting to note that this development of capitalism could have been predicted quite well theoretically on the basis of the market model itself, had it been applied in an iterative manner, rather than in the normative manner most common among economists. By iterating the market processes consecutively, in a sufficiently long series of cycles, we can find theoretically, and not only empirically and historically, that competitive markets operate in a self-destructive manner over time wherever the benefits of increasing size is greater than its costs.[1] When success breeds success among competing firms in an originally strictly competitive market this, over time, leads to oligopolistic, duopolistic or monopolistic structures which reduce or eliminate the competition which is supposed to be the singular and unbeatable vehicle of optimal resource allocation in a free enterprise economy.

Market theory itself thus allows us to predict the free markets of capitalism to be self-contradictory over time, in that they create a centralization of capital which undermines free competition. As a result of international competition, or of the emergence of innovations, and of variations in the time-span of designing, producing and selling different products, the process is slower in some areas than in others — and furthermore the state may more or less successfully try to

counteract this development; but the process itself app
within the parameters of the capitalist system, even if \
the premises and assumptions of mainstream econom
say, Marxist theory.

In his book *The Visible Hand* (1977) Alfred D. Cl   ., an
American historian, has convincingly shown that the competitive
market model fits the reality of contemporary capitalism rather badly.
His main thesis is that administrative co-ordination rather than market
forces determine production and distribution in big business. Chandler's
study covers the development of American capitalism from its begin-
nings in the early nineteenth century to the middle of this century.
To begin with the American economy did certainly conform rather
well with the image of a competitive market economy presupposed
by Adam Smith and more recent economic theory. Production and
distribution of commodities was handled by many small, independent
economic units. Market forces determined what was produced and
where production was located as well as transport and financing. The
growth of big business which in itself was a result of these market
forces successively changed the picture. Administrative co-ordination
proved to be superior to the co-ordination attainable by market forces.
Modern big business is composed of a multitude of units which theoretically could have acted quite independently; but the integration of
these units within a larger unit proved to be more advantageous. By
way of planning within such a larger economic unit, it is possible to
attain a more stable flow of products and a better use of buildings,
machines and labour. Costs for acquiring information about the market
as well as for business transactions can be minimized. On the basis of
his thorough historical studies Chandler concludes that production
and distribution nowadays are determined increasingly not by market
forces, as economic theory assumes, but by administrative co-ordination.
The invisible hand of market forces has been replaced by the visible
hand of corporate management.

Similarly John Kenneth Galbraith, in his book *The New Industrial
State* (1967, pp. 16 and 365) emphasized that big business, due to the
exigencies of advanced technology and large organizations, finds it
necessary to rely largely on planning rather than on market mechanisms.

To assess empirically the distribution of various types of markets —
monopolistic, oligopolistic, competitive, etc. — is a difficult task. In
the early sixties a Swedish government commission published a comprehensive study on concentration and centralization of economic
power (SOU, Koncentrationsutredningen, 1968) which produced some

relevant findings, however. One of the difficulties involved in this kind of study is that both markets and groups of products must be delimited. Even in cases where one particular commodity is produced by several different firms, it is theoretically possible for each firm to dominate the market in one particular part of the country. Furthermore the domination of one particular firm in the production of a commodity will not necessarily have monopolistic effects if competition is introduced through imports from the international market. In spite of these difficulties the government study just mentioned made an attempt to assess the distribution of three different types of markets involving monopolistic or oligopolistic tendencies:

1. High degree of monopolization at the level of firms: the largest firm accounts for at least 70 per cent of production; competing imports account for less than 30 per cent.

2. High degree of monopolization at the level of cartels: the cartel accounts for at least 70 per cent of production; competitive imports account for less than 30 per cent.

3. High degree of oligopoly at the level of firms: the four largest firms account for at least 70 per cent of production, or the eight largest firms account for at least 90 per cent; competing imports account for less than 30 per cent.

In 1963 the first type of market, with one dominant firm, accounted for 11 per cent of production value; the second type of market, the dominance of one cartel, accounted for 14 per cent; oligopolistic competition characteristic of the third type of market accounted for 25 per cent of total production value. Together these three types of markets thus accounted for 50 per cent of total production value which suggests that monopolistic and oligopolistic tendencies are rather pronounced in Sweden (Vem äger Sverige, 1968, p. 280). However, it is more difficult to say whether these monopolistic and oligopolistic tendencies have become more pronounced over time. Sören Wibe (1976), by comparing the findings of the Swedish government commission on 'concentration' based on data from 1963 with a similar study published in 1940, arrived at the conclusion that no further change in a monopolistic direction was discernible over this period. Furthermore, during this period, he found no evidence of monopoly prices and stagnation because of lack of competition, the correlates of monopoly capitalism predicted by Marx and his followers. However, he could empirically establish an increasing monopolization on the level of cartels in the first two decades of this century in Sweden after a period of competitive capitalism with a falling rate of profit during the last few decades of the nineteenth century. This monopolistic cartelization in the early twentieth century is seen by him as a response to the falling rate of profit within the competitive capitalism of the late nineteenth century. His general conclusion — arrived at empirically in contradiction to his basically Marxist outlook — is that monopolistic centralization, far from being the continuous, automatic and inevitable process explicated by some Marxists, is an intermittent and recurrent process slowing down and even reversing in times of industrial expansion and growth, and picking up speed in connection with more deep-seated structural crises of international capitalism, and thus perhaps related to the 'long waves' of such crises rather than to a continuous historical tendency.

Through his empirical studies Wibe has no doubt contributed to problematize the Marxian notion of monopolistic centralization, and thus rendered a significant stimulus to continued Marxist research in this area. However, his findings give rise to a number of theoretical and methodological questions which are not considered by him, and which relate to the role of finance capital in the kind of pyramidal structures which we have discussed earlier (p. 55). We have suggested that the frequency of *formal* mergers — monopolistic ones or those involving vertical integration or diversification — indicates only the tip of an iceberg. Hidden under the surface we may find business conglomerates which for all practical purposes display tendencies of diversification, vertical integration or even monopoly as forceful as those which are manifest in various kinds of *formal* mergers.

Similarly the formal criteria of monopolistic practice defining the data utilized by Wibe — criteria that may be reasonably valid as far as they go — do not exhaust the data needed to survey the tendency to monopolistic centralization. More data are needed here on the role of investment companies, and of the pyramidal structure of so-called conglomerates. Such data as are available — and we refer here to an illuminating article in *Veckans Affärer* (45/1978) and to Lundh (1973) — do certainly justify the statement that capital in Sweden has become increasingly centralized. Due to imports domestic competition is much less significant than international competition. The existence of such international competition certainly motivates great caution in using the label Swedish monopoly capital. On that point we agree with Wibe.

Even though the tendency to a self-destruction of competitive markets which is the subject of our present discussion, has been empirically substantiated for certain periods of Swedish economic history, through data on the monopolistic cartellization of the twentieth century, through the results of government studies of 'concentration' in the late 1930s and early 1960s, through data on the percentage of monopolistic mergers, and on the wide-ranging network of control of finance capital, it is obvious that this tendency has not resulted in any complete destruction of competitive markets in Sweden. The concentration and centralization of Swedish capital, in competition with international capital, would thus seem to have been less effective in generating monopoly profits and setting monopoly prices than in increasing the social character of the productive forces in contradiction to the private character of capital accumulation and investment decisions.

One particularly important aspect of increasing international competition is its effects on the movement of Swedish capital abroad to penetrate tarriff barriers and to capture new markets, and often no doubt also to exploit cheap labour, lack of effective unions and of labour legislation, and sometimes to meet the demands of Third World governments for investment in return for favourable treatment for foreign companies. In 1970 Sweden occupied the third place among industrialized countries with respect to direct foreign investments expressed as a percentage of domestic investments in industry and mining — after Great Britain and the Netherlands, and before the USA which occupied fourth place (Larsson, 1973, p. 11). In terms of direct foreign investments as a percentage of the value of export, Sweden occupied fourth place after the USA, Great Britain and the Netherlands. The direct foreign investments of Swedish companies increased greatly already during the 1960s. Formally speaking such investments can be made only after permission by the Bank of Sweden, but such permissions are virtually always granted. In 1965 the Bank of Sweden gave permissions for direct foreign investments amounting to about half a billion Swedish crowns. In 1970 this figure rose to over one billion Swedish crowns, and in 1975 2.3 billions of direct foreign investments were permitted (*Sveriges Riksdag*). In reality direct investments abroad were larger because the figures mentioned above exclude amounts for investments made directly from the profits of Swedish subsidiaries abroad. This rapid expansion of Swedish direct investments abroad is reflected in the levels of employment at Swedish firms in foreign countries. Table 6.1 reports the situation for 1960 and 1970. During this period the number employed by Swedish industrial firms abroad

Table 6.1: Changes in employment levels at Swedish industrial subsidiaries in certain countries 1960—70, and the corresponding changes of overall industrial employment in these countries for the same period

Country	Number employed at Swedish industrial subsidiaries abroad 1960	Number employed at Swedish industrial subsidiaries abroad 1970	Per cent change 1960—70	Overall percentage change of industrial employment in host country 1960—70
Federal Republic of Germany	26 446	32 604	24	11
France	13 641	21 237	56	4
Great Britain	11 707	13 927	19	0
USA	9 398	9 807	4	15
India	7 747	12 219	58	—
Brazil	3 964	12 981	227	—
Italy	3 668	15 526	323	20
Finland	2 811	5 870	109	22
Denmark	2 695	7 061	162	3
Belgium	2 581	6 020	133	6
Others	21 539	44 797	108	—
Total	106 197	182 049	71	

Source: SOU 1975:90, p. 91.

increased by 71 per cent, at the same time as there was a stagnation of industrial employment in Sweden itself.

Swedish firms which are troubled by costs at home, but who cannot move their production abroad for some reason, may find it profitable to use cheaper foreign parts for its 'Swedish' products. The proportion of such imported parts in Swedish export production has increased from 15 per cent in 1957 to 18 per cent in 1964 and 20 per cent in 1968 (Larsson, 1973, p. 15), and this trend has not been discontinued in recent years. As a result the Swedish trade balance, and our small and middle-sized industry may have been affected.

But what is the relevance of these figures, you may ask, from the point of view of our present topic – the self-destruction of competitive markets? Are not the changes indicated a reflection of the effectiveness of market forces rather than of their self-destruction? In strictly economic terms – yes. But these figures also highlight an important peculiarity of the market model – its complete neglect of political economy and of the *location* of destructive market effects on the map of political territorial units. With an increasing internationalization of markets, the market model becomes increasingly irrelevant for national economies, and for the very concrete and real human beings who depend on the survival and growth of national economies. Even if market forces bring about an optimal allocation of resources on an *international* market, we must ask ourselves: optimal for whom?

Given the assumptions of neoclassical theory the market is certainly optimally beneficial to everybody effectively involved in market operations. But who are involved, and who are excluded from what market? The theory does not specifically answer these questions. Obviously domestic capital and labour markets in some countries can be severely hurt by the 'optimal' allocation of resources on a more or less unregulated world market.

To a theoretical economist, capital, labour and commodities move in their abstract orbits in an abstract space, and there is no question whether or not the real human actors involved are in a position to allow factor and commodity markets to come to bear on each other within socially and politically meaningful political units, and much less within more local habitats.

Karl Marx once made fun of the 'vulgar economists' and their way of talking about factors of production without taking account of the social context in which they exist:

> It is an enchanted perverted topsy-turvy world in which Mr Capital and Mistress Land carry on their goblin tricks as social characters

and at the same time as mere things . . . Capital, Land, Labour! But capital is not a thing. It is a definite interrelation of social production belonging to a definite historical formation of society.

(Marx, 1971a, pp. 814 and 830).

A concrete example of the disastrous consequences of applying the disembodied abstractions of economic theory without taking the real world into account, can be found by having a closer look at the operation of so-called neo-colonialism where export goods are mined, cultivated or produced in underdeveloped territories, and sold in industrialized countries by companies possessed and controlled by metropolitan financial interests. In this case there is firstly *a territorial and political separation of labour markets on the one hand, and consumer markets on the other*. Secondly there are *vast differences in terms of income and development* between the territorial and political units involved. Most of the labour in underdeveloped territories employed in colonial or neo-colonial undertakings is recruited locally whereas the exports sold are consumed in Europe or the USA. In a case like this, as pointed out by Samir Amin (1974, p. 15) labour becomes exclusively a matter of *cost* to the entrepreneurs, and not a factor of consumer demand, because it does not buy the goods produced or any other significant portion of goods deriving from the industrialized world. Therefore there is no reason for capitalists, in this case, to worry about the underconsumption of labourers as conceived by Marx and later elaborated by Keynes, and about paying reasonable salaries to the labourers involved. Thinking in terms of economic theory, the neo-colonial system just described, given the proper conditions, will of course produce an 'optimal allocation of resources' within the unspecified but still well-known circle of persons corresponding to the major abstractions involved — that of capital and the sovereign Western consumer. But once we get down from this lofty level of abstraction to looking at the territories and peoples actually involved in all aspects of neo-colonialism, it becomes obvious that the calculations of marginalist theory are completely irrelevant to the needs of real people toiling in really dependent and underdeveloped territories.

Such consequences of non-correspondence between the abstract processes of economic theory, as used to justify the practice of international capitalism, and the real territorial and political world, may not be as severe in highly advanced industrialized countries such as Sweden, but our figures still suggest that international market forces may be somewhat less than optimal from a Swedish point of view, and many other industrial countries are in a similar situation. Even a Swedish management expert such as Ulf af Trolle (1978, p. 146), equipped with nothing but traditional economic theory and some facts of the case, has arrived at this conclusion; he suggests that Sweden should rely somewhat less on exports and imports than is presently the case, without of course isolating itself completely from the international market. But obviously such changes in our trade patterns will not be brought about by market forces; state interventions are necessary. This again points to what we have called the extended contradictions of capitalism to which we will return later on.

However, the self-contradictory character of market processes can be described not only in terms of the long-term, probably intermittent process toward centralization of capital, or in terms of the destructive effects of territorial and political separation of markets for capital, labour and commodities in the international economic system. There is also another well-known pattern of causation which results in cyclical fluctuations, so-called trade cycles. A thorough analysis of various theories of trade cycles is beyond the scope of this presentation.[2] In this context it is sufficient to point out that the theories of overproduction and underconsumption formulated by Marx, among others, and later elaborated by Keynes within quite a different theoretical framework, are insufficient to deal with the contemporary crisis of so-called stagflation. Marx's theory on the tendential fall of the rate of profit, or other similar conceptions, is inadequate unless supplemented with insights on profit- and price-maintaining mechanisms in response to recessions. Marxists would maintain, however, that this type of recession is generated by the internal contradictions of capitalism itself, whereas more conventional economists are groping in the dark at present, and cry for the advent of a new breakthrough in economic theory to resolve the riddle of stagflation.

As far as current debate goes this new economic predicament is attributed to several different factors. The 'mark-up prices' which are fixed or administered by international cartels, and more generally in branches with a high capital concentration, are mentioned as a major cause of stagflation by Wachtel and Adelsheim (1978, pp. 359f). Mark-up pricing becomes particularly pronounced in periods of recession; this accounts for the simultaneous appearance of inflation and stagnation.

According to the conventional theory of competition, the market generates prices, and price information is fed to single firms who respond to this, usually by adopting the market price, because it would be self-destructive to set higher prices. Within the single firm prices are thus set in the light of constraints *which lie outside the control of the single firm* – more precisely the constraints set by competitive market prices, available technology and the prices of factors of production.

But with the concentration of capital, the constraint of competitive prices becomes less significant. Monopolies and oligopolies can fend for themselves by attempting to attain a 'target rate of profit'. Profit is here no longer only a dependent variable subject to market constraints outside the control of the single firm. *The firm itself controls* the target of profit it wants to attain.

> Mark-up pricing suggests that firms first compute their labour and raw material costs, and then add a 'mark-up' over raw material and labour costs in order to attain their profits. Theoretically, prices cannot be raised too high (at least not on products for which there is an elastic demand) because sales will drop too low, and the firm would then lose more than it gained. As the economy becomes more concentrated, however, firms have greater control over the market, and correspondingly more freedom to increase their price mark-ups in order to attain their target profits. Here the two theoretical arguments intersect – the one about target profit rates and the other about mark-up pricing. Firms will establish a price in order to attain a target profit rate for any given level of sales.
>
> (Wachtel and Adelsheim, 1978, p. 361).

Wachtel and Adelsheim maintain that mark-up pricing as a cause of stagflation becomes particularly important in the recessionary phase of the business cycle. Losses through diminished sales will then be recouped by increasing the mark-up for remaining sales.

> Only when unemployment reaches a point where the firm encounters an elastic response to its price mark-up policy, will traditional macropolicy toward inflation be operational in the way it is designed to be. As the economy becomes more concentrated we need longer and deeper recessions, even a depression, before such policy becomes antiinflationary. Until the firm begins to face an elastic response to its own price mark-ups, a recession will feed inflation.
>
> (1978, p. 361)

Wachtel and Adelsheim have tested these hypotheses for the postwar period of US business. The hypothesis is supported by the data. Concentrated industries exhibit mark-up pricing in periods of recession more frequently than less concentrated industry. But it also turns out that 'the sectors of medium and low concentration are coming increasingly to resemble the sector of high concentration in their own pricing behaviour during recessions' (1978, p. 364).

The sector of high economic concentration would thus seem increasingly to set the tone for the sectors of less concentration — so-called price leadership. However, another explanation is that the data available to Wachtel and Adelsheim may conceal the circumstance that many of the firms which appear to be located in the sector of medium or low concentration in actual fact increasingly are becoming members of industrial conglomerates in the sector of high concentration — a fact not adequately reflected in the statistical records.

We cannot here go into all the details of Wachtel and Adelsheim's careful theoretical and empirical analysis — for instance of the role of foreign competition in partly offsetting the stagflationary effects of capital concentration (pp. 367 and 369). Nor can we summarize other contributions to this discussion (see for instance Rick Hurd, 1978, particularly his discussion of the Swedish model of manpower planning on p. 384). The main conclusion is clear: the root cause of stagflation is growing economic concentration and power, or in other words: the destruction of competitive market forces through the long-term operation of market forces themselves.

However, some attempt must be paid also on this point to the drastic increase of oil prices in the 1970s. Sweden is extremely dependent on imported oil. A decision by the OPEC countries to raise prices has serious effects for inflation and the trade balance. For example, between December 1978 and October 1979, fuel prices in Sweden rose by 30 per cent, and this increase alone accounted for nearly one-quarter of the 7.4 per cent increase in consumer prices during that period (Preliminär Nationalbudget, 1980). Higher costs are compensated by industry with higher prices, further worsening stagflation. The causes of higher oil prices are external to Swedish capitalism, but the effects must nevertheless be handled within that system.

Our conclusions so far on the stagflation caused by mark-up pricing, and more specifically in some cases by rising oil prices, can be supplemented on this point by reference to certain seemingly contradictory tendencies with regard to changes in profits and profit rates. Marx predicted both (i) a tendential fall of the rate of profit due to the increasing costs of capital-intensive investments — what he called the increasing 'organic composition' of capital — and (ii) increasing rather than falling profits because of the monopolization of capital. These two opposite trends could be seen as part of one dialectical process: the *tendency* for the rate of profit to fall as a result of the increasing costs of capital investments may give rise to the opposite tendency of increasing monopoly profits through both monopolistic mergers, and the destruction of less competitive and profitable firms.

In Sweden, which is much more exposed to international competition than the US and which also exhibits more of a 'profit squeeze' because of the swelling of the public sector, we cannot expect high concentration of capital to be as conducive to the creation of monopoly profits as in the US — except perhaps within Swedish multinational conglomerates which simultaneously exhibit high concentration *and* internationalization of capital. In the next chapter on the incentive patterns of mature capitalism we will have more to say about changing profit rates.

However, from the point of view occupying us here — the generation of recurrent crisis in the capitalist system — it is not necessary to have a definite answer as to whether the rate of profit tends to fall, remains stable or increases due to so-called profit targets. In whatever direction the capitalist system is heading, it would seem to generate crisis of different types. It generates at least two main kinds of crises: one type of crisis preceded by a *fall* in the rate of profit, and another one by *increasing* profits which however are not realized in the form of investments etc. (Wibe, 1978). Each of these two main types of crises can be subdivided into at least three sub-types:

1. Crises preceded by a falling rate of profit:
   (a) As a result of an unbalanced increase in the organic composition of capital; degree of labour exploitation roughly constant.
   (b) As a result of a decreasing degree of exploitation and a corresponding 'profit squeeze' which may be caused not only by effective class struggle, but also by heavy increases in the magnitude of 'unproductive' labour in the public sector; organic composition of capital roughly constant.
   (c) As a result of a simultaneously increasing organic composition of capital and a decreasing degree of labour exploitation.

2. Crises preceded by low degree of realization of surplus value when profit rate is high:
   (a) As a result of relative underconsumption on the part of labour; wages too low and/or unemployment too great to generate appropriate consumer demand.
   (b) As a result of underconsumption on the part of labour; commodities and services produced do not correspond to the needs of consumers.
   (c) As a result of the fact that capitalists fail to invest their profit.

A plurality of processes relating to technological developments, effect-iveness of class struggle in unions, the growth of government spending, intensity of international price-competition, particularly from the new industrial nations of the Third World, protectionist tendencies, etc. affect the elements which define these various types of crisis. The simplistic notion of a single cumulative process of crisis generation found among some Marxists is therefore not tenable.

It may be possible to place the different types of crisis here indicated in some kind of historical sequence relating to different phases in the development of capitalism, as suggested by Sören Wibe (1976 and 1978) and by E.O. Wright (1978, pp. 168f). The crisis of the very first years of the twentieth century would seem to have been of type 1(a); the crisis of the 1930s was a crisis of type 2(a). The crisis of the mid 1970s, from which Sweden still suffers, would seem to come close to a mixture of 1(c) and 2(c), in different sectors of the economy.

Summary

A competitive free market tends over time to undermine the free com-petition which constituted it in the first place; instead oligopolies, duopolies, monopolies and conglomerates with a firm vertical and horizontal grip over production emerge. Thereby the information obtained through volumes of sales and purchases, and from prices, no longer can operate to bring about an optimal allocation of resources. Complete monopolization is prevented in many areas of production by international competition. Market mechanisms also generate cyclical fluctuations in business — booms, recessions and crises — which recently have taken on a new shape in the form of stagflation, probably as a result of certain aspects of the concentration and internationalization of capital. In the absence of effective state interventions, cyclical market fluctuations may be further reinforced through the contradic-tion between the crisis-generating propensity of capitalism, and its ten-dency to react in a way which reinforces the crisis. But, as we will soon discover, state interventions may also neutralize the 'normal' adjustment mechanisms of capitalism, temporarily destructive as they may be, in a manner which rigidifies the structures of crises in the long run.

But before we proceed to discuss the role of the state and of trade unions both in responding to the basic crisis of capitalism, and in generat-ing further crisis, we will take a close-up view of the so-called monetary incentives which are supposed to operate not only among the capitalists responding to expected profits, but also among labourers in work and consumption.

7 Changes in the Incentive Patterns of Capitalism

Most economists today reject a psychologistic interpretation of 'economic man'. Modern economic theory does not assume that human nature is equipped with a psychological drive to 'economize', that is to attain the kind of relationship between costs and benefits implied by concepts of marginal utility or preference. Economic theory only implies, in a conditionally normative manner, that man must behave in conformity to economic theory, if he wishes to be economically rational.

However, because economic organizations to a large extent are set up and run in accordance with normative economic theory, it is not surprising that such theories often are 'empirically confirmed', by the study of the organizations which they have helped to mould (cf. Argyris, 1972, p. 16). Through processes of socialization based on economic incentives the capitalist order cultivates this rational drive to maximize economic benefits and minimize costs – a drive which after all is not completely absent in human nature. In fact capitalism could not exist and flourish without the cultivation of that drive; monetary incentives and rewards are the very mainsprings of the capitalist system, psychologically speaking.

A closer look at mature capitalism would seem to indicate, however, that this mainspring of capitalism is being hurt by the development of capitalism itself. This is another internal contradiction of capitalism which thus may emerge as capitalism develops and matures.

Firstly, as capitalism produces more widespread affluence – in collaboration with effective trade unions and welfare state interventions – it seems quite possible that we may encounter certain kinds of diminishing returns in private consumption among broad sections of reasonably well-paid employees. There are limits to the number of gadgets you find useful, and to the amount of good food you can consume, the number of holiday charter flights you can make, and the amount of leisure spending you can enjoy generally. These limits are not only physical, physiological and psychological but probably also social and structural. Apart from the fact that a strenuous work-day leaves you too tired to spend increasing amounts of money, such spending beyond a certain level, to become enjoyable, requires access to a certain high-class and service-intensive infrastructure and other leisure facilities. Such 'infrastructures of enjoyment' take time to build, and most often are partly inherited through an intergenerational or at least long-term accumulation of capital. This kind of enjoyment thus requires 'oligarchical wealth' (Harrod, 1958). The ordinary well-paid wage earner in an affluent society does not usually have access to this kind of class-determined, more or less inherited 'infrastructure of enjoyment', or the time to build it for himself or herself together with the rest of the family. Therefore the diminishing returns of increasing wages and consumption in affluent societies are a result not only of physical, physiological and psychological limits but also depend on socially determined structural limitations on the capability to *absorb* continuous wage increases in a meaningful manner. Fred Hirsch (1977, p. 21) has pointed out other structural constraints to increasing consumption in the form of 'consumption scarcities' caused by physical and social congestion. Finally, the tedium of work may in fact cause the ordinary well-paid employee in an affluent society to give higher priority to other improvements than wage increases and increasing consumption, such as improvements of the work environment, increased leisure and more public investments in environmental and leisure facilities.

These are not only speculative assumptions. In a theoretical and empirical study, *The Golden Chain* (1976), Göran Ahrne has provided quite convincing evidence to support some of these hypotheses. The 'golden chain' of wage increases which according to Marx would keep workers happy and contented in their bondage seems to have become so extended as a result of the relative affluence of Sweden that you do not have to be a Houdini to slip out of its entanglement. Ordinary people in Sweden no longer respond to the monetary rewards of capitalism quite the way they did, and the way they must, to keep capitalism alive. In another context Göran Ahrne (1978b) suggests that an increasing disinterest among relatively affluent wage-earners to further increase their consumption may be a greater threat to the capitalist order than the struggle for higher wages and salaries which for nearly half a century has been unable to shatter capitalism.

But the diminishing returns and limitations of monetary incentives just mentioned are less likely to operate among people who own capital. To a much greater extent they have access to money-absorbing 'infrastructures of enjoyment' — to high-class restaurants, to private ski-resorts, to a house on the Riviera — and much of this at the indirect expense of common tax-payers since the costs of using this infrastructure, with some elementary skills in tax evasion and tax-deduction, can be made to look like the costs of capital.

But even minor owners of capital who do not have full access to this infrastructure of enjoyment, may still continue to respond strongly to the monetary incentives of capitalism — much more strongly than ordinary wage-earners and tax-payers seem to do at present. The game of profit and capital acquisition — a game, with its own sources of hope and suspense — probably provides a thrill which is as strong a motivation to many small-scale stockholders and speculators as their desire to increase their everyday consumption. And most important of all: while there is a relatively low natural ceiling to consumption without full access to what I have called the infrastructure of enjoyment, there is no such natural ceiling for successful speculation in stocks or other valuables, apart from the financial resources which the speculator can command — and of course the availability of investment opportunities which seem profitable enough. However, there is probably also a limitation on the *number* of minor owners of capital who have a serious interest in the 'game' of profit and acquisition. Some empirical studies suggest that the great majority of minor stockholders in Sweden are interested in their shares only as a saving alternative superior to bank savings rather than as a speculative game; therefore they rarely buy and sell their shares but keep them for extended periods of time.[1] Furthermore, when profitability is falling and, we may add, welfare taxes remain high and the labour costs are roughly maintained if not increased by the strength of union demands, then there is a rapidly diminishing space for the game of speculative capital acquisition — at least in the sphere of production. There remains some space only for improductive speculative investments in diamonds, estates, art and stamp collections, etc.

To the extent that we can rightly say that a fall in profitability and these high labour and welfare costs are all requisites of mature capitalism itself rather than caused by sinister external forces of state and labour — and this would seem justified to say in view of the experiences of capitalist countries which have not for a long time been managed by labour governments — then the destruction of the game of productive speculation is a result of the development of mature capitalism, and another indication of its emerging internal contradictions.

We can thus conclude that mature capitalism in Sweden by its own development destroys the motivational force of monetary incentives, which provides the very mainspring of capitalist development, by creating affluence combined with alienation at work among the broad masses of blue-collar and white-collar workers, and by creating shortages of profit among speculators in productive capital.

These conclusions are supported by empirical data not only on the micro level of labour and consumer incentives explored by Göran Ahrne in a previous study (1976) and in Chapter 13 of the present book, but also on the macro level of aggregate rates of profit. Sören Wibe (1978, p. 14) has calculated rates of profit in a great number of countries, and found a falling rate in the USA, France, GDR, Italy, England, the Netherlands and Sweden during the period 1965-75. The fall is absent or less consistent in Canada and in Japan. In Sweden the rate of profit is lower than most other countries except England and Italy. This could be caused by the different criteria utilized in defining the data used for calculation of rate of profits, however. More interesting is the finding that the rate of profit has been falling less rapidly in Sweden than in most other countries. However, if the Swedish figures are broken down with respect to the size of firms (Wibe, 1976, p. 28) we find that larger companies display a greater fall in the rate of profit than smaller firms in the period 1951-73; the smallest companies in fact exhibit no clear falling trend at all (see Table 7.1).

Table 7.1: Rate of profit by size of enterprise 1951—73
(approximate figures; only trends are relevant)

Size: number employed	Period 1951—4	1955—9	1960—4	1965—8	1969—73
1000 or more	15.3	11.9	8.5	8.0	7.4
500—1000	11.3	8.4	6.9	6.6	7.9
200—300	11.0	8.7	6.8	7.4	7.6
100—200	7.8	7.8	7.4	6.7	7.6
50—100	7.3	7.1	6.9	7.9	8.7

Source: Sören Wibe, 1976, p. 28.

More conventional statistics on Swedish profitability show similar trends. Clearly profitability has fallen sharply after 1974 (cf. Trolle, 1978). So has the investment rate (see Figure 7.1).

Figure 7.1   Year-by-year changes (per cent) in industrial investment totals for Sweden

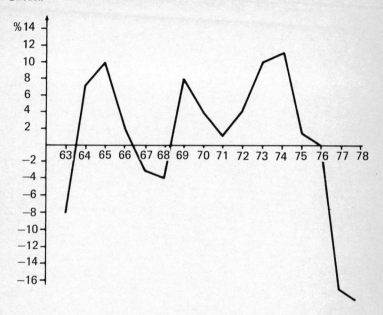

Source: Adapted from the Bjurel Report (Ds Ju 1979:1, p. 138)

However, profitability has been decreasing not only in Sweden but in a number of other advanced countries as well. Table 7.2 (overleaf) provides relevant figures for the period 1955-75.

Table 7.2: The development of profitability in six OECD countries
1955—75 (industry and private services)

	USA	Japan	FRG	England	Canada	Sweden
1955	36.2	34.1	45.3	16.6	21.0	15.1
1956	33.6	38.9	43.5	15.9	21.3	15.2
1957	31.8	44.0	42.4	15.3	18.8	15.5
1958	29.1	36.7	40.3	14.8	16.8	15.2
1959	32.0	37.4	40.8	15.4	17.0	15.4
1960	31.5	45.2	40.4	16.6	16.2	14.8
1961	31.0	45.3	37.2	15.2	16.2	14.2
1962	32.0	39.8	34.5	14.5	16.7	13.5
1963	31.5	39.7	32.2	15.3	17.2	12.5
1964	33.7	40.7	31.8	16.0	18.1	13.3
1965	34.7	37.2	32.5	15.5	17.3	13.9
1966	34.2	40.7	31.3	14.4	16.8	12.8
1967	32.0	44.9	30.5	14.2	15.8	12.7
1968	31.4	49.7	33.0	14.7	16.3	13.0
1969	29.1	50.8	32.0	13.8	15.9	13.4
1970	26.0	51.1	31.1	12.6	14.6	13.6
1971	26.0	45.9	29.6	12.7	14.4	10.8
1972	26.5	44.7	29.0	13.4	15.0	10.8
1973	26.4	44.9	28.4	13.4	17.6	11.9
1974	24.5	40.7	27.7	10.8	16.4	12.4
1975	25.2	40.3	26.9	9.5	14.1	10.6

Source: Peter Hill, *Measurement of Profit* (tentative title), forthcoming, OECD;
quoted from the Bjurel Report (Ds Ju 1979:1, Appendix 2, p. 50).

Note: Due to somewhat different criteria and data on profitability in different
countries, it is not advisable to make comparisons *between* countries in this
table. Trends *within* countries can be studied, however.

8 An Introduction to the Extended Contradictions of Capitalism

So far we have tried to clarify the contradictions of capitalism generated by the structures and processes intrinsic to its economic base, its mode of production. This limited focus is artificial, however, if a holistic analysis of society is the aim, because some of the processes in the economic base trigger off processes in social organizations and in the political, legal and ideological superstructure which then feed back on the economic processes in the base.

The artificiality of our distinction between basic and extended contradictions is indicated by the fact that, in the previous section on basic contradictions, we have been unable to avoid making references, for instance, to the operation of the welfare state which should be treated rather under the rubric of extended contradictions. However, clarity and intelligibility of exposition always demands some degree of artificiality. Now it is time to break the restrictions placed on our analysis by these demands. We now move into the domain of the superstructure, and closely associated with it the 'organizational field', while keeping in mind their close relationship with the base.

The 'organizational field' is not an original Marxian term. It has been introduced by Marxist analysts (Berntson, 1974, p. 23) to take account of the organizations which in modern societies mediate between the base and the superstructure, articulating if you wish the class forces inherent in the basis, transmitting them to the superstructure and responding to the resolutions and decisions made on the superstructural level. This is not to say that all organizations only or mainly reflect class forces. Religious, ethnic and other organizations may predominantly articulate forces other than those which are objects of class analysis, even though such organizations in addition may have a definite class content, or implications for the class struggle. Class organizations such as trade unions may also reflect religious or ethnic divisions in some countries. All these organizations are viewed as part of the organizational field between class and state, or in some cases rather between society and state.[1]

Trade unions introduce 'extended' contradictions in capitalism in the sense indicated earlier: trade unions can be considered in terms of 'agents or effects which were not originally part of the capitalist scheme but which have emerged in the process of capitalist development, provoked or demanded by it without being designed by the capitalist class itself' (see p. 43 above). But when we use the term 'extended' contradictions in this context, this should not be understood as implying that trade unions somehow derive from forces *external* to capitalism. Capitalists who complain about trade unions as if they were some kind of external nuisance. disturbing an otherwise beautifully efficient capitalist order, have simply not understood that capitalism itself has contributed to create trade unions.

Capitalism provided the subordinate class not only with good reasons but also with opportunities to organize to carry out its class struggle. Industrialization brought large numbers of workers together, exposed them to the same kinds of predicaments, enhanced their communications with one another, and thereby their will and ability to organize on the basis of their common predicaments. This is why trade unions introduce not an 'external' but an internal and extended contradiction of capitalism. This contradiction differs from the contradiction which led to the downfall of feudalism in that the victorious bourgeoisie at that time was in control of new means of industrial production ushered in through the emergence of factories. The workers under capitalism on the other hand have not introduced a new style of production; they have introduced a new style of organization, and may eventually throw off their shackles not by relying on their control over any new emerging forces of production but through their collective organizational strength which has grown as a result of the very capitalism to which the working class is subjected.

However, the dialectic of extended contradictions internal to the operation of capitalism turns out to be a lot more complex than assumed when we take a closer look at it. It has been pointed out that the growth of trade unionism does not necessarily introduce extended contradictions into capitalism but may in fact contribute to the reproduction of the capitalist order. From the point of view of capital an expansion of union organization may help to make the conduct of labour more predictable, and such predictability enhances the management of capital. Therefore more revolutionary, left-wing unionists have criticized the strong and centralized trade union organizations found for instance in the Scandinavian countries for being tools of capital rather than instruments of class struggle. But it could equally well be argued that more militant unions which usually become weaker and more fragmented as a result of the divisive dialectic of ideological rivalries, thereby strengthen capital. The cost of revolutionary troublemakers may be acceptable to capital as long as revolutionary ideologies constitute a divisive subjective element within the labour front which thus is prevented from acquiring greater organizational unity and strength.[2]

There is a dialectic within the dialectic here which may transform subjective revolutionary ideologies among workers and union leaders into a most forceful tonic of strength for capitalists, while the organizationally stronger, merely 'trade unionist' labour movement at some crucial moment might be transformed not only into a formidable adversary of capital in a reformist sense, but also into pursuing a class struggle with objectively more revolutionary implications than the struggle fomented by subjectively more revolutionary forces. Crucial for this 'dialectic within the dialectic' are the objective factors which constitute the growth of basic and extended contradictions within capitalism.

If and when the various contradictions of capitalism attain some point of culmination, even reformist working class organizations may be pushed into a struggle for a profound socialist transformation of society; and they could very well turn out to be more efficient in pursuing such a struggle than revolutionary groups lacking the necessary strength and unity. Certainly, the records of labour history do not exhibit a single case documenting the possibility of a revolutionary impact of reformist labour movements; this is sheer speculation. How possibly could a reformist labour movement whose members have been trained only to participate in trade unionist wage struggle within the framework of the existing capitalist order be transformed into a revolutionary force? One aspect of this crucial question is semantic: What is a 'revolutionary force'?

By 'revolutionary force' we mean a force which is instrumental in transforming our present system beyond the kind of welfare capitalism which we have today into a system where labourers have major control over production, the organization of work and the use of the surplus, regardless of whether 'revolutionary means' were used or not in attaining this measure of control. This definition makes it theoretically possible to conceive of a revolutionary transformation of capitalist society by reformist means. But to build a reasonably realistic scenario of a reformist 'revolutionary force' more than a definition is needed. We must answer a number of questions about structural options and constraints, working class mobilization, and related empirical questions about the existence of such options and constraints and levels of mobilization in a specific historical situation such as Sweden in 1979-80, and thereafter.

Our scenario of a socialist transformation by reformist means attaches more importance to objective than to subjective 'revolutionary conditions' — and attributes crucial significance in this context to the culmination of objective contradictions, and to the organizational strength and unity of reformist trade unions which usually are less struck by the divisive dialectic of internal ideological rivalry. However, we can certainly not neglect the subjective factor in system-transcending class struggle. These subjective factors will be discussed and empirically surveyed in Part III. Here our main point has been to call into question both the ideological claims of revolutionaries, and the alleged lack of revolutionary implications of reformist activities, as an introduction to our discussion of extended contradictions within mature capitalism.

The emergence, growth and shifting strategies and tactics of the labour movement is certainly a most significant aspect of the growth of extended contradictions within capitalism. Numerous volumes have been devoted to this topic. Therefore, and since we will devote several chapters in Part III to various dimensions and dynamics of the strength of labour as an actor on the stage of mature capitalism, we have chosen to cut this story short here. Instead we will proceed directly to other aspects of what we have called extended contradictions.

Among objective extended contradictions we will first pay attention to the private production and social significance of so-called negative externalities in the form of environmental effects inside and outside the work-place. Then we will discuss the role of state interventions. This sequence would seem to be natural since one of the main tasks of the state under welfare capitalism is the repair and prevention of negative externalities. Therefore these should be treated first.

9 The Social Character and Private Production of Negative Externalities

The term 'externalities' is used by economists for such results of production which do not appear on a market, and which consequently do not obtain prices according to the ordinary law of demand and supply.[1] These results of production are called externalities because they are external to the market; air and water pollution is not usually bought or sold at market prices. However, economists have suggested that a price could be set on negative externalities on the basis of trade-off curves between quantity of pollution and costs of production; decreasing pollution usually entails increasing production costs. In this manner it would be a matter of choice for each polluter whether to pay to the relevant agents of society the price set for a given marginal increase in the quantity of pollution, or to pay the cost of reducing pollution at its source — a type of decision which would save the logic of market forces and thus make superfluous any bureaucratic regulations and interventions.[2] Others have forcefully argued that quantity of pollution is a matter too serious to be settled by market forces. Binding rules, defining the maximum emissions allowed, should be legislated, according to this view. Market forces and the polluters' ability to pay compensation for increasing pollution should not be allowed to be the determining factors.

Pollution in Capitalist and So-called Socialist Countries

From this brief introduction it would seem to follow that a *pure* capitalist system necessarily will produce more negative externalities than a system which relies on public regulation of production. Says K. William Kapp (1978, p. 14), a pioneer in exploring the external 'social costs of business enterprise':

> The basic causes of social costs are to be found in the fact that the pursuit of private gain places a premium on the minimization of the private costs of current production. . . . The more reliance

an economic system places on private incentives and the pursuit of private gain the greater the danger that it will give rise to external 'unpaid' social costs unless appropriate measures are taken to avoid or at least minimize these costs.

However, it can be maintained that pollution and external social costs of production are a result of rapid industrialization, whether capitalist or socialist, rather than of capitalism as such. Whether this is a valid argument is rather difficult to judge because of both the scarcity of relevant comparative statistics and the tricky semantics involved in labelling certain countries as socialist. On theoretical ground, however, we can say with Kapp (1978, p. 14) that a planned economy 'which makes extensive use of private incentives such as bonuses to its managers in order to assure the attainment of its targets and objectives, will hardly be immune to social costs. Evidence of certain inefficiencies in the Soviet economy support this conclusion'.

On the other hand Kapp reports some evidence suggesting that China has shown more concern with reducing the external social costs of industrial and agricultural production (1978, Appendix 2). The crucial factor is the extent to which planners can be held accountable to those who bear the brunt of these social costs. 'In the last analysis this is a matter of the political structure of the planned economy, and whether or not the plan as an essentially political act of decision-making is subject to review at the polls.' (1978, p. 26).

However, we have considerable reservations about the implications of what Kapp has to say about the Soviet Union and China. Firstly, China is not known to make public issues 'subject to review at the polls' in any systematic manner, even though other means of public control of decisions on issues like social costs would seem to exist in the Chinese system. Secondly, our knowledge about the handling of pollution and other similar social costs in the Soviet economy is too limited to justify any firm conclusions, as we have already pointed out.[3] Thirdly, any comparison of, say, air and water pollution between the economic systems of Eastern and Western Europe must consider not only differences in economic and political systems, but also differences in levels of economic and technological development. Less developed industrial countries such as those in Eastern Europe may not find it as easy to afford the extra costs involved in reducing pollution levels as wealthier and technologically more advanced countries. Therefore, comparisons of pollution levels in socialist and capitalist countries preferably should be made between countries at about the same level of economic and technological development, in order to establish the effects of the different economic and political systems involved.

Finally, we have the notorious semantic and factual problem involved in assessing whether the countries which call themselves socialist are socialist in any reasonable sense, or have progressed sufficiently far on the socialist road. In our view the Eastern European countries are not sufficiently socialist in a number of respects, and cannot therefore be used for making straightforward comparisons between socialism and capitalism. In fact, there is at present no single country in the world satisfying our criteria of socialism. Therefore, when we speak of the negative externalities and social costs of capitalism, we do not accept references to environmental problems in the Eastern European countries as counter-evidence, and as proof of the thesis that it is the level of industrialization as such rather than the economic system which accounts for environmental problems.

For the same reason any implicit or explicit reference in the following to the advantages of socialism over capitalism in reducing negative externalities, and taking responsibility for remaining social costs, must remain theoretical. Because socialism, as we conceive it (cf. our discussion in Chapter 1), must include the kind of democratic accountability of planners and managers which was mentioned by Kapp, it follows theoretically that external and unsettled social costs of production will be less in a democratic socialist than in a capitalist system, other things being equal. Such a socialist system will address itself more consistently to the problems of external social costs of production, whereas capitalism is unable to eliminate the extended contradictions implied by negative externalities by its *own* internal logic of operation.

On the other hand there is now considerable evidence that at least water pollution can be significantly reduced under capitalism with the aid of efficient public municipal action, according to rules laid down by a welfare state. Whereas emissions of phosphorus and of organic pollutants from urban settlements in Sweden (83 per cent of the country's total population) increased rapidly from 1940 to the early 1960s these emissions decreased even more rapidly thereafter. Also emissions of organic compounds from industry have decreased after the early 1960s (Swedish Council of Environmental Information and the National Environment Protection Board, 1979, pp. 92f). As a result the quality of water in a number of streams and rivers has improved (pp. 127f).

One of the main reasons for the relative success of action to reduce water pollution is the high degree of 'centralization' of water pollution at large industrial plants, and the even higher 'centralization' of sewage plants cleaning the sewerage from multitudinous and dispersed local household polluters. This relatively high degree of centralization, and the high involvement of public and municipal agencies in this area has made it possible to focus anti-pollution activities on a few points on the local map even when the production of pollution has been relatively dispersed. However, some portion of water pollution is caused by pollution from the air. And air pollution does not always have the local character of most water pollution.

There is considerable evidence supporting the contention that air pollution from the European continent — particularly from the urban–industrial areas of North Western Germany — accounts for about 80 per cent of the sulphur which falls down over Sweden and thereby contributes to the acidification of lakes and land, particularly in Southern Sweden (Swedish Council of Environmental Information and the National Environment Protection Board, pp. 73f). This harms vegetation and leads to reduced forest production. The fish in some lakes have vanished completely.

Apart from not being entirely of local origin, the production of air pollution is less centralized than water pollution; a major portion of this pollution is accounted for by motor-car exhaust emissions. Here it is not the processes of *production* which are directly responsible for pollution, but the behaviour of *consumers*, or in less personalizing terms, rather the structures which make it necessary for us as consumers to use private cars so extensively. From the system point of view there is an interesting difference between 'consumer-generated' pollution from cars, and the equally 'consumer-generated' pollution of household sewage. The household is part of a publicly planned and regulated system of housing — at least in Sweden — and a sewerage system terminating in municipal sewage cleaning plants. State regulation certainly also affects to some extent what kind of cars are running on Swedish roads and streets, through specifications to be fulfilled by car-producers and by the legislated requirement of yearly inspections of used cars. This may have contributed to the diminishing frequency of motor-car accidents in Sweden — a decrease in spite of an increasing number of motor-cars.[4] But otherwise the car-owner epitomizes the concept of consumer sovereignty. He drives his car as much as he likes at his own discretion; the exhaust emissions of his car is a public ill for which he cannot take responsibility. To channel exhausts into a municipal cleaning plant is not possible. And on the side of the producers of cars and petroleum the requirements of the state must always be attuned to the constraints imposed by the need to maintain the profitability of the industry, because the whole national economy usually depends a great deal on the success of motor-car and petroleum industries.

Or to put it more bluntly: air pollution to a much higher degree than water pollution is a capitalist product. Even when attempts are made by governments to influence motor-car and petroleum producers to reduce the harmful components of exhaust emissions, these attempts are rarely as successful as could be desired, in spite of the fact that no insurmountable technical problems are involved.

Probably an expansion of collective municipal transport could have some beneficial effects on this point, but to make such municipal transport systems sufficiently competitive with motor-cars — particularly in suburbs with widely dispersed single houses — is an extremely expensive affair requiring greater public resources than most municipalities can command on their own without heavy subsidies from the state, that is from the tax-payers.

The capitalist character of a great portion of the air pollution produced in our societies appears in sharper profile if we consider the effects of expanding public commitments in this field. Sweden is heavily dependent on oil for heating in the cold season. During the last decades heating in urban areas has become increasingly centralized in municipal heating plants serving whole towns and cities. Instead of thousands of chimneys on apartment and single houses, spewing out the smoke from more or less properly adjusted oil burners, we now have just a few centralized municipal heating plants for each community, distributing hot water through heating networks to virtually all households at least in the central parts of each community. The quantity of harmful emissions into the air is thereby significantly reduced (Swedish Council of Environmental Information and the National Environment Protection Board, pp. 134f).

But whereas it would seem possible to reduce and control a significant amount of water pollution, and at least some of the air pollution, through a combination of state legislation, public municipal involvement and certain technical innovations within an overall framework of capitalist relations of production, there are other negative externalities relating more directly to the quality of life than the environmental externalities mentioned so far which seem so closely associated with capitalism itself that only a profound transformation of this economic system can be expected to substantially reduce or eliminate such negative externalities.

Unemployment and its Effects

Unemployment is usually not defined as a negative externality by economists, but as an adjustment mechanism of the market. From a Marxist point of view unemployment is an expression of the *basic* contradiction between capital and labour rather than of any so-called *extended* contradictions of capitalism (see our discussion above on p. 46). However, unemployment in its turn produces a number of undesirable effects. Long-term unemployment in particular has been shown to have harmful psychological and physical consequences as severe as many environmental effects. The social costs of unemployment are considerable.[5] Therefore, and because comprehensive time-series data are lacking on such negative effects and social costs of unemployment, we have chosen to introduce unemployment here as a marker for such negative externalities.

Open unemployment in Sweden, as registered by the Labour Market Authority (AMS), and in Labour Force Surveys (AKU), has been among the lowest in the world, varying within the range of 1.2–2.5 per cent from 1946 to 1977. However, such crude statistics tell very little about the real problems on the labour market. Below the surface of aggregate statistics which indicate a low and relatively stable rate of unemployment without any trend toward higher figures we find, for instance, a substantial increase in *long-term* unemployment. The number of persons struck by *shorter* periods of unemployment varies with the business cycle, and shows no tendential increase. Longer periods of unemployment, however, increased tendentially from 1963 to 1973; during this period the average length of unemployment nearly doubled in spite of all the efforts made by government authorities to keep this kind of unemployment down (see Table 9.1). In the years 1973–7 this increase in long-term unemployment was stabilized. As we will see later this stabilization of the figures may be partly accounted for by the exclusion of older persons from the labour force as a result of premature pensions.

At the same time as longer-term unemployment has increased there is also a diminishing probability of unemployed people being re-employed. (See Table 9.2).

In many cases the declining likelihood of a comeback on the labour market implies nothing less than a definitive exit from the labour force, or at least from the open labour market. In 1951 there were 17 413 applicants for vocational rehabilitation services; in 1960 there were 31 359, and in 1970 there were 95 599 persons applying for such services. In 1951 57 per cent of the applicants could be employed

**Table 9.1: Number of unemployed in Sweden 1963—78,
in thousands, by length of unemployment in weeks (yearly averages)**

Year	Light unempl. 0—4 weeks	Medium—heavy 5—12 weeks	Heavy unempl. 13—26 weeks	Very heavy 27 weeks	Average unempl. in weeks
1963	30.1	21.8	5.0	4.5	9.0
1964	31.4	16.6	5.4	4.7	9.6
1965	24.7	13.7	3.2	2.5	8.3
1966	31.1	16.4	7.5	3.2	8.4
1967	33.8	27.2	10.9	6.8	10.3
1968	35.3	28.2	12.2	8.4	10.8
1969	29.8	23.5	9.6	8.8	12.4
1970	29.5	15.6	7.7	6.3	12.0
1971	37.8	33.5	16.5	12.8	13.5
1972	35.3	33.0	20.2	18.8	16.2
1973	32.0	29.9	17.7	18.3	16.7
1974	30.5	23.0	13.5	13.3	15.8
1975	25.3	19.3	11.7	11.1	15.6
1976	25.2	19.4	11.2	10.6	15.2
1977	26.0	23.3	13.7	12.0	15.3
1978	31.6	26.9	18.2	17.0	16.2

Source: SCB Labour Force Sample Surveys 1963—78.

**Table 9.2: The probability for an unemployed person to become
employed next week, in per cent, for the period 1964—74**

1964	1965	1966	1967	1968	1969	1970	1971	1972	1973	1974
16	18	19	13	12	14	15	10	8	9	11

Source: A. Östlind, 1975, p. 24. Due to the somewhat arbitrary nature of certain assumptions underlying the calculations of these probabilities their *absolute* levels are not quite valid, but the trend is reasonably reliable.

in the open labour market; in 1960 34 per cent were thus employed, and in 1970 only 12 per cent could find jobs in the open labour market; most of the remainder were placed in so-called sheltered work.[6] This trend most conspicuously contradicts the official goal set up for vocational rehabilitation, namely to 'eliminate barriers preventing employment in the open market, that is to attain a rehabilitation consonant with labour market requirements' (SOU 1968:60, p. 127).

However, sheltered and semi-sheltered work also includes persons who have not applied for vocational rehabilitation. Table 9.3 presents the total figures for sheltered and semi-sheltered work for the period 1962—76. The increasing trend is obvious.

Table 9.3: Yearly averages of people employed in 'sheltered' or 'semi-sheltered' work 1962—76

	Sheltered work	Semi-sheltered work
1962	2 168	–
1963	2 581	–
1964	3 641	–
1965	4 658	–
1966	5 695	–
1967	6 809	–
1968	7 810	–
1969	9 254	713
1970	10 788	1 274
1971	11 877	1 682
1972	12 819	2 163
1973	13 796	4 021
1974	15 057	6 326
1975	15 996	8 302
1976	16 410	9 828

Source: SCB (1978).

Also the frequency of premature pensions has increased considerably in recent years. Earlier on premature pensions were awarded only on *medical* grounds, according to the formula laid down in the Act of 1962 on General Insurance. This act was amended in 1970 to allow premature pensions also to persons above 63 years of age (the normal age of pensions in Sweden is now 65) on the basis of *economic* indications — such as the inability to maintain or find gainful employment for the applicant. In 1974 a further amendment was introduced which accepted labour market indications for premature pensions from 60 years of age even without medical examination; but premature pensions on presumably medical grounds (see below) are not uncommon even in the 55—60 years age-bracket. At the same time other laws have been enacted to prevent the premature exit of older workers, but in spite of such laws premature pensions have been increasing in numbers virtually every year. In 1976 they were nearly twice as many as in 1·973 (Berglind, 1979, pp. 3—6 and 133; Östlind, 1975, pp. 61f).

Now it could be argued that the increasing number of premature pensions, far from being a source of worry, should be a source of pride. Finally, our society has become affluent enough to be able to care for older workers struck by partial handicaps by providing them with a permanent holiday from work for the rest of their lives. Disregarding for a moment the probability that the increasing number of premature pensions may also reflect a deterioration in the quality of working life (which is nothing to be proud of) this line of argument is supported by the fact that the overwhelming percentage of premature pensions were awarded not on the basis of labour market indications but on medical grounds. Labour market indications account for only about 6 per cent of premature pensions in recent years. However, Östlind (1975, pp. 63—4) has rather convincingly argued that this figure seriously underestimates the importance of labour market indications for awarding premature pensions. If premature pension awarding authorities for some reason wish to avoid making references to difficulties on the labour market even in cases where labour market considerations carry a lot of weight, then it is not particularly difficult to find some physical or medical fault with a worker in his fifties or early sixties. Labour market indications supporting premature pensions are thus dressed up in the more respectable cloak of medical indications. Further evidence supporting this interpretation has been presented by Berglind (1977) who found a significant positive correlation between various regional indicators of unemployment/underemployment, and the regional incidence of premature pensions. This correlation remains significant when Berglind controls for regional variations in age and sex distributions. Even though the majority of those involved were formally awarded their premature pensions on medical grounds, the real cause would seem to have been the diminishing capacity of the labour market to maintain the employment level for older workers below the regular age of pension.

Whereas the official unemployment figure in 1968 was 2.0 per cent, Öhman (AMS, 1970: 17, p. 22) calculated that 'real' unemployment that year was 7.3 per cent — that is if we refuse to exclude latently employable but not employed from the labour force. Öhman's calculation was based on findings from a Labour Force Survey. Respondents who were not employed and who had not applied for a job, but said they wanted a job, were included by Öhman as unemployed within the labour force. The fact that these employable but unemployed had not applied for a job was probably, in quite a number of cases, because there was no prospect of getting a job anyway.

If we include in our calculations those on relief work, on labour market retraining programmes and in sheltered work, and those who in fact (if not always formally speaking) were awarded premature pensions due to labour market considerations, then the percentage who would like to have a regular job but could not be absorbed by the open labour market would rise to figures even higher than 7.3 per cent.

Östlind (1975, p. 119) has attempted to give a more accurate picture of labour market problems by estimating the development of 'the problem sector'. The problem sector consists of officially unemployed, latently unemployed, prematurely pensioned, and those affected by various forms of government support such as vocational training, sheltered work and relief work. His calculations give an idea of what unemployment would look like if the government had not taken steps to keep the figures down. Table 9.4 contains a comparison between 1970 and 1974 which were both boom years for Swedish industry.

Table 9.4: Share of 'problem sector' of whole population, 1970 and 1974

		Problem sector in % of population		
Age		Men		Women
	1970	1974	1970	1974
16−24	5.0	7.4	6.6	8.6
25−44	3.5	4.4	7.7	7.1
45−54	6.1	8.0	9.6	10.2
55−64	13.0	18.7	12.7	15.9

Source: Östlind, 1975, p. 119.

It shows that the problem sector has grown for all groups, except for women aged 25−44. Especially for the youngest and the oldest age groups things have become worse from 1970 to 1974.

Whether to use the official unemployment figures which for quite some time have fluctuated around an average of 1.8, or to use the much higher figures calculated by Öhman and Östlind is a matter to be decided on the basis of the kind of questions you wish to answer. If our purpose is to answer questions about the efficiency of the Swedish welfare state in providing relief work and support to employable persons who are not absorbed in the regular labour market, then the lower official figures are most relevant. If our purpose is to illuminate one of the extended contradictions of capitalism — that is the increasing inability of capital to cope with the problems of employment in mature capitalism — then the higher unofficial figures are more relevant.

Many of the labour market problems mentioned above involve in particular workers in the older age-brackets. Even more serious, however, from the point of view of future developments, are the high unemployment figures in the lowest age-bracket of the labour force. Disillusionment, apathy, an increasing lack of self-confidence, and secondary effects such as alcoholism, drug addiction, prostitution and petty theft are more likely to strike less socially established younger people when they are unemployed for longer time periods. And such effects may be damaging the quality of life of young people not only for a few years but for a life-time — not to mention the hundreds of young people who are brought to premature death by drug addiction in particular.[7]

Official figures for youth unemployment (excluding latently unemployed, prematurely pensioned and those involved in vocational training, sheltered work and relief work) about doubled from 1963 to 1972. For those aged 16—19 years the increase was from 3.8 per cent to 8.2 per cent. Those aged 20—24 are a bit better off, but the trend is similar; an increase from 2.2 per cent to 4.5 per cent. For purposes of comparison we could mention that the overall official unemployment rate for 1963 was 1.7 per cent, and 2.7 per cent for 1972. After 1972 the situation improved somewhat as a result of government action and an upward turn in business. But in 1977 and 1978 the labour market was getting worse again for young people. The unemployment rate went up to 7.1 per cent for men aged 16—19 in 1978, and to 8.7 per cent for women of the same age (SCB Labour Force Sample Surveys).

But also here we can suspect that the real unemployment rate is considerably higher than official figures indicate. Relief work and labour market retraining absorb a large group of young people who have not been able to find a job, and an increasing number of youngsters are probably floating around in a passive existence without even finding it worthwhile to apply for a job; and some of them become involved in drug trade and addiction, petty theft, prostitution and the like. They are not officially counted as part of the labour force; in fact they have been expelled from the labour market.

So far we have focused most of our attention on the negative externalities of unemployment and underemployment. But negative externalities of an environmental nature manifest themselves also at work among those actually employed.

Occupational Accidents and Diseases

Experts agree that official statistics on occupational diseases, accident rates at work and their severity significantly underrate the actual incidence of these phenomena (Dahlberg and Grenninger, 1974, p. 18; Lagerlöf, 1975). If we take these official figures at their face value, however, we find that the accident rate has been relatively stable since 1960 — except for fluctuations positively correlated with business cycles (Dahlberg and Grenninger, 1974, p. 27). Accident rates are thus maintained at a relatively constant level in spite of the ongoing redistribution of the labour force to the less accident-prone branches of white-collar employment, and in spite of all the efforts made to reduce the frequency of accidents. However, the severity rates (number of working days lost per 1000 working hours due to accidents at work) have shown some improvements in the period 1955–74 for which there are official statistics available (SCB/RFS, 1977, p.23).

If we now control for different branches of employment (SCB/RFS, 1977, Table C, p. 24) we find an *increasing* accident rate in farming and forestry which have undergone rapid mechanization in recent years, and in the manufacturing industry. Mines and quarries exhibited increasing accident rates until 1968; thereafter these rates were substantially reduced even if they remain the highest in any branch of the economy. Also the severity rate was significantly reduced after 1968 in mines and quarries.

It is perhaps significant that this downturn of accident and severity rates in the branch of mining took place after the protracted 1969 wild-cat strike in the iron-mines at Kiruna which succeeded in calling forth not only conventional safety measures but also monthly salaries instead of piece-rates for mining workers.[8] Similar strike action took place among forestry workers in 1975, and here also accident rates have dropped, according to recent unofficial reports.[9] Unfortunately official statistics are presently available only up to 1974. But apart from such beneficial effects of class struggle there is nothing to indicate that our capitalist system as such contributes to reduce the negative externalities implied by accidents at work and occupational diseases. Dahlberg and Grenninger (1974, pp. 18 and 20) having cross-tabulated a simple index of capital intensity (organic composition of capital) with severity rates of accidents at work found that the higher the severity rate in a given sector of the economy the more likely this sector is to manifest a high degree of capital intensity (see Figure 9.1).

Figure 9.1 Relationship between severity rate of accidents at work and sectorial labour versus capital intensity

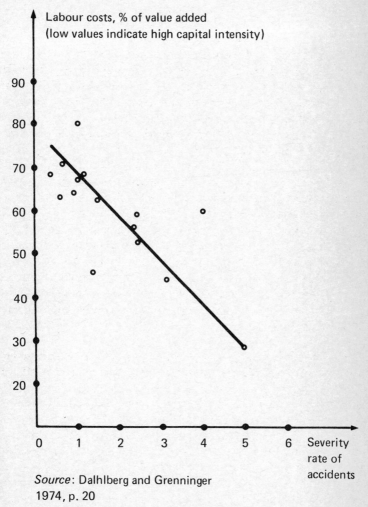

Source: Dalhlberg and Grenninger 1974, p. 20

In bringing to an end this section on negative externalities outside and inside the work-place, we would like to make two methodological points and then to summarize our main conclusions.

Firstly, practically all of the official statistics on accident and severity rates used in this chapter were calculated per million or thousand hours of work. This is of course highly justified in contexts of economic cost evaluation, or in time series and comparative statistical analyses, to control for variations in the incidence of part-time and full-time work over time, or between various branches of employment. But if we wish to pursue an analysis of human and social costs 'as if human beings mattered' it would perhaps be more relevant to use the human being struck by accidents or occupational diseases as a unit of analysis regardless of hours of work. In fact it is possible to conceive of decreasing accident rates per million working hours in spite of the fact that an increasing number of people are hit by accidents – namely if the total number of working hours increases at an even faster rate. Unfortunately figures on numbers of working hours in the various sub-categories of employment on which we have focused most of our attention are not available, and therefore we have not been able to calculate the number of *people* involved in accidents of various severity within each sub-category. Now it is a fact that *total* working hours have increased between 1955 and 1974 (Dahlberg and Grenninger, 1974, p. 23). We cannot therefore rule out the possibility that calculations more relevant from the point of view of estimating human and social costs, might indicate trends even worse than those we have actually found in some branches of the economy.

Secondly, there are human and social costs not covered by the medical and physical categories of accidents, disease and disabilities reported in official statistics. We have suggested some secondary effects of this nature in our discussion of youth unemployment. However, there are now also a number of empirical sociological studies (Gardell, 1976, Liljeström, 1976, and Karasek, 1976) reporting correlations and perhaps casual relationships between alienation, stress and fatigue at work, and an impoverishment of leisure time activities and of various individual and collective resources outside the working place. These also are negative externalities which should be taken into account in this context.

Summary

With regard to negative externalities of an environmental nature we have found that degree of *centralization* in production and/or cleaning of pollution improves the possibilities of introducing relatively effective public control even where the polluters are private units. This control becomes even more effective when production and/or cleaning of pollution are in *public* hands, for instance in municipal heating and sewage cleaning plants. The more private and dispersed the production of pollution is — as in the case of motor-car exhaust emissions — the more intractable become the problems of pollution control, unless of course th. interests of private capital can be checked or eliminated by public control.

However, these conclusions would seem to hold only *within* nations over time, and not in cross-national comparisons. In Eastern Europe where public control rather than the interest of private capital predominates it is quite possible that some environmental effects are as severe or more so than in some technologically advanced Western capitalist countries. In cross-national comparisons between countries with different mixtures of public and private control over pollution, it is therefore necessary to control both for level of technological development and the extent to which planners and industrial managers are really and not only formally accountable to those affected by pollution and the extent to which those affected can effectively voice their concern and opposition and channel their demands to relevant decision-makers. These attendant circumstances vary within as well as between capitalist and so-called socialist countries.

To the extent that long-term unemployment and other similar effects of labour marginalization generates negative externalities, it would seem correct to say that countries in Eastern Europe exhibit much less of this type of externality than countries in Western Europe, including Sweden. This is most probably due to the fact, mentioned in passing above, that this externality is much more closely related to the basic contradiction between capital and labour in Western capitalist systems.

With regard to figures on unemployment in Sweden we have pointed out that long-term unemployment has been increasing over the last fifteen years, particularly in the highest and the lowest age-brackets. Such unemployment is often a prelude to a definitive exclusion of labour from the regular labour market into so-called sheltered work, premature pensions, and among young men and women into various kinds of addiction, petty criminality and other types of social maladjustment. Official unemployment rates which are among the lowest in the capitalist world in Sweden, do not properly reflect these effects of capitalist production because official statistics are based on definitions of the labour force and of unemployment which exclude such effects. However, as indicators of the efficiency of the welfare state in taking some responsibility for marginalized labour, official unemployment rates are still quite useful. On this score Sweden has done very well in a comparative perspective (Korpi and Shalev, 1979b), but this fact should not be allowed to conceal the underlying failures of the capitalist system as such.

Overall official accident rates and severity rates as well as rates of occupational disabilities similarly underestimate the effects of capitalist production. Accident and severity rates have been shown to be cor related significantly with business cycles and with the trend toward more capital-intensive production. However, in cases where effective class struggle has forced employers in capital-intensive production to sacrifice some degrees of productivity and capital accumulation, for instance by substituting monthly salaries for piece-rate payment, accident and severity rates have dropped.

We have used the term 'negative externalities' as a label for these various effects, in spite of the fact that this concept fits rather badly into our Marxist framework, mainly for heuristic reasons in the hope that non-Marxist readers may thus find it easier to follow our presentation. However, now it is time to indicate some of the limitations of this terminology.

Negative externalities are defined as non-market effects of single production units, the costs of which are carried normally by those affected rather than by the units producing these effects. The conflict of interest which can be seen as emerging in such a context of negative externalities is most logically conceived as a conflict between those affected negatively by these non-market effects, and the units producing them. From a Marxist point of view, however, more than a conflict of interest is involved.

The logic of capital accumulation unavoidably implies attempts to minimize the 'external' costs involved, and as a result either the reproduction of labour or the reproduction of capital are threatened in the not so long run. Either the kind of labour power still needed in capitalist production fails to be reproduced at the level of motivation and physical ability required due to the damaging effects implied by negative externalities. Or the welfare state takes over responsibility for reducing these negative effects, perhaps not only to reproduce labour at required levels but also to care for those excluded from the labour market altogether as a result of such effects. The costs of such state intervention must be carried by production or by consumption; but decreasing consumption eventually also affects production.[10] Either way any attempt to minimize 'external' costs in the interest of capital accumulation strikes back on the reproduction of capital as well as of labour because of the system characteristics of capitalism. Capitalism is contradictory, and the contradiction involved is systemic and not just a conflict of interest between different groups of people, to be settled temporarily by bargaining agreements.

The role of the welfare state not only in responding but also in articulating and enhancing these contradictions is crucial in this context. This is the main topic of Chapter 10.

10 The Interventionist State and the Contradictions of Capitalism

So proliferate is current literature on the 'capitalist state', or on the role of the state in so-called 'mixed economies', that it defies any attempt to summarize briefly its analytical diversity and manifold disagreements.[1] Yet it would seem possible to discern a limited number of relatively well defined *problem areas* on which there is some consensus in spite of disagreements on relevant modes of conceptualization, and even on the conclusions to be drawn within each single mode of conceptualization. In some of these problem areas we are able to find empirical data, or at least empirical approaches, capable of eventually settling some of the disagreements involved. We will here concentrate on three dominant problem areas. We will do this by formulating a number of problematic conjectures around which agreements and disagreements seem to be focused. However our first conjectures would seem to be somewhat less problematic than the third.

1. Increasing state interventions in capitalist economies are an expression of increasing contradictions or inconsistencies in the economic systems of advanced capitalist societies

Gianfranco Poggi (1978, p. 129), applying a non-Marxist historical and constitutional approach, has pointed out that the competitive market was the economic environment presupposed by the liberal state/society distinction — and this for two reasons:

> First, the competitive market was self-equilibrating, and could thus dispense with *ad hoc* regulations and intervention by the state. Second, the competitive market did not appear to countenance the emergence of power relations between economic actors, and thus seemed to leave the state as the only entity wielding power within and for a given national society. The increasing dominance of large firms maximizing not only their profits but also their control over markets, their own growth, and their power over one another and the larger society contradicts both

the above assumptions and sharpens immeasurably that challenge I argued earlier the capitalist mode of production always poses to the state's power.

As a result of the destruction of self-equilibrating markets, the growth of centralized business power, and the increasing dependence of society as a whole on the success or failures of these highly centralized business empires, the state is faced with the necessity to equilibrate what is no longer self-equilibrating. The liberal distinction between state and society is thus blurred by far-reaching state interventions.

Up to this point many Marxists could easily agree with Poggi's analysis. In fact his non-Marxist approach is probably less attractive to some conservative liberal ideologists and neoclassical economists who refuse to acknowledge the destruction of competitive, self-regulating markets, and the growth of big business, and who accordingly view the interventionist state not as a result of capitalist developments but as an unwelcome intrusion of external forces promoting some kind of 'creeping socialism'. However, we maintain that there is a wide-ranging consensus among serious students of contemporary societies, whether Marxist or non-Marxist, namely that the interventionist state is an outgrowth of tendencies inherent in contemporary capitalism rather than a factor imposed externally by somehow autonomous political forces which cannot be accounted for by an analysis of capitalism itself. On this there is an extensive literature applying both historically more restricted statistical analyses (Wood, 1961), and a more historical longitudinal approach.[2]

Here we must warn against interpreting our first conjecture as saying that state interventions are generated only by *recessions* and *crises* of capitalism. Even though state interventions have expanded by leaps and bounds, particularly in periods of economic crisis, such interventions have also increased, even if not to the same extent, in less crisis-struck periods. The contradictions and inconsistencies of modern capitalism are structural. These structures are present also in periods of economic growth, and they call for state interventions to take account of residual growth-promoting tasks which the capitalist order itself cannot tackle on its own because of the private character of capitalist relations of production. Some state interventions play an integral part in economic growth by providing necessary infrastructural investments as well as directly productive investments of a size which private capital cannot itself afford. Other state interventions are rather aimed at stabilization and so-called crisis management in periods of recession or crisis (Gustafsson, 1977, p. 42). In either case it is the increasingly social character of capitalist productive forces which requires the swelling of the public sector.

Another aspect of this process can be explained by the strengthening of the labour movement, and its political impact within capitalism. The demands of labour for a more equitable sharing of the fruits of economic growth obviously has played a significant role in expanding the public sector — particularly in the Scandinavian countries where the labour movement has exhibited a considerable political strength (Wilensky, 1976; Gustafsson, 1977, pp. 30f; Korpi and Shalev, 1980). In view of our argument that the development of the labour movement is one aspect of the growing extended contradictions of capitalism, we can again conclude that these contradictions — extended as well as basic — explain a great deal of the swelling public sector in mature capitalism.

2. State interventions within the capitalist order are not only caused by the contradictions of capitalism; they introduce new contradictions which threaten the basic dynamic of further capitalist development

A highly respected Swedish management expert, Ulf af Trolle (1978, pp. 33f), acknowledging the operational efficiency of the mixed economy of Sweden for more than two postwar decades, with its extensive social welfare programme, argues that this mixed economy during the third postwar decade has drifted into inconsistencies which undermine the ability of the system to function at all. He calls for a more 'consistent economic system'; we must choose between returning to a basically self-regulating market economy or facing the necessity to adopt a more consistent centrally managed state-capitalist system of the kind existing in Eastern European countries. Compromises between these systems are inconsistent and not workable. The same call for a return to a more consistent market economy is found in the report published by a government commission on economic policy appointed by the new bourgeois government which took over after the defeat of social democrats in the 1976 election in Sweden (Ds Ju 1979:1), the so-called Bjurel-report.

Even though af Trolle finds a centrally managed state capitalism a much better option even from the point of view of management than the present 'mixture' (1978, pp. 137f), he prefers to speak for a return to the market economy — not for political reasons, he claims, but because he is unable to envisage how to carry out a transition to state socialism, a term which he uses as synonymous with state capitalism. He is not unaware of the *political* difficulties involved in a return to a more consistent market economy, but he has nothing to say about the *systemic economic* difficulties of such a return. How can a capitalist system with such a high degree of concentration, centralization and internationalization as the Swedish economy be returned to a 'wholesome and efficient national market economy'? Such a 'return' to an idealized market model would seem to entail difficulties as great as a transition to some kind of state socialism. Are there no other options? This is a question to which we will return.

Ideas similar to those expressed by af Trolle can be found in one of the volumes published by the so-called Trilateral Commission (Crozier, Huntington and Watanuki, 1975). In this volume, again, the political difficulties of a return to an efficient market economy are emphasized, and systemic constraints of an economic nature neglected. Some authors in this volume complain about dangers inherent in excesses of political democracy (p. 113), and dream of a political system characterized by the kind of political apathy among its citizens which at one time was postulated as a basic requirement for a workable and stable democracy by political scientists and sociologists such as Tingsten (1937) and Lipset (1960).

Apart from these attempts to find faults with active democratic citizenship rather than with contemporary capitalism there is, however, considerable similarity between statements by some Marxist writers and bourgeois experts on the workability of so-called mixed economies, given the conditions which confront capitalism today. As Ernest Mandel (1968, p. 649) says,

> A system based on private property and private profit cannot function adequately unless the capitalist 'rules of the game' are respected. It can resort to *supplementary* techniques of 'planning', especially where it is a question of nationalising losses, or of subsidising new (or sick) industries. It cannot in the long run cohabit with important sectors of production, and above all with an overall management of the economy, which are not guided by the criterion of profit. . . . Instead of genuine planning, what we have is a half-hearted, clumsy, embarrassed attempt to manage the economy, which often interferes in a contradictory way, and whose balance of achievement is most 'positive' in periods of war economy and of reconstruction, that is in periods of acute shortage.

This diagnosis of 'late capitalism' could have been formulated by Ulf af Trolle, the Bjurel or Trilateral Commissions rather than by Ernest

Mandel. If there is agreement between Marxist and bourgeois writers on the inconsistency and long-run dysfunctionality of so-called mixed economies, there is also considerable agreement on the mechanisms involved. As long as state interventions exhibited a reasonable degree of 'market conformity' (Mayntz and Scharpf, 1975, pp. 15f), as they did in the early Swedish attempts to fight the depression of the 1930s, and in the state interventions of the first two postwar decades in quite a number of Western countries, the capitalist 'rules of the game' were certainly respected. By counter-cyclical regulation of aggregate consumer demand in relation to business cycles, by adjusting interest rates, and by providing incentives overcoming the 'frictions' and 'imperfections' of the labour market, capital accumulation and economic growth was enhanced. The market conformity of these state interventions had the support of trade unions in Sweden, and was actively pursued by the governing Social Democratic Party.[3] The very rate of economic growth which was a characteristic of most Western countries at that time but which manifested itself with particular force in Sweden because its machinery of industrial production was left untouched by the destruction of war, made it possible for labour as well as capital to gain in absolute terms from this kind of development. But as other countries in Europe as well as in the Third World caught up with Sweden, and as stagflation emerged as a new phenomenon on the international scene, state interventions took a new direction, orienting themselves no longer simply to the smooth operation of consumer and labour markets but also to commodity production itself. In addition increasing public pressure on the state to tackle the various society-wide effects which we have discussed under the rubric of negative externalities brought forward new types of interventions which were neither geared to the needs of the market nor to commodity production but to a costly non-commodified production of use values with respect to environment, child welfare, the welfare of the increasing population of aged, handicapped, etc.

The Boston Consulting Group (1978, p. 86) in their commissioned study of Swedish industry shows that greater state support to stagnating rather than to expansive sectors of industry is a more common pattern in Sweden than in other, leading European countries.

This pattern of state intervention obviously breaks a fundamental rule of capitalist development: profit and growth should be basic mechanisms of dynamic progress. Subsidies to stagnant enterprises not only violate this fundamental rule in an abstract sense. It redistributes financial resources in a manner which deprives expansive sectors of industry of their competitive advantage and growth potential. But this tendency — most clearly manifested as it is at present in Sweden, even with a bourgeois government in power — is probably far from absent in other European countries. In the international debate it has often been emphasized that the sheer size of crisis-struck enterprises today makes it too costly politically and too disruptive economically to allow a free play of the classic mechanisms for advancing long-term productivity — bankruptcies, unemployment, devaluation of capital, etc. — and therefore the state may have to intervene to control and discipline individual capitalists as well as the working class (Wright, 1978, p. 177). Therefore this pattern of state intervention is a latent force even in countries which have not pursued this approach to the same extent as Sweden.

The fact that such forces, breaking into the capitalist 'rules of the game', seem to have been more powerful in Sweden than in some other countries may be a result not only of the greater unity and strength of the Swedish labour movement (even when it is not represented in the cabinet), but also of the size of the country and the structure of its economy. Sweden is a small country dominated by big companies. Therefore the total bankruptcy of one or two such companies would play greater havoc with the whole web of economy and society in Sweden than in other comparable countries in the Western hemisphere.

We have thus found a rather broad-based agreement that the inconsistencies of so-called mixed economies become ever so more pronounced, the further we move from (1) toward (2) and (3) in the typology of state interventions indicated below:

1. Early state interventions subject to the rules of 'market conformity';
2. Later selective interventions directly in the sphere of production (often for the purpose of salvaging sick companies or adjusting regional imbalances);
3. Improductive and costly welfare interventions to tackle negative externalities, and 'to reproduce labour power even when it cannot be sold as commodity on the labour market' (Wright, 1978, p. 235), for instance in the relatively mild form of unemployment insurance or in the more clearly improductive forms of support to the handicapped, to premature pensions, care for the aged etc.

The increasing transfer of resources, that is of tax-payers' money, to sector (3) is sufficiently well documented internationally, and its extensive nature in Sweden sufficiently well-known, to allow us to limit ourselves to an empirical investigation into sector (2), that is state subsidies to industrial enterprises.

Such an investigation confronts us with a number of difficult problems related to the availability of materials relevant to various definitions of the term 'subsidy'. We have found that these technical problems can be minimized, if not completely solved, if we limit ourselves to a rather narrow definition of subsidy. The figures now to be reported refer only to subsidies in the form of *payments* to *private* industry in response to *applications* from single enterprises. This is a selective type of state intervention contrasting sharply with the non-selective, generalized measures characteristic of the first type of state interventions mentioned above.

This narrow definition of subsidies excludes loans and credits, tax reductions, investments in industry made by state pension funds, joint ventures involving state and private industry, nationalization of enterprises, etc. It is well-known that all these forms of state participation in industrial production have increased greatly during the last decade, and particularly after the change of government in 1976, but it is difficult to estimate quantitatively the volume of such state participation in terms of money, and even more difficult to assess what forms and volumes of such state participation go beyond the limits of market conformity. Therefore we have chosen to focus our attention on subsidies in the more limited sense indicated. The schema used to assess the volume of such subsidies has been described in a separate project report (Lundberg, 1979, p. 24 and Appendix 2).

We do not claim that our figures are free of errors. They may include small fractions of support to industries and services in the public sector, and they certainly exclude loans which for all practical purposes eventually become subsidies as a result of remittance. However, even if our figures may be somewhat incorrect with regard to the absolute volume of subsidies per year, they are valid enough as trend indicators.

In Figure 10.1 we can see that state subsidies allocated in 1978/9 were about *eighty* times as large as in 1961/2. We have not been able to find any counter-cyclical relationship between the volume of state subsidies and the business cycle. In the recession year 1967/8 subsidies to private industry were only one-third of subsidies in the boom year 1970/1. There is rather a monotonous upward trend which probably reflects a steady but long-term structural change in the economy. Such structural change may in some cases paradoxically imply a lack of needed structural change in certain branches of industry. When such branches are exposed to structural changes in market composition and competition, while rigidly maintaining their internal structure, this implies a changing strategic position of such branches in their economic environment; and such changes certainly are structural.

Figure 10.1 State subventions to private enterprise in Sweden 1961/62−1978/79. (1961 prices, in million crowns)

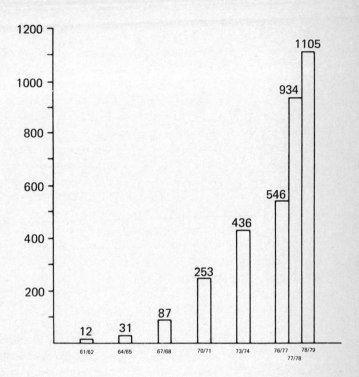

Source: Government Bills

Note: Subventions 1978/79 are probably underestimated due to the fact that data were available only for 1978. Current prices have been deflated with the consumer price index. For 1979 we have used predictions in the preliminary national budget.

But while subsidies to private industry have increased as much as indicated by Figure 10.1, overall state expenses have increased as well. We may therefore ask whether such subsidies have remained stable or in fact increased also in proportion to the national budget as a whole. In Figure 10.2 we find that subsidies to private industry have indeed increased even when expressed as proportions of the national budget. Yet this proportion is still rather small in comparison with other sectors of the budget − only 2 per cent in 1977/8.

Figure 10.2 State subventions to private enterprise in Sweden 1961/62–1978/79.
(per thousand)

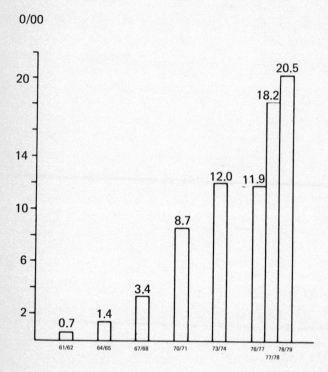

0/00

Source: Government Bills

Note: Subventions 1978/79 are probably underestimated due to the fact that data were available only for 1978. Current prices have been deflated with the consumer price index. For 1979 we have used predictions in the preliminary national budget.

State subsidies are not uniquely Swedish. When measured in terms of per cent of GNP most capitalist countries exhibit an upward trend in state subsidies to private industry (Blackhurst, Marian and Tumlir, 1978, quoted from the Swedish Bjurel report, Ds Ju 1979:1, Appendix 2, p. 105).

Other empirical studies than our own (Wiking-Faria, 1976) show that, apart from subsidies specifically destined to small-scale industry, the bulk of other subsidies in Sweden are allocated to large companies or concerns with more than 1000 employees. Perhaps this could be explained with the downward trend in the rate of profit reported for bigger companies (see above, p. 86).

Nationalized industries have not been included in the figures previously reported. In recent years, that is during the period of bourgeois government from 1976 to 1980, more nationalizations of industries have taken place than during the forty-four preceding years of social democratic rule. Between 1977 and 1980 the recently nationalized shipbuilding industry is receiving 8.1 billion crowns in added capital from the state (covering of losses and new capital). Favourable loans amount to 2.5 billion crowns. During this period the state also is giving guarantees for another 17.5 billion crowns. Of these guarantees, 3.7 billion crowns are offered to private shipowners (Ds Ju 1979:1, p. 128). Thus, the support to shipping and nationalized shipbuilding alone is quite comparable to the 'ordinary' subsidies allocated to private industry as a whole for the years 1977–80 (see Figure 10.1 above).

The textile industry has been partly nationalized in the last few years, and has also received considerable support both within the support to private industry reported above and through nationalizations.

As late as 1974 the Swedish steel industry had a very good year. But the crisis in recent years has brought forward considerable state subsidies and new joint ventures between state and private industry in Sweden. While in France about 30 000 steel-workers were being pushed out into unemployment in the spring of 1979, the Swedish government made serious attempts to contain this trend.

These are just a few examples of increasing state involvement directly in production. In most of the cases mentioned we can speak of a *socialization or nationalization of losses* – in obvious violation of the logic of the capitalist market economy.

So far we have focused most of our attention on the intrinsic *economic* inconsistencies of state interventions in late capitalism. But there are also contradictions between the demands of the capitalist economy and the demands of political democracy. We have pointed out the uneasiness expressed in a report from the Trilateral Commission with regard to 'inflated' political demands. Marxist writers have not been unaware of this contradiction but expressed it in different terms (Habermas, 1973; Offe, 1972; O'Connor, 1973).

The Marxist authors just mentioned – Marxist not in a dogmatic sense but in terms of their basic queries – all agree that 'advanced' capitalism involves an increasing contradiction between the requirements of capital accumulation and efficiency on the one hand, and political legitimacy on the other.

According to Habermas the market provided both for capital accumulation and legitimacy in the earlier 'liberal' stage of capitalism. The wonders of the self-regulating market were in themselves a source of ideological legitimation (cf. Lane, 1977) at the same time as the market provided for capital accumulation and optimal efficiency. In 'advanced' capitalism, however, market forces are partly breaking down, an inconsistent mixture of economic forces and state interventions is emerging, and as a result political legitimacy and economic efficiency also become contradictory. If too much emphasis is placed on economic efficiency and capital accumulation, this will necessarily imply that less resources than otherwise are devoted to consumption, social services, the fighting of unemployment and negative externalities, etc. Thus, the legitimacy of the regime is undermined because voters demand that the state concerns itself with these problems; and this loss of political legitimacy may eventually give rise to state interventions which again undermine capital accumulation and efficiency. But as capital accumulation, manifesting itself in statistics on economic growth, is not only a requirement of capitalism but another source of political legitimacy in industrial societies,[4] there seems to be a vicious circle here which is extremely difficult to tackle. To strike the right balance between efficiency and legitimacy often seems too problematic to be handled adequately by the political—administrative resources which the state can command.

To this diagnosis James O'Connor has added his notion of 'the fiscal crisis of the state' (pp. 5f). Attempts to care simultaneously for the requirements of capital accumulation and political legitimacy heavily taxes the citizen up to a point where the 'fiscal crisis' emerges, for instance in the form of tax protests. On p. 121 we have quoted passages from a keynote speech by the chairman of SAF, the Swedish Employers' Confederation, Curt Nicolin, giving his views of the situation.

These various writers differ among each other in several respects with which we cannot deal at length in this context. O'Connor, for instance, emphasizes more strongly than Habermas that state welfare policies eventually benefit total capital (p. 7). This belief which justifies the use of the label 'capitalist state' is obviously empirically wrong. State interventions of the third type mentioned above — improductive support to non-commodified services — do not necessarily contribute to 'total capital'. The modern state is not only a capitalist state; it is a contradictory state.

INDUSTRY MUST RELY ON ITS OWN ABILITY
Politicians cannot provide dynamic leadership!
Keynote Speech by Dr. Curt Nicolin, chairman of SAF,
March 23, 1979

Ten or fifteen years from now Sweden will be a socialized country, perhaps not according to the classical definition, but for all practical purposes. Decision-making at that time will be in the hands of politicians and corporations, with consequent restrictions on freedom for individual citizens. To establish new private enterprise will be virtually impossible and the proportion of private enterprise in the country has been drastically reduced. However, the fiction that we are a democracy based on a market economy with personal freedom for individuals will be retained.

This is my evaluation of the probable development for the future.* This development is not absolutely inevitable, however, But powerful forces are needed to prevent this probable development. Great moral courage will be required to bring about necessary changes — or to speak with Dante: 'The hottest places in Hell are reserved for those who retain their neutrality in times of great moral crises.' . . .

What are the motives behind the actions of the politicians? Well, there are the great ideas. The necessity to win elections is another motivation for politicians. It is in fact quite natural that the activities of politicians are determined by this fact. We might say that politicians buy marginal voters from different categories of people by providing new subventions or by introducing new or expanded services. . . .

Politicians have at most twenty years to relearn. Because they cannot dispose of more than 100 per cent of GNP. Before then they must learn to get votes without providing new subventions. Similarly they must learn to adjust public administration to the resources available. . . .

But when the Swedish people discover the truth, can't we expect opposition? Yes, I believe so. But the question is whether we at that time will have any leaders who are capable of changing the direction of events. Will we not have destroyed our economy and our morality so thoroughly that our task becomes insurmountable? . . .

From what I have said it is obvious that the state is rather unlikely to help in adjusting the costs of the more dynamic part of our economy. Industry will be wise to fend for itself and rely only on its own ability. The leaders of industry must exhibit forceful initiatives and an element of daring which is not based on calculations of profits and losses or on balanced accounts. They must act forcefully and take the necessary steps in collaboration with the employees. The pleasant line no longer holds; a strong will, a drive toward ambitious goals become a necessity.

---

*In his comments after this speech Nicolin pointed out that his prediction about the probable development might hold regardless of whether labour or bourgeois parties were in political command.

Habermas on the other hand would seem to have a stronger belief in the ability of advanced capitalism to resolve some of the contradictions mentioned, as a result of an increasingly fruitful collaboration with the state and a weakening of class forces in advanced capitalism. The class character of social conflicts which, according to Habermas, was obvious in liberal capitalism, is masked under advanced capitalism, Habermas believes, because of the piecemeal character of welfare policies directed toward 'quasi groups' such as consumers, house-dwellers, school children and their parents, the sick and the aged — categories which cut right across class divisions. Therefore Habermas does not consider a crisis of political legitimacy as imminent. A greater threat to the capitalist order is the 'cultural crisis of legitimacy' caused by the fact that the cultural system under advanced capitalism is unable to produce the necessary social norms for system maintenance. Here Habermas comes very close to a structural-functionalist sociologist, Daniel Bell (1976), who speaks of 'the cultural contradictions of capitalism'.

Habermas has been heavily criticized by other Marxists, particularly those of the Althusser school, for his 'idealism', that is for being a heretic within the historical materialist tradition. Be this as it may. More important in our view are the following two considerations.

Firstly, the insistence of Habermas on analysing mechanisms which may delay a socialist transformation of capitalist society strikes a healthy note of scepticism questioning some of the most facile Marxist predictions on the downfall of capitalism. Secondly, however, his downgrading of the critical role of a *political* legitimacy crisis in favour of a crisis of *cultural* legitimacy seems to be quite questionable not because it is heretic but for empirical reasons. Class struggle was not as undisguised and manifest under liberal capitalism; and it is not as masked and latent in advanced capitalism, as Habermas claims. We will have more to say about this matter in Part III. The class struggle is one of several threats against political legitimacy at present. Furthermore, there are also empirical data which disprove the assumption that trust in the democratic party system is maintained. Even in a country such as Sweden, reputed for its relatively high level of political legitimacy, there are many signs of a diminishing trust in the system, according to repeated public opinion surveys among the electorate (Petersson, 1978, pp. 258f).

Claus Offe, who belongs to the third generation of Frankfurter Marxists, has elaborated on the ideas of Habermas, particularly that of the *internal* operation of the state. He has pointed out the potential capacity of capitalism to adjust its strategy to the new situation, namely by developing 'functional equivalents' to the politicization of production implied by state interventions. If capitalism can take it upon itself to tackle the problems which now are the objects of state interventions, we may ask whether the politicization of the economy indicated above is really inevitable. It is, we assert, in our third problematic conjecture.

3. The politicization of the economy in capitalist countries through state intervention violating the capitalist 'rules of the game' is the inevitable result of capitalism itself.

That state interventions violating 'market conformity' have in fact increased in virtually all advanced capitalist countries is a demonstrable fact; but its inevitability is a conjecture which can be questioned on both logical and empirical grounds. If we can find one single capitalist country which has abolished the far-reaching state interventions discussed in the preceding section, and in practice endorsed the kind of classical economic strategy proposed by, say, Milton Friedman, the well-known economist and Nobel Prize winner, then we can also empirically reject the inevitability of a politicization of advanced capitalist economies.

There is such a country — Pinochet's and Milton Friedman's Chile. Perhaps it is significant that free enterprise, liberated from the shackles of the state interventions which distort the superior logic of market forces, could be salvaged in Chile only through one of the most repressive and cruel regimes in the world. If the state does not intervene in the economy, it must intervene all the more forcefully and brutally to crush civil rights and the struggle of the working class, it would seem. We think that there is a lesson to be learnt from this. A return to a market economy undisturbed by state interventions violating the rules of the market is possible only through authoritarian repression. Therefore our third conjecture should be amended to take account of this fact. A politicization of the economy in capitalist countries is inevitable only in countries which operate reasonably well according to the rules of pluralist democracy, unless such democracies are disfigured by authoritarian take-overs.

So much for the attempted empirical refutation of our third conjecture. But as the critical discussion of Karl Popper's (1963) schema of conjectures and refutations has shown, the power of valid refutation through single deviant cases is somewhat less than Popper thought.[5] Logical theoretical arguments are also necessary in rejecting a conjecture.

It has been argued that representatives of capital who view a politicization of the economy with apprehension could decide to join hands to take responsibility for what presently is seen as 'residual' tasks for the state to take care of. The German Frankfurter Marxists Offe (1972) and Ronge (1978) have emphasized that this possibility at least should be discussed and evaluated before we assume the inevitability of a politicization of the capitalist economy. To deal with highly speculative possibilities of this nature falls outside our competence and interest in the present context. Ronge speaks about 'relatively equifunctional mechanisms of socialization' within the framework of capitalism. The fact that he uses the term *relatively* equifunctional seems to imply that the kind of reformed and socialized capitalism he has in mind would give priority to a capitalist socialization of credits and investments while neglecting the predicaments of the working class. Even if such 'relatively equifunctional mechanisms of socialization' ever would materialize within the framework of a flexible capitalist system, they would have to do so by repressive means directed against a working class which already now is protesting unemployment, wage restraints and working conditions all over Europe.

What do we mean by 'repressive means'? Not necessarily what it means in Pinochet's Chile. Repression can be found along an extended scale ranging from the killings, brutality and intimidations of authoritarian states to certain forms of 'law and order' found even in democratic societies. In addition there are more subtle forms of ideological repression in pluralist democracies. Claus Offe speaks of the repressive exclusion of certain items from the political agenda; anti-capitalist demands and interests simply cannot be effectively articulated on the political arenas of our capitalist societies since they are lacking necessary and respectable means of articulation. If such demands surface anyway they are immediately stamped as threatening individual freedom and social order.

However, in Sweden in recent years this kind of repressive ideological selection does not seem to have been as effective as earlier. Established social democratic leaders have increasingly come out with critical remarks about 'capitalism' and the 'market forces' in a way which would have been conceived as impossible some ten or twenty years ago. But when the 'repressive selection' of agenda-setting political bodies thus turns out to be inefficient, there is instead a tendency of the business community to disavow democratic politics as a whole. And to the extent that these voices of the business community are skilfully advertised to the public, they may reintroduce 'repressive selection' into politics through a back-door.

Leaders of the business community in Sweden, and commentators closely associated with big business, are indeed starting to voice warnings against 'excesses of democracy' similar to those expressed in the Trilateral Commission Report mentioned earlier (Crozier, Huntington and Watanuki, 1975). One example is the speech by Curt Nicolin quoted above (p. 121). 'Independent economists' and economic commentators offering to save us from the inconsistencies of our present 'mixed economy' by a return to a more full-fledged market economy, often remark that they realize the lack of political feasibility of their suggestions, and may add that our democratically elected politicians are one of the greater threats to further progress (see, for instance, an article by Sven-Ivan Sundqvist, respected economic commentator, in the liberal newspaper *Dagens Nyheter*, 25 February 1979). Such remarks come very close to what Samuel Huntington, in his contribution to the Trilateral Commission Report mentioned above, conceived as the root of our problems (p. 73): 'What the Marxists mistakenly attribute to capitalist economics, however, is, in fact, a product of democratic politics.'

Commentators like those just mentioned obviously do not realize that democratic politicians, unlike economists and other spokesmen of capital, cannot define their task as if people did not matter. Capitalist societies are inhabited by people. An increasing number of them are exposed to the extended effects of capitalism in the form of environmental pollution, health hazards, bad working conditions, unemployment, impoverishment of family life, etc. These are problems created by our industrial societies which happen to be capitalist, and not by democratic politics. If class struggle and welfare state interventions (which also happen to be products of capitalism) are undertaken to tackle these problems, and in their turn create problems for capitalism, it would seem rather myopic to attribute these additional economic problems to democratic politics rather than to the systemic characteristics of capitalist societies themselves.

On this point it is interesting to note the change of style and argument exhibited by the Swedish management expert Ulf af Trolle when he writes on economics on the one hand, and on politics and trade unions on the other (1978, pp. 18f, 35 and 149). He emphasizes the urgency of applying a sober and scientific approach to our problems; but again we notice signs of myopia. The scientific approach is reserved for the problems of the economy in a narrow sense. When he writes about politics and working life he starts sermonizing, and forgets the scientific approach. While incentives for investment are seen by him as objects of scientific analysis, the motivations of workers to be diligent, hard-working and willing to accept wage-restraints are topics for sermon and exhortation. But these are not the only revealing inconsistencies in the scientific—ideological stance of business.

Spokesmen of the business community would do well to remember their own rhetoric that only capitalism can generate and maintain a liberal and pluralist democracy. There may be some limited historical truth in this assertion, in spite of the fact that it most often has been used for propagandistic purposes in Cold War contexts. But if this assertion contains some element of truth, then it is not logical to view democratic politics in the age of welfare state interventions as some kind of external nuisance for which capitalism itself is not responsible. Pluralist democracy and our trade union organizations have been generated and maintained by the dynamics of capitalism itself — even though we can point to capitalist states which have not yet been able to remove oligarchical or dictatorial rulers. Therefore it is quite possible that attempts to restrict the so-called 'excesses' of democracy in the interest of capital and economic growth, actually hit back on the functioning of capitalist economies. If political democracy at present is seen by spokesmen of business interests as a nuisance from an economic point of view, the nuisance of increasing political conflicts and class struggle which probably will be generated by attempts to restrict democratic rule may become even worse — also for the business community itself.

The Quandary of Mature Welfare Capitalism

In whatever direction you turn, your back remains behind. Whether we are socialists or liberals or conservatives, hired labour power or capitalists, we seem to have been locked into a quandary. Regardless of ideologies or personal predicaments many can agree that (i) the capitalist 'mixed economies' are contradictory and doomed to stagnation from most points of view. On the other hand a return to a more consistent and comprehensive type of free and competitive economy may require (ii) a politically apathetic citizenry ruled within the framework of a rather restricted formal democracy. If this political apathy fails to emerge, (iii) a brutal authoritarian repression is needed for a return to a consistent system of free enterprise. The only other option seems to be (iv) a consistent and centralized type of state socialism, or state capitalism as some prefer to call it, which functions reasonably well as an egalitarian welfare state, and not so badly as an industrial society, but quite poorly as a civil and humane society, at least as far as we can judge from the historical experience of Eastern Europe.

Now, there are democratic socialists in the West who claim that the historical experience of Eastern Europe is invalid as far as Western Europe is concerned. Eastern European socialism was first introduced in a country without any democratic tradition. The Russian revolutionaries had to overthrow a tsarist oligarchy, and must face external and internal counter-revolutionary forces during those first formative years of the new Soviet state. None of these conditions would be present if a Western European nation decided, with majority support at the polls, to take significant steps on the road to socialism. Here in the West state socialism could certainly be combined with civil liberties and humanitarian values, according to this view. Once socialism has been made constitutional, just like general elections and political democracy were once made constitutional, socialism would cease to be controversial just as democracy today is uncontroversial in stable pluralist democracies. Respectable political parties would organize around other issues than for or against socialism, just as respectable political parties after the introduction of general elections stopped fighting about the pros and cons of political democracy; and thus a multi-party system could very well be combined with a state socialist economy.

To us this argument seems quite reasonable — particularly in comparison with the false and propagandistic attacks levelled by conservative and even liberal forces against democratic socialists in our Western countries. But even if the compatibility of centralistic state socialism and pluralistic democracy is at least as high, or perhaps even higher, than the compatibility of concentrated capitalism and pluralist democracy, this is not a sufficient reason to advocate centralistic democratic socialism, in our view. Even if pluralist democracy and a civil society were left intact after the introduction of centralistic socialism in a Western European country, there are other reasons for disliking that kind of socialism. Its centralized economy would probably become rather bureaucratic, and leave rather little space for decentralized creativity. Over time a socialist as well as a bourgeois bureaucracy may become ossified, feeble and passively obstructive. Alternatively a socialist bureaucracy could become too powerful, vital and demanding, producing a 'new class' of economic power-holders occupying much the same positions as the monopoly capitalists of today, while the multi-party parliament and the cabinet would be struggling over more or less peripheral issues.

We should look for another socialist option — but not in a speculative, idealistic manner. Some men in quandaries start dreaming about new systems resolving all the contradictions inherent in their present predicaments. Dreamers and visionaries are not necessarily wishful thinkers. Utopias can emerge from an innovative, scientific approach with due consideration for all the situational parameters involved. But to break out of a quandary it is usually not sufficient to have bright, innovative and scientifically based ideas; you also need forceful support to implement them.

Some visionary social scientists like to act as 'architects' of the future. Their visions could possibly become useful in some contexts, but it is the context which matters. A decisive context usually consists of large groups or classes of people struggling with the help of their organizations to find a way out of their predicaments. In such contexts solutions can be invented, usually not by social scientists but by creative practitioners, which suggest more or less piecemeal or seemingly incidental solutions to the problems at hand. Sometimes such solutions turn out to have implications which go far beyond the piecemeal significance originally anticipated. We propose that more or less visionary social scientists can play a role in transforming society to build a better future only if they immerse themselves in such contexts of class or group struggle, refraining from enacting the grandiose role of architects of the future and rather helping critically and constructively to evaluate and modify the solutions advanced from below by practitioners participating in such struggles, by helping to place them in a larger holistic context.

Even though we claim, as social scientists, that the quandary outlined above is real and not a figment of an ideological imagination, we do not pretend to have any detailed 'scientific' solutions of our own. We prefer to look for solutions which are proposed from within the working class which is suffering most from the contradictions of mature capitalism. Such proposals may or may not turn out to be the best possible solutions for dissolving the quandary in a manner beneficial for most people — but they have the strength of a broad-based support. If we are serious about the need for a transformation of our capitalist society, such broad-based support is absolutely essential not only because that is most democratic, but also because the momentum of change can be provided only by such a support. Therefore we would rather occupy ourselves with somewhat incomplete half-baked proposals for social change emanating from the labour movement than with complete, thoroughly analysed blueprints prepared outside a labour movement context — even if such blueprints were designed by the most brilliant and progressive social scientists around. Brilliant designs of society emerging not from below but from an excellent mind cannot be implemented unless they are imposed from above. If such an imposition is at all possible, it may also be dangerous. On this point at any rate we concur with Popper's criticism of utopian social engineering (1969, Chapter 21). But let us not forget that Karl Marx voiced an equally severe criticism of utopianism much earlier than Popper.

Fortunately, there are very few good utopians around. To the best of our knowledge there are no progressive blueprints for the future prepared by the most brilliant social scientists of today. Not even one of the most brilliant minds of the nineteenth century, Karl Marx, had any utopian designs for the future.

In the next chapter we will refer to some concrete proposals toward wage-earners' capital funds drawn up originally on the request of the Swedish Metal Workers Union, and later modified and supplemented through discussions within LO, the Swedish Federation of Trade Unions and within the Social Democratic Party. These proposals will be one of the focal points of political debate and reform in Sweden for the next few years. Similar but not identical designs have emerged in other European countries like the German Federal Republic and Denmark (see Chapter 19).

The main question in the next chapter is the following. To what extent do the wage-earners' capital funds proposed within the Swedish labour movement actually address themselves to the contradictions of late capitalism, and can they help us to break out of the quandary in which we find ourselves? In the course of our attempt to explore this question in a preliminary fashion (Chapter 19 contains a more thorough discussion of various alternatives) the main conclusions of Part II will be summarized.

11 Resolving the Contradictions of Capitalism: Options and Constraints

To various extents and in somewhat different patterns all advanced capitalist societies exhibit the tendencies described and documented in this book: capital undergoes concentration, centralization and internationalization, and whole nations as well as international transactions are now totally permeated by capitalism and its effects, good and bad. After a prolonged period of sustained economic growth which diverted attention from the social costs of capitalism, we now see these effects more clearly.

But while capitalism has permeated society, and exposed an increasing number of people to increasingly negative aspects of capitalist development, social interests have far from penetrated into the centres of capitalist decision-making; at most such broader social considerations have been allowed to influence the various policies of democratic states aimed at reproducing labour power, at restoring the market mechanisms which capitalism itself at the same time requires and destroys, and aimed also at repairing some of the damage done by the negative externalities of capitalist production. As long as these social costs were taken care of in a manner which concurred with market conformity and the reproduction of necessary labour power, this system of collaboration between state and capital could be conceived as reasonably workable — at least among those who were not devoted socialists. Even if the increasingly social character of productive forces as yet are unmatched by corresponding changes in social relations of production, the state has taken over responsibility for some of the social effects and social costs of capitalism in a way which ameliorates the situation to make the contradictions of capitalism less dreadful than they would have been without such state interventions.

But in recent years democratic states have increasingly broken the rules of market conformity and labour reproduction. The state now often intervenes directly in production in a manner violating the most elementary criteria of capitalist business, and also allocates increasing resources to sustaining people whom the labour market no longer can absorb. This is done not only or even mainly for ideological reasons. Bourgeois — and not only labour — governments do it, even though there are differences in the way it is done or proposed to be done by bourgeois or labour parties. State violations of market conformity emanate from the contradictory development of capitalism itself. Simultaneous industrial stagnation, unemployment and inflation — so-called stagflation — is the most visible symptom of this capitalist predicament. The so-called mixed economies no longer seem workable, because the state is forced, by the development of capitalism, to disturb the basic dynamics of capitalism itself. State medication sometimes has effects as serious as the original illness of capitalism itself.

Does this mean that we now can expect the 'final demise' of capitalism — or as Marx wrote: 'The knell of capitalist private property sounds.'

As Sam Bowles and Herbert Gintis (1979, p. 17) have sarcastically remarked, Marxists have 'successfully predicted nine out of the last three final collapses of the capitalist order'. But capitalism has survived. However, our notion of a transition from capitalism to socialism does not presuppose the realization of such prophecies of capitalist doom. Contemporary capitalism can survive because of state interventions and other arrangements, however contradictory, which both assure survival and contain collective uprisings. The crucial point of social transformation in mature capitalism therefore, is not a dramatic collapse of the system, but the trivial fact that mature capitalism is performing badly, and that the relative strength of the labour movement within the framework of political democracy makes it possible to articulate demands for a better economic system. We stand at a cross-road, and the issue is not to wait for any breakdown of capitalism, but to be aware of the cross-road itself, and to make a political choice of the right way in order to reduce and eliminate the contradictions of capitalism.

But the statement that capitalism performs badly must be qualified to make explicit the specific character of the present situation. Even in countries which are relatively well off in economic terms — not just Sweden but also countries such as the Federal Republic of Germany — there are a number of economic indicators which suggest that the present situation is more than just another cyclical and passing downturn in the economy (Altvater, Hoffman and Semmler, 1979). In addition there are several political indicators which suggest that the present ills of mature capitalism no longer can be treated effectively with the conventional medicine within the framework of the present system. Spokesmen of both capital and reformist labour demand changes in the system itself, and not only a more effective application of previously accepted methods of crisis management. It would seem that the current crisis puts the innovative capacities of capitalists to a completely new test.

How innovative are the recommendations of the Trilateral Commission, and other similar proposals, calling for a return to a pure market economy, with drastic cut-backs on public welfare expenditures, and an extended role of the state in the accumulation of capital for profitable private investments?

And what are the systemic innovations proposed by the labour movement? Is democratic socialism an alternative answer to the ills of mature capitalism? Let us not jump to conclusions. From an intellectual point of view it would be interesting and perhaps revealing to put capitalism to a final test, an intellectual test only, in the form of a simulated theoretical experiment.

Assume that the fault of capitalism lies not mainly in its reliance on market mechanisms — at least not as far as commodity markets are concerned. Assume that the main fault lies with the *actors* responding to market forces. Modern capitalism operates with a number of different actors: capital owners and speculators, managers responsible to capital owners, workers in direct production, consumers (working or not), and the state responding both to the conflicts among these actors and to the needs of capitalist system maintenance. Among these actors there is an asymmetry of power in the capitalist system. Capitalists are most powerful — not because they 'command' or are most 'influential' but because the system is theirs. They have the systemic power.[1]

Our theoretical experiment takes off from the observation that the actors mentioned above are involved in a contradictory and asymmetric division of functions and power. It proceeds with the query whether some of the actors may be in a better position than others to integrate the various functions and the power involved in a less destructive and costly manner.

We have already rejected the ideal of state capitalism. The state is not the actor we are looking for. The actor we are looking for must be directly and locally involved in production, must depend directly on success and innovation in production at his place of work. At the same time our actor must be personally concerned with employment, with prices of consumer goods, and with the environmental effects hurting common people, families and children. In short the main actor must be able to integrate in one multi-dimensional judgement the requirements of capital accumulation and investment, the requirements of the commodity market, the effects of productivity and wage levels on employment and on commodity prices, and the damage done by negative externalities. Finally he must know that no deliberate sacrifice of satisfactions on any of these dimensions will be unduly exploited by other actors, because otherwise he could not properly balance the various interests involved in his multi-dimensional judgement.

Does such an actor really exist? Not if an optimal multi-dimensional judgement is required. Yet as Herbert Simon (1968, p. xxv and Chapter 5) has pointed out most actors in the real world can 'satisfice', if not optimize. Our next task therefore is to rank the actors mentioned above in terms of their capacity for multi-dimensional satisficing. This capacity will be evaluated primarily on the basis of rather conventional *structural* criteria, that is in terms of the pattern of incentives which operate on actors with different positions in the given mode of production. We consider criteria of judgemental *competence* as secondary.

The main incentives of capital owners and speculators are profit, and perhaps stability or at least predictability of profits. When profitability declines capital owners and speculators are therefore likely to move their capital into more profitable production elsewhere, or into non-productive speculation in diamonds, art, etc. if there is a more general decline of profitability. This is done without concern for the destruction of productive capital, and the unemployment which may ensue.

To managers who are responsible to capital owners profit is also a main incentive, but they are likely to be somewhat more concerned with capital investments which in the short run may somewhat detract from profits. Managers may also have a marginal concern for maintaining smooth relations with workers in direct production in order to sustain productivity and the predictability of production. But when profitability shows a tendential decline, managerial incentives for investments also tend to decline.

To workers in direct production *profitability* is also an important incentive because a profitable company is more likely to pay reasonable wages. But if increasing profits are siphoned off to shareholders rather than to wages and investments for improvements of production at a given plant, workers are less likely to look at profits as an incentive. Unlike shareholders who can easily move their money to other companies or to improductive speculation, workers can view profits as an incentive only if most of it remains in the company for the benefit of further investments and wages. Workers have no incentives allowing the *movement of capital abroad*, to Swiss bank accounts or fictitious agencies in Lichtenstein. In addition continued and stable *employment* is a main concern of workers in production. Therefore if workers are assured that wage restraint ensures employment and productivity, and is not exploited by 'profiteers', we may even find incentives for *wage restraint* among workers when that is required. But if wage restraint is seen as conducive only to the 'super profits' of shareholders, then obviously incentives for wage restraint will be less pronounced. In his capacity as consumer the worker is more concerned with *consumer prices and living costs* than other actors. Basic living costs account for a larger proportion of the expenses of workers. And furthermore workers to a much lesser extent than capital owners and even managers can convert part of their costs into tax deductibles. Workers are usually also more exposed to *negative externalities* in and outside of their work, and therefore should have more of an incentive to reduce such externalities.

This means that the decisions of workers in a system of workers' self-management are subject to a much wider spectrum of productive and social incentives than the traditional owners and managers of capital. The present system of capitalism (i) divides different incentives between actors who hold contradictory positions in the system, (ii) gives most systemic power to the actor(s) with the most limited repertory of incentives and, as a result, (iii) requires costly state interventions to rectify the imbalances and externalities ensuing from the operation of these limited incentives.

Workers' self-management operating within competitive commodity markets implies a shift of power in the production for such markets. *Most systemic power is given to the category or class of actors which exhibit the least limited spectrum of productive and social incentives, that is to workers.* Within this relatively wide spectrum of incentives, many incentives remain contradictory, but here these various incentives are instantaneously integrated in the multi-dimensional satisficing process of a *single* collective actor. In contrast to this we have the non-integrated separate processes of satisficing, with *different* actors responding to different and partly contradictory incentives, which characterizes the present system of private enterprise, and which calls for constant and costly corrections when more or less irreversible damage has already been done as a result of non-integrated satisficing processes dominated by the actors least capable of multi-dimensional satisficing.

Having taken account of the capability for multi-dimensional satisficing of different actors within a market economy we now turn to their judgemental competence. As a result of not only the mass educational standards of modern society but also the competence available in unions and among labour consultants, we can assume that judgemental competence is increasing within collectively organized labour. Furthermore, there are sound psychological reasons to assume that the judgemental competence of labour will increase with workers' self-management. Melvin Seeman (1967) has pointed out that motivation to acquire the knowledge and competence required in order to exercise power increases with power exercised. But in addition to such reasonable theoretical assumptions we can here also rely on observations. In the Swedish shipbuilding industry local unions were first to voice warnings about the coming crisis of this industry, and to suggest workable solutions (Beckholmen, 1979). But these warnings were not heeded by owners and managers because of their narrow capitalist perspective, nor by the social democratic government at that time because of their weak position in parliament. When the crisis erupted, the damage and the costs involved were greater than they probably would have been if the judgemental competence of labour and its more multi-dimensional incentive structure had been combined with more decision-making power.

Socialists who refuse to consider workers' self-management within a commodity market economy as an instance of genuine socialism often characterize such a system as a refinement of capitalism, as 'capitalism without private capitalists'. We leave these points for later discussion. Here our intention has been precisely to explore intellectually whether the efficiency of a decentralized market economy could be salvaged in a manner which integrates social considerations not by bureaucratic state interventions but through a redistribution of power among the actors within a capitalist system according to the principle of maximum multi-dimensional satisficing capability. A Swedish economic historian, Bo Gustafsson (1978, p. 12), has indicated that the system thus emerging may be most adequately characterized as 'democratic collectivist capitalism' rather than socialism — but he has also suggested that such a system might be a crucial step toward a democratic form of socialism. After all Karl Marx himself (1971b) did assume what might be called a refinement of capitalism as a precondition for a socialist transformation of society: 'No social order ever disappears before all the productive forces for which there is room in it have been developed; and new higher relations of production never appear before the material conditions of their existence have matured in the womb of the old society.'

But even though a system of workers' self-management may eliminate some of the contradictions of present day capitalism — particularly with reference to the whole pattern of capital accumulation, investment rates, job motivation, wages, prices, employment, content of production, and negative externalities — some problems will remain which require state intervention. In an increasingly complex economy there is always a need for co-ordination, corrective redistributions and some degree of overall planning; and the state could partly meet such needs by setting the parameters of economic activities rather than by detailed regulation (Brus, 1972, pp. 132f) and rely on regulation only in specific cases. Various ways of combining workers' self-management and state intervention will also be discussed in Chapter 20.

In a simplified and perhaps provocative form Figure 11.1 depicts a structural change from present day capitalism to a system of workers' self-management supplemented by state interventions of a much more limited nature than those in existence today. A similar diagrammatic representation with a somewhat different emphasis has been suggested by the Yugoslav economist Branko Horvat (1977).

In Figure 11.1 the hierarchical subordination of labour under management and capital, with a heavy superstructure of state interventions expanding beyond the limits of market conformity, is contrasted with a system where these company hierarchies are turned upside-down, and the tasks of the state become more limited. Labour takes decisive even if not immediate majority control over capital; management is appointed and employed mainly by labour. In Chapter 19 the details of such a system will be discussed.

But these are not simply the visions of some free-floating architects of an utopian future. The system of wage-earners' capital funds, and social development funds recently proposed by LO, the Swedish Federation of Trade Unions, and by the Social Democratic Party, does not go quite as far as our figure suggests, but could quite possibly provide a starting-point for a movement in that direction. This proposal is presently being investigated together with other related proposals by a Swedish government commission. Depending on the outcome of future political elections, a system with at least some of the general characteristics indicated above may be introduced over the next ten or fifteen years in Sweden — but not without struggles.

The struggle has already started in the form of campaigns and pamphlets attacking the proposed wage-earners' funds as a threat against democracy and pluralism (Norling, 1977; Lindbeck, 1979) and in the polemics of bourgeois political parties accusing the Social Democratic Party and LO for pushing the country toward an Eastern-European kind of state socialism.

Figure 11.1 Some structural characteristics of present day capitalism contrasted with a system of workers' self-management

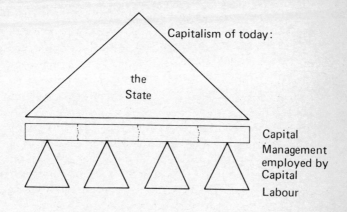

Capitalism of today:

the State

Capital
Management employed by Capital
Labour

A system of workers' self-management:

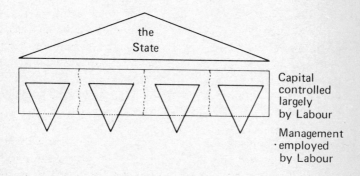

the State

Capital controlled largely by Labour

Management employed by Labour

Here the Marxian metaphor of the 'fetters' of capitalist relations of production constraining the development of new productive forces seems quite appropriate. The introduction of a new system of work organization which shifts the powers of management from directors responsible only for capital accumulation to actors with a greater capability for what we have called multi-dimensional satisficing implies a development of new productive forces not only in the organization of work, but in the long run probably also with respect to the technology of production (Hansson, 1976). But the growth of these new productive forces are constrained by forces wishing to preserve existing capitalist relations of production. Only the 'bursting asunder' of these constraining production relations to make them more compatible with the new emerging productive forces will release the dynamic of these forces for the benefit of the great majority of working people. This is the classical Marxian hypothesis about the transition to socialism in the terminal phase of capitalism. But this transition is not automatic. The strength of struggling actors on the political scene in terms of numbers, organization, social consciousness and systemic power will determine the outcome.

This is the topic of Part III.

PART III

Actors on the Stage:
Labour and Capital

by Göran Ahrne, Leif Lundberg
and Ulf Himmelstrand

12 Social Structures, Actors and Predicaments

Macro-structures and macro-processes such as those discussed in Part II of this book set the stage for action. Actors on the stage take action determined by the way in which the stage has been set, and the play organized.

This theatrical metaphor may serve some heuristic purposes in organizing a complex subject matter. But if pursued in detail metaphors may be misleading. The theatrical metaphor we have used to structure the content of this book certainly is misleading if it is taken too seriously. Even if we accept the idea that social action is largely determined, in a structural sense, by the way the social stage has been set, we may not find a script specifying the roles of actors, and the unfolding of the plot. Or if we find such scripts, a closer scrutiny of their content and representation on the stage may convince us that they must be 'burst asunder' to allow the action needed to resolve the structural contradictions figuring prominently on the stage of society. What then becomes of the concepts of role and play? If we are too infatuated by our theatrical metaphor just to forget about it, once it has been used for organizing our subject matter, we may be unable to find any notion on this point other than the concept of 'happening' to replace the concepts of role and play in trying to understand historical processes of change. But is history really a 'happening'?

Let us forget our metaphor for the time being, and concentrate rather on a scientific analysis of the ways in which macro-structures and processes are seen as linked to micro-notions of actors and action in social science, and how micro-events are understood as feeding back on macro-events. This may help us to discover how to deal with the shortcomings of our metaphor.

In marginalist economics actors on the micro-level take action on the basis of *incentives* to maximize marginal gain and minimize marginal cost on the market. The result is marginal *utility*. The relationship between the micro and macro-levels is basically one of statistical aggregation. Because the aggregated outcome may turn out to be quite different from the outcomes expected by the majority of individual economic actors, disequilibria may emerge on the macro-level. Equilibrating adjustment mechanisms which again are based largely on incentives to maximize marginal gain and minimize marginal cost then come into play to correct the disequilibrium. This presupposes another link between macro and micro-levels: channels of information on emerging disequilibria.

We will not here elaborate on the nature of these assumptions in marginalist theory, nor on the complications introduced by notions of trade-offs, and by Keynes's emphasis on the role of state intervention in bringing about equilibrium on the macro-level. For our purpose it is sufficient to emphasize the crucial position of the concepts of *incentives* and *utility* in marginalist theory, and of the actual *behaviour* revealing the preferences of aggregates of individual consumers, investors and producers — that is 'the ways in which people strive to obtain whatever it is they want' (Olson Jr., 1969, p. 147) — as indicators of incentives and utility.

The concepts of wants, incentives and revealed preferences, whether they are used in a causal or a normative sense, all refer to the subjective dispositions of actors. As Göran Therborn has pointed out (1976, pp. 270f) this provides a conceptual link between marginalist economics and academic sociology. Social exchange theory (Homans, 1961; Blau, 1964; Ekeh, 1974) is the most obvious contemporary instance of this linkage, but Therborn also suggests such a linkage between Max Weber's interest in marginalist theory and his preoccupation, as a sociologist, with values, action and rationality.

The preoccupation with values finds a more socio-psychological twist in *symbolic interactionism* with its focus on the processes and outcomes of interpersonal evaluation (Rose (ed.), 1962).

When *structural-functionalists* specify various structures such as social institutions, statuses and status-sets, ranks, roles and role-sets, etc. they usually do this in terms of social norms, rights, obligations, role expectations and similar concepts which all refer to some kind of shared standards of evaluation. In addition there are shared belief-systems and systems of knowledge. These, when seen in their combination with standards of evaluation constitute shared ideologies. Society as a whole is seen as structurally embodying various evaluative principles, belief-systems and ideologies which define the functions and dysfunctions entailed by the various sub-structures of society. Structural differentiation, role differentiation (a more disembodied way of speaking about division of labour), and diffusion of innovations, being the main processes of societal change acknowledged by structural functionalists, again are attributed to driving forces of a subjective nature, for instance the drive toward greater efficiency. This drive may be balanced by other drives which strive to maintain the values of unity, continuity and identity. The mix of values and beliefs in a given society is determined by and in its turn influences the degree of structural differentiation, the role differentiation and the diffusion of innovation in that society, be it traditional or modern, *Gemeinschaft* or *Gesellschaft*.

In terms of our theatrical metaphor, the stage of economic processes, as understood by classical and marginalist economists, is the *market*, whereas the stage of social processes, as understood by the kind of sociologies we have mentioned, is the normative community, or to use the more comprehensive notion suggested by Göran Therborn (1976, Chapter 5): the *ideological community*.

Statistical aggregation and information feedback takes care of macro—micro relations in economics. In sociology social institutions of child-rearing, education and law on the macro-level — that is families, schools and courts — take care of the reproduction of the macro-patterns of the ideological community on the individual micro-level through socio-psychological processes of socialization and social control, while the individual contributes to this reproduction by enacting the norms and roles prescribed and, marginally, by making innovations which may be accepted by the ideological community at large, and thus influence the conditions on the macro-level, if these innovations are attuned to dominant values; otherwise they are treated as deviant behaviour.

It should be obvious by now that the theatrical metaphor of stage, actors and play fits the structural—functional conception of sociology rather well, if not completely. This whole conception of society as a normative or ideological mould which shapes individual lives on the micro-level through processes of socialization and social control, has been criticized not only by Marxists, but also by several sociologists. Dennis Wrong (1961) did this in his well-known paper on 'the over-socialized conception of man', and Ralf Dahrendorf (1959) in his defence of the conflict perspective on social processes. More recently Alain Touraine (1979) has called for the complete rejection of the concept of society, because of its common interpretation as a social mould, and its use as a legitimation of structurally repressive social policies disguised in the cloak of a consensus ideology.

But while Dennis Wrong would seem to emphasize immutable biological and psycho-dynamic characteristics as a counterpoint to 'the oversocialized concept of man', Alan Touraine opens the stage to struggling actors — groups and classes in conflict — acting on and producing a society rather than being produced and moulded by it. He outlines a research methodology resembling radical action research where the sociologist 'takes the role' of an actor without taking the actor's 'standpoint', to use Ralph Turner's (1956) important distinction. The contribution of the sociologist in this kind of research is 'to continually push the actor to conduct his self-analysis, while continuing to be an actor. It is the actor's ability to conduct this analysis which informs us best about the nature of his actions, since this ability increases with behaviour which can be defined as *production of society*.' Touraine goes on to ask: 'How can the researcher play this role? How can he avoid either being an ideologist or destroying the actor by observing him as a dead butterfly? I think that he can do this by representing for the actor the highest possible meaning of his action.' This implies that the relationship between the researcher and the actor is one of dialogue by which the researcher contributes to the self-analysis of the actor (Touraine, 1980).

To the extent that Touraine's concept of man as a producer of society rather than as a product of society is seen as an antidote to structural functionalism we sympathize with his conception. But we take exception to its apparent voluntaristic and idealistic implications. In a Marxist perspective man appears as both a product and a producer of society, in a dialectical interplay which involves not only conflicts between actors but also contradictions between structural elements of 'society' which when reflected in the consciousness of actors compel them to act in order to produce a different kind of society. However, Touraine's formulations on the whole are generous enough to allow for such a dialectical Marxist approach as long as it does not restrict itself to the simplistic structuralism 'without a subject' vindicated by the school of Althusser. As we conceive the dialectical approach, it also implies the necessity to do research on 'society' not only within the limited perspective of subjective action research but also in the more objective structuralist sense illustrated in Part II of this book. Structure and action are dialectically related to each other, and this should be taken account of also in what we might call dialectical action research (Himmelstrand, 1978).

In our view it would in fact be possible for a Marxist to admit the validity of the structural—functional model as a near-sighted *description* of 'bourgeois society', a description excluding the foundation of this society in the exploitation of labour, and therefore of course also excluding the possibility of understanding the basis of bourgeois society, and its consequences for the society as a whole, including the working classes. Bourgeois society certainly produces bourgeois people playing bourgeois roles in bourgeois structures in the manner described by structural functionalists.

If Touraine's call for a complete rejection of the concept of society means that the limited bourgeois concept of bourgeois society must be abolished, then we agree with him. But a broader concept of society (or the social formation, as Marxists like to say) is certainly necessary both in order to locate the causal nexus which moulds the predicaments of people, and to identify the targets of struggle for those who wish to eliminate the structures generating such predicaments.

The Notion of Predicament

The notion of predicament refers to a position at the intersection of the realms of necessity and freedom, of objective and subjective circumstances. It would seem to be a notion quite useful in a dialectical analysis of historical processes linking the macro and micro levels of structure and action.

Dictionaries say that a predicament is 'a dangerous or trying condition or state' or 'a condition or situation, especially one that is dangerous, unpleasant, embarrassing or sometimes comical'. A predicament 'implies a complicated, perplexing situation from which it is difficult to disentangle oneself'. Approximate synonyms are the concepts *dilemma* and *quandary*. An example of a quandary can be found in our previous discussion on p. 126. A more general concept which would seem to subsume all these is the concept of *problem*. However, these latter concepts are too general for our purpose because they include both difficulties which appear only in the mind, and difficulties of a more objective nature. A predicament would seem to have a more limited meaning implying something objectively physical or social, involving material threats as well as social impositions by other human beings, or (when defined in terms of unpleasant effects) mainly such effects which are physically and not only mentally 'trying'. The dictionary definitions speak of 'dangerous', 'embarrassing' or 'perplexing' situations. That these situations are 'sometimes comical' clearly indicates the social element involved. What is dangerous or embarrassing to one person, sometimes looks comical to an observer in a socially protected and dominant position.

If you believe, as we do, that the notion of predicament could occupy the same kind of position in Marxist theory as occupied by the role concept in structural—functional theory, while of course serving a quite different function in that position, then we need a more conceptually precise definition of predicament than provided by ordinary dictionaries. As a first attempt we tentatively suggest the following somewhat simplistic definition: *a predicament is a negatively valued position from which it is difficult to escape due to the constraints of material and social structure.*

A closer consideration of concrete cases of predicaments would seem to indicate, however, that this definition is unnecessarily restrictive. There are situations which may be defined as predicaments which entail positively rather than negatively evaluated positions, or positions of great potential, which however are threatened in one way or another — situations which are subjectively good, beautiful, enjoyable, or inspiring hope, but which at the same time are objectively hazardous or dangerous.

Our second attempt at a definition would then run as follows: *a predicament is a negatively valued position from which it is difficult to escape because of material or social constraints, or a positively valued but weak and objectively threatened position.*

According to these attempts at a definition of predicament, it would seem that no objectively observable position in a material or social constraining or threatening structure is *objectively* a predicament. It becomes a predicament only as a result of a subjective definition of the value of the given position by actors involved. This is why we speak of predicaments as located at the intersection of objective and subjective realms.

Operationally speaking our definitions imply that predicaments can be observed only through a combination of (i) intersubjectively valid observations of positions in material and social structures from which it is either difficult to escape or which are threatening, and (ii) subjective attributions of negative or positive values to such positions by (iii) actors occupying or understanding such positions. By speaking about actors occupying *or* understanding the positions involved, we have deliberately left some leeway for the definition of predicaments by external expertise as well as by those occupying predicaments.

However there is nothing particularly dialectical about the conceptual and operational definitions of predicament suggested so far, except that they suggest the possibility and necessity to reduce or destroy the objective structural constraints which make it difficult to escape from a negatively valued position, or to overcome the threats involved. Another theoretically but not particularly dialectical possibility, however, is to redefine subjectively a negatively valued position so as to make it positive; to make virtue out of suffering.

A more dialectical interpretation is possible if you define a predicament in terms of a structural context which introduces not only constraints but also contradictions. Imagine a situation structured in such a way that regular attempts to escape a 'bad' position tightens the constraints preventing your escape. Or a situation such that regular attempts to overcome threats directed against a 'good' position in fact strengthen those threats. These situations exhibit structural contradictions in the form of a unity of opposites. Some aspects of the working class predicament display such a dialectic.

Labour power, by being part and parcel of the development of productive forces, thus in a sense helps to enhance the contradiction emerging between forces and relations of production. In this case the constraints imposed by the given capitalist relations of production may not be 'tightened' in an absolute sense by the development of productive forces; but by remaining essentially unchanged while productive forces expand, they more and more appear as 'fetters' upon the productive forces, and thereby also on labour power. Similarly the wage struggle and the relative affluence which as a result may be achieved by the working class in advanced capitalist societies, may under certain, if not all conditions, lead to an *embourgeoisement* of the working class weakening its class organization and, relatively speaking, increase the threat against labour from organized capital.

Dialectical class predicaments in this sense can no doubt be found also in the capitalist class in late capitalism, as we will suggest later (p. 217f). Attempts by capital to safeguard capital accumulation may enhance the visibility of anti-social characteristics of capitalist relations of production, so as to mobilize the working class and the white-collar strata in a manner which increases the threats against capital accumulation and the position of the capitalist class.

Having tentatively defined the meaning of predicaments as produced by the structural contradictions of society within the 'realm of necessity', having suggested furthermore the limitations of 'regular' piecemeal attempts to break out of such structural predicaments because of the tightening of constraints and increase of threats, and having indicated also the possibility of struggle to transform the given structures to attain the 'realm of freedom' (which of course in its turn may entail new 'necessities'), we can now go on to suggest how the concept of predicament can be used in a study such as ours.

The concept of predicament occupied a very prominent place in our first conceptualizations for this research project. We made distinctions between the 'classical' working class predicaments of severe exploitation and absolute deprivation so visible to Marx and Engels in nineteenth century England, the 'neoclassical' predicament of relative deprivation discussed by sociologists such as Robert Merton (1957, Chapter VIII) and Gary Runciman (1966), and the 'modern' working class predicament as conceived by one of us, even if in a different terminology (Ahrne, 1976). The 'modern' working class predicament was conceived as a position of relative affluence with a real potential for improvements in the quality of life and leisure, threatened however by alienating structures of power, work and marginalizing unemployment, and by congestion and environmental effects.

However, as we proceeded on the project the focus on predicaments was successively dissolved, and it turned out that we had used this notion rather as a sensitizing concept alerting us to the structural contradictions presumably generating various kinds of class predicaments, but also drawing our attention to some aspects of subjective consciousness such as the awareness of system-transcending class struggle. This may appear as an anti-climax given the attention we have paid to the concept of predicament on the preceding pages. However, this is the function of some concepts in research: they help to crystallize and to contrast one approach with another, and they trigger a search for related concepts and facts.

It should also be said that a more thorough study of various kinds of predicaments, at the present stage of conceptualization of this notion, probably would require more detailed individual case studies than we had in view, or could afford in this largely macro-sociological project. However, many of the objective and subjective variables for which we have assembled empirical data were originally suggested to us by our original preoccupation with predicaments, and we certainly hope to make more of this preoccupation in future research.

Our macro-sociological orientation implies that our notion of *actor* for the most part refers not to single individuals but to groups, organizations and even social classes. An actor in our understanding is usually an organization or category of individuals sharing approximately the same predicaments. An actor as defined by us does not enact a 'role' which 'expects' him to strive for certain prescribed goals with certain prescribed means. An actor is facing a certain predicament of which he may be aware in terms of perceived constraints and threats, and he may attempt to break out of this predicament, or to change its character as a predicament, by getting involved in or supporting attempts to overcome the threats or constraints involved, or even the structures presumably generating these threats and constraints.

This means that our theatrical metaphor of stage, actor and play, in order to be applied within our theoretical framework, must be stretched beyond recognition. Certainly there is a stage; and the stage is set in such a way that actors confront predicaments. But there are no predetermined roles nor any predetermined intrigue which constitutes a predetermined play; or if there is a play with given roles, we are not particularly interested in it, but rather in how actors relate to their predicaments and use whatever subjective and objective resources they have in order to change the stage, the roles and the play by their action, defying established theatre directors if necessary. This new play is written as it proceeds — through the struggle between actors facing different situations, predicaments or not, with or without the aid of Touraine-style action researchers, and with or without plagiarizing historical events of the past, as if they were a play with roles to emulate.

Struggling Actors and Dimensions of Class Struggle and Power

The kind of struggle which is the focus of our attention is class struggle. Now the term class struggle may seem quite alien to some of our readers — even to some who are actually involved in it, on the side of labour or the side of capital. It may not have entered the mind of everybody involved, say, in the more technical aspects of collective bargaining, or in a political debate about legislation on the work environment, or industrial air pollution, that she or he is involved in 'struggle', and much less in 'class struggle'. Not only bourgeois hegemony but also labour reformism with its emphasis on more or less institutionalized agreements probably tend to make us uneasy about terms such as 'struggle' which seem to have the connotations of violence and even revolution.

But even though such connotations of violence may in fact be intended in some leftist political agitation, the term 'class struggle' in Marxist theory is a *technical* term with much broader but also more precise implications. It is in this sense we use it here. Class struggle refers to any action which results in changing or, as the case may be, in maintaining and reproducing given relationships between capital and labour. Capitalists as well as workers are involved in it. The *wage struggle* taking place within the existing system is an instance of class struggle. So is *system-transcending struggle* by revolutionary or democratic political means. But in opposition to such attempts to transform the system there is also the *system-reproducing struggle* of the capitalist class and its allies.

The linguistic awkwardness of the term system-transcending struggle is deliberate. This awkwardness may help to dispel some of the more romantic, agitational and idealistic connotations of the term revolution, thus opening our minds to queries about the possibility and adequacy of *different* ways of transforming capitalist relations of production, ways which are democratic and not only or necessarily violently revolutionary.

Class analysis and the class struggle approach have their limitations, real and alleged. In some societies the demographic complexity, the pervasiveness of kinship organization, geo-ethno-political structures and the like (Himmelstrand, 1973 and Lijphart, 1977) introduces lines of cleavage which seem more important than class cleavages. Historically rooted religions and other cultural criteria of cleavage may also have to be taken into account. Local versus national, and rural versus urban affiliations similarly go beyond class analysis (Rokkan, 1970). Even if such distinctions are intertwined with variables relating to class and economy, such diverse affiliations cannot usually be reduced to these latter variables. Therefore class analysis can never validly claim to account for the whole domain of conflict analysis. Class analysis, Marxist or not, is limited to its own object of knowledge.

There is a well-known sociological tradition which takes off from this fact that variables relating to class may be more or less intertwined or correlated with variables related to kinship, ethnic, linguistic, religious, rural—urban and other non-class affiliations. The degree of 'criss-crossing' or 'crystallization' of such different variables (Coser, 1956 and Galtung, 1966), or the presence or absence of 'superimposed cleavages' (Dahrendorf, 1959) have been assumed to sharpen or soften cleavages of class, culture and kinship, to influence the intensity of conflict and to influence political attitudes, (Lenski, 1954).

We do not question this line of analysis, as far as it goes. If you choose as your main dependent variables only the subjective intensity of antagonism and conflict, or political attitudes, then the theoretical and empirical findings of this sociological tradition must certainly be given a prominent place in your analysis. But our own main focus is different. We are concerned with the 'production of the categories of practice' (Touraine, 1980), that is with the generation of contradictions and latent issues, by the capitalist economic system and its class structure, and the extent to which these contradictions and issues appear as non-issues, or are reflected in the subjective consciousness and class action of actors, seen in their class contexts. A structurally generated contradiction or issue is not necessarily less real and urgent if the criss-cross of class and other cleavages blurs the emerging conflict and reduces its subjective intensity. False consciousness – a problematic concept which we cannot discuss in this context (see for instance Gabel, 1975) – may also be generated by criss-crossing cleavages, but cannot be evaluated as such without going beyond the kind of variables so prominent in most criss-cross analysis.

Apart from these justifications for our neglect of criss-crossing relationships, we can also find a justification for this in the fact that Sweden is a homogeneous country in terms of religion and culture, in spite of the recent wave of immigration which has complicated the picture somewhat (Soydan, 1975, pp. 74f). Therefore we do not have to pay as much attention to the criss-cross of class and culture in the Swedish setting as in some other countries. However, there are several studies which indicate that in Swedish politics there is a centre-periphery or local–national dimension of cleavage cutting across the class-related left-right dimension (see for instance Petersson, 1978b, p. 117). When that is required we will of course pay attention to this fact. But our main focus is on class-divisions and on class struggle in the sense indicated above.[1]

In addition to the conceptual limitations of class analysis and the class struggle approach, this approach also allegedly has political limitations. If our book receives the broad spectrum of readers which we hope, we can imagine that some readers of this chapter may find our theoretical framework inadequate, and in its consequences destructive, for explicit or implicit political reasons. Why look for 'struggling actors' and their relative strength when we need to learn more, both as analysts and political or managerial practitioners, about conditions for collaboration between political parties on the left, the centre and the right as well as between management and unions? 'We cannot solve the problems we have created in an atmosphere of confrontations', said the management expert Ulf af Trolle in an interview for a weekly magazine.[2]

We do not claim that our analytical and empirical focus on struggle rather than on harmonization and collaboration is politically unproblematic. Even though we claim that a thorough philosophical, methodological and sociological analysis of our approach will prove it to be fully acceptable in a scientific sense, this would not constitute an adequate rejoinder to the kind of political objections mentioned above. But it would seem that our approach can be justified in political terms of a rather common-sense nature, acceptable regardless of political inclinations.

The basic contradictions of mature capitalism, and of social classes within this mode of production, which we are documenting empirically in this book, will not disappear by any act of wishful harmonization or well intended collaboration. Contradictions not resolved, but wishfully neglected in the phase of policy formation, will tend to forcefully re-emerge in the policy implementation phase, and there make implementation unsuccessful, and confrontations even more serious. From this common-sense point of view it is quite possible that confrontations may be avoided for the future if the challenge of contradictory social processes and class conflict are faced and not avoided.

To paraphrase af Trolle: We cannot solve the problems created in our kind of society without squarely confronting them, and the social structures and classes which prevent their solution.

But this point of view should not be construed as a defence for a hard-nosed and uncompromising style of political action, under all circumstances. Harsh confrontations always take their toll, on all sides. The circumstances must decide whether this price must be paid in order to resolve the underlying contradictions. If circumstances permit we can even see some political merit in the low-intensity conflicts fostered by criss-crossing cleavages, as long as this criss-cross does not conceal the basic issues under the placating formulas of false consciousness. This is one point where social scientists can play a significant role in politics, that is in unravelling basic issues and dissolving such placating formulas.

In addition to a proper understanding of the basic issues related to the basic and extended contradictions of capitalism, some strategic and tactical thinking is also necessary on this point in order to formulate the most adequate style of political action. In such a strategic and tactical context, we need an assessment of the strength of actors struggling to solve or to evade the kinds of problems we have tried to document through our research. The strength of struggling actors is the main topic of Part III of this book.

An Outline of Part III

In the following we will present some theoretical considerations and empirical data relevant for assessing the strength of labour and of capital in Sweden. Readers less concerned with specifically Swedish conditions may hopefully find interest in the methodological aspects of our work.

We distinguish five main dimensions of strength:

1. Numerical strength
2. Organizational strength
3. Strength in terms of consciousness or ideology
4. Political strength
5. Systemic power.

The numerical strength of capital is negligible. But labour has considerable numerical strength. Crucial for the determination of the numerical strength of labour, however, is a definition of the working class which lends itself to empirical assessments of its numerical size. Therefore we will briefly discuss various types of definitions of the working class, and question some of the notions implying that its size is diminishing.

Numerical size alone does not provide strength. The larger the number of working class members who are *organized*, however, the greater their strength. We will also report on the organizational strength of capital, but this will be done in the context of our analysis of the ideological dimension of capitalist strength.

Ideology and consciousness help to fortify the organizational bonds which unite the members of a class; but membership itself may also help to articulate and strengthen consciousness and ideology. Within the working class and among its potential allies in the middle strata, we are particularly interested in exploring empirically to what extent the contradictions and predicaments generated by mature capitalism are reflected in working class consciousness and in the views of the middle strata. In capitalist ideology we do not expect to find a true reflection of the contradictions of capitalism. There are other aspects of ideological strength and weakness more relevant to study within the capitalist class.

Politics is supposed to translate popular opinion and public issues into political action. We ask: Does labour find the labour parties trustworthy enough to deserve the vote of labour? Are the bourgeois parties which came to power in Sweden as a result of the 1976 election, after forty-four years of social democratic government, adding political strength to the systemic power which the capitalist class already possesses? These are questions which we will try to answer.

The notion of capitalist systemic power will be discussed extensively in the following. Here it is enough to indicate that systemic power accrues to the capitalist class by virtue of the fact that our economic system is capitalist. The capitalist system is the hub around which a

great deal of politics and union activity revolves. We will devote particular attention to the question whether the systemic power of capital
is increasing or decreasing.

Once we have surveyed these various dimensions of strength of
capital and labour, the question emerges whether we can assess the
relative strength of these two main actors on the arena of class struggle.
In spite of the prevailing pluralist ideas of countervailing power, according to which there could be virtual parity between capital and labour
(see Korpi and Shalev, 1980), we find little or no evidence to support
such an assumption. However, because of the multi-dimensional nature
of our notions of strength of struggling actors, and because of the
incommensurability of the various dimensions involved, it is impossible
to arrive at an overall quantitative assessment of the relative strength of
labour and capital. But we can determine whether the strength of
labour, and of capital, is increasing or decreasing. The only final test
of their relative strength is the 'scratch test' of present and future
practical action and struggle.

But in that struggle the so-called welfare state also participates,
often in a contradictory and confusing manner, acting both to keep
capitalist business running and to intervene where it does not run, or
runs amok, thus successively affecting the very dynamic of capitalist
growth in a way which calls for even more state interventions, and
perhaps leading eventually to capitalist demands for the dismounting
of state involvement, and not only in public welfare.

In Part II we explored some of the objective economic and structural
aspects of state interventions in mature capitalism. In this part we will
concentrate mainly on the ways in which the state appears in the minds
of our struggling actors.

13 The Delimitation and Organization of the Working Class

> The complexities of the class structure of pre-monopoly capitalism arose from the fact that so large a proportion of the working population, being neither employed by capital nor itself employing labour to any significant extent, fell outside the capital—labour polarity. The complexity of the class structure of modern monopoly capitalism arises from the very opposite consideration: namely, *that almost all of the population has been transformed into employees of capital.*
>
> H. Braverman (1974) p. 404

Numerical Strength: Three Approaches to Defining the Working Class

It has often been alleged that traditional labour parties — whether reformist or 'revolutionary' — are likely to receive decreasing support as a result of changes in the occupational structures of advanced capitalist societies. The proportion of wage earners in the working population is certainly increasing all the time but the core of the working class — industrial workers — is decreasing while the white-collar strata are swelling in size. Consequently, to the extent that labour parties attempt to bring about a socialist transformation of society, such a transformation becomes less rather than more likely in advanced capitalist societies, it is argued. No wonder that devoted socialists have been looking elsewhere for support to socialist change — for instance to intellectuals and students.

In Sweden as elsewhere there has been a steady increase of the proportion of wage earners in the working population. In 1940 they were about 74 per cent while in 1970 they were 91 per cent of the labour force, according to census data. This increase is still going on. The numerical size of the *industrial* working class reached its maximum in the 1950s. At that time industrial workers comprised about 40 per cent of all gainfully employed. Since then this proportion has slowly but steadily decreased. In 1975 industrial workers were only 28 per cent of all gainfully employed. In the year 2000 it is quite possible that only 10 per cent of the gainfully employed can be classified as industrial workers.

At the same time as the contradiction between labour and capital has become more dominant in our society both as a result of the steady increase of 'employees of capital' and of the more pronounced contradictions between forces and relations of production, we can thus assume that the emergence of new categories of employees has changed the very character of this contradiction.

In our perspective of societal change we are thus faced with the following kinds of questions: How will the changing composition of the wage earning strata affect the content of the increasingly pronounced contradiction between labour and capital, between forces and relations of production? What categories of wage earners in particular are bearers of these contradictions? What problems contribute to unite and what problems separate wage earners from each other, thus influencing the unity and the numerical strength of what might still constitute a working class?

We distinguish three different theoretical approaches to these compositional changes within the wage-earning category.

The *first* approach implies a very narrow delimitation of the working class; only those who are directly involved in industrial production (production of surplus value) are included. From different theoretical vantage points Poulantzas (1975), Giddens (1973) and also Mandel (1975) have taken this approach. According to this view class society is based on the contradiction between those who are 'productive' workers, and those who live on the work of others. The 'improductive' workers depend on the surplus labour of 'productive' workers, it is argued. Whatever the merits of the distinction between productive and improductive labour in other contexts, we find it extremely difficult to apply this distinction in categorizing individual employees in different social classes (see Wright, 1976, p. 15). There seems to be an increasing number of employees who are involved both in 'productive' and 'improductive' labour. This distinction can also be criticized on theoretical grounds (Olsson, 1978).

The *second* approach would seem to imply a neglect of the compositional changes taking place among wage earners, and a strong emphasis on the relative stability of the working class in the labour force as a whole due, for instance, to the decreasing number of self-employed small-scale farmers and entrepreneurs. In Sweden this approach is represented by Therborn (1972) and Korpi (1978).

The *third* approach deemphasizes the criterion of 'productive work' (production of surplus value) and instead points to the significance of the ongoing processes of division of labour, and the social implications of work and technology. According to this approach a substantial section of the growing stratum of white-collar employees could be assumed to belong to the working class. Mallet (1975), Braverman (1974), E. O. Wright (1976) and Nilsson (1977) represent this third approach. The increasing impoverishment of industrial work and the increasing distance between planning, control and execution of labour in industry, is a process which now increasingly is penetrating also into white-collar strata, according to Harry Braverman. Even functions of control and planning are subject to a minute division of labour.

> These management functions of control and appropriation have in themselves become labour processes. They are conducted by capital in the same way that it carries on the labour processes of production: with wage labour purchased on a large scale in a labour market and organized into huge 'production' machines according to the same principles that govern the organization of factory labour. Here the productive processes of society disappear into a stream of paper — a stream of paper, moreover, which is processed in a continuous flow like that of the cannery, the meat-packing line, the car assembly conveyor, by workers organized in much the same way.
>
> (Braverman, 1974, p. 301).

It is this routinization of work, this degradation of labour, which create new, common conditions of work for a very large portion of all gainfully employed, whether blue-collar or white-collar, thus constituting the basis for our assumption of a common objective interest among these various strata. With increasing productivity and rising levels of material standards of living among the employees of capital it also becomes less natural to define capitalist exploitation in terms of surplus value than in terms of this increasingly visible degradation and routinization of work (Ahrne, 1976, p. 210). In this context the distribution of supervisory functions in a given division of labour is a significant factor (Wright, 1976, p. 28).

Thus, according to this third approach to class analysis, an estimate of the numerical strength of the working class today must rely less on the position of employees in economic production as such; the distinction between productive and non-productive labour becomes less relevant. Much more relevant is the degree of social subordination within a given division of labour. More important than the distinction between productive and improductive labour, or even between manual and non-manual labour is the distinction between what we would prefer to call de-skilled or routinized labour and intellectual labour. Intellectual labour involves elements of planning and access to the 'secret knowledge' of production. Manual 'de-skilled' labour involving a manipulation of machines and a performance of administrative routines without access to the privileged and secret knowledge embodied in such technical and administrative machinery has become increasingly common among so-called 'non-manual' white-collar employees. Another aspect of this process is the increasing number of such employees in the public sector.

Having found the third approach to class analysis to be most realistic and also most reasonable from a theoretical point of view, our next task is to assess on the basis of empirical data the actual numerical scope of this 'extended' working class.

The Extended Working Class: Some Empirical Data

On the basis of a questionnaire study carried out on a stratified two-stage random sample of work units and employees in Stockholm and Kopparberg provinces[1] we have tried to assess the numerical size of the so-called extended working class, and have explored the extent to which various objective working conditions really are more similar within this extended working class than between this class and the middle strata.

As a crude measure of the division of labour and the routinization of work in a given occupation we have used requirements for vocational training in each given occupation. We assume that on the whole lower requirements for such training in a given occupation implies more routinized labour and less control over the work in the labour process. However, we are aware of the fact that the requirements for training attached to a particular occupation sometimes are lagging behind the process of job degradation and impoverishment. To assess the magnitude of this systematic error is not possible; but it definitely deflates rather than inflates our estimates of the numerical size of the extended working class.

The specification of requirements for vocational training in given occupations we have derived from the socio-economic categories defined by the Swedish Central Bureau of Statistics (SCB). They classify five groups by requirements for vocational training: no need for vocational training; less than two years of vocational training; two but not three years of vocational training; three but not five years of vocational training, and at least five years of such vocational training. The overwhelming majority of those employed in production and distribution, that is 99 per cent, need less than three years of vocational training according to SCB's classification. Among clerical personnel, technicians, etc., about 46 per cent fall in this category of required training. This means that about half of those whom we usually count as belonging to the middle strata work in occupations demanding no more vocational training than occupations in the core of the working class. We can thus assume that about half of these white-collar strata encounter about the same amount of routinization of work and about as little control over the labour process as the large traditional categories of workers.

We can now test our assumption that working conditions, specifically *physical* and *psychological work environment, income* and *supervisory functions*, are similar for employees in the traditional working class and white-collar employees in occupations which do not require more training than occupations among blue-collar workers. In Table 13.1 we have presented data not only on these variables but also on a few others which may be of some interest. From this table it is obvious that blue-collar workers and white-collar employees in occupations demanding less than three years of vocational training are very similar indeed in terms of psychological work environment, salary and supervisory functions. There is a clear discontinuity between the percentages for these two categories of the extended working class on the one hand, and the remaining part of the middle strata and those in management positions.

However, with regard to physical work environment there is a three-step rather than two-step discontinuity between the various strata involved. Industrial workers have a considerably poorer physical work environment than others; but there is also some difference between the physical work environment of lower level white-collar strata on the one hand and the remaining part of the middle strata and those in management positions on the other.

If we made the rather reasonable assumption that de-skilled and routinized labour is reflected most clearly in the psychological work environment, the data presented in Table 13.1 clearly support the inclusion of lower level white-collar strata in what we have called the extended working class, as suggested by the third approach to class analysis. The simplest operational criterion for assessing the numerical size of this extended working class is thus to look for the percentage

Table 13.1: Selected attributes of employees and work situations in various strata (percentages)

	Industrial workers	Workers not immediately involved in production	Lower white-collar employees	Higher white-collar employees	Managers
Women	10	63	60	23	4
Public sector	8	42	25	32	19
Part-time work	4	38	25	9	0
Supervisory functions*	14	8	27	62	80
Low income; part-time employees excluded	63	80	62	24	27
Poor physical work environment	51	28	9	5	4
Poor psychological work environment	36	42	31	20	16

*The term 'supervisory' is not entirely adequate here, due to the inclusion of higher white-collar and managerial strata, but we were unable to find a more comprehensive term. In this table 'supervisory' should be understood as including staff and managerial functions for the higher strata.

of employees in occupations demanding less than three years of vocational training. Slightly more than 40 per cent of white-collar employees would then be included in the working class (cf. Nilsson, 1977, p. 55; Olsson, 1978, p. 54). Within this extended working class we can distinguish two strata — industrial workers and what we will henceforth call 'service workers'. The term 'service worker' is a literal translation of the Swedish word *tjänstearbetare* which itself is a terminological innovation suggested by Göran Ahrne (1977). What we call 'service workers' does not include only employees in the so-called service trades.

Among employees who work in occupations requiring vocational training for three years or more we can distinguish the middle strata proper and managerial positions. This means that the term middle strata as used in this book henceforth will exclude white-collar employees in occupations demanding less than three years of vocational training, that is the so-called service workers. In Table 13.2 we have summarized the strata and classes conceived in our discussion so far and their proportions among wage-earners according to census data.

Table 13.2: Percentage of wage-earners 1975 in different classes

Industrial workers	31	}		
			Working class	77
Service workers	46	}		
			Middle strata	20
			Managerial functions	3
Total				100%

Source: Folk- ach bostadsräkningen 1975 samt SCB:s undersökning om levnadsförhållanden. (Population and housing census 1975 and The Investigation on Living conditions 1975.)

Industrial workers are those immediately involved in production, and thus correspond to the narrow definition of the working class found in works by Poulantzas, Giddens and Mandel. *Service workers* is a category including those employees in the traditional working class who are not immediately involved in production: warehouse workers, drivers, sales personnel and employees in services such as restaurants, hospitals, etc. In addition this category includes a significant number of what is called *tjänstemän* in Swedish, more precisely white-collar employees on lower skill levels where educational requirements are less than three years of vocational training. Table A.1.1 in Appendix I (p. 316) presents a more detailed breakdown of strata within the working class as well as in the middle strata.

If we return now for a moment to Table 13.1 we discover some findings which do not fall quite as neatly into the pattern of class analysis applied so far. Female employment is by far highest among so-called service workers — 62 per cent as against 10 per cent among industrial workers, 23 per cent in the middle strata and 4 per cent in managerial positions. Part-time work consequently is much more common among service workers than among other categories of employees. This should be kept in mind when we interpret some of our later findings.

Obviously, our definition of an extended working class including service workers as well, does not imply that a distinction between the core of the working class (industrial workers) and service workers is irrelevant in all contexts. Particularly with regard to the physical work environment, but also with regard to female employment, there are significant differences between industrial workers and service workers. With Olin Wright one could also argue that some service workers are more likely to occupy 'contradictory locations within class relations'; they represent positions 'which are torn between the basic contradictory class relations of capitalist society' (Wright, 1976, pp. 26f). Wright also argues that political and ideological relations are more likely to influence the class positions of employees occupying such contradictory positions within social relations of production than those occupying more unambiguous positions. 'A strong union movement among white-collar employees . . . could constitute a political factor which pushed them closer to the working-class.' (1976), p. 40). This brings us to the question of the organizational strength of the working class.

The Organizational Strength of the Extended Working Class

In Sweden unionization of blue-collar workers has been very high for a long time; more than 90 per cent of blue-collar workers are presently organized in LO, the central confederation of mainly blue-collar unions. Among white-collar employees unionization has been less pronounced. However, the trend is clear: whereas only about 50 per cent of white-collar employees were unionized in 1950, about 70 per cent were unionized in 1975. Furthermore the collaboration between TCO, the federation of white-collar unions, and LO on the side of blue-collar labour has become more and more intimate in recent years. Certainly this collaboration is not without its problems – partly because TCO claims political neutrality whereas LO is intimately related in various ways to the Social Democratic Labour Party. It has been asserted that a closer collaboration between TCO and LO might bring about internal frictions within TCO as a result of differences in political affiliations among TCO members. However this is a matter relating to the political strength of the extended working class, and therefore we will have more to say about these problems later on. Here we will concentrate simply on some aspects of the organizational strength of unions.

Swedish labour is not only very highly organized and unified; it has also tended to become bureaucratic and centralistic (Korpi, 1978, Chapter 8). The increasing number of wildcat strikes in the late 1960s and early 1970s (Korpi, 1972; Ohlström, 1977) could be interpreted as partly directed against this centralistic trend in trade unions, and not only against employers and management. The fact that quite a number of wildcat strikes have been fairly effective in bringing about desired change at least to some extent (see for instance our discussion on p. 104), plus the emergence of demands for a more responsive trade union leadership, might be interpreted as signs of trade union weakness. Paradoxical as it may seem it is also possible to consider these recent developments as a source of increasing strength of organized labour in Sweden. The same union leaders who officially condemn wildcat strikes – and must do so for formal reasons – have privately condoned such strikes as significant symptoms of underlying problems, and as hopeful signs of worker mobilization and sources of strength – a collective resource to be tapped in future union work. The rise of a new generation of union leaders may have been significant on this point. Another source of increasing strength of organized labour is some of the most recent laws, partly in response to growing worker unrest, to enlarge the decentralized control of workers over their own work environment (see below). Even when these laws have turned out to be rather ineffective for reasons that we will discuss later on it is quite possible that such failures of the legislative approach will increase the desire of workers to use their organizational strength to come to grips with these failures.

Even if the increasing frequency of wildcat strikes in the late 1960s and early 1970s cannot be interpreted unambiguously as indicators of union weakness, such unofficial labour disputes are equally unsuitable as indicators of union strength, of course. Unless we can find other more convincing evidence of union participation, involvement and efficacy, the figures indicating extremely high level of unionization among industrial workers and sharply increasing levels of unionization for white-collar employees may indicate nothing but a hollow strength.

One of the most careful studies of union government and membership influence made in Sweden has been carried out by Walter Korpi and published in his recent book on *The Working Class in Welfare Capitalism* (1978). Most of his data derive from a study of the Swedish Metal Workers Union. He distinguishes three types of union involvement: 'solidaristic' involvement (41 per cent), instrumental involvement (37 per cent), and reluctant involvement (17 per cent). 'Solidaristic' members think of their union membership as an expression of solidarity to the labour movement as a whole. They also tend to buy the LO-owned social democratic evening paper rather than its bourgeois competitor, and they prefer shopping in a co-operative store rather than in privately owned stores. Instrumental union involvement is indicated where workers feel that they personally benefit from being members of the union without finding it necessary to express a solidarity to the labour movement. However the majority (63 per cent) of these 'instrumental' union members also prefer buying the LO-owned evening paper and shopping in a co-operative store. Reluctant union members are those who simply felt obliged to join or joined in spite of not being very interested in union membership (1978, p. 171).

It may seem that 17 per cent reluctant union members (plus 4 per cent non-members) is a relatively low figure, and thus an indication of rather strong support for the union among its members. However a breakdown of type of union involvement by birth cohort shows that reluctant workers are much more common in the younger age groups, and 'solidaristic' workers much less so (1978, p. 173). After a rather careful statistical analysis Korpi arrives at the conclusion that variations in the reluctance to join the union movement is a result of varying degrees of union socialization rather than an effect of generational differences, whereas the level of solidaristic union involvement would appear to be largely a generational matter. The language of solidarity obviously is more congenial to those who have experienced the climate of manifest class conflict in the 1930s and earlier. Younger union members thus more frequently take an instrumental view of their union involvement, and this view can be expected to emerge also among younger reluctant union members once they have been exposed to the socialization process demonstrated by Korpi (1978, p. 179). Korpi suggests that the decline in the level of solidaristic union involvement 'indicates that the younger generations of metal workers probably have a more critical and questioning attitude to the union than their elders. As we have seen, however, this more conditional orientation to the union is congruent with a very high level of union membership and reliance on collective action through the union.' (1978, p. 180).

Basic to an instrumentalist union involvement is, by definition, a belief in the utility and bargaining power of the union. Korpi shows that the youngest age group believe in the bargaining power of unions to a significantly larger extent than middle-aged union members. In fact the relationship between reported bargaining power on the one hand and age as well as length of employment on the other is curvilinear; the oldest and the youngest union members exhibit a stronger belief in the bargaining power of unions than the middle-aged. That such beliefs are based largely on objective realities rather than on subjective illusions is suggested, for instance, by findings on average percentages reporting a high bargaining power of local unions by frequency of membership meetings and size of firm. These are objective rather than subjective variables. In smaller firms the perceived bargaining power increases considerably with frequency of membership meetings.

On the whole Korpi's findings do reject the assumption that the organizational strength of metal workers is a hollow strength. However, his study has two limitations from our point of view: it does not contain much data on the lower level white-collar employees which we have included in the stratum of so-called service workers, nor on the middle strata. Furthermore, his data were collected in 1967, and since then the mood of the union movement and the political climate would seem to have changed a great deal. Our own surveys which were carried out in 1976—7 may shed light on more recent conditions.

According to our surveys there seems to be a larger percentage of workers now than in 1967 who believe that union work is instrumental in improving the situation of workers. Surely our questions are not identical with Korpi's, but they are similar. Among industrial workers 81 per cent believe strongly that union work provides *great* possibilities for improving the situation of workers. Corresponding figures among service workers and in the middle strata are 63 and 68 per cent respectively. The significance of these percentage figures may be better understood if they are compared with corresponding percentages concerning belief in the effectiveness of party political work. These percentages are about 55 per cent for all the three categories mentioned.[2]

The most significant factor of all in determining union involvement and participation is political involvement and political support for the labour movement (1978, p. 200). And such political involvement is not a generational matter like the use of the language of solidarity but a matter of political socialization and length of employment, as indicated by a number of findings in studies by Korpi and others.

Having surveyed some important aspects of the organizational and numerical strength of the working class, we may now ask to what extent our findings point to the possibility of obtaining a majority support, within our democratic institutions, for significant changes in the relationship between capital and labour in Sweden. Certainly a numerical strength of the working class amounting to about three-quarters of all gainfully employed, of whom the great majority are organized in unions, and with a steadily increasing degree of union-ization among white-collar employees, would seem to provide for the majority needed. However this is only a necessary but not a sufficient condition of a majority electoral support for a labour party aiming at profound structural changes of the capitalist order. To understand the nature and content of such majority support we must take a closer look at some of the ideological components of class relations, and the subjective consciousness displayed by different strata within the extended working class and beyond.

14 The Social Consciousness of the Extended Working Class

Marx's own vision of the proletariat and its social consciousness was by no means simplistic. His belief in a revolutionary consciousness arising from the exploitation of the working class was tempered by an understanding of social processes counteracting the development of such a revolutionary consciousness:

> The advance of capitalist production develops a working class which by education, tradition and habit looks upon the requirements of that mode of production as self-evident natural laws. The organization of the capitalist process of production, once it is fully developed breaks down all resistance . . . the silent compulsion of economic relations sets the seal on the domination of the capitalist over the worker.
>
> K. Marx (1976) p. 89

This 'silent compulsion' demobilizes rather than mobilizes the revolutionary potential of the working class. More appropriate perhaps for the understanding of the predicament of the working class of today is another quotation from Marx which indicates the possibility of a 'golden' rather than a 'silent' compulsion:

> A rise in the price of labour, as a consequence of the accumulation of capital, only means in fact that the length and weight of the golden chain the wage-labourer has already forged for himself allow it to be loosened somewhat.
>
> K. Marx (1976) p. 769

The notion of a 'golden chain' would seem to contradict Marx's conception of a successive impoverishment of the working class. However, a closer reading of Marx clearly indicates that he had a relative rather than an absolute impoverishment in mind;[1] such a notion of relative deprivation can very well be combined with the notion of a 'golden chain'. Nevertheless it is doubtful whether Marx could foresee the high level of affluence within the working class that we find in some capitalist countries today. His notion of the 'golden chain' would still seem to fit well with present-day theories of *embourgeoisement*. Such a process of *embourgeoisement* is supposed to affect the working class of today as a result of their increasing affluence. This process implies that an increasing number of affluent workers come to see themselves not primarily as members of a working class opposing the bourgeoisie but as individual citizens and consumers in a consensual consumer society offering a choice of commodities on the consumer market, and an agreed-upon set of welfare measures provided by a democratic welfare state. The sense of conflict and opposing class interests, class exploitation and injustice is lost; a privatization of consciousness takes place, and as a corollary demands and complaints directed toward society become individualized and piecemeal rather than collective and structural (Compare Gorz, 1964).

Social Consciousness in an Affluent Society

That Sweden is an 'affluent society' is sufficiently well-known not to need further corroboration in this context. Comparing the Swedish working class as a whole, and not only the best paid workers, with corresponding occupational categories in other wealthy countries, one could surely claim the Swedish working class to be one of the most, if not the most, affluent in the world. And the most *embourgeoisé?* Let us look at the facts.

A recent Swedish survey reported by Göran Ahrne (1976) presents findings indicating that an overwhelming majority of full-time employees consider a transfer of national income to solving environmental and social problems to be equally or more important than a pay rise or an increase of private consumption. Figures around 85 or 90 per cent supporting this view were found even in the lesser paid rungs of the working class. Similar findings are reported from other empirical studies (Zetterberg and Busch, 1975, pp. 79f).

Workers do not accept the ideal of leisure time consumption as a compensation for the tediousness and strain of work. They do not predominantly exhibit an instrumental attitude to work, accepting work purely as a means of earning the money to be spent in leisure (Korpi, 1978, pp. 130f). Work itself must be made more meaningful, and integrated with considerations of the quality of life. These empirical findings do not confirm the image of the Swedish worker as a privatized consumer unconcerned with any aspect of his work other than its relation to his ability to consume.

Nor do existing empirical surveys confirm the image of the Swedish worker as unconcerned with structural injustice and class conflict. Richard Scase has made a survey of different images of social structure and social inequality in Sweden and England suggesting that Swedish workers are more aware of economic inequalities than English workers, and more likely to view them in a conflict perspective, or to use Frank Parkin's terminology, according to an 'oppositional' interpretation of class inequality (Scase, 1974a, pp. 208f; Parkin, 1971, Chapter 3). Another well-known sociologist Erik Allardt (1975, pp. 132, 136–8) in a comparative survey of the Nordic countries has made similar findings indicating that the sense of conflict and social inequality is more pronounced in Sweden than in the other Nordic countries, except Finland, in spite of its greater affluence and more pronounced welfare on a number of different dimensions.

In our own empirical surveys we have tried to assess the existence of an 'oppositional' interpretation of class interests, by asking our respondents whether they felt that they had interests in common with a number of different groups, categories, classes and other units such as relatives, workmates, the enterprise, the place or region of domicile, those voting for the same political party, one's social class, or the Swedish nation. Among these it is of special interest in this context to look at interests held in common with the enterprises in which our respondents were employed, with the workmates or the social class to which they feel they belong. If a respondent indicates little or no common interest with his enterprise, but great common interest with his social class and workmates, then he or she is considered to have an oppositional interpretation of class interests. Later on some findings deriving from the use of this simple indicator will be reported.

Another way to assess popular images of structural contradictions in society is to ask questions about perceived threats to social development. In a recent Swedish national sample survey (Hedman, 1978, pp. 226f) quite convincing evidence has been found to the effect that a majority of Swedes tend to look at the influence of capitalism, multinational corporations, industrial waste, pollution and unemployment as considerable or serious 'threats against the future development of the world'. In the working class this majority is even greater. We have re-analysed Hedman's data by combining the methods of factor analysis and class analysis, that is by factor analysing responses to the threat questions mentioned above separately for the working class and the middle strata. The results obtained are presented in Table 14.1. The most striking result of this combination of factor analysis and class analysis is that the threat variance is accounted for by four factors in

Table 14.1: VARIMAX-rotated factor structures of threat images by social class

Threat variables	Factors in middle class N = 651				Factors in working class N = 637	
	1	*2*	*3*	*4*	*1*	*2*
Differences in living standards	-0.07	0.20	0.25	0.19	0.46	-0.02
Environmental problems	0.01	0.02	0.61	0.10	0.51	0.13
Communist influence	0.71	-0.04	0.10	0.03	0.12	0.57
Nuclear power	0.06	0.29	0.35	-0.12	0.41	0.12
Population explosion	0.08	0.13	0.14	0.59	0.53	0.12
Multinational firms	-0.03	0.52	0.04	0.19	0.57	0.09
Distribution of world resources	0.02	0.43	0.25	0.20	0.54	0.18
Mechanization of production	0.14	0.29	0.29	-0.20	0.49	0.24
Capitalist influence	-0.04	0.67	0.13	-0.08	0.57	0.06
Arms race	0.14	0.44	0.20	0.15	0.62	0.07
Socialist threat	0.80	0.10	-0.00	0.06	0.14	0.69
Lack of energy resources	0.08	0.13	0.46	0.22	0.46	0.20
State influence	0.66	0.01	0.10	-0.02	0.11	0.64
Unemployment	0.14	0.19	0.35	0.04	0.50	0.19
PCT of common variance	47.5	30.5	12.0	10.0	77.3	22.7

Note: This factor analysis was based on a probability national sample. As a result of a lack of detailed information about occupations it was impossible to reliably distinguish strata within the upper and middle classes. What is here called the 'middle class' consists of a small percentage of upper class respondents plus middle class respondents *minus* those middle class respondents who in response to a separate question declared themselves as closer to the working class.

the middle strata while two factors appear in the working class. We have tested and falsified the hypothesis that this finding is a statistical artefact due to a greater homogeneity of the middle strata.[2]

The first factor in the working class we interpret as a factor referring to *the total structural complex of capitalism.* It includes high factor loadings not only for the 'threat of capitalism' itself and for multinational corporations, etc. but also for threats pertaining to environment, nuclear power, mechanization of work, energy problems and unemployment, not to mention the arms race. This factor accounts for 77 per cent of the common variance.

The second factor in the working class accounts for 23 per cent of the common variance and refers to the *threats of socialism, communism and state power.* It is interesting and highly indicative that threats of socialism cut across the capitalism factor orthogonally rather than appearing as negative loadings in a bi-polar capitalism factor. Such a bi-polar factor had been more consistent with a coherent view of society. The orthogonality of the capitalism and socialism factors would seem to corroborate our conjecture in Chapter 1 (p. 6) that socialism in the Swedish political vocabulary, as conveyed by dominant bourgeois newspapers and understood in significant segments even of the working class, is a bad word rather than an analytic concept. Even if the word socialism is less tainted by ugly associations in Sweden than in the US and parts of continental Europe, its bad connotations are significant enough in the Swedish context to warrant further attention when we discuss the 'socialist' mobilization of the working class later on in this chapter.

Returning to our combination of factor analysis and class analysis we find that the middle strata, in contrast to the working class, do not look at environmental problems, energy problems, the problems of unemployment and mechanization as part of the complex structure of capitalism, but rather as an *independent* factor (factor 3 in the middle strata). The first factor in the factor matrix of the middle strata refers to the *threats of communism, socialism and state power*, and it explains 48 per cent of the common variance. The second factor which explains 31 per cent of the common variance is a capitalism factor but of much less complexity than the corresponding factor indicated in the working class factor matrix. It would seem to correspond most closely to notions of the *military—industrial complex.* In comparative terms, however, it would seem that the middle strata have a much more piecemeal image of the threats to 'the future development of the world' whereas the working class exhibit a more holistic and structural image of these threats.

In our own more limited survey of blue-collar and white-collar workers from two provinces in central Sweden, we have used much the same threat questions as in Hedman's study, but now as seen not in relationship to 'the future development of the world', but in relation to the respondent himself, and people like him. Because of the small-ness of the middle strata in our sample we could not utilize the same class distinctions in our analysis, however. We have simply distinguished blue-collar and white-collar employees in this case.

The factor structure among blue-collar workers turns out to be exactly the same as for the working class in Hedman's study in spite of the fact that we are now considering threats to 'people themselves' rather than to 'the future development of the world' — but factor loadings are somewhat higher. White-collar employees in this particular analysis of our empirical data include part of the 'extended' working class — namely service workers, and the lower middle strata, and we cannot therefore expect the same results among our white-collar employees as in the middle strata of Hedman's study. In fact the factorial structures found among white-collar and blue-collar employees in our own study are very similar indeed (see Table 14.2). The main difference is that the 'threat' of state power is more closely linked to the 'threat' of socialism among white-collar than among blue-collar employees. In the latter category state power exhibits a lower factor loading on the socialism factor and a higher loading on the capitalism factor than is the case among white-collar employees. If anything, this would seem to indicate a higher awareness among blue-collar employees of the close relationships between capital and state.

By way of summary of these two studies it would seem justified to say that the middle strata to a much higher extent look upon the threats included in our factor analyses as piecemeal problems separated from the systemic features of a capitalist economic order, whereas the working class, including service workers, take a much more holistic, structural view of capitalism and its attributes, but quite frequently are confused about the analytic meaning of socialism.

On the other hand, it is not unreasonable to assume that the upper middle strata and the top stratum of managers and administrators also have a 'structural' image of threats, but relating rather to the increasing influence of state intervention, and to socialism. Looking at these two types of conceivable threats separately, we find that 36 per cent of the top stratum see a *great* threat in the influence of the state, and

Table 14.2: VARIMAX-rotated factor structures of threat images among white-collar and working class employees

Threat variables	Factors among white-collar employees		Factors in working-class	
	1	*2*	*1*	*2*
Inflation	0.41	0.39	0.49	0.22
Environmental problems	0.63	0.17	0.69	0.22
Nuclear power	0.61	0.18	0.53	0.30
Mechanization of production	0.57	0.13	0.46	0.21
Capitalist influence	0.63	0.03	0.55	0.09
Socialist influence	0.11	0.76	0.15	0.86
Concentration of private economic power	0.53	0.30	0.43	0.37
Big-city growth	0.61	0.22	0.59	0.29
State influence	0.22	0.81	0.36	0.61
Unemployment	0.63	0.26	0.62	0.19
PCT of common variance	79.4	20.6	84.5	15.5

Note: This factor analysis was based on our own probability sample from the Stockholm and Kopparberg provinces.

42 per cent in the threat of socialism, as against 32 and 22 per cent in the middle strata, and 27 and 15 per cent in the extended working class. However, in the top stratum all the various threats about which we have asked questions in our survey are rather weakly correlated, which would seem to indicate a piecemeal rather than a structural image of threats. Another interesting finding is that as many as 42 per cent within this top stratum perceive no threats at all, while only 17 per cent in the extended working class fail to see any threats.

To enable us to analyse threat awareness in more detailed breakdowns of strata within the extended working class we have used the results of our factor analysis to construct a scale of the *awareness of structural threats as related to the capitalist mode of production*. In Table 14.3 we have dichotomized this scale in the following manner: if respondents *combine* the perception of threats of unemployment, inflation and nuclear power with threats considered as relating to more systemic aspects of society such as the influence of capitalism, the increasing mechanization of work, and concentration of decision-making power in the economy, we classify such respondents as exhibiting a strong awareness of *structural* as distinct from piecemeal threats. Obviously this combination of responses to a rather large number of threat questions provides a quite demanding criterion (i) of structural awareness. In Table 14.3 we have also supplied a somewhat weaker criterion (ii) enabling us to assess the numerical strength of those who exhibit at least some structural awareness in the various strata of the extended working class.

Table 14.3: Working class identification, oppositional interpretation of class interests, and awareness of structural threats by strata (%)

	Working class identification	Oppositional interpretation	Awareness of structural threats		N
			A	B	
Industrial workers	71	34	45	61	453
Service workers	48	22	43	55	486
Middle strata	31	12	27	38	292
Managers	15	9	4	15	26

Note: With regard to awareness of structural threats the more demanding criterion A has been indicated in the main text. The less demanding criterion B defines an awareness of structural threats as present if a given respondent acknowledges some threat or a great threat with reference to both unemployment, environmental problems and the influence of capitalism.

In Table 14.3 we find that about 45 per cent of industrial workers *as well as* service workers perceive structural threats related to the capitalist mode of production, according to our stronger criterion. With regard to this indicator we thus find a clear similarity between these two strata within the extended working class. Outside the working class we find that the middle strata contain about 27 per cent who perceive this kind of structural threat; and in the small stratum of managers and top administrators only about 4 per cent perceive such a structural threat.

Further breakdowns of strata within the extended working class, and the middle strata, illuminates the existence of some 'weak spots' in terms of *embourgeoisement*. In Table 14.4 we find, for instance, that blue-collar workers in storage, transport and sales manifest a slightly lower level of structural awareness than industrial workers and workers in the service trades and in social reproduction (hospitals, schools, etc.). Perhaps the fact that transport workers like taxi drivers and lorry drivers work individually rather than together with other workers, and the fact that sales workers have closer relationships with customers than with other workers accounts for this finding.

On the whole, however, the empirical findings reported so far would seem to refute the *embourgeoisement* hypothesis, that is the assumption of a close correlation between affluence and social welfare on the one hand, and a destruction of a structural social consciousness of class conflicts, threats and injustice on the other. The Swedish working class would not seem to have undergone this process of embourgeoisement to the extent one could expect. Using the somewhat less demanding and stringent criterion of structural threat-awareness in Table 14.3 it is quite obvious that a clear majority of the extended working class (55–61 per cent) are quite aware of the structural contradictions and threats supposedly inherent in our capitalist economic order.

However, if we speak of a *process* of *embourgeoisement* this would seem to indicate a change over time. Unfortunately there are no previous studies using the same kinds of threat questions included in our survey which would allow us to report such changes over the last few decades. Therefore we will here instead use some data derived from some other interview questions which however would seem to be closely related to the kinds of structural images we have in mind. In the late 1940s Torgny Segerstedt and Agne Lundquist (1955, p. 281) carried out a study among industrial workers on class consciousness and images of power and influence of different classes, among many other variables. The relevant findings were obtained in reply to the following interview questions:

Table 14.4: Aspects of social consciousness by strata of the working class and the white-collar category (horizontal percentages)

Social strata	Working class identity			No working class identity			Total	Total
	Awareness of structural threats	Piecemeal view of threats	No threats at all perceived	Awareness of structural threats	Piecemeal view of threats	No threats at all perceived	%	N
1 Workers in industrial production	37	19	11	8	14	11	100	462
2 Storage, transport and sales workers	26	20	7	12	21	14	100	99
3 Workers in the service sector	30	26	6	16	6	16	100	55
4 Workers in 'reproduction': hospitals, schools etc.	30	19	11	15	10	15	100	74
5 Technicians in industrial production	14	14	4	13	32	23	100	169
6 Office clerks	16	10	6	22	31	15	100	175
7 White-collar employees in sales, banks, etc.	8	5	3	23	41	20	100	80
8 White-collar employees in 'reproduction'	22	7	8	16	23	24	100	99
9 White-collar employees in service sector	4	33	8	17	17	21	100	24
								1235

Note: The stratification scheme here employed has been developed by Göran Ahrne (1977) on the basis of a paper by Göran Therborn (1972). Originally storage and transport workers were kept separate but due to the relatively small number of transport workers in our sample they have here been combined into one stratum with sales workers.

What social class would you say you belong to?
What social class would you say has the most influence in Sweden
— your own or some other social class?

Table 14.5 presents some relevant breakdowns of the data from the
Segerstedt—Lundquist study. We note that as many as 58 per cent of
workers who identify with the working class are convinced that their
own social class is equally or more powerful than other classes. Another
remarkable finding is that among those who identify with the working
class, the higher one is in the employed ranks of a company the more
likely he is to think that his own class has the most influence in Sweden.
As many as 70 per cent of the white-collar employees who think of
themselves as working class (and most of whom have been upwardly
mobile) are convinced that their own social class is equally or more
powerful than other classes, while only 31 per cent of white-collar
identifying as middle-class think of their own social class as having
such a share of influence in Swedish society.

These findings from the late 1940s could be interpreted in terms
of the distinction between political and economic power and influence.
It would seem reasonable to assume that blue-collar and white-collar
employees in the late 1940s interpreted the term 'influence in Sweden'
in political rather than economic terms. The Social Democratic Labour
Party at that time had been in government for more than two decades.

If we now look at the data we collected more than thirty years
later in 1976 while the Social Democratic Labour Party was still in
government, and had been so for forty-four consecutive years, we find
a significant change in response distributions. In 1976 only 23 per cent
of industrial workers were convinced that the working class has the
greatest influence in Sweden as against 47 per cent in 1949. And among
those workers who were less than forty years old in 1976 only 14 per
cent said that the working class has the greatest influence (cf. Scase,
1977, Chapter 6). These differences in findings between 1976 and 1949
would seem to indicate that workers, when asked a question about
'influence in Sweden' tend to think more frequently about economic
than political power in 1976 in comparision with 1949. This change
from interpreting influence in economic rather than political terms
could be interpreted as a change from a more bourgeois to a more
socialist interpretation of the power structure. When in 1976 a majority
of workers consider social classes other than the working class to have
the greatest influence in Sweden, in spite of forty-four years of social
democratic government, they must obviously have been thinking of

Table 14.5: 'According to your opinion, what social class has the greatest influence in Sweden?' Horizontal percentages

	Own class	Classes have equal influence	Other class	Don't know + don't want to say	Total	(N)
Total	42	11	39	8	100	(1214)
White collar	41	10	43	6	100	(195)
With middle class identification	21	10	62	7	100	(83)
With working class identification	60	10	25	5	100	(112)
Blue collar	46	10	37	7	100	(1 019)
With middle class identification	40	—	54	6	100	(48)
With working class identification	47	11	36	6	100	(971)

Source: Segerstedt and Lundquist, Människan i industrisamhället. Del II p. 281

something other than political power, namely economic power and influence. If this interpretation is correct this implies that our data reject the assumption of a *process* of *embourgeoisement* in the Swedish working class.

On the other hand it is possible to argue that the radical structural image of society unravelled by these various findings about the social consciousness of the Swedish working class still indicate nothing more than a *private* kind of radical consciousness shared with others only in a statistical sense, not in terms of a working class *Gemeinschaft.*[3]

This argument about the possibly private character even of radical working class consciousness gives rise to a number of important questions about the anchoring of subjective consciousness in objective cultural and material conditions. A sound sociological conjecture in response to such questions is the following: images about society, fears and expectations about the future, and other such aspects of subjective consciousness among workers will be rather irrelevant from the point of view of worker mobilization — even if they are shared by large statistical aggregates — unless they are clearly related to objective conditions such as union membership, and shared conditions of work which are objects of union and political party debate and action. Only if a radical subjective consciousness, as revealed for instance by individual questionnaire responses, is connected with union membership, and with conditions of work that are salient issues of union and political debate and action, only then can such a subjective consciousness be transformed to an objective, material force of collective mobilization, and not only appear as private expressions of radicalism.

However, this sociological conjecture may be a bit too restrictive. Even if such a relationship between subjective and objective factors is relatively weak among certain groups or strata within the working class, this could be compensated for by what Korpi has called a solidaristic involvement with the labour movement (see above), or by an explicit identification with the working class. Such a solidaristic identification will make workers prepared for a collective worker mobilization even if their subjective consciousness is less radical or, while being quite radical, remains private in the sense indicated above.

Before investigating the relationship between some objective conditions and the radical structural image of the threats of capitalism, let us therefore look at some figures on working class identification.

Working Class Identity

As an indicator of class identification we have used responses to a very common type of question: What is the social class to which you feel most close? This could be considered an indicator of 'traditional' working class consciousness expressed in *Gemeinschaft* terms, and linked to traditional labour movement solidaristic ideology. With the indicator we have used, we seem to come very close to what Giddens calls 'class awareness' (Giddens, 1973, p. 111). In Table 14.3 (see p. 174) we found that nearly three out of four industrial workers in our sample exhibit this traditional type of class awareness, whereas only about half of the service workers show such awareness or identification. In spite of the fact that we have included service workers in our extended working class on objective grounds, a significantly smaller percentage of them identified subjectively with the working class. Obviously this traditional manifestation of a labour movement ideology does not attract a *significant* majority within this 'new' stratum of the working class. The language of working class solidarity and identity does not come as easily to this 'new' stratum as to the core of the working class, the industrial workers.

Richard Scase (1972, pp. 205f) has made a very comprehensive summary of the evidence of class consciousness in Sweden and England which rather conclusively shows that Swedish workers in the period 1950—65 were much more inclined to identify with the working class than were English workers. Furthermore, Scase has carried out surveys of his own in the early 1970s comparing Swedish and English manual workers (Scase, 1974a and b). His figures on the absolute level of class consciousness of that time are not quite comparable with our own and other Swedish studies — partly because his questions were differently formulated than those used in other surveys — but the differences he found in his own surveys in the early 1970s confirm earlier findings that Swedish workers are much more inclined to identify with the working class than are English workers. Unfortunately there is a lack of other Swedish studies from the late 1960s and early 1970s using questions about class identity, comparable to questions asked earlier. However, in studies carried out in the late 1940s and early 1950s (Segerstedt and Lundquist, 1955, p. 281 and Dahlström, 1954, p. 56) we find figures around 80 per cent or more for explicit working class identification among industrial workers in Sweden. These figures are slightly higher than our own figure of 71 per cent among industrial workers, and may indicate a slight decrease of traditional class awareness among Swedish industrial workers. On the other hand there would seem to be a more widespread working class identification today among younger white-collar employees than was the case in the late 1950s and the early 1960s. However, we should remind the reader on this point that our category of white-collar employees is somewhat different from the white-collar category in the late 1940s and early 1950s, due to the process of 'de-skilling' of white-collar occupations indicated earlier – a process which has lead us to include some segments of the white-collar category into an extended working class under the label of service workers.

So far we have made no distinction between working class *awareness* in the sense of Giddens, and working class *identity*, but rather equated these two terms. However, it would seem possible to distinguish between an awareness of the *existence* of social classes, and a readiness to *identify* oneself with the classes perceived. Given such a distinction it should be possible to find people who are aware of social classes but fail to identify with any one social class. White-collar employees who occupy 'contradictory locations within class relations', according to Erik Olin Wright (see p. 162 above), are most likely to exhibit this combination of class awareness and lack of class identity. Lowe Hedman (1978, p. 101) has made this distinction between class awareness and class identity, and addressed a question using this distinction to the national sample survey which we have referred to earlier. One of the response categories to his question on subjective class affiliation runs like this: 'Certainly there are classes, but I can't say to which one I belong.' About 28 per cent of his respondents answer the class affiliation question in this manner. Cross-tabulating responses to this question on class affiliation by a scale of structural threat awareness very similar to the one we have used in our own analysis, Hedman arrives at a very interesting finding. Those who show class awareness *without* class identity manifest an awareness of the structural aspects of a capitalist order percentage-wise as often as those who clearly identify with the working class (1978, p. 105). We have reanalysed Hedman's data, and found that this combination of class awareness and lack of class identity with a structural threat awareness is particularly common among service workers and the lower middle strata – a finding which is rather close to the finding reported in Table 14.3 above on the basis of our survey.

By way of summary, the differences we have found within the extended working class between industrial workers and service workers refer primarily to what we have called traditional working class consciousness expressing itself in terms of class identity and *Gemeinschaft*.

However, as indicated in Hedman's survey a lack of working class identity among service workers does not preclude an awareness of the existence of social classes. No differences at all have been found between industrial workers and service workers when we employ this criterion of class awareness and our criterion of perceived structural threats relating to the capitalist order. On every point, however, there is a clear difference between these two strata within the working class, on the one hand, and the middle strata, on the other. There are also clear differences in class identity and structural threat awareness between the middle strata and the top stratum of managers and administrators.

Perhaps we can interpret these results as a progression from traditional types of solidaristic class consciousness to a class consciousness more clearly related to an image of the contradictions within the capitalist mode of production itself. If this interpretation is correct, the 'newest' members of the working class in our extended sense would seem to have skipped the early stage of traditional solidaristic class consciousness while exhibiting a modern type of structural class consciousness to the same extent as industrial workers.

Some Correlates of Working Class Consciousness

We will now analyse how variations in type of class consciousness relate not only to variations in working conditions and union membership, but also to a traditional working class heritage as indicated by a working class occupation of the respondent's father and mother. We assume that so-called traditional working class identification relates most clearly to a cultural heritage, whereas the awareness of structural threats emanating from the capitalist mode of production is assumed to relate more strongly to present working conditions and type of union membership.

In Table 14.6 we have summarized our findings with regard to the relationships between father's/mother's occupation, working conditions and union membership on the one hand, and our different types of consciousness on the other.

Cultural heritage mediated by parental influence is related primarily to *class identity*. In all strata — working class as well as middle strata and the top stratum — subjective working class identity is more common among respondents whose parents have been workers. Class identity also seems to be influenced by type of union membership. Among service workers, those who are organized in LO are much more likely to identify with the working class than those who are members of TCO.

Table 14.6: Working Class Identification (WI), Oppositional Interpretation of Class Interests (OI) and Structural Threat Awareness (ST) as related to Social Class of Parents (CP), Work Environment (WE) and Union Membership (UM) in various Social Strata

(a) *Coefficients of association: gamma*

Social strata	Gamma WI/CP	Gamma WI/WE	Gamma WI/UM	Gamma OI/CP	Gamma OI/WE	Gamma OI/UM	Gamma ST/CP	Gamma ST/WE
Industrial workers	0.40	0.17	0.57	0.05	0.24	0.45	0.05	0.10
Service workers	0.37	0.42	0.36	0.15	0.31	0.09	0.02	0.06
Middle strata	0.39	0.27	0.36	0.02	0.23	0.06	0.06	0.17

Note: The variable of union membership (UM) was dichotomized in two categories: (1) Members in LO, TCO or in SAC, a very small syndicalist organization and (2) others, consisting mainly of employees who were not members of any union, but in addition a small number of employees organized in SACO, a union of academically trained employees (see below).

(b) *Structural threat awareness by stratum and type of union membership (percentage)*

Social strata	LO (N=)	TCO (N=)	SACO (N=)	Non-members (N=)
Industrial workers	46 (357)	44 (18)	—	35 (53)
Service workers	41 (193)	45 (160)	—	36 (93)
Middle strata	—	30 (183)	6 (18)	22 (56)

Note: The more demanding criterion of structural threat awareness (A) presented on p. 174 has been used in this table.

Among service workers there is also some correlation between a poor physical and psycho-social work environment and working class identity. The degree of *oppositional interpretation of class interests* (see above p. 169), on the other hand is related primarily to variations in the physical and psycho-social work environment among industrial workers and service workers. In the working class we find twice as many workers with a strong oppositional interpretation among those who work in a poor physical work environment than among those who are exposed to better working conditions in this respect. Oppositional interpretations of class interest would thus seem partially to reflect objective conditions in the work situation, in contrast to working class identity which is part of a cultural heritage across generations. Among service workers union membership also seems to have a certain influence on the extent of oppositional interpretation of class interests. Service workers who are members of LO exhibit a somewhat higher percentage with an oppositional interpretation than those who are members of TCO.

Structural threat awareness is completely unrelated to parental background but is weakly related to variations in work environment, and clearly related to union membership. However, we find no differences between those employees who are members of LO and TCO respectively; they manifest a structural threat awareness to the same extent. But in the middle strata there is a considerable difference in the percentage exhibiting structural threat perception between those who are members of TCO — the percentage here is very close to the percentage exhibited by the working class — and those who are members of SACO. SACO is a relatively small organization recruiting only academically trained employees, usually in the upper middle strata and in the top stratum of administrators and managers. SACO members in the middle strata only very rarely show proof of a structural threat awareness; in fact their percentage figures are very similar to those exhibited in the top stratum of managers and administrators.

We pointed out earlier that images of society, and fears and expectations about the future as well as other aspects of subjective consciousness among workers will be rather inconsequential from the point of view of worker mobilization unless they are clearly related to more objective conditions such as union membership and shared conditions of work which are objects of union and political party debate and action. A purely 'private' type of radicalism may not in itself be sufficient to guarantee a broad mobilization of workers even if such radicalism is shared, statistically speaking, by very large aggregates of blue-collar and white-collar employees. However, the empirical findings reported above prove that the oppositional interpretation of class interests found among Swedish workers are indeed related to such objective conditions of work and union membership.

A Summary

We are now in a better position to draw more definite conclusions about the strength of the Swedish working class in terms of numbers, organization and consciousness. Numerically the working class is not diminishing in size. The decreasing percentage of industrial workers is more than compensated for by the processes of division of labour, numerical growth, unionization and consciousness production within the lower white-collar strata; and these processes are still at work.

Service workers, these new entrants into the working class, do not subjectively affiliate themselves with the working class as easily as industrial workers do. But they exhibit an emerging new type of structurally defined social consciousness to an extent equal with that found in the core of the working class, and their increasing degree of unionization would seem to promise a continued expansion of this structuralist ideological tendency within the extended working class. It is also interesting to note that this ideological tendency extends beyond the working class into a significant minority of the middle strata, where, consequently, the extended working class might be able to find a significant number of allies in supporting political attempts to bring about structural reforms to reduce the structural threats seen as inherent in the capitalist order.

However, a structuralist interpretation of the threats perceived as inherent in the capitalist order only contributes to set the stage for the future. This type of social consciousness only implies a certain definition of the *problems* of capitalism. Often a certain way of defining the problems of society becomes generally accepted long before relevant and adequate *problem solutions* come to be accepted generally. The process of defining such problem solutions, and making them acceptable, has picked up speed in Sweden recently. We will have more to say about this in the following section on the political strength of the extended working class. The speed of this process depends not only on the objective processes of division of labour and unionization mentioned above, but also on the responsiveness of political party leadership, and the tempo of political decision-making. The fact that the Social Democratic Labour government was removed from power in the 1976 general election is relevant here, as well as the very close race between socialist and bourgeois parties in the election of 1979 (see below).

On this point it becomes necessary to turn from the question of the *class bases* of political parties to that of their *electoral bases*.[4] The electoral and class bases of a given political party are certainly overlapping to a considerable extent, but they are not identical. Whereas the class basis of any given party contains only those who are gainfully employed, the electoral basis of a party also includes many who are not thus employed — for instance housewives, students and pensioners. Furthermore the electoral base excludes immigrants who occupy class positions in production, but have not obtained full citizen and voting rights.[5]

15 The Political Strength of the Extended Working Class

The actual strength of labour and bourgeois parties in the electorate is not only a reflection of their potential strength in the electoral basis. It is also a matter of the responsiveness of political party leaderships to the class and non-class issues salient in the electorate, and their ability to spell out these issues and problem-solving action needed in terms that are understood in the electorate. If political parties fail to respond to the issues felt as most urgent in the respective electoral bases, and if they fail to address these issues in terms and in action felt to be relevant to the issues involved, then this will result in an increasing sense of distrust in politics and in politicians. Therefore our question about the strength of the parties representing the extended working class cannot be answered simply by a piecemeal analysis of any one aspect of this complex of political strength. It rather calls for an analysis of both the electoral bases of these parties, of party responsiveness to salient issues, and their ability to translate these into understandable political messages and political action, thus mobilizing the voters and preventing distrust in politics within the electorate. The common thread through all these levels of analysis is the concept of issues: the generation of issues inside and outside the class basis of parties, party responsiveness to salient issues, the translation of issues into political proposals and action, and electoral mobilization in view of the electorate's distrust in politics due to whether or not political parties fail to address themselves to salient issues.

The Electoral Bases of Parties Competing for the Vote of the Extended Working Class

The working class is defined in terms of the contradiction of labour and capital. Its empirical delimitation is another matter, however. We have delimited the extended working class in terms of the routinization and de-skilling of work, as reflected in skill requirements within the division of labour. We have found that those who share such working conditions — whether they are blue-collar or white-collar — also share an awareness of the structural threats of the capitalist order. It seems as if the issues of concern to the various strata within the extended working class are generated largely by their experience of work and union membership. On the basis of these various analyses we have suggested that the extended working class contains about 70 per cent of all gainfully employed. But the electoral bases of labour parties must also be considered beyond their class basis, and they also exclude part of this class basis. The relevant electorate includes housewives, students and pensioners, and excludes immigrant workers without voting rights in national elections, as we have just suggested. We know that housewives in Sweden tend to vote in a slightly more bourgeois fashion than their husbands, and that Swedish students also tend to vote mainly for bourgeois parties, even though quite a number also vote for the communist parties.[1] Immigrant workers who are not eligible to vote, would have voted overwhelmingly for the social democrats and the communists; here the labour parties are thus deprived of a substantial number of voters.[2]

This means that the proportion of the electorate which the labour parties can count on as their electoral basis is smaller than their class basis as a percentage of all gainfully employed. If we estimate the class basis of labour parties among all gainfully employed as about 70 per cent, as we have indicated above, the basis of these parties in the whole electorate is bound to be less percentage-wise. But how much less? It should be possible to make an assessment of the potential maximum support for labour parties in the electorate by re-analysing national electoral surveys, and other national surveys of social class, political attitudes and behaviour. Unfortunately, no such study is available, and our own limited resources of time and money have not allowed such a secondary analysis of available data. However, after some paper calculation of our own, and an interview with a political scientist specializing on electoral research[3] we have arrived at the informed guess that the two labour parties in Sweden — the larger Social Democratic Party and the small Communist Party — together could obtain support from a maximum of 55—60 per cent of the electorate in a general election. To obtain such support these parties must perform well in translating salient issues into political proposals and action, and in effectively mobilizing their potential electoral base. However, the actual attainment of this potential is due not only to the political skill and competence of the labour parties themselves, but also to the skill of competing political parties — particularly the centre and liberal parties — in addressing those parts of the electorate which they share with the labour parties. Clearly there is an overlap between the electoral bases of labour and non-labour parties among service workers and in the middle strata, but probably also among first-generation workers with a background in a relatively conservative peasantry or petty bourgeoisie.

It is not our intention here to predict how this competition between labour and non-labour parties will turn out where their electoral bases overlap. If we disregard for a moment the social psychology of electoral mobilization, and look only for objective trends which affect the size of the potential electoral base for labour parties, we find a regrettable lack of systematic research. We would need to know past and present trends with regard to the volume of recruitment, through geographic and/or social mobility, from one set of class or non-class positions to another. We would also need to know the political 'conversion probabilities' for those who move in various streams or patterns of class recruitment, and the trends for such probabilities. Is the probability of being converted to another party-political allegiance in the process of geographical or social mobility becoming greater or less? Finally, we would need information on the times of onset, culmination or termination of the processes underlying such trends. In the absence of any comprehensive and systematic study of this nature we have summarized some relevant observations in a note for those readers with a special interest in this matter.[4] Here we will only provide some tentative conclusions which are based on these observations not in a stringent quantitative sense but only with the somewhat impressionistic method of close and thoughtful reading of available data on the patterns of mobility, and conversion probabilities involved.

We have concluded that the potential electoral basis of the labour parties was shrinking somewhat for a period *after* the fifties when the percentage of industrial workers was at a peak level and started declining, and when the inflow of immigrant labour without voting rights was just beginning, but *before* the actual onset of other counteracting trends. Such are the upsurge of unionization of routinized white-collar labour, the inflow of women in the labour force, the increasing number of students with a working class background, the recent decrease of labour immigration, the increasing number of immigrant workers gaining Swedish citizenship, etc. It is our informed contention that these recent upsurging processes which counteract the shrinking of the potential labour electoral base now are becoming more predominant than the processes which shrink that base. This means that the potential electoral base for Swedish labour parties presently is expanding.

The Responsiveness of Political Parties and Types of Political Mobilization

The greatest threat against the political branch of the labour movement — that is, mainly against the Social Democratic Party — is not the threat against its class basis, and its potential electoral base. Most threatened is the community of social relations, the web of local activities which in the past constituted the texture of politics and leisure in labour communes all over Sweden in periods between elections. Certainly, the Social Democratic Party together with the trade unions still prove to be rather efficient in mobilizing their constituencies in election campaigns, but increasingly this mobilization must be based on extraneous techniques of mass communication and canvassing rather than on appeals to the sense of community and solidarity among workers, young and old, which in the past was a given social reality already at the onset of an election campaign. Increasing centralization of politics, the decline of local politics, increasing geographical mobility of the so-called labour force, the collapse of an increasing number of local labour newspapers, including the only labour morning paper in Stockholm, the withering away of labour issues in the programmes of the workers' adult education movement, the de-politicization of the labour youth movement, working class family disintegration and a disruption of the links between working class families and the public sphere of working class life through mass media and commercialization of leisure activities can all be seen as elements in this destruction of a living class culture of labour.

More forcefully than by anybody else these points have been made by Jan Lindhagen, a sociologist working in a research group affiliated with the Social Democratic Party (Lindhagen and Nilsson, 1971; Lindhagen, 1976 and 1977). Above we have criticized some of his views on the 'privatization' of working class consciousness with the help of data from surveys made by ourselves, and by Walter Korpi (p. 179, see above). However, in all fairness we must admit that his words of warning seem to us more justified when we move from the question of the size and composition of the *electoral base* of labour parties to the question of *mobilization* of the working class not only in elections but also in political and parapolitical activities between elections. Lindhagen does not himself make any explicit distinction between these two levels of analysis; he could be wrong on one of these levels — that is with regard to questions of class and electoral bases of labour parties — but still be right on the other level.

Which are then the premises of working class and labour party mobilization today? In the following we will take account of six different types of basic premises of such mobilization:

1. Traditional working-class solidarity and corresponding labour party loyalty
2. Weaknesses in the common front and action of competing bourgeois parties
3. Party-leader appeal
4. Diminishing trust in the politicians and an increasing contempt for politics
5. The appeal of labour and bourgeois party programmes on piecemeal issues
6. Labour party responsiveness to new structural issues emerging in the electorate, or in the objective structure of mature capitalism.

These bases of electoral mobilization or demobilization are not typically Swedish but exist in most political democracies. What is rather typically Swedish, however, is that religious affiliation and linguistic or ethnic identity and similar cultural variables are estimated to be of minor or no significance in the context of electoral mobilization. World events and foreign policy orientations have influenced some Swedish elections, but are probably much more important in countries such as the USA, England and France with heavy commitments abroad. Here such premises of electoral mobilization will be disregarded.

In Table 15.1 we have summarized our conclusions regarding the relative advantages or disadvantages of different bases of electoral mobilization, from the point of view of Swedish labour parties — mainly the Social Democratic Party. We will now comment upon these relative advantages and disadvantages — in some cases at greater length.

1. With regard to the first basis of electoral mobilization — traditional working class solidarity and corresponding labour party loyalty — we have nothing to add to our previous analysis except one point. The extension of the working class into the lower 'middle class' strata of what we have called service workers makes it necessary for the Social Democratic Party to appeal less to traditional working class solidarity and the *Gemeinschaft* of the labour movement and more to electoral

Table 15.1: The relative advantages or disadvantages of labour parties with respect to different bases of electoral mobilization

Bases of electoral mobilization or demobilization	Relative advantages or disadvantages of labour parties in electoral mobilization + relative advantage; − relative disadvantage; 0 neither advantage nor disadvantage; (+) untapped advantage
1 Traditional working-class solidarity and corresponding labour party loyalty.	1 Still an extremely important basis for labour party mobilization; but its importance is diminishing due to the 'embourgeoisement' + of certain working-class strata (transport − and sales), and the emergence of new working-class strata (so-called service workers) which only partly respond to traditional working-class appeals but still may vote for labour due to their concern for certain issues.
2 Weaknesses in the common front and action of competing bourgeois parties.	2 Probably one of the most important sources + of strength of the Social Democratic Labour Party.
3 Party-leader appeal.	3 The Social Democratic Party has no particular advantage on this point. All party leaders − except perhaps the conservative 0 leader Gösta Bohman − are somewhat controversial among minorities of party supporters, and probably even more so among floating or marginal voters.
4 Diminishing trust in politicians, and an increasing contempt for politics.	4 If we assume that radicals who distrust politicians and feel contempt for politics fail to vote, while conservatives who feel − the same distrust and contempt vote for the Conservative Party which favours a depoliticization of economic and other issues, then such an increasing distrust and contempt disadvantages mainly the Social Democratic Party.
5 Appeal of labour and bourgeois party programmes on piecemeal issues.	5 In the past the social democrats had an advantage over the bourgeois parties due to their record of piecemeal reform. But this advantage has been partly undermined by their less good record in fighting unemployment in the mid-seventies, and by the fact + that some of the piecemeal reforms of the − past have turned out to have undesirable side-effects. Furthermore, social democrats no longer to the same extent monopolize the concern for unemployment and other piecemeal social welfare issues; bourgeois parties have increasingly incorporated such issues in their programmes and policies.
6 Labour-party responsiveness to new structural issues emerging in the electorate, or in the objective conditions of mature capitalism.	6 Here the Social Democratic Party has an important potential source of strength which (+) is still largely untapped, and which is less easily tapped by bourgeois parties.

concern for crucial ideological issues, piecemeal or structural. For an early statement on this need for a change in social democratic electoral strategy, see Himmelstrand and Lindhagen (1970).

2. The fact that the bourgeois side of Swedish electoral competition consists of three parties with rather different programmes in some important policy areas has been a source of strength of the Social Democratic Party for many years when the social democrats were in charge of the Swedish government. But paradoxically this source of strength became even more visible after the defeat of the social democrats in the 1976 election, and the instalment of a three-party bourgeois government. Where normally the parties that gained the most in an election for a while keep on gaining public support, according to public opinion polls, this time the support for the Social Democratic Party was growing remarkably after its defeat to a point where, since March 1977 and up to October 1978, public opinion polls gave it an absolute majority either alone or together with the Communist Party (see Figure 15.1). Political commentators have agreed that this was largely a result of the weaknesses in the common bourgeois front which in October 1978 led to the collapse of the three-party bourgeois government. The three bourgeois parties then found it impossible to go on ruling together — mainly but not exclusively because of the nuclear power issue.

A minority liberal cabinet was then formed with the tacit support of the Social Democrats who could not then rally sufficient parliamentary support for a minority social democratic government. Such a government would not only have been more broadly based in parliament than the Liberal cabinet but could also have announced immediate elections, to exploit the majority electoral support for Social Democrats reported by public opinion polls at that time.[5]

The instalment of the liberal minority cabinet caused an increasing support to the Liberal Party, and a sudden drop in the support for Social Democrats who were not able to regain sufficiently much lost territory before the regular elections held in September 1979. This turn of events would seem to support our contention that cracks in the bourgeois front are a main source of electoral support for the Social Democratic Party. With *one* bourgeois party in government — namely the Liberal Party — the electorate seems to have formed a rather favourable image of determination and unity which dispelled some of the disenchantment with the previous three-party bourgeois government, at least to begin with.[6]

3. With regard to the appeal of the party leader we have little to say.

Figure 15.1: Support for political parties in Sweden in the interelection period 1976—9 according to public opinion polls carried out by SIFO

Scource: *Dagens Nyheter*, September 1, 1979, and Table A.1.4 in Appendix I

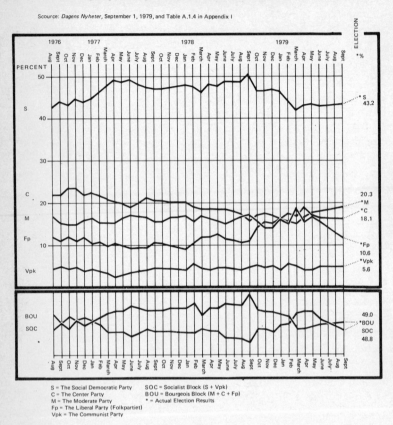

S = The Social Democratic Party
C = The Center Party
M = The Moderate Party
Fp = The Liberal Party (Folkpartiet)
Vpk = The Communist Party

SOC = Socialist Block (S + Vpk)
BOU = Bourgeois Block (M + C + Fp)
* = Actual Election Results

It is quite possible that the Social Democrats could win greater victories among marginal voters by having a party leader less controversial and with a more general and popular appeal than Olof Palme. It is also possible that a poorer image of the Social Democratic party leader could reduce the electoral support for the Social Democratic Party even more than was the case in the 1976 election. These matters are important for electoral strategists. But for us, and probably also for a Labour Party hammering out a stand on political issues of concern to the party and the electorate, a concern for such *issues* comes more naturally than studies of the salesmanship of leadership-image production. But before we proceed to a discussion of issues in electoral mobilization we will look briefly on the possibly demobilizing role of diminishing trust in politicians and the increasing contempt for politics which can be found in many countries, also in Sweden.

4. In Sweden the belief that politicians are corrupt would seem to play an insignificant role in causing a contempt and distrust in politics and politicians. Unfortunately, there are no sufficiently detailed Swedish studies available on the class bases, and the psychological or party-political implications of such contempt and distrust — even though there are studies which establish the existence of this phenomenon itself (Petersson, 1978, pp. 258f). Therefore our hypothesis about the demobilizing effects of this phenomenon on electoral support for the Social Democratic Party remains unsubstantiated. But we still believe that it is a reasonable hypothesis, at least in settings where such distrust and contempt can find expression in votes for more or less 'anti-political' bourgeois parties, whether conservative as in Sweden, or reactionary populist or Poujadist as in some other countries. However, this hypothesis should be further qualified.

Intuitively, and on reading large numbers of 'letters to the editors' and the like, we believe that one source of contempt for politicians in the Swedish setting is the fact that people dislike 'quarrels', and perceive televized debates between party-leaders as 'quarrelsome'. If we assume that this dislike for 'quarrels' implies an essentially bourgeois distaste for a conflict-perspective on society, then a contempt for the 'quarrelsome' aspects of politics might demobilize bourgeois rather than socialist voters, to whom conflict and struggle are more natural categories of social action. However, we do not believe that this counter-hypothesis alone carries much weight.

We believe that it is the *irrelevancy* of political 'quarrels' which counts the most among potential voters who are demobilized by their contempt for politics. If the structural issues which seem so salient in the minds of common people in Sweden, according to the studies we have reported above, fail to be reflected in party-political stands, then political debates which are concerned only with piecemeal issues may certainly be perceived as irrelevant 'quarrels'. Because the Social Democratic Party, being the largest 'socialist' party, could be expected to devote itself particularly to such structural issues of welfare-capitalism, it would be the party to lose the most from a failure to address such structural issues. But has it failed in this respect?

5—6. The advantages and disadvantages from the point of view of labour, of mobilizing the electorate in terms of piecemeal or structural political issues, is the most important question of all in assessing the political strength of labour, in our view. These two aspects of electoral mobilization should therefore be treated together and not separately.

Piecemeal and Structural Issues: The Performance of Political Parties, and Two Processes of Electoral Mobilization

Political issues can be presented and perceived either in a piecemeal or a structural fashion, that is either in terms of complaints about piecemeal problems to be solved by piecemeal political action or reform, or in terms of faults of the social system as such which cannot be remedied without launching a programme of structural reform and eventual transformation. Such structural transformation may have to be initiated also be piecemeal reform — unless there is a revolutionary situation which violently overturns the existing social structure. The situation in Sweden like in most other mature capitalist societies is not revolutionary, however, and therefore somewhat piecemeal action is involved in cases of both piecemeal and structural reform. But piecemeal action which is part of a project of structural reform cannot be understood as such without taking the broader structural context into account.

During the 1972—6 electoral period the Social Democratic government instituted several reforms concerning the work environment, and the relative power of labour and capital. These were certainly piecemeal reforms, but they can be understood fully only as part of a broader project of structural reform aiming at profound structural changes of the Swedish economy. Undoubtedly these reforms were speeded up in response to pressures from below; without the drastic increase of wild-cat strikes in the late 1960s and early 1970s, and worker articulation of alienation and protest, the Social Democratic Party leadership may very well have been content just to administer the capitalist order in a progressive and liberal manner. At least it would have been easier to find excuses for doing so while still verbally maintaining a more radical 'political will' or, in Swedish, *viljeinriktning* which is a key term in social democratic language on this point. Nevertheless, the responsiveness of the trade union movement and the Social Democratic Party to these pressures from below, even in a situation where the parliamentary majority of the party was undermined, turned out a number of results. The following list of legislation enacted during this period may not speak for itself without comments — such comments are forthcoming with regard to some of these legal acts in Chapter 17 — but may still give a first impression of the responsiveness of the Social Democratic Party to the issues of work environment and labour—capital relationships which were so salient already during the early 1970s:

· Act on Board Representation for the Employees in Joint Stock Companies.

- Statutes on Obligations to Inform on Certain Planning Matters.
- Several Amendments to the Industrial Safety Act of 1949; these amendments greatly expanded the powers of union-appointed safety stewards (*skyddsombud*).
- Act Concerning Employment Security.
- Act on the Position of a Trade Union Representative at the Workplace.
- Act Concerning an Employee's Right to Educational Leave.
- Act Concerning Public Board Members in Certain Joint Stock Companies and Foundations (in order to provide public interests with more information rather than with opportunities for control or influence).
- Act on Co-Determination at Work (MBL).

Sociologically speaking the most important aspect of many of these new legal acts was that they were intended to counteract the centralism which otherwise has been such a pervasive trait of Swedish society — without, however, destroying the significant and centralized unitary power of the national federation of trade unions, LO. Genuine, not fake, *local* controls were being placed in the hands of workers in local unions by some if not all these pieces of legislation — particularly through the new amendments to the Industrial Safety Act — amendments which greatly expanded the powers of union-appointed safety stewards.

One possible effect of these acts even when their implementation has been delayed and met with the obstruction of company management and employers, may have been to create a new social climate, and new arenas for exercising new ways of thinking and acting about relations of production; and this in turn could make for new, more structural demands in these respects.

The pieces of legislation we have mentioned are illustrations not only of responsiveness on the party level to pressures from below. They also illustrate piecemeal reforms which can be seen as part of a long-term project to change the structure of relationships between labour and capital, as indicated above.

Reforms with this kind of structuralist aim in focus came to an end with the defeat of the Social Democrats in the elections of 1976, and in fact some of the reforms which were already in the pipeline at the time of this shift of government power, have later been watered down by the new bourgeois government, or efficiently obstructed by the employers' confederation SAF.[7] However, at the time of the shift of government, the Social Democrats were making two further proposals for future legislation which deserve special attention in this context because they may bring about more profound changes in relationships between capital and labour than the legal acts mentioned above — at least if the Social Democratic Party is returned to political power in future elections.

One of these proposals suggested the establishment of 'restructuration' funds (*strukturfonder*) controlled by worker majorities, for the purposes of changing the structure of certain branches of industry which exhibit a proliferation of small firms with manifest problems of investment and competitiveness. Competitiveness and profitability are goals which labour shares with capital in these cases. But the approaches to these goals are looked upon differently by labour and capital, capital interests being more prone to closing down firms in trouble and to move capital to locations abroad or at home which are more profitable in the short run without taking human and social costs into account.

Even less piecemeal are the proposals for wage-earners' funds — or *löntagarfonder* in Swedish — originally initiated by the Federation of Metal Worker Unions, and explored by Rudolf Meidner et al. (1976). In his study Meidner and his collaborators explored the possibilities and implications of successively transferring company profits to a capital fund, controlled collectively by trade unions, both locally and branch-wise, which would make trade unions hold a decisive proportion of the shares in these companies within a certain span of time. These funds would imply a corresponding increase in the decision-making power of labour in relationship to the traditional holders of capital. The Social Democratic Party was not prepared to make this an issue in the 1976 election campaign, but has later accepted the aims of the proposal with some additions and amendments (see Chapter 19).

Social democratic political historians now tend to describe the development of the Swedish Social Democratic Party in three periods: the first period was the struggle for *universal suffrage* undertaken together with liberal politicians; in the second stage of *welfare capitalism* the main issues were economic growth and social welfare redistribution; in the third phase which has just barely begun, the main issue is *economic democracy* which implies a stepwise but thorough overhaul of power relationships between capital and labour (Johansson, 1976). From the point of view of academic historians as well as from the point of view of communist writers to the left of social democracy, this neat and logical sequence of periods may seem a bit too neat and logical to be historically true. Whatever the case may be — and we will return to this matter in the last chapter — my point is that this periodization of social democratic history itself is an indication of a new approach of the Swedish Social Democratic Party, implying a greater responsiveness to demands based on an awareness of the structural contradictions of mature capitalism.

But in politics it is not an easy matter for a political party to change and go beyond an earlier approach. The past history of a party has shaped its image and established its identity. To give up or rather to transcend such an image or identity, and to switch to a new approach is probably as difficult as to change unsynchronized gears in an old-fashioned motor-car negotiating a steep upward gradient — particularly if you lack the necessary skills in double-clutching. In such a situation you are likely to maintain the car in second gear as long as possible, until the vehicle is nearly at a standstill, before you try to change into first gear. And then, if you fail, you may come to a complete stop, or even roll a bit backwards until you finally make it.

Metaphorically speaking this is what seems to have happened to the Social Democratic Party in its transition from the stage of welfare capitalism to the stage of economic democracy. The party has been identified as a party of piecemeal social reform within the framework of capitalist economic growth. Those who were satisfied with that approach, and fail to understand the objective need for another approach, are likely to become confused about the identity of the Social Democratic Party in this transitional phase; and others who certainly would favour structural reform toward some kind of economic democracy might fail to understand or to believe that the party is really about to transcend its previous identity as a party of capitalist economic growth and welfare redistributions.

Even though the Social Democratic Party in its previous legislative activities, and in its internal debate about the transition to economic democracy, has proved itself to be reasonably, if not totally, responsive to the new structural issues emerging on the stage of mature capitalism, its record in recent election campaigns is a different matter.

Before we proceed to characterize the campaign performance of the Social Democratic Party in 1976 and 1979 election campaigns, a few words should be said about two types of electoral mobilization — in terms of either piecemeal or structural political issues:

1. If people translate their image of society, as documented by empirical studies reported above, that is their sense of social inequality and their awareness of the structural threats of mature capitalism, into party

affiliation, and add to this their sense of relative affluence and their documented willingness to sacrifice part of possible future increases of private consumption for more of social investments, then the Social Democrats and the Communists should be able to mobilize a majority in general elections at present.

2. If on the other hand the 'privatization' of social consciousness (which also exists in the Swedish public and even in some strata of the extended working class) becomes the more salient process among significant numbers of marginal voters, then these voters will be mobilized politically not in terms of structural images of capitalist society, or in terms of the threats which are inherent in a capitalist order, but in terms of private complaints and demands. Bourgeois parties have been rather good at waging electoral campaigns in such privatized terms. However, such campaign methods may seem less adequate, or at least more dangerous from a bourgeois point of view now that bourgeois parties have themselves for some time occupied government positions, and can be held responsible by those entertaining such piecemeal and private complaints.

Unfortunately, political scientists and political sociologists interested in the issue-orientation of voters have not devoted much attention to studying the conditions which determine which of these two alternative processes of electoral mobilization become dominant, and which electoral appeals can be used to switch such mobilization to being regulated by one process rather than by another, particularly among voters who easily can be mobilized either way.

In the absence of any empirical studies of these crucial theoretical questions of electoral mobilization, we can only venture a few conjectures based on observations on past election campaigns in Sweden, and particularly of the 1976 campaign which led to the first serious defeat of the Social Democratic Party in forty-four years.

In the 1976 election campaign the Social Democrats were fighting an uphill battle, and rather effectively as various empirical studies suggest, at least until the last few weeks of the campaign when the Centre Party forcefully reintroduced the nuclear power issue into the campaign (Petersson, 1978, p. 231). From that point on the Social Democrats started losing votes (Korpi, 1977, p. 149) Petersson (1978, p. 219) has shown that about 55 per cent of those voters who shifted their allegiance from the Social Democratic to the Centre Party did this because of their stand on the nuclear power issue. Certainly there were also other issues involved in this election campaign — such as negative attitudes to state bureaucracy and 'socialism' (Petersson, 1978, Chapter 5, particularly pp. 214f), but such issues have also been involved in earlier elections without causing the defeat of the Social Democratic Party. However, it would seem that the anti-socialist slogans of the bourgeois parties this time were a bit more intense than in most recent elections, because the trade union movement with a somewhat reluctant support from the Social Democratic Party leadership at this time advocated a proposal for the transfer of a certain percentage of company profits to wage-earners' funds.

The social democratic defeat can be diagnosed in the following terms. While a large group of voters in marginal categories among service workers, and even in the middle strata exhibited a structural interpretation of social problems (including the problems of energy production and nuclear power) the Social Democratic Party failed to appeal to the electorate in the structural terms which it could have handled better than any of the bourgeois parties. It never acknowledged the connection between the fears of nuclear power and the fears with respect to the capitalist order which we have documented through our factorial analysis above. Its approach to the nuclear power issue was narrow, piecemeal and technocratic. It did not dare to counter effectively the crudely propagandistic notion of socialism disseminated by the bourgeois parties, by clearly spelling out its own notion of socialism as a democratic way to resolve the contradictions of capitalism which so many marginal voters were aware of — again according to our empirical surveys.

The Centre Party could thus easily reap the fruits of popular concern about nuclear power without ever being pressed to explain how they would be able to abolish nuclear power without radically changing the parameters of the capitalist economy also favoured by the Centre Party — an economy which structurally as well as vocally is demanding more not less nuclear power.

As Jan Lindhagen (1977, p. 490), the social democratic critic of the Social Democratic Party, has emphasized, nuclear power is more than just another piecemeal technological and political issue — even though electoral analysts and politicians tended to treat it in that piecemeal fashion after the 1976 election. Nuclear power symbolizes our technological and economic order; and the opposition to nuclear power therefore must be interpreted partly as a more or less well understood opposition to this order — even though many voters probably also tended to be against nuclear power just on the basis of piecemeal fears.

This connection between fears of nuclear power and fears about our present technological order under capitalism creates a dilemma for the Social Democratic Party in Sweden, and for any other progressive or socialist party which believes that further technological development within and beyond welfare capitalism is necessary as a means of improving conditions of life for the broad masses of the people. This is not the right place to discuss how this dilemma can be resolved. In our final chapter we will briefly return to this problem.

In the second election lost by the Social Democrats – the election held in September 1979 – this party waged a low-key campaign in the public media. With regard to the nuclear power issue the Social Democratic Party leadership seemed to have softened their position somewhat after the Harrisburg nuclear-reactor accident in the spring of 1979, by approving a referendum on this issue to be held in March 1980. The structural issue of wage-earners' funds was again soft-pedalled since a final proposal on this matter would be submitted to trade union and party congresses in 1981, in preparation for the election in 1982. This cautious and defensive posture, in response to bourgeois attacks, could certainly not have impressed many marginal voters. Again, here was another crucial issue which was removed from the agenda of the 1979 election campaign, and referred to future decisions. What remained were a number of piecemeal issues concerning some environmental hazards, taxation of single-family dwellings, a new system of taxation directly on production, the bourgeois mismanagement of the economy, etc.

But the bourgeois parties at the centre of the political spectrum – the Liberal Party and even more the Centre Party – seem to have suffered even more from this low-key campaign, and of course from the lack of popular enthusiasm for the performance of the two bourgeois governments in the period 1976–9. Only the Conservative Party increased its support, and quite substantially (see Figure 15.1).

According to political science experts[8] this move of bourgeois voters to the right should not be interpreted as a reflection of a move toward more conservative attitudes in the electorate. The key for understanding the movement of voters *between* the bourgeois parties, according to these experts, is not electoral attitude change but the changing images of the three bourgeois parties. Whatever bourgeois party happens to convey a more vivid image of dynamic vigour and growth will attract the largest number of bourgeois voters. In the 1976 election the Centre Party seemed to be *the* bourgeois party – vigorous and emphatic in its vindication of an anti-nuclear stand, and its 'decentralist' philosophy. In the 1970 election the Conservative Party was the only bourgeois party which clearly deviated from the low-key campaign pattern which otherwise dominated the scene.

But the story is not complete without pointing out that the Social Democratic Party in the 1979 election in fact increased its support significantly for the first time in ten years. Only about 8000 votes separated the socialist block from winning the election. The main Communist Party (VPK) in spite of, or because of, having been subjected recently to the secession of a Moscow-oriented fraction, increased its support remarkably for the first time in nearly thirty years. Its 'Eurocommunist' orientation is now firmly established.

A Look into the Future

This is the point of departure as we move into the 1980s. After considerable difficulties a new three-party bourgeois cabinet was formed in October 1979 after nearly a month of inter-party negotiations. The bourgeois block now have only a one-vote majority in Parliament. In the very first instance of parliamentary voting — the election of a new Speaker of the House — the bourgeois side lost due to defection, which is very unusual in highly disciplined Swedish party politics. The outlook for this new bourgeois government is not better than for the previous ones, to venture an understatement which will be tested over the next few years.

For the Social Democrats the great task ahead is to tap the largely untapped latent sources of strength which we have documented by our surveys of the social consciousness of the extended working class and part of the middle strata. But as we have indicated elsewhere the existence of a broad-based and realistic awareness of the structural contradictions of mature capitalism is not in itself a guarantee of electoral support for the Social Democratic Party or for the Communists. An awareness of our main social problems can be widespread in the electorate long before sufficiently broad segments accept or even understand the relevance of the problem-solutions suggested by trade unions and political parties.

Thus, it is not a main task for the labour movement to lecture the electorate extensively on their own problems and predicaments, or even on the structural contradictions which generate these predicaments. From their own experience and mass media exposure the voters already know a lot about these things. What is needed on this level is probably just some anecdotal or aphoristic formulations which help to condense and strikingly illuminate the contradictions of our welfare capitalism.

The main task lies on a different level. Trade unions and the labour parties must be able to show that their concrete proposals for wage-earners' funds, new techniques of energy production or whatever, *address themselves* to the problems and structural contradictions which are troubling people. A cognitive link must be established between the problem and the problem solution. This is no mean intellectual and educational task in view of the limited access of the labour movement to the daily press which is dominated by bourgeois papers. This bourgeois hegemony mattered less in the past when traditional working class solidarity and party loyalty were more crucial in mobilizing the labour vote. Now, with a larger number of marginal and floating voters, press and media hegemony is certainly much more crucial than before.

If the labour movement in spite of the cultural constraints of bourgeois hegemony, succeeds in bridging the cognitive gap between problems and problem solutions, and in establishing its new identity in the opening stage of economic democracy, then there are no significant structural constraints preventing a new era of labour party majorities in Parliament, and a stepwise change of Swedish society to resolve the contradictions of welfare capitalism.

Whether or not such an era is initiated in the near future, the Liberal and Centre Parties will have some difficult years ahead, unless they can find a better way to relate to current problems and events than to collaborate with the Conservatives, and to continue falsely exploiting the fears of Eastern European socialism in their relations with Social Democrats. They cannot compete in vigour and force with the Conservatives except by vigorously expounding the non-conservative views of their own, if they have any. They cannot compete with the more dynamic and path-breaking efforts which we expect from the Social Democratic Party unless they find a new and competitive angle to address the growing and structurally conscious extended working class strata which we have called service workers. But this the Liberals and the Centrists cannot do except by moving closer to the Social Democrats, just like TCO, the Centralist Organization of Salaried Employees, has moved closer to LO, the Swedish Confederation of Trade Unions. If they move closer to the new brand of social democracy which is about to emerge, the likelihood of parliamentary collaboration with the Social Democrats increases, with or without coalition governments depending on the temporary strength of the Social Democratic Party in Parliament.

This scenario is rather optimistic with respect to the support we expect for broad-based solutions based essentially on the emerging new identity of the Social Democratic Party. The only caution we have voiced so far is the possibility that the Social Democrats may bungle the intellectual and educational tasks which are now on the agenda of this party. In the next section we will briefly survey some other more objectively based vulnerabilities of the Swedish labour movement.

The Future of Working Class Power: Vulnerabilities

So far we have shown how changes in the productive forces and in degree of unionization have affected the numerical, organizational and consciousness strength of the working class. In our analysis we have emphasized how developments in the economy of production, the increasingly social character of productive forces, routinization of jobs — particularly through the introduction of machines and computers in the occupations of the lower-middle strata — have created conditions for a system-transcending struggle beyond the mere struggle for wages, involving an extended working class which is growing in size rather than diminishing. Finally we have in a rather speculative manner related these changes to what we expect with regard to the political strength of the extended working class as expressed in the electoral support for labour parties.

In this section, however, we will rather emphasize processes which may counteract or undermine the incremental trend in working class power described so far. How realistic is our relative optimism about the present and future strength of the working class? Again our discussion must necessarily be rather speculative because it concerns the future rather than the present or the past. We will discuss processes reducing the numerical size of the extended working class, processes diminishing its organizational strength, and processes dissolving the structural orientation of working class consciousness. None of these processes is inevitable. But they all constitute threats to the future of working class power. If these threats are not counteracted in time, that is before the critical point beyond which the working class and its organizations no longer can mobilize the strength needed to turn the direction of events, these processes may very well run their course. Once again we wish to emphasize the time dimension involved. The problem of timing is extremely important in any working class strategy aiming at a structural transformation of a capitalist society.

With regard to *processes affecting the numerical size of the extended working class* we have pointed out that the diminishing size of the stratum of industrial workers has been more than compensated by the 'proletarianization' of the lower middle strata of service workers. But the question is whether the dynamics of productive forces and division of labour comes to a halt at this point. Is it not possible that this dynamic will continue and produce not an extended working class but a new 'class' of permanently unemployed who at best may receive a 'social wage' for their survival but would definitely be deprived and segregated in relationship to the class of fully employed?

In his analysis of 'late capitalism' Ernest Mandel (1975, p. 180) emphasized the great significance of the falling rate of unemployment during the 1950s and the early 1960s, for the strength of labour in class struggle. Particularly in the wage struggle the diminishing size of the 'reserve army' of unemployed increases the strength of labour. If the rate of unemployment increases again, as it has recently done in a number of European countries, if not in Sweden (see Table 4.1 on p. 47) working class power will again diminish. Increasing robotization and computerization of industrial and clerical work could very well speed up this process of marginalizing labour.

However, as André Gorz (1978) has pointed out, this trend toward robotization and computerization has an element of promise as well as of threat. If the logic of capitalist accumulation is replaced increasingly by the production of use value related to social and human needs, a production which could be financed largely through transfers from the automated sectors of production, then free time, human time and social time could expand with a new content which has not yet been discovered by the labour movement. But in order to take advantage of this promise, the labour movement must soon, very soon, make this discovery, and take the first steps to move beyond the present system of welfare capitalism. Otherwise unemployment, whether or not it is contained by various kinds of make-believe welfare programmes of care or retraining, may reach that critical point beyond which the cohesion and numerical size of the gainfully employed working class has dropped to a level which makes it difficult to wage a struggle against the threats inherent in the anticipated development of automated productive forces.

What has just been said relates very clearly to what we discussed earlier about the responsiveness of labour parties to the structural issues of mature capitalism. Obviously it is not enough to be responsive to the structural issues which are clearly visible today. Future structural changes must be anticipated. The vulnerabilities of the working class and the labour movement generated by such structural changes must be taken into account right now, in order to formulate a strategy for the future.

With regard to *processes affecting the organizational strength of the working class*, we suggest that the attempts which are being made in Sweden and elsewhere to expand not only workers' co-determination but also in the near future to transfer ownership and power over capital from private capitalists to some kind of wage-earners' capital funds, while being expressions of the organizational strength of labour, may in the not so long run undermine this very strength — unless necessary precautions are taken.

The foremost dangers in any system of workers' co-determination, and in the early phase of a transition to wage-earners' fund, are the dangers of union technocracy, the rule of union experts, and a growing gap between the higher ranks of union decision-makers and the rank and file. There are also the dangers of capitalist co-optation; workers' co-determination may imply more obligations than real benefits to labour.

If and when the present capitalist system has been transcended, e.g. by a full-fledged system of wage-earners' funds, the problems of co-optation have disappeared, and the problems of union top level technocracy can be dealt with in due course by rank-and-file members within the system itself.[9] *The critical point is the period of transition to such a system.* It is then, before such a transition has been successfully achieved, that a reduction of the organizational strength of the working class, because of an increasing gap between union officials and the rank-and-file members, is most dangerous from the point of view of the working class.

For instance, the 1976 Act of Workers Co-determination (MBL = *Medbestämmandelagen*), which was designed during the final period of postwar economic growth, is now being applied in a period of protracted stagnation. Thus one of the main functions of MBL at present is to make union representatives participate in decisions on what workers should be fired. Such co-determination would not seem to contribute to the organizational strength of the working class.

But if union participation in administering sick companies within a capitalist order undermines the strength of unions, this process could be at least partly counteracted if trade unions at the same time wage a forceful system-transcending struggle which is sufficiently successful within a sufficiently short time-period. The struggle for wage-earners' funds which is now under way could be such a struggle.

However, the transition to wage-earners' funds which we will discuss at greater length in Part IV, would also seem to imply a number of problems for the organizational strength of the working class. If the transition is too slow, and is not supplemented with other measures to safeguard the power of labour, the capitalist class can easily make a number of counter-moves before the collective control of labour over capital has attained sufficient strength. The disillusionment thereby caused among workers could be a real blow to the organizational strength of labour.

Therefore the great organizational strength achieved up to now by the extended Swedish working class is not a guarantee for the future. This strength can cause its own demise if used mainly to administrate problems arising within the capitalist order, or in the early period of a transition to a system of wage-earners' fund. It would seem that the only way to maintain and improve the organizational strength of labour during the present period of transition is to step up the processes of democratic mobilization and participation of union members in the struggle to change the system and to make the new system emerging more consistent and effective.

A sore point about the organizational strength of labour at present is the fact that the trade union movement until now has paid less attention to external environmental problems than to the work environment and problems of employment and production. Some union spokesmen have juxtaposed the problems of employment with external environmental effects, and emphasized the traditional union concern for employment problems. Among those who consider external environmental effects — including the effects of nuclear power — as a main threat to people like themselves, such a union approach is not likely to maintain trust in union activities. This is reflected in the results of our survey where we find that service workers more frequently trust the ability of environmental or ecology groups to improve their situation than they trust trade unions. The difference in trust is rather small — 68 as against 63 per cent — but contrasts markedly with corresponding figures for industrial workers who trust trade unions much more frequently in this regard than environmental and ecology groups. However, the number of industrial workers is decreasing.

As regards vulnerabilities related to *processes affecting the social consciousness of the extended working class*, we have already pointed out that a traditional working class identity and solidarity are found mainly in the industrial working class, particularly in the older generations. As the number of industrial workers diminishes, and the older generation disappears, the consciousness strength of the working class will depend entirely on what we have called the 'modern' type of working class consciousness — namely an awareness of the structural threats and contradictions of capitalism. Here, as we have already pointed out, the vulnerability of working class strength depends primarily on the responsiveness of trade union and labour party leaders to these structural issues, and on their ability to address their policies and programmes to these structural issues in a manner which can be understood by ordinary people.

But even though service workers exhibit an awareness of the structural threats inherent in capitalism as frequently as industrial workers, the composition of their threat profiles are somewhat different.

Unemployment is seen as the greatest threat by more industrial workers than service workers; for environmental problems it is just the opposite. (See Table A.14 in Appendix I). As we have already pointed out the trade union movement has traditionally emphasized problems of employment and production more than external environmental problems — a position which now must be reassessed in a manner which proves the responsiveness of the labour movement to new issues arising.

Finally one of the more sensitive spots in the social consciousness of service workers in particular, is their image of socialism and the state as indicated in Chapter 14 and in Tables A.I.2 and A.I.3 of Appendix I. Even if service workers realize the threats inherent in the capitalist order, just like industrial workers do, 'socialism' does not seem to inspire great hopes among a majority of service workers. While 68 per cent of service workers see capitalism as a threat, as many as 36 per cent see both capitalism *and* socialism as a threat. Even though part of this negative image of socialism could be a result of the efficiency of bourgeois attempts to link the term socialism exclusively to the Soviet political system, we do not believe that this explains everything. There is the state with its bureaucracy and red tape — and quite probably many of our respondents think that this is what socialism will be like. Even those who rationally find it necessary to embark upon a 'socialist' development, as they conceive it, in order to combat the threats of capitalism, may not be exactly enthusiastic about the increasing influence of the state which they, according to our empirical findings (see p. 173), associate with socialism.

In some strata of the extended working class, socialism is thus not seen as the rising sun sometimes depicted on old trade union banners, but as a 'necessary evil' in a contradictory world. Unless the notion of socialism can be disassociated from its connection with state bureaucracy, as we have suggested in Chapter 11, the social consciousness of the new growing strata of the extended working class will remain a highly vulnerable spot in the working class struggle for new and more appropriate social relations of production.

16 The Strength of Capital: Systemic, Ideological and Political Aspects

We have discussed the strength of labour in terms of numerical strength, organizational strength and strength in terms of consciousness and political support. Several of these dimensions of power are applicable also to capital. Numerical strength, however, capital does not have. Largely because of the concentration and centralization of capital the size of the capitalist class has decreased to a point where today it probably does not count more than a few per cent of the adult population of Sweden. But the capitalist class has other sources of power which effectively compensate for this lack of numerical strength, namely the systemic power engendered by their control over the structure and dynamics of the economy.

However, an attempt to assess empirically capitalist power or strength — these two terms are used as synonyms in the following — cannot be pursued without a brief conceptual clarification of the concept of power and its dimensions.

On Definitions of Power

Concepts of strength and power have been extensively discussed by social scientists. We assume that this discussion is well-known by our readers (see for instance Dahl, 1957; Bachrach and Barratz, 1970; Burns and Buckley, 1976, Chapter 10). Therefore we will in this context limit ourselves to indicating roughly where we stand with regard to the various definitions of power proposed.

Dahl's analysis of power in terms of influence (A has power over B to the extent that he can get B to do something that B would not otherwise do) is at best applicable within a given system and its parameters. It is not particularly helpful in the study of *systemic* power, that is the 'meta-power' to reproduce or restructure a given system (Burns and Buckley, 1976, p. 224). 'Meta-power' is often exercised not through decision-making and influence but through non-decision.

Neither is Dahl's analysis satisfactory in dealing with the vulnerability of power. This is because Dahl defines power in terms of its effects (= influence) rather than in terms of its means or its basis. The vulnerability of power can be observed in terms of variations in its effects but cannot be understood except by reference to the bases or the means of power. In discussing the dimensions of power we also must take account of contextual circumstances affecting the capability to employ given power resources.

In the following we will try to apply the concept of systemic power (meta-power) to an exploration of the question whether the systemic power of the Swedish capitalist class is diminishing or increasing.

Is the Systemic Power of Capitalists Decreasing?

We can answer the question in the heading with reference to Sweden relying largely on data provided in Part II of this book, and also on some of the conceptual distinctions introduced there. But of course these conceptual distinctions have a much more general relevance for an exploration of capitalist systemic power than the case of Sweden alone.

We tentatively define the systemic power of capital in terms of two partly interdependent aspects of a capitalist social formation: (i) the degree of *penetration* of the capitalist mode of production into all the corners of that social formation, and (ii) the degree of *autonomy* (self-financing and self-regulation) of the capitalist sector. The higher the value of both variable (i) and variable (ii) the higher is the systemic power of capital. A high degree of systemic power of capital is thus indicated when the given social formation is greatly dependent on the capitalist mode of production, whereas capitalism itself is less dependent on society, except as a market.

However, on a historical and empirical level the construction of a joint measure of (i) and (ii) is rather problematic not only because of the difficulties of finding or developing commensurable quantitative indicators of (i) and (ii), but also because of variations in certain historical trends of change with regard to these variables.

It can be established both theoretically and empirically (see Part II of this book) that capitalism, up to a point, tends to expand and to penetrate into most segments of the economy of a country in terms of people employed in capitalist production. Later on, however, we find an increasing percentage of employees in the so-called public sector. For the moment we do not count those employed in nationalized industries because it is debatable whether or not they are involved in non-capitalist production, but concentrate on those employed in non-commodified production of services. Leaving aside for the moment the tricky problem whether these non-commodified services should be interpreted as inputs in capitalist production, and assuming that at least a considerable part of these services detract from rather than contribute to capitalist production (see our discussion on p. 115) we envisage a downward trend of capitalist penetration in advanced capitalism. In Figure 16.1 the full-drawn line represents such a trend.

Figure 16.1 Changes over time in capitalist penetration and autonomy; an illustrative case

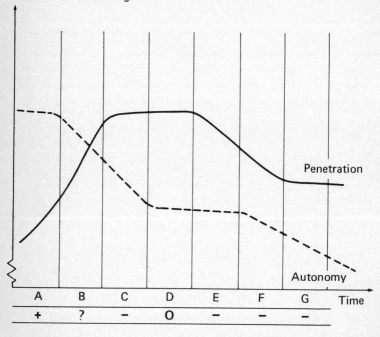

At the same time there is a rather typical trend of diminishing autonomy of purely capitalist production, as industry becomes more dependent on infra-structural state investments, subsidies of various kinds, and dependent also on various state regulations or concessions.[1]

Again we must leave aside here the discussion whether these state interventions are simply inputs into an unchanging capitalist order, or whether they actually are infringements on capitalist autonomy, by asserting, according to our previous discussion in Part II, that capitalism in fact is losing some of its autonomy.

The curves in Figure 16.1 are not representations of any particular empirical case, but rather an illustration of possible and rather typical trends which, however, may have somewhat different shapes in different countries. Figure 16.1 illustrates some of the difficulties but also some of the possibilities of combining trend indicators of variables (i) and (ii) in attempts to assess whether the overall systemic power of capital is increasing or decreasing. In Figure 16.1 we can discern the following cases (A—G):

A: Capitalist autonomy high and stable; capitalist penetration low but increasing. Since autonomy is constant, the problem of how to combine the incommensurable measures of autonomy and penetration does not emerge in this case — at least not if our only task is to answer the question whether the systemic power of capital is increasing or decreasing. Obviously systemic power is increasing in this case, since one of its components exhibits a rising trend while the other is constant.

B: Capitalist autonomy decreasing; capitalist penetration increasing. In this case it is absolutely impossible to say anything definite, based on fact and logic, about trends of development of capitalist systemic power, unless a formula can be found for transforming at least one of the variables involved into an indicator commensurable with the units used to scale the other variable. We leave this task to more competent toolmakers in the field of political economy, and we can do this without endangering our subsequent analysis since contemporary Sweden, like most other advanced capitalist countries, has already passed through this stage of development. We simply do not need the empirical tools required to characterize changes in the systemic power of capital at this stage, for the most important part of our analysis.

C: Capitalist penetration high and stable; capitalist autonomy decreasing. In this case the systemic power of capitalism is decreasing by virtue of the fact that one of its components shows a decreasing trend while the other is constant.

D: Capitalist penetration high and stable; capitalist autonomy relatively low and stable. The systemic power of capitalism in this case is constant at the level terminating the previous stage.

E: Capitalist penetration decreasing; capitalist autonomy rather low and stable. The systemic power of capitalism continues to drop. But due to the fact that this is now caused by decreasing values of another variable than in the previous stage, we cannot say anything definite about whether or not it is falling at a faster or a slower rate than before.

F: Both capitalist penetration and capitalist autonomy are decreasing. In this case we can definitely say that the systemic power of capitalism is falling at a faster rate than in the previous stage since *both* of the component variables exhibit falling trends.

G: Capitalist penetration stable; capitalist autonomy decreasing. This case is structurally identical with stage C, but in this case we can also assert that the systemic power of capitalism is falling at a slower rate than in the previous stage F since now only one of the component variables exhibits a falling trend.

In the lower part of Figure 16.1 we have summarized the changes in the systemic power of capitalism derived from the upper part of the figure. Note that nothing definite can be said about the level of systemic power in stage C in comparison with the terminal phase of stage A due to the impossibility of arriving at definite conclusions about changes in stage B. In the later stages, however, the determination of the relative levels of systemic power is unproblematic. When both of the component variables of systemic power are changing in the same direction or when one of the variables is changing and the other one is constant, the problems of incommensurability mentioned earlier do not prevent us from drawing logical conclusions about changes and relative levels of systemic power.

So far our discussion has been concerned only with a model case for the purpose of illuminating the methodological problems involved in assessing the direction of change of systemic power as we have defined it. Before proceeding to an application of this methodology to the empirical case of present-day Sweden, it would seem theoretically justified to add a third and a fourth component variable to the definition and measurement of changes in systemic power.

We assert that *changes in economic efficiency* as indicated for instance by conventional measures of growth rate, or growth rate adjusted for distributional changes (Chenery et al, 1974, Chapter II) is an important component of changes in the systemic power of capitalism: the more efficient capitalism is in delivering economic growth, preferably with a more equitable distribution of economic resources, the greater its systemic power, other things being equal. As we will soon indicate this statement is not entirely unproblematic, however.

The fourth and final component of capitalist systemic power concerns the *ability to discipline labour*. Access to repressive measures which anyway often have unpredictable double-edged effects will not be considered here, since this factor is of limited importance in Sweden.[2] The threat of unemployment generated in the labour market, and the existence of a large 'reserve army' of unemployed, is probably the most effective means available to capital in disciplining labour.

We can now add changes in the third and fourth components of capitalist systemic power to the changes indicated by plus and minus signs in the lower part of Figure 16.1 by using the same technique suggested for combining the first two components. We can then arrive at conclusions concerning the joint effects of all four components on capitalist systemic power.

In order to assess recent changes in the systemic power of capitalism in Sweden we should thus look at the trends of change in capitalist penetration, capitalist autonomy, economic growth and unemployment. Only if these trends turn out to move in opposite directions do we face the problems of incommensurability mentioned above. If we disregard short-term fluctuations and pay attention only to long-term trends, our data, fortunately, do not confront us with problems of that nature.

Official statistical figures on occupational distribution trends (briefly summarized on pp. 52f), more precisely on percentages employed in the capitalist and public sectors, clearly show that percentages employed in the capitalist sector culminated in the 1960s, and in fact for some time have exhibited a falling trend, while percentages employed in the public sector have been rising rapidly. Even if we allow for reasonable assumptions about the proportion of public services to be considered inputs into the capitalist sector, we cannot find support for any assertion that capitalist penetration has been increasing recently. In the absence of more precise estimates of the proportion of public services which should be considered inputs into the capitalist sector, our most conservative estimate leads to the conclusion that capitalist penetration has been approximately constant for the last fifteen years. But most probably it has been decreasing. Our strongest argument for this assessment is the increase of public services which are clearly improductive from a capitalist point of view, as indicated not only by spokesmen of Swedish capital but also by the fact that other capitalist states less influenced by a strong labour movement have found them unnecessary (see our discussion on pp. 115 and 119).

With regard to trends concerning *capitalist autonomy* our data on the magnitude and character of state subsidies to industry after 1964 (see p. 116f) would seem to indicate a falling trend for this component of capitalist systemic power. Another indicator of capitalist autonomy is financial solidity. In the early 1960s the average solidity of Swedish firms, that is the relationship between equity capital and total capital, was just above 40 per cent; in the early 1970s it was just about 30 per cent (Meidner et al, 1976, p. 215). In 1976 the average solidity of the 200 largest companies in Sweden was 24 per cent *(Veckans Affärer,* 26/77).

The decreasing solidity of companies reduces the freedom of action of private capital, and increases the dependency on external sources of capital such as the state. On this particular point it would seem possible for the state to exert some control over the use of capital, by imposing certain conditions that restrict the freedom of movement of equity capital. But this does not affect the freedom of action of more solid companies, of course, and of those companies who can find other external sources of financing than the state.

Therefore it would be wrong to make exaggerated claims about the weaknesses of systemic power of Swedish capital. Swedish capitalism is still quite strong. But as far as the first two components of its systemic power are concerned, it is obvious that the systemic power of capital in Sweden has been falling for the last ten or fifteen years.

The third component of capitalist systemic power — the growth rate of the economy — has failed to show any long-term tendency to rise or even to stay constant. Ever since the late 1960s the Swedish growth rate has been falling (see Table 16.1):

Table 16.1: **Yearly percentage growth of Swedish GNP from 1960 to 1970 as measured from the production side**

1960−5	5.3
1965−70	3.8
1970−4	3.0
1974−7	0.3

Source: DsJu 1979:1, p. 57.

After many decades of sustained economic growth in Sweden, interrupted only by regular recessions of a 'normal' nature, we have now for a number of years found ourselves in an 'abnormal' period of prolonged recession with stagflation. In 'normal' recessions within a longer period of sustained economic growth, it was rather natural for a government concerned with welfare redistributions to stimulate the economy without violating the basic rules of market conformity in order to provide for an expanding tax base for the financing of welfare measures. Social democratic welfare policies *depended* on the growth of capital. Capital thus possessed a great deal of bargaining power in exhorting the state to facilitate its growth. Therefore we cannot flatly state, as we have done before, that the systemic power of capital increases in a linear fashion with the rate of economic growth. Within longer periods of sustained economic growth we may rather find that capitalist systemic power increases even more in shorter periods of 'normal' recession, particularly in countries which are highly dependent on its export trade. Sven Lindqvist (1974, p. 190) has pointed out this 'inversion effect' in Latin American countries exhibiting a large component of export in their production. Because the whole country depends greatly on export production in these countries, export companies can apply a great deal of pressure on the state to fulfil their demands. However this seemingly paradoxical 'inversion effect' — that is an increase of capitalist systemic power when GNP shows a decline — seems less likely in prolonged 'abnormal' recessions, particularly in countries with relatively strong states such as Sweden.

The 'abnormal' recession and stagflation in the years after 1975 would seem to illustrate the inability of capitalist dynamics, including state interventions, to find a way out of a prolonged crisis. It highlights the fiscal crisis of the interventionist state (O'Connor, 1973), and it gives increasing visibility to the threat implied by the trend for Swedish companies increasingly to invest abroad rather than at home (see p. 174f). The present situation would therefore seem to create distrust in capitalism among larger segments of the population. Such distrust is reported even among leading personalities and spokesmen of the international and Swedish capitalist class itself (Greenspan, 1977; af Trolle, 1978). It would seem that this 'abnormal' context makes it more difficult for the business community to use its remaining systemic power as effectively, in some respects, as in 'normal' recessions. Still, of course, the state 'depends' on capital for maintaining social welfare measures; but it cannot at present, to the same extent, count on capital to deliver the goods. Capital no longer has the bargaining power which follows from a trust in its ability to deliver growth.

And the strength that Swedish capital can maintain through investments abroad, and through the growing influence of investment companies and capital concentration may turn out to be a hollow strength, because these trends increase the public visibility of basically anti-social attributes of capitalist relations of production, particularly in the present period of prolonged recession when the most attractive asset of capitalism — its capacity for economic growth — is left in doubt. Slight improvements in the growth rate may not be sufficient to dispel doubts of this nature. Therefore, nether empirical data nor theoretical considerations on changes in Swedish economic growth in recent years lend any credibility to assertions that this third component presently contributes to strengthening the systemic power of Swedish capital. On the contrary.

The same conclusion applies, but perhaps less strongly, with regard to the fourth component of capitalist systemic power, namely unemployment. Open unemployment did increase in the first few years of the bourgeois government which was seated in 1976, but in an international perspective the Swedish 'reserve army' is still very small. All the bourgeois parties in Sweden have come to accept the need to give priority to the fight against unemployment. Social Democrats have voiced suspicions about the sincerity of the Conservative stand on this issue, but the Liberal and the Centre Party ministers in charge of Labour and Industry in the bourgeois government of 1976 certainly did whatever they could to reduce unemployment, with policies adopted largely from previous social democratic governments. This was even publicly acknowledged at that time by the leader of the Social Democratic Party, Olof Palme, even though he, naturally, maintained that the Social Democrats could have done an even better job. For reasons to be listed in the next section no Swedish politician with a normal sense of self-preservation will accept the levels of unemployment found for instance in the USA, England, France, West Germany and Italy (see Table 4.1).

Considering all four components of capitalist systemic power, our conclusion is clear: the systemic power of Swedish capital has been falling during the last ten or fifteen years, and particularly after 1976.

Political and Ideological Sources of Strength and Weakness of Capital

In our previous discussion of declining economic growth we mentioned a subjective aspect of capitalist power: the trust or distrust in capital, and in its ability to efficiently deliver economic growth.

Later on we will present some empirical data on the trust or distrust among Swedish capitalists — more precisely a sample of company-board members and managing directors — with regard to their own influence and power relative to state and labour. Here we will present a more general view of ideological themes and political sentiments among leading bourgeois politicians who predominantly support the 'market economy', that is the capitalist order, in spite of the fact that no modern Swedish government has gone as far as the bourgeois government after 1976 in breaking the 'rules of the capitalist game' by providing state subsidies and socializing the losses of industry, and generally by preventing the adjustment mechanisms of the market to work it all out on their own.

This discrepancy between a verbal homage to the forces of the market economy, and a discrepant political practice, could be interpreted as a sign of ideological weakness. But to attribute this weakness only to the compelling nature of a 'temporary' economic crisis calling for extraordinary and exceptional political action or to explain it in a more Marxist fashion by indicating that the contradictions of current capitalism generates a contradictory bourgeois politics, is not sufficient.

The present ideological inconsistencies of some bourgeois parties — particularly the Liberal and Centre Parties in the middle of the political spectrum — are no doubt also a result of the strength of the Swedish labour and trade union movement, and to the fact that these parties in 1976 were supported by significant segments of voters organized in LO and TCO, the blue-collar and white-collar unions.[3] The Liberal and Centre Parties cannot afford to antagonize these voters. The role of TCO is particularly important on this point. As we have indicated earlier (p. 162f), this organization has moved closer to LO not only in terms of its stand on a number of issues, but also in synchronizing and co-ordinating its collective bargaining with its sister-organization of blue-collar workers.

At a time when Mrs Thatcher in United Kingdom and Monsieur Barre in France are calling for a return to a more pure or 'raw' capitalism, and have initiated a dismounting of significant welfare institutions, and at a time when the chairman of the Swedish Employers' Confederation (SAF) makes similar appeals (see p. 121), we find leading liberal and Centre Party politicians and commentators voicing opinions in a quite different direction. Realizing the political hazards in seriously challenging the views of LO and TCO in matters of concern to employees, these two parties in the middle have moved perceptively closer to the standpoints of these two union organizations without in any way whole-heartedly identifying themselves with their views. This is obvious not only with regard to the question of unemployment, as mentioned above, but also to some extent with respect to the more controversial questions of workers' co-determination and wage-earners' funds.

While the former Liberal Party leadership in the 1960s and early 1970s vocally espoused individual profit-sharing, which was opposed by LO, and while a former Liberal Party leader, Per Ahlmark, in a much publicized statement explained that he could find no better place for significant trade union proposals than the waste-paper basket, the present Liberal Party leadership has expressed quite different views. It has expressed cautious support for collective wage-earners' funds with some added provisions for individual utilization of such collective arrangements. This is a far cry from the previous denunciation of collective arrangements, and the purely individual profit-sharing schemes favoured earlier by the Liberal Party. The favourable even if tentative attitude of the TCO-leadership to some kind of collective wage-earners' funds (TCO, 1978) with some restricted individual rights of withdrawal, is likely to have influenced the Liberal Party on this point. Traditionally this party has recruited quite a large portion of its voters from the white-collar strata.

But the Liberal Party is still quite strong in its support for a market economy — much more so than the Centre Party, its closest companion in the three-party bourgeois government which collapsed in October 1978 because of the nuclear-power issue. The liberal standpoint on the crucial role of the market economy was reiterated in a Government Bill on Industrial Policy in the spring 1979. It also seems as if the new role of the Liberal Party as the basis of a minority cabinet between October 1978 and September 1979 again made it more reluctant to express views on the role of employees and wage-earners' funds in economic development. Our impression (which must be substantiated by future research) is that the Liberal Party has retreated to its traditional generalizations about the significant role of market forces, and refused to voice publicly its recently expressed interest in wage-earners' funds.

The Centre Party, on the other hand, has become more explicit and positive with regard to wage-earners' funds after it left the three-party cabinet in October 1978. Earlier, however, the leader of the Centre Party, Thorbjörn Fälldin, Prime Minister in Sweden's first bourgeois government since 1932, rather brusquely rejected the whole idea of wage-earners' funds, falsely labelling it as a step in the direction of Eastern European totalitarian state-socialism. Later on Nils Åsling, Centre Party Minister of Industry in that government, similarly rejecting the idea of wage-earners' funds, instead proposed a more extensive and directed use of the giant National Pension Insurance Fund (AP-fonden) for crucial investments in Swedish industry. The irony of Åsling's proposal was not only that the Centre Party most emphatically fought the creation of these pension insurance funds in the late 1950s when they were introduced by a social democratic government which at the time was under heavy bourgeois fire for its creeping socialist centralization of the economy. Another irony was that Åsling, being a leading proponent of a party always advertising its belief in 'decentralization', still preferred the 'creeping socialist centralization of the economy' implied by this particular use of the National Pension Insurance Funds, rather than the building of a more decentralized system of wage-earners' funds for this purpose.

Åsling's main arguments for rejecting wage-earners' funds at that time, and for recommending a more extensive use of centralized national pension funds for investment purposes was that the use of these pension funds would guarantee a more adequate democratic control of such investments through the politically chosen representatives seated on the boards of these several funds. Wage-earners' funds under union control would undermine political democracy, according to Åsling. Again it is ironic that Åsling and his party rarely if ever questioned the capitalist system which always had reserved crucial investment decisions for itself without any substantial democratic control. How could political democracy in the economic context possibly be undermined by wage-earners' funds in a situation where democratically elected political bodies had virtually no control over the use of profits and the making of investments?

We will return to the important problematic indicated by Åsling's somewhat inconsistent but still quite interesting early interventions in the debate about wage-earners' funds in the concluding part of this book. Here it is more relevant simply to report the changing views of the Centre Party on this issue after it left government, as they have been revealed in a book by Åsling on *Industrial Crisis and Renewal* published in the summer of 1979, a few months before the election in September that year.

> Wage-earners' funds in one form or another is an inescapable element of the solidaristic wage-policy which the trade union movement has vindicated. In principle wage-earners' funds are necessary in a modern industrial society which exhibits both growing needs for capital resources in industrial development and strong demands from union organizations concerning the participation of employees in capital formation. The re-evaluation of the role of labour in economic life which has taken place

simultaneously with the emergence of a new perspective on capital implies a self-evident democratic right for employees in a firm to have a share in the growth of wealth in that firm.

(p. 114)

Later on Åsling emphasizes the role of greater stability in economic life in order to create a better climate for investments, and adds that this probably presupposes a system of wage-earners' funds which safeguards collective capital formation and compensates for the effects of the solidaristic wage policy maintained by the trade union movement (p. 121).

These recent statements by Åsling should not be construed as a complete change of the Centre Party's position on wage-earners' funds. In his book Åsling still defends his earlier proposal on the use of national pension funds. He also mentions individual profit-sharing with approval, but rather vaguely with regard to new 'employees co-operatives' (whatever that is supposed to mean) fashioned after the widespread Swedish system of farmers' producers' co-operatives. Trade union and social democratic proposals for wage-earners' funds are still criticized by Åsling, but in a less high-pitched ideological manner than Fälldin did in his references to Eastern European state socialism. What emerges in Åsling's book is a variety of quite different proposals supposed to supplement each other in what he calls a 'synthesis'. From our point of view the most important aspect of Asling's book is that the Centre Party here for the first time seems to take wage-earners' funds seriously.

Åsling is also adamant in his criticism of 'market forces' (1979, pp. 109f). These, he maintains, may operate satisfactorily on the large and diversified markets of the North American continent, because of the rather limited dependency of the US economy on the rest of the world. But in a small country such as Sweden with its extensive dependency on international trade, market forces are unable to generate a balanced outcome satisfactory to the interests of various groups in Sweden, he asserts.

The market economy should be maintained wherever possible, but within the framework of strict rules and an active government planning of the economy. This planning should involve regional balance and decentralization. If the state does not actively intervene in such a manner in the play of market forces, the damaging social effects of such forces may eventually give rise to demands for a much more centralized and bureaucratic form of state planning than would have been necessary if the state had intervened more intelligently and actively earlier, according to Åsling.

In his evaluation of the role of market forces and state planning, Åsling comes much closer to the present position of the Social Democratic Party than to the Liberals. As a result it would seem that references to the 'self-healing forces of the market' which conservative and some liberal politicians still make, are becoming increasingly unsuitable for establishing the legitimacy of the present economic system (cf. Lane, 1977).

The significance of these accounts of Centre and Liberal Party standpoints even to readers who lack any interest in the details of Swedish politics is twofold. Firstly, they indicate that bourgeois parties of the centre in an advanced capitalist country, with a strong and comparatively radical trade union movement involving white-collar as well as blue-collar employees, to some extent will adjust their views on labour issues to incorporate at least some aspects of the proposals made by trade union organizations, in order not to antagonize potential voter support among employees. Secondly, this means that capital now less than before, when TCO was weaker and less close to LO, can count on the bourgeois parties in the centre to act as ideological and political tools of capital. In these respects the ideological and political strength of capital would thus seem to be diminishing in spite of the fact that bourgeois parties took over government posts in 1976 after forty-four years of social democratic government.

However, in the 1979 election campaign the Liberal and Centre Parties were careful not to reveal any changes in their position with regard to wage-earners' funds. This was probably because public opinion polls had indicated a move of voters toward the Conservative Party at the expense of the Centre and Liberal Parties. Probably in order to contain this defection toward the Conservatives these parties did partly revert to older positions on the issues of wage-earners' funds. But they did not succeed: they lost votes both to the right and the left (see above, p. 194). However, once this issue is introduced as a matter for the consideration of Parliament in the early 1980s the bourgeois parties in the centre of the political spectrum must consider it more seriously than in election campaigns.

Finally, we must admit that our account of Liberal and Centre Party standpoints in this section are more journalistic than strictly scientific. This was unavoidable because many of the changes reported here took place during the last few months before completion of this manuscript. However, we have checked our interpretations with political commentators who are in closer touch with current affairs than ourselves.

In the next chapter we will base our interpretations and conclusions on somewhat better even if not quite as recent empirical evidence collected by ourselves.

17 Subjective Aspects of Relationships between Capital, Labour and State

Having drawn attention to some of the more objective aspects of capitalist systemic power, and to some recent changes in Liberal and Centre Party standpoints which may influence the political strength of capital, we will now go on to look at more subjective ideological elements among company-board members in a sample survey of fifty Swedish companies.

We have carried out a questionnaire of board members of companies in Stockholm and Kopparberg provinces; the same companies were covered in our survey of employees reported above. Our board member survey was carried out in March 1977 in a period of unusually bitter collective bargaining between the Swedish Employers' Confederation (SAF) and central trade union organizations. Within the prevailing system of private ownership of the means of production almost all the firms included in our survey are joint stock companies in which shareholders elect a board, which appoints a managing director. However, according to the Act of 1972 Relating to Board Representation for the Employees in Joint Stock Companies, as amended in July 1976, local unions have a right to appoint two board members, and alternates, in joint stock companies having at least twenty-five employees. Our survey includes these union-appointed board members as well as other board members and managing directors, altogether 165 respondents. More details about the sample are provided in Appendix II (p. 323).

Members of company boards were asked the same question about various threats against the development of Sweden that we used in our sample of employees in these companies (see above p. 172f). In Figure 17.1 we have combined our findings on employees and on company board members. The latter have been divided into trade union representatives on the board, and those representing capital (managing directors and representatives of shareholders).

On the average our representatives of capital perceive lower levels of threat than union representatives or employees. Two obvious exceptions

Figure 17.1 Subjective threat awareness by categories of respondents; means for employees, company board members appointed by the local union (union), and company board members appointed by shareholders meeting plus managing directors (capital). Survey question asked: 'We sometimes hear about different factors which may THREATEN development. A number of possible threats are listed below. Please indicate to what extent (none, some or big) each factor may threaten people in your position'

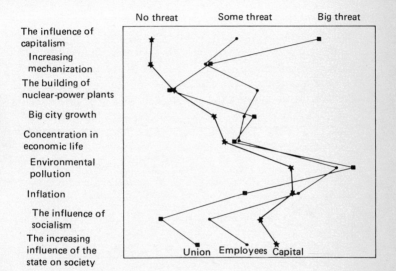

are the threat of increasing state interventions, and the threat of socialist influence where representatives of capital see threats but employees and trade union representatives hardly see any. Capitalism, not surprisingly, is considered to be no threat at all by representatives of capital whereas it is considered a considerable threat by union representatives, and as some threat by employees.

However, as implied by our preceding discussion of dimensions of capitalist power (Chapter 16), we are here primarily looking for cracks in the ideological facade of capitalism. Incongruities between the cognitive elements of such an ideology, or between such cognitive elements and corresponding aspects of objective realities are indicators of such cracks. Our findings on threat perception alone cannot provide a sufficient empirical basis for establishing the existence of such 'cracks', but these findings at least provide a convenient starting-point for our analysis. Of particular interest here are the threats perceived with regard to concentration of economic power, environmental pollution, inflation and state interventions.

Even though capital concentration is not on the average perceived to be a great threat by representatives of capital, it is considered some threat by quite a number. Representatives of capital come rather close to union representatives and employees in the assessment of this particular threat. Because concentration, objectively speaking, is a regular feature of mature capitalism there is an incongruity between the perception of concentration as a threat, and the fact that representatives of capital see no threat in capitalism itself. Furthermore, the admission that environmental pollution is a considerable threat (together with the threat of inflation this threat in fact is seen as the greatest threat of all by representatives of capital) is another source of incongruity, because environmental pollution is an obvious effect of the industrial activity for which capitalists are responsible.

But the responsibility for initiating measures to reduce environmental pollution rests mainly with the state (see below p. 242f). Still representatives of capital view state interventions as a considerable threat as well. If the reduction of industrial pollution were the main or only task of state interventions, then the simultaneous perception of pollution and state interventions as considerable threats would have been very incongruous indeed. But state interventions have other aims as well. Therefore our main conclusion on this is that cognitive congruity can be maintained in this limited context only by carefully differentiating (Abelson, 1959) between the various tasks of the state, and by emphasizing other aspects than state pollution control in attributing a considerable threat to increasing state interventions. But in a wider context incongruity may re-emerge. Probably there is an isolation of the cognitive elements involved, more precisely a cognitive isolation between the blanket disapproval of state interventions in response to our threat questions, and the more differentiated views on the state held by representatives of capital in response to other questions to be reported later on.[1] Such a cognitive isolation which helps to maintain cognitive congruity in limited and isolated cognitive units may, however, easily break up under the pressures of entrepreneurial and political practice.

Labour Law and Management

Management decisions take place within the framework of company law and labour law. Company law has not changed much in recent years. Labour law has changed a great deal. A great deal of labour legislation could be conceived of as a codification and explication of previous practice established through negotiated agreements between the main actors on the labour market. A typical sequence is the following. After a period of more or less satisfactory operation, important agreements negotiated between the parties on the labour market achieve legal status by political decision-making in Parliament. On issues not regulated by law – and these no doubt form the great majority of cases – the employer traditionally has had the prerogative to decide. A cornerstone of management ideology is that ownership entitles such prerogatives. Even though such prerogatives have not been codified in Swedish law, but only in Paragraph 32 in the statutes of SAF, they have been considered as binding. In the following we will see to what extent this cornerstone has been gradually displaced. In applying such a perspective of change we should not forget, however, that the baseline from which such change should be evaluated is the proposition that the employer has the exclusive prerogative to make all significant decisions on the content of production, investments, the hiring and firing of workers, distribution of work, and relations to external agents such as customers and suppliers.

In this context we cannot possibly survey the history of Swedish labour law. Here are just a few examples relating to the questions we have asked in our survey. The Industrial Safety Act of 1974 greatly expanded the powers of union-appointed safety stewards. Safety stewards now have a right to be released from their jobs, on their own initiative, to be able to carry out the functions of a safety steward; they have the right to obtain access to documents that are relevant for their stewardship, and the right to decide on their own initiative to order a work stoppage if they consider the work to be an immediate and serious hazard to the life or health of workers, unless the hazard can be immediately removed. The prerogative of interpretation of what constitutes a hazard belongs to the safety steward, not to the employer. In order to safeguard further the integrity of the safety steward, the legislators – a majority of social democratic MPs responding to a social democratic government bill – made explicit that no safety steward can be sued for economic losses by the company even if his decision to order a work stoppage eventually turns out to lack a sound foundation. A safety steward can thus call for a work stoppage even if he only reasonably *suspects* a hazard, without fearing later demands for compensation of losses, and may thus initiate a careful study of the suspected hazards by the relevant government authority, the National Swedish Workers Safety Board.

Another example of the sequence from negotiated agreement to law is the Employment Security Act of 1974. Already in the Basic Agreement

(*Huvudavtalet*) between SAF and LO of 1938 it was specified that disputes concerning notices of termination, and dismissal, should be resolved by *negotiations*. In 1964 this agreement was amended to include the requirement that notice of termination must be based on *reasonable grounds*. The 1974 Act on Employment Security made this a *legal obligation*. This legislation has made it possible for employees, through their unions, to influence significant aspects of the employment policy of companies, with less dependence on their current bargaining power.

The Acts mentioned so far have contributed to diminishing but not eliminating the prerogative of capital in labour—management relations; and such legislation more generally has typically been initiated by union struggle and negotiated agreements between the main actors on the labour market.

On one point, however, SAF has consistently and stubbornly refused to negotiate their prerogatives; it has claimed an exclusive right for the management to decide on investments, on the direction of production and distribution of work. Originally these prerogatives were accepted by the trade union organization LO as part of the so-called December compromise of 1905. This compromise implied that SAF, the Swedish Employers' Confederation, recognized LO as a partner in collective agreements, in return for LO's acceptance of these prerogatives. SAF safeguarded these prerogatives by explicitly establishing in its statutes (Paragraph 32) that SAF members are prohibited from negotiating any questions of this nature, as indicated above. The Act of July 1976 on Co-determination at Work, valid from 1 January 1977, has removed this prerogative, however, and made all the questions concerned negotiable. This Act, then, does not *prescribe* co-determination but makes it possible to *negotiate* co-determination on most issues which previously were included in the prerogatives of management. In other words this Act has removed the obstacle to negotiated agreements contained in the statutes of SAF; it has thus initiated the characteristic sequence of negotiated agreements, a period of practical tests of the agreement, and perhaps in the future some final legislation prescribing co-determination. It has thus maintained the traditional pattern of 'development from below' which is characteristic of Swedish Labour Law.

As for the present the main significance of the Act on Co-determination at Work is that it has vastly expanded the negotiable area. In fact employers have a so-called primary obligation to negotiate with unions before any decisions are made about important changes at the place of work. The primary obligation to negotiate also includes important changes for individual employees — for instance significant changes in his work situation. Furthermore, the employer is obliged to negotiate matters on demand from the trade union organization. Wherever negotiations have been initiated along the lines indicated above, the employer is not allowed to implement his plans until negotiations have been concluded. The employer is also obliged to inform unions about various economic and technical aspects of production at his enterprise, and about guidelines for personnel policy.

The primary aim of this Act is to create favourable conditions for collective agreements about workers' co-determination. The Act does not specify any limitations for such agreements; in principle such an agreement can include any issues concerning labour–management relations, that is also questions concerning management itself.

In case of disputes about the interpretation of rules or agreements regulating the relationship of labour and management, management has traditionally had the prerogative of interpretation. This has now been changed: in disputes about the implementation of collective agreements on co-determination the unions now have this prerogative.

But since the Act as such only expands the area of negotiation, and prescribes certain rules about the initiation and interpretation of agreements on co-determination, its results in practice depend entirely on the bargaining power of the parties involved. If unions are in a weaker position from the point of view of their bargaining power, as they have been for the last few years, this new law may have very limited effects indeed. So far this is the case. Trade union organizations have not been able to force the organization of employers to any acceptable agreement on workers' co-determination in private industry since this new Act came into play in 1977. As a result labour demands for a more direct, legislated control over capital, for instance in the form of so-called wage-earners' capital funds (see Part IV) have become more vocal.

In our survey of company board members we asked a number of questions intended to assess how these members view the actual distribution of influence between representatives of capital and of labour on a number of issues relating to the kind of legislation we have just sketchily described.

Assessment of the Actual Influence of Capital and Labour within Enterprises

Often power-holders prudishly reject any suggestion that they hold power. But this is probably not only a matter of prudery. The assessment of relative influence or power is a complicated matter. A managing

To what extent did the bodies listed below *actually*, in 1976, have an influence on decisions within your firm on the following topics. Please answer by allocating 10 'scores of influence' among the different bodies.

	The shareholders' meeting	The board	The managing director	The employees	The state	'Union'	Total
Decisions concerning							
Employment policy	___ +	___ +	___ +	___ +	___ +	___ =	10
Investments	___ +	___ +	___ +	___ +	___ +	___ =	10
Appointment of managers/directors	___ +	___ +	___ +	___ +	___ +	___ =	10
Uses of profit	___ +	___ +	___ +	___ +	___ +	___ =	10
Questions concerning work environment	___ +	___ +	___ +	___ +	___ +	___ =	10
The direction and distribution of work	___ +	___ +	___ +	___ +	___ +	___ =	10
Other aspects of production	___ +	___ +	___ +	___ +	___ +	___ =	10

director or a union representative on a company board may therefore find it difficult to give a straight answer about his relative influence as regards various aspects of labour—management relations, even if he can at length describe the decision-making process itself. However, for our analytic purposes we have constructed a relatively simple type of question asking board members to allocate ten 'scores of influence' among various agents of capital and labour, and the state, with reference to their influence over decisions in a number of specified areas. More precisely our question was designed as illustrated opposite.

Naturally some valuable information is lost when such a complex reality as influence over decisions is forced into a distribution of numerical scores among various agents. But the advantages of obtaining numerical measures of relative influence are so great, and our research aim on this point limited enough to compensate for the disadvantages. Our aim is twofold: firstly to establish subjective assessments of the *actual* situation with regard to relative influence over decisions in a number of areas covered by legislation in 1976, the year before the Act on workers' co-determination was put into force, and secondly to provide a base for comparisons with assessments of *desirable* changes in relative influence.

Our findings about assessments of the actual distribution of influence have been summarized in Figure 17.2. In this figure we have excluded the influence of the state because it is less extensive and important in this particular context. To some extent the figure speaks for itself. One obvious feature is the virtually complete agreement among various categories of board members for the ranking of decision areas about the relative influence of capital and labour.

However, the influence of capital can reasonably be assumed to be greater than indicated *prima facie* in Figure 17.2. The various areas of influence have different weights. Generally speaking the areas represented closer to the top of the diagram — where company board members agree that capital is most influential — simply are more crucial. Decisions in these areas condition and limit the range of decisions which can be made in the areas indicated in the lower parts of the diagram. With the terminology we have used earlier to distinguish the various dimensions of strength of capital in the economy as a whole, we can say that there is a systemic power of capital also within single enterprises.

Decisions about what investments to make are limited by 'higher' decisions on how to use company profits; and capital has a virtually exclusive control over these higher decisions, as indicated in the diagram. Similarly 'employment policies' are limited by decisions on

Figure 17.2 Assessments of the distribution of influence within firms between the sectors of capital *(the shareholders' meeting, the board and the managing director) and of* labour *(the employees and the union) with regard to a number of decision-making topics. These assessments were made by managing directors* (Man. dir.), *board members appointed by the shareholders' meeting* (Board), *and board members appointed by the local union* (Union).

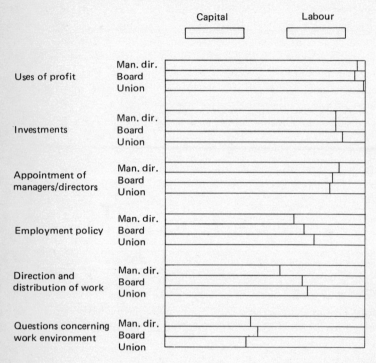

investments. For all practical purposes, the size and range of employment has been settled by 'higher' decisions on investments; and also matters relating to the skills, experience and other qualifications of needed labour power are thus determined. Within the limits thus set, subordinate personnel may counsel with representatives of labour about decisions on employment. The influence of labour on employment policies as perceived by company board members, is not insignificant, but it must be seen as being exercised within the limits set by the systemic power of capital within the enterprise through decisions on crucial systemic issues such as the use of profit and the making of investments.

It is also possible that the term 'employment policy' has been interpreted by our respondents as relating mainly to dismissal, notice of termination and lay-off; and on these points labour unions have a significant influence, according to law and collective agreements. Still representatives of capital, more precisely managing directors, have a greater influence on employment policy, according to our findings, even apart from the systemic power involved.

'Direction and distribution of work' similarly are conditioned by decisions on higher levels, higher both in the company hierarchy and in Figure 17.2; the influence of labour can be exercised only within the limits thus determined from above. And our respondents clearly estimated this influence to be significantly less than the influence of capital.

Representatives of both capital and labour agree, however, that labour has won considerable influence over matters relating to the work environment. In fact all three categories of board members assess the influence of labour as being slightly larger than the influence of capital on this point. Thus it would not seem to be a matter of labour over-estimating its own influence. In fact labour estimates of its own influence are more conservative than the estimates of labour influence made by the two other categories of board members with respect to all the other areas of influence — except influence on the appointment of directors.

Earlier on we have indicated the importance of legislation on labour-appointed safety stewards whose main task is to care for matters relating to the work environment. It would seem that this legislation, backed by unions and the Social Democratic Labour Party, has succeeded to break the systemic power of capital within enterprises at least on this point. Most of the limits set on the activities and decisions of safety stewards by the systemic power of capital before this new legislation was enacted have been removed. We will soon report findings which indicate that representatives of capital on company boards view this legislation as having gone too far.

The significance of our findings on the influence of labour on matters of work environment is that political, legislative action indeed can change the balance of power between capital and labour — if legislation moves beyond formulas of collective bargaining power, and allocates *legislated* power to labour. In this regard the new statutes on labour safety stewards can be contrasted with the Act on workers' co-determination which only allows labour to collectively *negotiate* workers' co-determination.

Until now we have spoken of 'the influence of capital' without distinguishing the relative influence of the annual shareholders' meeting, the company board and the managing director. The influence of capital has been calculated as the sum total of influence of these three categories.

By analysing their relative influence separately, we can establish that the shareholders' meeting has some influence only over the use of profits; their influence over investments, appointment of the managing director, personnel policy, etc. is negligible or zero.

With regard to the use of profits our respondents attribute about 20 per cent of the influence of *capital* to the annual shareholders' meeting, but 60 per cent to the company board appointed by that meeting, and 20 per cent to the managing director. However, in terms of systemic power which is most likely to be exercised in potential or actual crisis situations, the influence of shareholders is likely to be considerably larger. A potential crisis thus may cause a realization of shares endangering the financial situation of the company; and a crisis furthermore may be seen as an indication of the incompetence of the board and the director, and result in their replacement by new people.

With regard to decisions on dividends of shares, recent legislation has introduced certain limits on the power of the annual shareholders' meetings (Government Bill, 1975:103, p. 237). The shareholders' meeting is not 'normally' allowed to decide larger dividends than those proposed by the company board. This legislation has been motivated by the assumption that the board generally is more concerned with the long-term interests of company consolidation and stable employment, while individual shareholders are more likely to consider short-term interests of maximum gain from their capital investments.

Assessment of the Ideal Distribution of Influence between Capital and Labour

The findings reported in the previous section were not intended to tap the *ideology* of influence among representatives of capital and labour, but to assess the *actual* distribution of influence within enterprises in 1976, the year before the law on workers' co-determination came into force, and the year before our survey of company board members was carried out. However, this assessment of the *actual* distribution of influence provides a suitable reference point for establishing the ideological positions of board members on the *desirable* distribution of influence between capital and labour, and the state as the case may be. Data on the desirable or 'ideal' distribution of influence were collected with a question designed in the same fashion as the previous question on the actual distribution of influence. But the question now asked for an assessment of the 'most appropriate' distribution of influence between capital, labour and the state. Just as in the previous section on the *actual* distribution of influence, we here eliminate the relative influence of the state from our report on the ideal distribution. On the level of the single enterprise, the influence of the state is less interesting than the balance of influence between capital and labour.[2]

In Figure 17.3 we have combined assessments of the actual distribution of influence with assessments of the ideal distribution. The differences between these two assessments have been indicated by arrows. At the tail end of each arrow we find the average assessment of actual influence; at the tip of each arrow the average assessment of ideal influence is indicated.

In most of the areas included in Figure 17.3 representatives of capital are prepared to accept a somewhat enlarged influence of labour. This is the case even with respect to the use of profit. But the changes accepted are rather small, as the length of arrows indicate; and within the areas which represent the traditional prerogatives of management, the ideal accepted by representatives of capital still implies a considerably greater influence for capital than for labour. In most cases managing directors are willing to give away a little more influence to labour than are the representatives of shareholders on company boards. With regard to the direction and distribution of work, managing directors would seem to wish a slight increase in the influence of capital, however.

Assessments of the influence on matters relating to work environment is an exception to the general rule. Here representatives of capital wish to re-conquer some of the influence they have lost through legislation, to achieve parity between capital and labour in this regard.

Trade union representatives on company boards demand much greater changes with regard to the balance of influence. In four of six areas of influence they demand more influence for labour than for capital, but in no case do they ask for a complete take-over of power. However, if we take account of the notion of systemic power introduced above, it is significant that union representatives wish to attain near parity with regard to influence over the use of profits and the making of investments, the two areas of decision-making which ensure the greatest systemic power in the enterprise. In fact this implies an even greater influence at lower levels of decision-making than indicated in our diagram, because labour then will partake in exercising the influence of *capital* at these lower levels.

It is also significant that labour demands for a considerably larger influence over the use of profit goes far beyond what existing legislation and practice makes possible. Decisions on the use of profit are in

Figure 17.3   Actual and ideal distribution of influence within firms between Capital *(shareholders' meeting, the board and the managing director) and* Labour *(the employees and the union). Survey questions asked: 'To what extent did the bodies listed below ACTUALLY, in 1976, influence decisions within your firm on the following topics? Please answer by distributing 10 'scores of influence' between the different bodies.' and 'The Act on Co-determination at Work states that agreements can be made with regard to co-determination for workers on several issues. Answer in the same manner as in the previous question by distributing 10 'scores of influence' according to what you find most appropriate with respect to the following topics.' The actual distribution of influence between the sectors* Labour *and* Capital *is found at the tail end of the arrows, and the most appropriate distribution is found at the tip of the arrows. The length of an arrow thus indicates the discrepancy between the actual and the most appropriate distribution of influence. Answers from managing directors (MD), board members (Board) and unions (Union) are presented separately.*

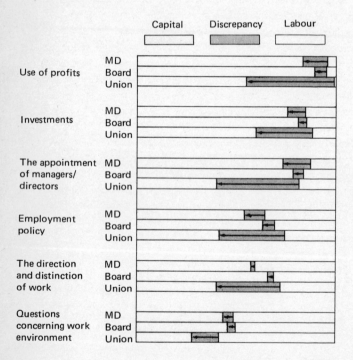

principle made at annual shareholders' meetings. Representatives of shareholders on company boards, and managing directors, as a rule make proposals for the use of profit to these meetings of shareholders. Labour representatives have neither formal nor any real influence on this point (cf. Figure 17.2). A greater influence for labour in this regard can be achieved through new legislation — such as suggested, for instance, in the proposal for wage-earners' capital funds (Meidner, 1978). By implication, representatives of trade unions on company boards would thus seem to be in favour of such a new legislation entitling them to a greater influence over the use of profits.

So far we have spoken about 'the influence of labour' without taking into consideration that labour, in the question directed to our respondents is represented by two categories — the employees and the unions. Up till now the 'influence of labour' has been assessed by adding up the influence scores of these two categories. If we now separate these two scores, we can make some interesting observations. But first some references to the Act on co-determination.

In more general terms, the relevant Government Bill (1975/76:105, p. 1) states that the main purpose of the Act on Co-determination in Work is to 'open the door for a democratization of working life by giving the employees a right to co-determination by virtue of their work'. Here only the employees, not the unions, are mentioned. How the 'rights of employees' are to be implemented is not specifically stated in the Bill except that this should be determined by negotiations between unions and management. Here unions enter the scene. But the two parties involved in such negotiations may have different views on the role and influence of employees as against their unions in labour—management relationships. This is corroborated in Figure 17.4, which has been designed somewhat differently from our previous figures. Figure 17.4 takes account only of the influence of employees relative to their unions, and furthermore combines the relevant influence scores for all the various areas of influence which were indicated separately in the previous figure.

Figure 17.4 The influence of employees and unions, actual influence at the tail ends of arrows, and ideal influence at the tip ends, according to managing directors (man.dir.), board members appointed by the shareholders' meetings (board) and board members appointed by the local union (union). The figure reports only the mean for all the topics listed in Figure 17.3.

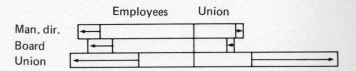

The representatives of capital — company board members and managing directors — assess the *actual* influence of employees as about two-thirds of the total influence of labour, while unions are assumed to account for the remaining third. Furthermore, to the extent that these representatives of capital find an increasing influence of labour desirable (the arrow in the diagram), they obviously shun the thought of more influence to unions; they only accept giving more influence to employees in direct man-to-man situations without union mediation.

Union representatives on company boards assess the *actual* influence of labour as evenly shared between employees and unions; and the increasing influence of labour which they desire is also rather equally divided between employees and unions. Obviously then, labour representatives do not wish to centralize and monopolize the influence of labour to unions.

The attitude of representatives of capital — a little more influence for employees, but nothing more for unions — has also been expressed in informal conversations with employers: 'I find no difficulty in collaborating with the chaps on the floor, my employees. We have been able to solve many difficult problems together in a manner beneficial to both sides. But once the unions get involved — particularly their "ombudsman" — then frictions start to develop. Stalemate, prestige and endless negotiations ensue.'

In a broader context this attitude is not surprising. Given the great collective strength of employees through their unions in Sweden, it is quite natural that employers favour individual man-to-man relationships with their employees because this strategy allows them to 'divide and rule'. Whether this is a conscious strategy or not is immaterial as long as it has the effect of dividing employees from each other, and from their main source of strength in labour—management relations — their unions.

It is also in this context we should understand a certain passage in the keynote speech by the chairman of the Swedish Employers' Confederation, Curt Nicolin, quoted above on p. 121. After castigating democratically elected politicians, and the state, he went on to ask for 'forceful initiatives' from industry 'to fend for itself and rely only on its own ability'. Industry should 'take the necessary steps in collaboration with the employees'.

Nicolin does not mention unions, and he already had dismissed the role of political parties representing the broad interests of employees, among others. What emerges is the image of corporatism, imposing a community of interests on capital and labour, as against independent unions and democratic politics.

On the next few pages we will see to what extent representatives of capital go along with Nicolin in his extremely negative view of the state. That they, on the average, seem to agree with him on the necessity of immediate collaboration with the employees rather than with unions is pretty obvious. We will see that there is less agreement with Nicolin on the justified influence of the democratic state.

In fact the historical record shows that the Swedish Employers' Federation has a history of internal cleavage between hawks and doves, the hawks taking a more explicitly negative attitude to social democratic labour politics, and promoting open ideological and not only financial support to conservative bourgeois political parties, while the doves maintained a more pragmatic and, officially a more politically neutral posture. For most of the postwar period the doves were in command (Söderpalm, 1976). Just before the bourgeois victory in the 1976 elections, however, a new more hawk-like leadership emerged in the Confederation, with Curt Nicolin as chairman. But signs of internal dissension are still there, and the hawkish posture of the present leadership could very well contribute to making this internal weakness even greater, particularly in view of the possible comeback of the Social Democrats to governmental power in the future. The more pragmatic wing of the Confederation, and its rank-and-file, might maintain with some justification, that the present leadership of the Confederation by its militancy has polarized class conflict, discredited capital in the eyes of broad segments of the population, and antagonized trade unions and the Social Democratic Party to an extent that will make it more difficult to promote the interests of capital if and when the Social Democrats are returned to government. Socialists, on the other hand, could be expected to regard this polarization with some degree of satisfaction.

The Potentially Political Nature of Questions on Working-life and Business Enterprise

So far we have mainly considered relative influence, actual or desirable, over decisions made *within* single enterprises. We have pointed out that the struggle for influence has been pursued according to rules made by employers and employees themselves, usually in the form of collective agreements. The main role of the state in Sweden has been to confirm by law the agreements already reached by the parties on the labour market. In addition it is customary for the state to follow and evaluate the effects of such legal rules and, in cases where these effects have not sufficiently benefited the weaker side, to change the rules of the game for the benefit of the weaker party.

There are many examples of such changes in the rules of the game, for instance with regard to the position of tenants on the housing market, and the consumer on the commodity market.[3] We have already given some examples from labour legislation. Depending on the outcome of future elections, we may still see further changes in this legislation because of the obvious weaknesses of the recent Act on workers' co-determination, from the point of view of labour which remains the weaker party in this context.

However, according to Swedish custom the state has on the whole refrained from actively influencing wage negotiations.[4] Its studied neutrality in such contexts is increasingly eroded, however, not only by the fact that the state itself has become one of the main employers on the labour market, but also because wage settlements are a main factor in the general economic policy of the government.

In order to find out to what extent our respondents find a political involvement of the state justified in matters relating to working life and business enterprise, we asked their reaction to the influence of a number of areas from the most 'internal', from the point of view of the single enterprise, to the most 'external'. The question is illustrated opposite.

In this case we did not ask a similar question on the *actual* distribution of influence, but only the present one on the desirable or recommendable distribution. Our intention was to assess the extent to which representatives of capital and labour on company boards could accept and recommend political interventions from the state in the areas mentioned in our question.

In Figure 17.5 we have, as usual, combined the agents of influence into a smaller number of rubrics — in this case capital, labour and the state — and furthermore rank-ordered the different areas of influence from those with the smallest amount of desirable state influence to the highest.

One finding is that representatives of capital and labour rank-order the different units in virtually the same way with regard to the desirable influence of the state, with two slight exceptions. Representatives of labour see a slightly larger role for the state in influencing the prices of commodities and services, and in the employment of older and handicapped workers than is indicated by the overall rank-order of areas.

With regard to the influence of capital as against the aggregate influence of labour and state there are more obvious differences between representatives of capital and labour.

Representatives of labour recommend parity or near parity of influence between capital on the one hand and labour on the other only

To what extent should the following units or categories have influence with respect to the following general problem areas? Please answer by allocating ten 'scores of influence' among the different units or categories.

	The single firms	The employers' unions	The trade unions	The employees	The state	Total
Structural rationalization within the economy	__ +	__ +	__ +	__ +	__	= 10
Levels of wages and salaries	__ +	__ +	__ +	__ +	__	= 10
Forms of wages and salaries	__ +	__ +	__ +	__ +	__	= 10
Employment of older employees and employees with reduced working capacity	__ +	__ +	__ +	__ +	__	= 10
Industrial pollution	__ +	__ +	__ +	__ +	__	= 10
National co-ordination of production, and removal of market imperfections etc.	__ +	__ +	__ +	__ +	__	= 10
Balancing of interests related to social versus private costs and benefits	__ +	__ +	__ +	__ +	__	= 10
Support to economically weak regions and branches	__ +	__ +	__ +	__ +	__	= 10
Prices of commodities and services	__ +	__ +	__ +	__ +	__	= 10
The establishment of multi-national firms in Sweden	__ +	__ +	__ +	__ +	__	= 10
The investment rate in Sweden	__ +	__ +	__ +	__ +	__	= 10

Figure 17.5 Ideal distribution of influence between Capital *(the single firms and the employers' unions),* Labour *(the trade unions and the employees) and the state* (State) *with respect to a number of topics, according to managing directors* (Man. dir.), *board members appointed by the shareholders' meeting* (Board) *and members appointed by the local trade union* (Union).

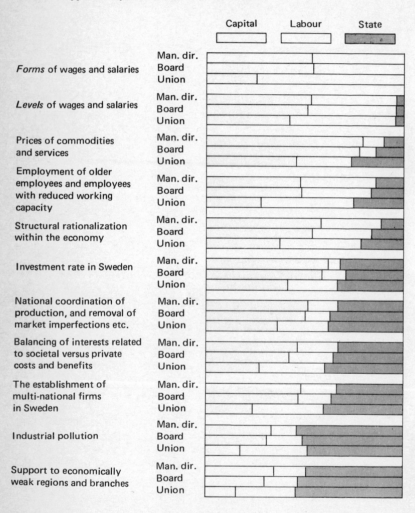

in questions on the size of wages or salaries. In the upper part of the diagram where recommended state influence is particularly low or even zero, representatives of labour recommend only a small influence of capital on the *form* of remuneration to employees (hourly wages, piece-rates, monthly salaries, etc.). Here labour wants for itself a major influence over decisions, while accepting near parity of influence (with a slight edge for labour) on the *size* of wages and salaries. It is also clear that labour representatives can accept only a minor influence of capital with regard to the employment of older and handicapped workers. Here they wish to give labour and state together significantly more scope than capital.

The Act on Employment-promoting Measures (1974) attempts to make employers take social considerations into account in employing new people. Larger companies in particular are expected to hire a reasonable proportion of the older labour force. However, the statutes do not specify general rules about this matter, but only directs that deliberations between employers, trade unions and the County Employment Board can be called for by this Board in matters relating to the employment of older or handicapped workers. The County Employment Board can then enjoin an enterprise to increase its proportion of older and handicapped employees. However, in practice matters such as these have been handled within so-called 'adjustment groups' composed by representatives of employers, employees and the County Employment Board — if not by premature pensions (see above, p. 100f).

Our findings seem to indicate that representatives of capital favour a situation of parity between employers on the one hand, and unions and state (= County Employment Board) on the other, while representatives of labour ask for a significantly greater influence for labour and state, particularly for labour unions.

Structural rationalization, the rate of investment in the business sector, co-ordination of production and elimination of market imperfections, the balancing generally of private business and social considerations, and the control of multinational firms in Sweden are areas where representatives of capital accept and recommend a significant influence of state and labour, but never significantly beyond parity. On the other hand they do not go all the way, like Curt Nicolin, the chairman of the Swedish Employers' Confederation, and ask for industry to 'rely *only* on its own ability' (see above, p. 121; my italic). A minor, but still significant state influence on these matters is recommended. Here we can trace a certain lack of consensus between the rank-and-file and the top leadership of the Swedish Employers' Confederation.

Only in two problem areas do representatives of capital accept and recommend that the state assume a major influence and responsibility — namely with regard to industrial polluting emissions, and support to industrially weak regions and branches. In these areas it is seen as desirable to give state and labour together more influence than capital.

Problems emerging in these areas are thus defined, by representatives of capital, as predominantly political questions to be resolved by political decisions. This is quite consistent with the fact that representatives of capital view environmental pollution as one of the greater threats to the future development of the country (see above, p. 225). Representatives of labour concur with representatives of capital about the need for state interventions in these areas, but in addition they desire a much greater scope for the influence of labour in these contexts which further reduces the scope for the influence of capital.

It is interesting, however, that representatives of capital, in response to the much more general question on who should influence the balance of private business interests versus broader social interests, are less prone to see state interventions as desirable. Only when pressed on concrete problems such as environmental pollution and regional policy, are representatives of capital willing to admit the importance of state interventions.

Another interesting observation is that representatives of capital on company boards are willing to accept and recommend much more far-reaching infringements on the influence of capital with regard to external environmental pollution than with regard to the internal work environment (compare Figure 17.5 with Figure 17.3 on p. 236). Representatives of capital wish to retain about 55 per cent of the influence over the *internal* work environment, while accepting and recommending a reduction of this influence to about 30 per cent with regard to *external* environmental pollution. External pollution of course is much more visible to the general public, and may therefore affect the public relations of industry, whereas the internal work environment is much less visible to the general public. On the other hand the strain, the noise, the dust and chemical exposures of the industrial work environment are not only more severe but usually also more permanent than external disturbances of the environment.

It would thus seem that representatives of capital are more sensitive to the external public relations of enterprise than to the objective strains and dangers of the internal work environment.

18 Images of the Future and Subjective Sources of Weakness

We have reviewed empirical findings on how company board members perceive current threats to development, and how they assess the actual and desirable distribution of influence among capital, labour and state in a number of different problem areas. In the following we will present findings on how these company board members view probable developments for the next ten years — not only the relative influence of capital, labour and state, but also certain other aspects of social development such as employment, capital concentration and international competition.

Analytically such images of the future are interesting to us mainly in their relationships to assessments of the current situation, and to the ideals expressed in response to our previous questions.

If someone expresses as ideal that trade unions should receive no more power and influence than they have today but predicts that in fact they will acquire considerably more influence over the next ten years, then this implies a significant cognitive incongruity between factual and ideal expectations. Such incongruity may lead to greater *militance*, if the respondent thinks that he and his group or class have enough resources of power to struggle against a probable but undesirable development, or else if he is prone to act irrationally. But such an incongruity between facts and ideals may also lead to greater *defeatism* or cynicism in the face of the inescapable, if the respondent believes that he and his group or class have insufficient resources of power to affect the momentum of change. Such defeatism inevitably contributes to weaken the subjective forces of resistance to the developments expected — except perhaps in the form of rear-guard skirmishes.

Our analytical interest in findings on the images of future developments is conditioned mainly by our interest in this subjective source of weakness — particularly with regard to the strength or weakness of capital in resisting a development toward economic democracy involving a much greater influence for labour and the general public in determining the course of enterprise. The empirical findings to be reported should be viewed in this light.

We have asked our company board members whether they believe that the influence of various segments of capital, labour and state will (i) decrease greatly, (ii) decrease moderately, (iii) remain unchanged, (iv) increase moderately or (v) increase greatly. The segments of capital, labour and state which were assessed with regard to their likely future influence were employers' organizations, private banks, owners of 'big capital', smaller shareholders, shareholders' meetings, company boards, managing directors, employees, trade union organizations, the Bank of Sweden and the state. The various centres of power and influence mentioned above can easily be grouped under our three main categories — capital, labour and state.

As usual we have calculated average assessments for representatives of labour and capital. In order not to make Figure 18.1 unduly complicated we have in this case combined managing directors and shareholders' representatives on the board into one category.

In Figure 18.1 we have ordered the various centres of influence and power from those exhibiting the most decreasing influence on the left to those assessed as attaining the greatest increases of influence on the right. The ordering has been made on the basis of the assessments of representatives of capital. On the whole representatives of labour on company boards order the various centres of influence in the same sequence. Exceptions are for instance 'private banks' and 'owners of big capital' which are seen by labour representatives as acquiring considerably more influence than assessed by representatives of capital. This is significant for our coming discussion of subjective militance versus defeatism as sources of strength and weakness of labour and capital respectively. Otherwise we should not attach too much importance to the smaller discrepancies between assessments of representatives of capital and labour respectively. Representatives of labour constitutes a much smaller sub-sample than representatives of capital, and therefore some degree of random error may be involved with regard to the assessments made by representatives of labour.

The general impression conveyed by Figure 18.1 is that those centres which represent various segments of capital are seen as most probably losing some of their influence while state and labour are believed to gain influence over the next ten years. According to representatives of capital the big capital owners and shareholders' meetings will suffer the greatest loss of influence, with managing directors and company boards suffering somewhat smaller losses. In the assessments of labour

Figure 18.1 Expected future changes in the influence of various bodies and units within the economy according to managing directors and board members appointed by shareholders' meetings (capital) *and board members appointed by the local union* (union). *Survey question asked: 'What changes do you expect for the next ten years with regard to the following conditions?'*

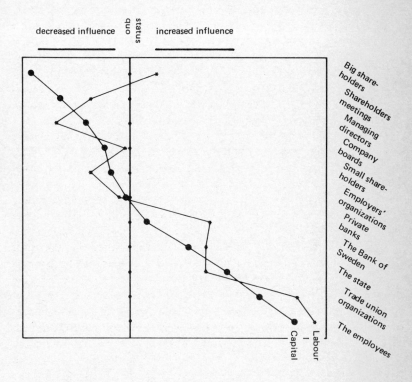

representatives the largest decrease of influence will be felt by managing directors with shareholders' meetings next, while company boards will retain their current influence. Quite possibly labour representatives on company boards believe that labour will be better represented in company boards in the future, and therefore the fact that influence of the board remains unchanged in the assessments of labour representatives cannot be interpreted unambiguously as a status quo with regard to the influence of *capital* on this particular point.

The fact that representatives of labour on company boards to a larger extent than representatives of capital assume that big capital owners and private banks will increase their influence somewhat during the next ten years may be interpreted as implying that the more centralized segments of capital not only will retain but actually increase their influence, while the less centralized units will suffer losses of influence. Both representatives of labour and capital assume that the centralized influence of employers' organizations will be retained.

Both representatives of capital and labour agree that the state and the Bank of Sweden (which formally speaking is subordinated to the political directives of the Parliament) will attain a greater influence in the future — another centralistic trend. However, the greatest increase of influence is attributed to employees and unions. Representatives of labour and capital agree on this point, and also in attributing the greatest increase of influence to the employees — that is to more decentralized units than unions.

In another, and perhaps more unconventional perspective, we might say that those segments of the overall economy which today bear the greatest risks are believed to gain most in influence over the next ten years. Conventionally, terms such as 'risk-assuming capital' would seem to indicate that capital bears most of the risks. In a modern, diversified and relatively well-managed so-called mixed economy this view is difficult to sustain. Obviously the employees of a company which is less profitable or even goes bankrupt run the greatest risks. They can lose their jobs, be exposed to long periods of unemployment, be forced to uproot themselves from their domicile and the like. Unlike capital owners they cannot spread their risks but must commit all they have — their labour power — into one enterprise. Capital owners do not have to put all their eggs in one basket. Not only can they spread their risks; they can easily move their capital from less profitable to more profitable companies without uprooting their human existence.

Furthermore, the counter-cyclical measures taken by modern states, and the 'socialization of losses' so common today in Sweden and other capitalist countries (see above, p. 119), relieves capitalists from suffering the kind of losses which in the past were the joint result of a less diversified capital market and the lack of remedial state interventions.

Conventional wisdom has it that those who bear the greatest risks should have the most power and influence. If conventional wisdom is maintained while conventional assumptions about the risk-assuming nature of various 'factors of production' are adjusted to the current facts, it follows logically that labour should have a greater influence over the use of capital than traditional capitalists.

Furthermore, what has been said and documented earlier about state involvement in the 'socialization of losses', and in crisis management generally, supports the contention that the state, and more directly the taxpayers, bear a great deal of the risks involved in private enterprise. Thus, according to conventional wisdom, they deserve the greater influence which our respondents predict they will get within the next ten years.

Taxpayers must accept not only the paying of higher taxes but also the price of cost-inflation. Business enterprises may be able to compensate themselves for higher costs — particularly in situations of weak competition — by raising the prices for their products, while taxpayers and employees usually are less able to do so. And if the state tries to compensate for its higher costs by raising taxes, this may result in election defeats, in tax-evasion or tax-revolts of various kinds — revolts often fomented by elements in the business community which would seem to be in a better position to compensate themselves for losses and rising costs than nearly everybody else. But there is nothing abnormal about this favoured position of capital in spite of the fact that employees, taxpayers, politicians and the state run greater risks and bear more costs relatively speaking; it is simply the basic logic of capitalism. As long as our economic systems are capitalist, this logic will remain. Even as state interventions increasingly tamper with the capitalist dynamic of market forces, as we have documented in Part II of this book, this is usually done in a manner which favours capitalism, if anyone.

These are ideological considerations. Ideological considerations such as these may quite likely have determined the assessments of labour representatives on company boards in their predictions about a substantial increase in the influence of labour and state over the next few years. Labour and state may be seen as ideally deserving more power and influence as a result of their running equal or greater risks than capital. But these predictions remain wishful thinking unless they are also based on realistic assumptions about the current strength of labour and state to pursue and eventually attain a greater influence in relation to capital. In the Swedish context such assumptions would seem reasonably realistic.

Among representatives of labour we thus find a high degree of cognitive congruity between ideals, perceptions of threats, expectations about actual future developments and the current objective strength of labour and state. This cognitive congruity constitutes a further subjective source of strength to be added to the objective strength of labour.

The situation among representatives of capital is different. Here we find rather pronounced cognitive incongruities with regard to the cognitive elements mentioned above. The state is seen as one of the largest threats to the development of Sweden. At the same time far-reaching state interventions are recommended not only with reference to concrete issues like environmental pollution and regional policy but also — even if to a lesser extent — with regard to the more general issue of balancing social versus private business interests.

Trade unions and employees are seen by representatives of capital only as junior partners to capital. For most issues of business and working life more than parity influence is recommended for capital in relationship to labour and state. With regard to their influence on work environment the influence of labour is even seen as being somewhat too great.

In contrast to these ideals and rather limited recommendations on the influence of labour and state in relationship to capital we have found that assessments about future developments predict a decreasing significance of a number of centres of capitalist influence while state and labour are expected to increase their influence quite substantially, or even greatly. Ideals, realistic assumptions and expectations about actual future outcomes are clearly incongruous in this case.

In addition we can assume that employers vary a great deal with regard to the strength and power they command for struggling against the likely future predicted. If we apply here our earlier conjecture about militancy and defeatism, these variations in power imply that the business community easily may become split between militants and defeatists, hawks and doves — a split which not only reproduces but deepens the historical hawk-dove cleavage within the Swedish Employers' Confederation (SAF) to which we have already alluded.

On this point we venture a hypothetical sociological generalization which claims validity not only for the Swedish case but for other capitalist countries as well:

Cognitive incongruities between ideals and expectations concerning the most likely future, shared among a category of actors A, combined with significant power differentials among those sharing these incongruous views, will lead not only to greater militance in order to change this likely course of events among those wielding more power, and greater defeatism among those wielding less power, but will thus affect the overall organizational strength of category A:

(1) In societies where A is organized in one unified or federated organization the emergence of both militance and defeatism among its members will result in deepening cleavages between hawks and doves in the organization, and a loss of organizational unity and strength.

(2) In societies where *A* is organized in several organizations differentiated according to resources of economic power, the lack of organizational unity and strength will become even more pronounced as a result of conflicts between more hawkish and more dovish organizations.

(3) In societies where *A* is relatively unorganized, this lack of organizational strength will make it possible for the more militant and hawkish elements of *A* to come together and, by virtue of their militance, to dominate the scene while the more dovish elements will lack organizational channels for articulating their conflicting views and therefore possibly in the end may acquiesce to the dominant tenor of hawkishness. This means that, paradoxically, the lack of organizational strength of *A*, at the time when cognitive incongruities between ideals and expectations for the future emerge, will be a source of subjective and even collective strength since this allows the militant response to dominate the scene.

Sweden certainly is a society of type (1) even if there are some elements of type (2) as well. Readers are invited to consider the validity of our conjectures with regard to their own countries.

Capitalist Power — A Hollow Strength?

On concluding our assessment of the strength of labour (pp. 205f) we asked a number of questions on the vulnerability of this strength which we — as far as Sweden is concerned — had assessed as increasing in spite of the decreasing number of industrial workers.

Similarly we should now ask a number of probing questions about what we have said so far about the strength of capital. Will the systemic, ideological and political power of capital really continue to decrease in the manner we have described in Chapters 16 and 17? Is the power of capital increasingly becoming a hollow strength? Or are there processes at work which will change the direction of this falling trend?

To answer these questions fully and systematically is a futurological task much more complicated than to assess the vulnerabilities of working class power. Here we will restrict ourselves to a few conjectures.

The crisis of stagflation which has characterized capitalism during the 1970s is certainly not a sign of the 'final demise' of capitalism (see our discussion in Chapter 11). Capitalism has enough strength to survive yet for a long time, with all its contradictions. Increasing centralization and concentration of capital creates problems for society and for the working class, but for capital it is a solution, a source of strength which makes it easier for capital to survive. The vertical integration, diversification and internationalization of corporations and business conglomerates help capital to create internal markets which it can itself control, and to spread its risks, and to hide its profits where profits are highly taxed, and to reap profits where fiscal costs are less. Finance capital and big business can pass on many of the burdens of the crisis to medium-sized and small companies, and indirectly to the interventionist state and the taxpayer.

We leave the economists to assess the short-run and long-run vulnerability of capital to the new types of crisis which are emerging. Our assessment is of a different nature. We are asking not how vulnerable capitalism is to crises, but how vulnerable it is to class struggle of the type we have in countries such as Sweden. With reference to this latter question we will make some observations with regard to the ways in which capital and labour, respectively, fortify themselves in situations of weakness or crisis.

In its attempts to overcome repeated crises of a type which it has not before confronted, capitalism brings into play new mechanisms such as fixed or administered mark-up prices and state interventions breaking the rules of market conformity (see above pp. 79 and 115) which contradict the basic principles of free enterprise capitalism itself. If the uncontrolled nature of trans-national capitalism generates further problems, capitalists may very well come to accept trans-national political agreements (which they themselves of course can help to design) in order to resolve the problems generated. Again, capitalists are forced to accept and design mechanisms which contradict the basic nature of capitalism.

Thus capitalism is doomed to preserve its strength by sacrificing the very principles on which it was built, and which still are used to legitimize the capitalist system. A stronger shell is being built around a content which is continually eroded by a *politicization* of the economy — a hollow strength as seen in the perspective of capitalist ideology, and not only in the perspective of the working class.

The working class, on the other hand, even though it may also be temporarily weakened, can fortify itself in a manner which does not contradict its system-transcending struggle which is by its own nature *political*.

This is the main difference between the two mechanisms of fortification applied by capital and labour, respectively. While the mechanisms of fortification which mature capitalism must apply in periods of weakness successively deprive capitalism of its very nature, its intrinsic strength, by politicizing the capitalist economy, the mechanisms of political and organizational fortification applicable by the labour movement in critical periods contribute to its intrinsic strength, to the very nature of organized political struggle.

Therefore, as the Yugoslav economist Rikard Štajner (1979, pp. 220f) has suggested, we may very well encounter a temporarily fortified but in the long run weakened capitalism, and a temporarily weakened but in the long run strengthened working class and labour movement.

PART IV

Action on the Stage

by Ulf Himmelstrand

19 Wage-earners' Funds

A pedestrian wants to cross a busy boulevard. You see him coming down the pavement. But he is not alone. A strange little team of people follow in his footsteps, one of them pulling a rickety little van on four wheels. Slowly, at the same pace as this little group, follows a mighty ambulance, white with a red cross, on the other side of the street.

The men stop at the pedestrian's crossing. There are no traffic lights. The man who wants to cross the boulevard places himself on the van. The ambulance stops at some distance on the other side of the boulevard. The man pulling the van places a blindfold over his eyes. So does another man who now clutches a rope attached to the van at the back — a braking assistant, it seems. Two men remain — one on each side of the van — without blindfolds.

At times the traffic is lively. Random shocks of cars and other vehicles come rushing down the boulevard, in both directions. One of the men without blindfolds looks attentively to the right, the other one to the left. Suddenly you hear one of these men yelling 'Go!'. But the other man, watching the traffic in the other direction, shouts 'Stop it!'. The blindfolded pulling and braking assistants drag in opposite directions, and with a tremble the van remains where it is on the pavement.

Only when both of the traffic watchers shout 'go', at about the same time, does the van start moving across the boulevard.

The boulevard is broad, and some motorists, approaching the crossing at great speed, obviously are quite insensitive to the predicament of the street crossers. At the middle of the boulevard the little van gets stuck, with busy traffic running on each side.

Barely audible above the traffic noise you hear the watching assistants shout their various instructions. Or are they quarrelling with each other and the blindfolded assistants who pull in various directions, back and forth? Finally, the van starts moving over the remaining part of the boulevard. OK — it all seems to work out.

There is a second of inattention followed by the sound of a crash.

Well, nobody has eyes in the back. This man should have employed at least one more assistant walking backwards — but labour costs must be kept down, of course.

Moral of the story: It is handy to have an ambulance around.

The Art of Street-crossing

Every experienced urban pedestrian knows how to negotiate a street crossing without traffic lights, even at rush-hours. Visual and auditive information, the perception of motion, distance, speed and sound, but also of the whole pattern of vehicles moving at various speeds at various locations in space, is fed through eyes and ears to the brain of the pedestrian. This marvellous data-processing and calculating machine then directs the muscular tonus, the motion, speed and trajectory of the pedestrian swiftly across the street. In this whole process, operating at split seconds, there is a complete unity of command and action, no division of labour among different individuals often working at cross purposes with each other, with various time lags of communications and reaction which slow down or speed up the process perhaps at the wrong rather than the right moment.

But on the other hand every experienced sociologist knows that division of labour is a social mechanism most conducive to increasing efficiency in production. How come that this mechanism is so ill-fitted to making the art of street-crossing more efficient?

In a well-constructed production line every task in the given division of labour is carefully scheduled with regard to time, place and operation. The flow is uni-directional with no random shocks of dangerous crossing, meeting or passing 'traffic'. Occasional bottlenecks in the flow of materials or components may slow down the process, but does not usually endanger it. In addition to workers allocated to various tasks and places along the production line, the division of labour also includes engineers specializing in designing and adjusting the production line itself. The production line is constructed such that most decisions which require judgement and skill have been taken away from the workers. The machines, by embodying the skills and judgement of the engineers, carry out more difficult tasks. At his station the worker only has to go through the motions required by his machine. At the same time as there is a division of labour, there is also unity of command — the command of machines integrated into the production line.

The parable of street-crossing at the beginning of this chapter is a parable of division of labour, but under conditions very different from those prevailing in a well-constructed production line. Under the kind of conditions implied by our parable it would seem that a division of labour is much less efficient than the kind of unity of command and action which characterizes the conduct of a normal pedestrian crossing a street.

If any expert on management happens to read these lines he is likely to be both happy and puzzled. Unity of command is often hailed by such experts as the only efficient principle for running a business in response to intermittently crossing, passing and meeting 'traffic' which characterizes commodity and factor markets. Workers' co-determination and the adding of local and state representatives to the governing boards of enterprises only creates a mess, it is maintained. Unity of command is sacrificed. What might be puzzling to management experts is the fact that I seem to recommend unity of command rather than a division of functions and responsibilities between actors with different and even opposite interests, while in other parts of this book workers' co-determination has been treated quite respectfully. Is that consistent?

Consistency in idealized blueprints of a system does not guarantee consistency at the level of concrete reality. In the idealized blueprints of management experts, the demands of labour appear as just another constraint in addition to constraints appearing on commodity and factor markets. Management regularly assesses these constraints and acts accordingly with full unity of command — just as the experienced pedestrian crossing a street at rush-hours.

But in reality the demands of labour have developed to a point where they no longer can be viewed just as given constraints; and similarly the position of management and capital can no longer be viewed simply as a given constraint on labour demands.

When representatives of capital and labour sit around a table for half a year, every or every other year as they do in Sweden nowadays, in protracted centralized collective bargaining with the purpose not only of assessing mutual constraints, but in fact to change the nature of these constraints, then it is difficult to maintain the idealized image of swift action and unity of command on the level of management.

When representatives of capital and labour increasingly appear as actors representing not only conflicting interests operating within a system of constraints, but as actors trying to change the system itself — either back to a more consistent market economy, or to a system of economic democracy involving a much greater power of labour and state — then it is folly to dream about a unity of command of management in the manner presupposed by the blueprints of our management experts. Those who persist in recommending these blueprints have screened themselves off from reality. Labour cannot simply be told to act as if it were just another constraint on a market now when in fact the labour movement actively opposes some aspects of the market economy. It will not work.

But still unity of command must be considered a most essential principle in the kind of situations which we have illustrated with our parable of street-crossing, and with reference to the situation of management. If such unity does not exist, nor the conditions for such unity, then the only practical line of action is to create this unity, and its pre-conditions. Of course this cannot be done simply by restricting one's view in such a manner that the system-transcending struggle of labour is defined as non-existing.

In Chapter 11 at the end of Part II we suggested how such a new unity of command can be created — even though we did not there use the term 'unity of command'. We based our argument on the following diagnosis of the situation (p. 134): 'The present system of capitalism (1) divides different incentives between actors who hold contradictory positions in the system, (2) gives most systemic power to the actor/s with the most limited repertory of incentives and, as a result, (3) requires costly state interventions to rectify the imbalances and externalities ensuing from the operation of these limited incentives.'

There are some parallels between this description of contemporary capitalism and our street-crossing parable — even though these parallels are far from complete. The ambulance is there — that is the state picking up the debris of this inconsistent system. But in the parable the assistants respond to contradictory information rather than to incentives. Furthermore because parables should be relatively simple we assumed only one direction of movement. By seating two haggling persons in the van, with different ideas about the direction of movement, with differential influence over their assistants, and with different degrees of protection against accidents, we would come a bit closer to the kind of situation we find in mature capitalism. But the point should be clear anyway. The division of 'responsibilities' or functions among capital, labour and state in mature capitalism is too inefficient and costly in economic, social and human terms.

Our formula to reduce this costly and inefficient division of functions, and to approximate the necessary 'unit of command' is very simply to redistribute power within larger enterprises (p. 134f). Power is removed from the category of actors which exhibit the most limited spectrum of productive and social incentives — namely capitalists

— and instead allocated to actors who are more capable of 'multi-dimensional satisficing' — that is to labour.

Within the wider spectrum of incentives which is characteristic of labour by virtue of their position in the economy, 'many incentives remain contradictory, but here these various incentives are instantaneously integrated in the multi-dimensional satisficing process of a *single* collective actor'. In more concrete terms this means that management is employed by labour rather than by capital; and in that position management no longer must respond to the largely contradictory demands of independent capital and subject labour, but is responsible primarily to labour as both producer and controller of capital. Unity of command has been attained as far as it is possible in a contradictory world, and this unity resolves the contradiction between forces and relations of production in mature capitalism. To resolve this latter contradiction more fully the democratic state must also play its role with respect to those social effects of the conduct of single enterprises which cannot be resolved at the enterprise level.

As indicated in Chapter 11 this resolution of the contradictions of capitalism is not just a visionary design in the dreams of some independent 'architects of the future'. In Sweden various proposals for wage-earners' funds address themselves to the problems we have discussed, and they have been proposed not by utopians and ideologists but by the trade union movement and the Social Democratic Party which however, after its second electoral defeat in 1979, must reassess its ability and its electioneering methods with regard to the crucial task to make the scheme of wage-earners' funds understandable to the electorate.

We will now briefly summarize the Swedish debate about wage-earners' funds by outlining the construction of the proposed funds, the reasons and aims stated for advocating them, and some of the most interesting arguments against funds of this nature.

Wage-earners' Funds: Why and What?

We have suggested that a major control over capital by labour and the democratic state, through some kind of workers' self-management within state-determined parameters of economic activity could be a way to resolve the contradictions of mature capitalism. These contradictions were investigated in Part II of this book. The Swedish debate about wage-earners' funds has also included references to the structure of modern capitalism, but references to various ethical or ideological objectives have been as common, or more so, in the advocacy for such funds. In particular the debate has invoked the objectives of distributive justice and equality. In addition democratic control over the economy has been emphasized as a value in itself. Wage-earners' funds were thus proposed as a means to rectify the unequal distribution of wealth and influence created by private ownership of industry (Meidner, 1978, pp. 14f). This emphasis on equality calls for solutions which do not run counter to the LO-principle of solidarity in wage policy which requires equal pay for equal work regardless of the profitability of the firms involved, in addition to decreasing wage differentials between better and less paid workers: 'any profit-sharing scheme which gave rise to disparities in income within the total aggregate of employees would not be acceptable to the trade union movement' (Meidner, 1978, p. 17).

Even though various proposals addressing themselves to these problems of inequality had been made within the Swedish labour movement from the 1930s and on (Meidner, 1975, pp. 9–15), these proposals did not gain a greater appeal until the late 1960s and early 1970s. At that time it was felt that the successful application of the principle of wage solidarity aimed at reducing wage differentials between better and less paid employees within the LO collective came into conflict with the principle of a fair distribution of wealth in industry (Meidner, 1978, pp. 30f). By accepting some measure of wage restraint for better paid employees in order to give room for pay increases among the lesser paid, LO made it possible for the successful companies at which this wage restraint was applied to reap 'excess profits' which further aggravated the already very unequal distribution of wealth in industry. A solution had to be found which at the same time allowed success and profitability in industry, reduction of inequalities in wealth, and a policy of wage solidarity.

At the 1971 LO-Congress Dr Rudolf Meidner, a senior economist employed by LO, was invited to head a working party within LO to study these problems in depth. When Meidner and his collaborators submitted the first version of their report in August 1975, suggesting a legislated transfer of a certain percentage of yearly company profits to wage-earners' funds, it became obvious that Meidner's proposal for so-called wage-earners' funds addressed itself not only to the lofty ideals of equality and economic democracy, but also to the concrete realities of capital concentration and centralization, and to the inability of the capitalist system to ensure stable investment and employment rates. In the ensuing debate the emphasis was shifted to the problems of power over decisions on investment and employment. In the words of the programme of the Swedish Social Democratic Party (1975, p. 11): 'Decisions affecting the development of the entire country and the living conditions of individual citizens are still the prerogative of a limited number of persons guided by considerations of capitalist profit.' And furthermore (p. 16) 'Decisions concerning the orientation of production are coming to have more and more far-reaching and wide-ranging effects. Consequently the need for democratic control of the economy is being thrown into progressively sharper relief. Both national economic planning and local initiatives are needed. One of the central tasks of social democracy must be to reconcile planning for society as a whole with local and individual aspirations.'

These extracts from the programme of the Swedish Social Democratic Party were quoted in the opening paragraphs of a revised proposal for wage-earners' funds submitted jointly by LO and the Social Democratic Party in February 1978. This revised proposal contained not only Meidner's original proposal for successively transferring a certain portion of yearly company profits to wage-earners' funds, but also a proposal for the creation of a system of national and regional development funds based not on company profits, but on fees on incomes from wages and salaries. The aim was to increase collective savings for the benefit of industrial investments, particularly in the export-oriented industry. Henceforth we will call this joint proposal of LO, the Swedish Federation of Trade Unions, and SAP, the Swedish Social Democratic Party, for the LO—SAP Report of 1978.

The proposal for national and regional development funds was added to the original profit-sharing plan in order to cope with the trend toward decreasing rates of public savings after 1972 (LO—SAP, 1978, pp. 22f). During the 1960s and early 1970s the General Pension Fund, created by the Social Democratic government in 1960 contributed significantly to the expansion of the investments in Swedish industry. After 1972 this role of the General Pension Fund became less significant as the paying of pensions became more extensive.

Incentives for private saving, and an increasing solidity of private industrial firms through increasing profits, as a means to satisfy the needs for industrial investments, could not be accepted unconditionally by LO and SAP. In view of their wish to decrease distributive inequality, and to influence investment allocations, only collective savings under joint labour and public control were acceptable. The Meidner scheme of profit-sharing alone would not be sufficient to increase savings, however.

In September 1978 the new LO—SAP proposal was discussed at the Social Democratic Party Congress. In principle the Congress accepted the proposal for various development funds, the new component added to promote capital formation for investments, particularly in export industry. With regard to the original profit-sharing proposal by Meidner, the Congress supported the main idea, but did not find the 1978 LO–SAP version sufficient as a basis for political decisions (SOU 1979:8, p. 43). The Congress decided to study that proposal in preparation for a decision at the next party congress in 1981.

Some left-wingers within the Social Democratic Party considered this decision a betrayal.[1] However, two things were obvious after the Congress. The party had indeed supported LO's original profit-sharing idea in principle. But it could not in detail, without further study and debate, accept the rather complicated scheme suggested in the joint LO–SAP proposal. Perhaps the party leaders also felt the need for buying time in order to prepare for the inevitable struggle about this proposal in the coming 1982 election campaign. In the 1979 election campaign they soft-pedalled the issue — not always successfully — referring to the fact that a government commission, appointed in 1975, was still studying the issue, and that no political decisions on the matter would be taken until after the 1982 elections.

Even though the profit-sharing component of the LO–SAP Report was tabled at the 1978 Party Congress, its general outline is of considerable interest from the point of view of our study. To what extent does this part of the proposal, together with the regional development funds, address themselves to the contradictions and problems of mature capitalism?

The LO–SAP Report, including the proposal for regional development funds, stated the following objectives (LO–SAP, 1978, p. 27):

- To support the principle of solidarity in wage policy,
- To counteract the concentration of wealth and power which is a corollary of self-financing (solidity) of business firms,
- To strengthen the influence of labour through capital ownership,
- To contribute to collective savings and capital formation for productive investments.

Figure 19.1 summarizes the 1978 version of Meidner's profit-sharing scheme. Business firms with more than 500 employees — all in all about 200 concerns in the whole country — would be required by law to issue shares every year amounting to 20 per cent of their profits to wage-earners' funds. In Meidner's original proposal firms with more than 50 or perhaps 100 employees were included. To prevent 'business egoism' tied to each firm, the increasing number of labour seats at shareholders' meetings to which labour would be entitled by virtue of their increasing ownership of shares, would be allocated equally between representatives of the local union and a provincial labour representative body, until the representation of labour attains 40 per cent of the seats at the shareholders' meeting. From that point on all additional seats would be allocated to representatives from the provincial body of labour representatives according to the LO–SAP Report.

Figure 19.1

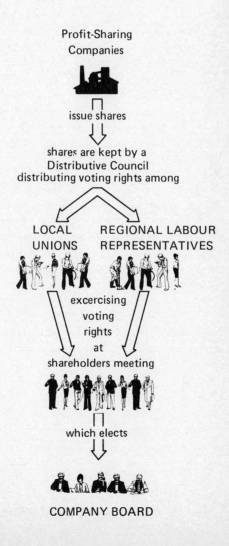

Profit-Sharing
Companies

issue shares

shares are kept by a
Distributive Council
distributing voting rights among

LOCAL   REGIONAL LABOUR
UNIONS   REPRESENTATIVES

excercising
voting
rights
at
shareholders meeting

which elects

COMPANY BOARD

The shares are kept by a Distributive Board which also is responsible for keeping track of the size of labour representation on shareholders' meetings, and for allocating seats between local and provincial bodies.

Shares in wage-earners' funds cannot normally be sold on the stock market. They are the collective ownership of labour, and therefore no individual dividends will be paid to workers. A main objective of wage-earners' funds is to increase and consolidate the collective control of labour over their firms through representation on shareholders' meetings and in the appointment of company boards. However, it has been suggested that yields from wage-earners' funds, once they have become large enough, could be paid to workers for specific purposes such as participation in training programmes, paid leave for certain family reasons, etc.

Today it is usually sufficient to own about 10—15 per cent of the shares in a Swedish company to have a decisive influence over the deliberations of shareholders' meetings, and the appointment of company boards. If wage-earners' funds are introduced in the future, it is quite possible, however, that this limit may be displaced upward. Larger shareholders may try even harder than today to obtain the right to vote by proxy for smaller shareholders who usually do not attend shareholders' meetings. In any case it will take quite some time before labour attains a crucial vote at shareholders' meetings, with the profit-sharing scheme outlined in the LO—SAP Report. With 20 per cent of the profit issued as wage-earners' shares it will take ten years before labour attains 17 per cent of the vote if the profit is 10 per cent. If the profit is 15 per cent, about 24 per cent of the vote will be attained by labour in these ten years. In order to attain 50 per cent of the vote it will take twenty-five years in companies with an average profit of 15 per cent, and as much as twenty-nine years in companies with an average profit of 10 per cent. (LO—SAP, 1978, pp. 37f).

It is anticipated that the arrangements outlined above will be reviewed by Parliament every five years to oversee the functioning of the system, and to improve it if necessary.

Obviously this profit-sharing proposal will meet resistance from private shareholders who quite possibly may consider the issuing of shares from 20 per cent of yearly company profits to wage-earners' funds as a confiscation of part of their property. In order to placate private shareholders, and also to stimulate their continued interest in buying and holding shares during a long transitional period the LO—SAP Report suggests a number of measures (1978, pp. 39f) which will not be discussed in detail here. For instance, the LO—SAP Report supports Meidner's original suggestion that companies should be allowed to deduct the shares issued to wage-earners' funds from taxable profit. This would largely neutralize the effects of the issuing of wage-earners' shares, from the point of view of private shareholders.

The fact that companies with wage-earners' funds, for the foreseeable future, also would need privately owned capital is probably as important as these legal measures and guarantees. It would thus be counter-productive for labour representatives, even when they have a decisive vote at shareholders' meetings, to tamper with dividends to private shareholders who contribute risk-assuming capital to the company. Wage-earners' funds are not designed to deprive *present* shareholders of their current assets, but to distribute increases in wealth and profits more equitably, with decisive labour control as a final goal.

The LO–SAP Report suggests that such a change in the distribution of power over capital in fact may turn out to be quite beneficial to smaller shareholders in the long run (1978, p. 40). Increasing solidity combined with greater equity and labour control — a combination which is impossible within the present system — and the wider range of economic and social incentives of labour as compared to capital, could be more conducive to a stabilization of investment rates, to a diminish-ing flow of capital abroad, to wage restraints when such are needed to combat inflation, to a greater tolerance of increasing profits, because part of the profit then would go to labour, and to a greater involvement in work and productivity generally. The LO–SAP Report seems so con-vinced of these long-term benefits of wage-earners' funds even for minority private shareholders' interests, that it seriously considers the possibility that business firms with fewer than 500 employees (who will not automatically become part of the system) volunteer to join the system to reap these benefits — including the tax deductions derived from the issuing of wage-earners' shares.

Before we go on to look into some of the substantial or at least inter-esting objections raised against the LO–SAP Report, some space should be devoted to the new national and regional development funds proposed in this report (1978, pp. 52f), and the partial support for wage-earners' funds expressed in a report from the Central Organization of Salaried Employees, TCO.

As we have mentioned earlier the national and regional development funds will be based not on a profit-sharing scheme but on incremental fees to be paid yearly by every company on the basis of a certain per-centage of wages, salaries and other income deriving from each company. The fee would increase with 0.75 per cent every year until a ceiling of 3 per cent has been reached in the fourth or fifth year. In return LO has accepted the idea of a roughly corresponding wage restraint in collective bargaining. Within these four or five years the development funds would thus attain a level of savings amounting to about 40 per cent of gross investments in the manufacturing industry. However, the increase of total net savings would be only 1 or 2 per cent of GNP. Every five years Parliament would reassess the fee percentage (LO–SAP, 1978, p. 53).

The LO–SAP Report emphasizes that in the short run it would be justified to give labour a significant influence over the management of development funds in view of the fact that these funds require some wage restraint on the part of labour in return for the fees paid on the basis of wages and salaries. At least two competing *national* development funds would be set up, one with an earmarked labour majority, and one with a majority for representatives of public interests, to be appointed by government. These representatives will of course include representatives of labour parties in some proportion to their strength in Parliament. The governing bodies of regional development funds would be appointed by regional political bodies.

In the long run when the influence of labour over the economy may have increased considerably as a result of the increasing number of labour representatives on shareholders' meetings, the earmarked majority representation of labour in one of the national development funds, could be reduced in favour of members appointed by government, to represent broader social interests.

It is significant that the other major trade-union federation, TCO, representing white-collar employees in the business and public sector, has come out with a proposal (TCO, 1978) which on major points coincides with the principles laid down in the LO–SAP Report. The TCO Proposal is much less detailed about the organizational structure of wage-earners' funds than the LO–SAP Report, but quite detailed in its discussion of basic principles. With regard to the profit-sharing scheme the TCO Congress was more cautious in its assessment. Again, there seems to be a need for buying time to explore the matter more thoroughly, to make the profit-sharing scheme better known, and more firmly rooted among TCO members, with their wider spectrum of party-political affiliations.

Comparisons between Profit-sharing and Savings Schemes in Sweden and some other Countries

In an international comparative perspective it should be emphasized that wage-earners' profit-sharing and savings schemes became an issue in Sweden later than in some other European countries such as West

Germany, France, the Netherlands and Denmark.[2] One possible reason for the earlier introduction of these ideas in some other European countries could be the greater organizational strength of the Swedish trade union movement, and its close collaboration with a relatively stable and enduring labour government which in 1960 introduced a General Pension Fund which also implied some public control over investments.

This strength of labour in Sweden made it realistically possible to attain, or to hope for an improvement of the position of labour within the traditional framework˙ of wage struggle, and labour legislation. Furthermore, the Swedish labour movement did not wish to become too closely involved with capital and management, beyond the collaboration entailed by collective agreements about wages and salaries (Hedborg, 1976).

The fact that the Swedish labour movement changed its view about these matters in the early 1970s by advocating an involvement of labour not only in workers' co-determination but also in the ownership of capital and control of its use through wage-earners' funds, implies a break with the past which calls for an explanation. Shortly I will return to this question. First some differences should be pointed out with regard to the profit-sharing and savings schemes initiated or proposed in some other European countries and the proposal for wage-earners' funds in Sweden.

In France and Holland the schemes introduced or proposed aim at some redistribution of wealth and income rather than a redistribution of power and influence. Profit-sharing and savings schemes are introduced or proposed not to change the balance of power between capital and labour, but to make it possible for individual workers to obtain a return from profits in the form of individual payments or improved pensions. Furthermore, these schemes were introduced from above — in France already by de Gaulle under the slogan of 'participation'. The labour movement in these countries have been sceptical about the long-term benefits of such schemes from the point of view of labour; workers are said to be simply 'bought off', pacified and privatized by these schemes in a manner which diminishes the collective strength of labour.

In West Germany various schemes of profit-sharing, savings and workers' co-determination were introduced as early as in the late 1950s — often without the support of the trade union movement, and not in a particularly systematic manner which would integrate workers' control over capital and the more traditional schemes of workers' co-determination.

In Denmark, however, the labour movement itself demanded 'economic democracy', involving a greater control of labour over capital accumulation, already in the late 1960s and early 1970s. Several rather radical proposals have been put forward, but due to the difficult and unstable political situation in Denmark none of these earlier proposals has as yet been legislated and put into effect. A main argument of the Danish labour movement in trying to convince even bourgeois and capital interests about the merits of their schemes has been that labour would be unable to accept an income policy and reasonable wage restraints unless labour was allowed to partake in the accumulation of capital which would be generated by a stringent income policy. This argument is similar to the one advanced in Sweden with regard to the effects of solidarity in wage policy on the generation of 'excess profits'.

Clearly both the Danish and Swedish proposals for wage-earners' funds are more radical, more in tune with working class interests than corresponding schemes in West Germany, France and the Netherlands. Why, we may ask, and why did these more radical schemes emerge later in Sweden than the less radical ones on the continent.

At Swedish trade union congresses from 1956 and up to 1971 only sixteen motions were submitted demanding more employee influence in enterprises. Most of these motions expressed vague discontent with the existing system of joint consultation, and asked for rather limited and piecemeal inprovements. Then suddenly, at the 1971 LO-Congress, twenty-five motions appeared, all at once, asking for much more far-reaching and precise measures.

A LO-economist, Anna Hedborg (1976), has recounted these telling statistics on the number of motions on 'industrial democracy' in a brilliant and sociologically illuminating article, published in the Social Democratic magazine *Tiden*, where she tried to explain why the Swedish trade union movement was so relatively late in seriously addressing itself to the issues of 'industrial democracy'. Her story goes back to the 1920s when Ernst Wigforss, a social democratic theoretician and Minister of Finance (1932—49), led an inquiry into the problems of industrial democracy (1920—3). Hedborg points out that this inquiry presented a radical diagnosis of the situation but a cure which was very limited indeed. The time was not ripe for proposals which were both radical and realistic. Existing power relations in the 1920s and the 1930s imposed severe constraints on industrial democracy. The Wigforss inquiry did not produce any practical results.

At a time when a real change of power was virtually unattainable, Hedborg argues, small reforms in the field of industrial democracy would have entailed several obligations and responsibilities on the part of labour, but scarcely no rights, no real influence. A co-optation of labour on the side of management in running the enterprise was not particularly palatable to the Swedish trade union movement; only in the field of collective bargaining did trade unions find it beneficial for labour to establish a system of collaboration with the other side in the interest of stability and economic growth. This collaboration, which over the years has been severely criticized from the left, must be understood in the context of the increasing *political* strength of the Swedish labour movement. With Social Democrats in government positions from the early 1930s, and with the welfare policies of the Social Democrats being paid by progressive taxes on the yields of economic growth, the trade unions found it rather natural to take a positive and responsible view of economic growth as the main source not only of wages but also of social welfare generally. But 'industrial democracy' was another matter; there no real benefits were anticipated, only obligations and co-optation.

Anna Hedborg argues that the recent change of attitude of LO to industrial democracy, and the emergence of the broader concept of economic democracy, is a result of a slow but persistent change in the relations of power between labour and capital from the 1920s onwards. Only when the labour movement, with its union and political branches, had been rather firmly established and acknowledged as a power which no one could neglect except at his own peril, only then could a limited reform such as labour representation on company boards, which had previously been rejected by the trade union movement, be accepted without fears of co-optation.

> Representation on company boards was now a limited or indeed a small part of a larger package of measures, in which other parts actually were more important in the sense that they made it possible to fruitfully utilize the information gained by company board representatives. All this strengthens the assertion that demands for [industrial] democracy in too small doses are rather ineffective. . . . Only when time is ripe and power-relations are such that it is possible to make rather comprehensive demands *all at one and the same time* will the limits of the existing system be transcended.
>
> (1976, pp. 222f)

In this context Anna Hedborg points out the importance of the proposal of wage-earners' funds as a particularly significant system-transcending element in the total package of measures toward industrial and economic democracy. More details about other elements in this package were provided in Chapter 17.

I have summarized Hedborg's article at some length not only because it gives a comprehensive review of changes in the LO posture to industrial and economic democracy, but also because it suggests some important sociological generalizations about reformist strategies for transcending the limits of contemporary capitalism.

Postscript: In March 1981 a working group appointed by the Social Democratic Party (SAP) and LO presented a third, but probably not final version of the proposal for wage-earners' funds (*The Labour Movement and Wage-Earners' Funds,* Stockholm: Tidens förlag). The aims are the same as in the 1978 LO—SAP report, but the new version introduces a number of rather substantial changes intended to simplify and, I think, to make for a smoother transition from the present system.

The 1981 SAP—LO proposal, instead of two sets of funds financed in two different ways, now suggests one single set of 24 regional wage-earners' funds financed both by profit sharing and fees on income.

Profit sharing, however, would not be based on the compulsory issuing of shares on 20% of yearly profits, but on the paying of cash (20% of "excess profits") from all registered companies (not only those with more than 500 employees). Wage-earners' funds would use this money (2—3 milliards crowns) for the purchasing of shares not only in the stock exchange but also in companies not registered in the stock exchange (compare my discussion on page 281, paragraphs 4 and 5). This implies a more heavy reliance on the capital market than was the case in the 1978 version.

If a big company with at least 500 employees refuses to issue new shares which can be purchased by a wage-earners' fund or other potential buyers, then the local union should have the possibility of taking the company to a tripartite council of arbitration.

The wage-earners' funds would be required to pay a certain proportion of their return to the General Pension Fund.

The 1981 SAP—LO report discusses two alternative principles for electing representatives to the board of each regional wage-earners' fund: *either* with an electorate of every citizen who ever has been a wage-earner *or* through local trade unions. In the latter case a minority of the board would be elected as representing provincial and local government. Without taking a definite stand between these two alternative principles, the report still would seem to favour the second alternative.

The elections of delegates to share-holders meetings in companies where wage-earners' funds have purchased shares will follow about the same rules as those suggested in 1978, according to the most recent SAP—LO proposal.

20 Some Objections to Wage-earners' Funds

In the Swedish debate about wage-earners' funds a number of arguments have been advanced against this reformist strategy of transcending the present economic system. Some of these objections have been raised by social democrats and communists, but most of them by bourgeois politicians, economists and spokesmen of the business community. These objections will be systematically summarized here not in order to convey an image of the current Swedish debate, but to clarify the logic of definitions and proposed solutions of problems which are endemic not only in Sweden but in most mature capitalist societies, and which sooner or later call for action both on the political and the trade union level. Therefore I will not make detailed references to the Swedish debate about wage-earners' funds.[1]

The various objections raised against the kind of wage-earners' funds proposed by LO–SAP can be roughly subdivided into those which concern effects on the *system* level — including both the political and economic system, the *intermediate organizational* level, and the level of *single enterprises*. In Table 20.1 these various objections have been summarized in such a way that the reader can distinguish those objections which have come from social democrats and communists on the one hand, and from bourgeois participants in the debate on the other. Most of the objections deriving from social democrats are virtually identical with some objections raised in bourgeois quarters, even though they may have a somewhat different slant.

When Meidner's first proposal for wage-earners' funds was submitted it was rather severely criticized by communists for being just another refinement of capitalism (see above, p. 135). Later on communist criticism of the Meidner proposal has softened a great deal; after all Meidner did bring into focus the classical socialist concern with the private ownership of capital. However, the development funds based on fees derived from a certain percentage of wages and salaries are still a target of communist attacks. It is maintained that these funds are

Table 20.1: An overview of objections against
wage-earners funds (WEFs)

Communist and social-democratic objections	Objections from spokesmen of bourgeois parties and the business community
THE SYSTEM LEVEL	
WEFs are nothing but a refinement of capitalism.	The aims of WEFs can be attained within the existing economic order without WEFs.
A too slow transition to WEFs may threaten the stability of the capital market.	Transition to WEFs threatens the capital market and the interests of shareholders.
	The market economy is threatened.
Political democracy may be threatened.	WEFs imply the complete dominance of one kind of capital ownership.
The interests of the country as a whole may suffer for the interests of workers in direct production.	Pluralism and countervailing powers are threatened.
	Political democracy is threatened.
	The rights of workers in direct production takes precedence over the rights of 'people' and consumers.
THE ORGANIZATIONAL LEVEL	
The principle of solidarity in wage-policy may be threatened.	Trade union bureaucracy in control.
Dual roles of unions in representing both owners and employees.	Trade unions must fulfil the dual roles of representing ownership as well as employees.
THE ENTERPRISE LEVEL	
	Unity of command is sacrificed.
	Innovation, creativity and the initiation of new enterprise is sacrificed.

basically an attempt to solve the needs for capital accumulation within the capitalist order rather than a system-transcending reform. So far the main Communist Party — VPK — has not detailed any alternative scheme but only introduced the general idea of a 'social fund' of a much more centralistic nature than the wage-earners' and development funds proposed by LO—SAP.

From the bourgeois side the first line of attack waged by a number of economists was simply that the main objectives which LO had in mind in making their first proposal could be attained as easily without changing the economic system. A more even distribution of income and wealth, a resolution of the problems of 'excess profits' as a result of the application of the principle of solidarity in wage-policy, desirable changes in the structure of ownership, and more savings for productive investments could be attained, according to this line of argument within the framework of traditional legislative, regulative and bargaining activities. There is no need to discuss this line of argument in detail here. In Part II we have already pointed out a number of contradictions of the capitalist system which makes it extremely difficult to achieve simultaneously these various goals within the framework of the present system.

More interesting is an argument voiced in a little book with the title *The Passing of Ownership Power* (*Ägarmakt på avskrivning*; Lidén, Lindencrona et al., 1979). This book, published by an organization (SNS) closely associated with the business community, takes the problem of capital ownership and power quite seriously but suggests a way other than wage-earners' funds to solve this problem. Rather than transferring ownership from shareholders to labour, the problem can be solved by dissolving the linkage between ownership and power, and by transferring some power over company management directly to labour, without tampering with the economic benefits of shareholders. We will discuss the logic of this proposal later on.

Another line of attack has been to paint a dark picture of the effects of an introduction of wage-earners' funds on the economic system during the first period of transition. In anticipation of an increasing control of labour over capital it is predicted that the domestic capital market would stagnate, more and more capital would move abroad and the investment rate drop to a catastrophic level while the representatives of labour are still too weak to prevent these destructive trends. This kind of argument which only perfunctorily, if at all, acknowledges the real problems to which wage-earners' funds might be an answer, and the possibly beneficial long-term effects of wage-earners' funds, still indicates a very serious difficulty attached to any slow and reformist transition to a partly new system. While the grass keeps growing, the cattle starve to death.[6]

On the social democratic side there is a keen awareness of this danger. But obviously this danger is partly of a psychological nature only. Those who have a strong interest in preserving the present structure of ownership can use their positions to foster quite unrealistic fears which operate as self-fulfilling prophecies destroying shareholders' incentives, and motivating large-scale mobility of capital abroad. The *real* danger of such destructive trends, however, can certainly be considerably reduced not only by the kind of tax incentives mentioned earlier, but also by more strict government control of the movements of financial capital.

Another possibility is to make the transition to a fully fledged system of wage-earners' funds much more rapidly. But such a swift change would require much broader parliamentary support than is available today if political legitimacy is to be maintained. As we shall point out, it is not at all impossible that such political support will be forthcoming. But, anyway, the main limitation of the kind of objection which we have just indicated is that it takes certain alleged dangers for granted without exploring to what extent a system of wage-earners' and development funds actually would have implications which *objectively* constitute a threat to most shareholders.

The Government Commission appointed in 1975 to study various proposals for wage-earners' funds has carried out a preliminary study on the probable effect of wage-earners' funds on the stock market. The tentative result of this study is that the value of shares may decline in certain types of companies as a result of the introduction of wage-earners' funds of the type proposed by LO–SAP, while remaining stable or even increasing in other types of companies. (SOU 1979:9, pp. 163f). Psychological effects, and the possible effects of increasing or decreasing productivity etc. have not been considered in that study, because they cannot be assessed within the framework of conventional economic theory.

In my view, the objections summarized so far – even the early fears of the Communist Party that wage-earners' funds may only constitute a refinement of capitalism – should be taken quite seriously. Those who have advocated the possibility of attaining the objectives of wage-earners' funds in more traditional ways within the framework of the present system have done so on the basis of a serious exploration of the matters involved with the help of established scientific paradigms of economic analysis, and so have those voicing the objection that wage-earners' funds might seriously affect the stock market, and the flow of capital abroad. On the other hand it is understandable that social democratic proponents of wage-earners' funds are sceptical about these objections. In the late 1950s when the Social Democratic government introduced the idea of a compulsory general pension scheme based on fees from employers, similar objections were heard from highly respected and competent economists, among them a later Nobel Laureate, Professor Bertil Ohlin, leader of the Liberal Party (1944–67). Not only was it predicted that the economy would suffer, but also that democracy and pluralism would do so. None of these predictions was borne out. Today those who attacked the General Pension Scheme introduced in 1960 not only acknowledge the importance of this scheme, but also suggest that its extension would provide a better solution than wage-earners' funds to the problems we are now facing.

We have seen it all before. The objections now voiced against wage-earners' funds by bourgeois politicians and economists closely follow the pattern of objections raised against the General Pension Scheme more than twenty years ago.

The objections which will now be summarized are less technical and analytical than most of the objections mentioned above. Quite a number of them prove to be ill-conceived and untenable when subjected to criticism based on fact and logic. Their propagandistic nature is often quite obvious. But some of them seem to have at least some substance, and should be dealt with a bit more seriously than the others.

For instance, some social democratic intellectuals – most of them professors of sociology or political science – have maintained that the type of wage-earners' funds proposed by LO–SAP would violate the following passage in the Social Democratic Programme (SAP, 1975, p. 4): '. . . the Social Democratic Party wishes to transform society in such a way that the right of determination over production and its distribution is placed in the hands of the entire nation. . . .' Keeping this objective of Swedish social democracy in mind, it would seem illogical to allow the employees of Volvo, for instance, to make their own decisions on investments and production within a system of wage-earners' funds because such decisions may have consequences for the economy of the nation as a whole. Some social democratic proponents of this view have suggested the building of 'citizens' funds' as an alternative to wage-earners' funds. The board of such 'citizens' funds' would be elected on a separate ticket in connection with elections to Parliament (Korpi, 1978, p. 333).

This approach places citizens' rights in opposition to the rights accruing to man by virtue of his work. This latter right has been derived by some proponents of wage-earners' funds from Marx's labour theory of value (Abrahamsson and Broström, 1980), by others from the simple fact that most people spend most of their time awake at work. In my view neither line of argument seems particularly relevant to the problem at hand, quite regardless of whether you otherwise accept the usefulness of the concepts of citizens' or workers' rights.

Proponents of wage-earners' funds, and of the kind of workers' self-management which can be envisaged in the future as a result of this reform, rarely claim that decision-making in firms controlled by local or even regional labour is sufficient to meet the needs of 'the entire nation'. Such a claim could be based only on a strange combination of syndicalism and classical Manchester liberalism. The LO–SAP proposal for wage-earners' funds quite explicitly rejects the 'egoism of the firm' by requiring not only local but also a more broadly based representation at shareholders' meetings, and by suggesting a parliamentary representation in the boards of regional development funds and in at least one of the national development funds. Furthermore, even where local and regional labour control predominates, the economic activities of any firm take place not only within the constraints of the commodity market (which assures the interests of consumers if the market is sufficiently competitive), but also within the parameters of economic activity determined by a democratically elected government supposed to cater for the needs of the nation as a whole.

The arguments and counter-arguments in this part of the debate help to expose two quite different conceptions of how 'the right of determination over production is placed in the hands of the entire nation'. One concept, by combining the ideas of political democracy with the notion of a 'citizens' ' rather than a private control of production, ends up in some kind of centralistic democratic socialism with all the risks of bureaucratic regulation and stagnation so characteristic of the much less democratic version found in Eastern Europe.

Here I venture the guess that proponents of this first conception of democratic socialism, with its centralistic implications, have arrived at their standpoint not because of any particular preference for such centralism but rather because of their limited normative approach based on normative conceptions of political democracy and citizens rights.[3]

The fact that an equally normative approach — more precisely a normative reinterpretation of Marx's labour theory of value, prescribing more power to the worker by virtue of his work — has been juxtaposed against the citizens' rights approach, has certainly not helped to make the debate more realistic. It has rather locked the proponents of these two normative views in a fold where the material implications of wage-earners' funds are completely overlooked.

Only if the broad-ranging material implications of wage-earners' funds are brought into focus is it possible to discover how 'a determination of production and its distribution' can be 'placed in the hands of the entire nation', by a *combination* of decentralized local and regional workers' control over capital, competitive commodity markets, and state control of significant parameters of economic activity. This is the second conception of democratic socialism.

Because labour has a broader spectrum of interests and incentives of labour than has private capital, state interventions into a system where there are considerable elements of workers' control will, firstly, have a much more limited task to perform than in contradictory capitalism. Secondly, where such state interventions are necessary anyhow, they will meet with less resistance and more understanding where labour is in control (Södersten, 1976, p. 205). It is only the operation of this multi-level system of decentralized labour control, competitive commodity markets and the determination of significant economic parameters by the democratic state which can assure that production is determined in a way which satisfies broad national interests rather than only the interest of private capital accumulation, the interests of local or national unions, or the interests of a new class of state bureaucrats. Locating the control only on the national level of parliamentary decision-making would imply a system of bureaucratic regulation which most probably would hamper the dynamics of the economy, to the disadvantage of 'the entire nation', including the working class.

If the objections raised against wage-earners' funds in terms of political democracy and citizens' rights by some social democratic intellectuals can be understood as a consistent but somehow too narrow application of normative political theory, the same kind of objection when voiced by some bourgeois politicians and spokesmen of business interests appears as confused or perhaps propagandistic. If the introduction of wage-earners' funds in private industry is a threat against political democracy and citizens' rights, is not the capitalist system of private enterprise favoured by these critics also such a threat![4]

When it has seemed expedient from a bourgeois point of view to picture wage-earners' funds as an Eastern European, *centralistic* and bureaucratic system which would stifle the economy, then spokesmen of bourgeois parties and the business community have used this image as a target of propagandistic attack (Norling, 1977). When such attacks have turned out to be less successful because the audience knew the complete difference between wage-earners' funds and the centralistic Eastern European systems, then such funds have been attacked by the same bourgeois and business groups for the opposite reason: they give too much *decentralized* power to those directly involved in production, and too little power to consumers and to 'the people' as represented in the centralized representative bodies of political democracy.

To watch the remaining parade of objections against wage-earners' funds could seem uninspiring. But it may still be worth watching. Soon this parade is history — and history is not necessarily less illuminating when the events and catchwords which make it up are dull or perhaps theatrical.

An objection against wage-earners' funds which has been voiced with considerable theatrical abandon and chest-beating would have it that pluralism and the balance of countervailing powers in our society is seriously threatened by such funds. Because the weaknesses of this objection are so clearly related to the weaknesses of the previous objection, we will not dwell on it at any length. However, arguments concerning the balance of countervailing powers have some interesting implications beyond those so skilfully criticized by Korpi and Shalev (1980) in a paper also providing a historical and comparative perspective. Their main point is that there is no parity or balance of countervailing powers in our so-called pluralist societies. I agree. But even if they were wrong, even if there were a real pluralist balance of power, this whole approach evades all the crucial questions about the content and character of the interests and policies of those who are supposed to be involved in this balance of power.

Assume that a given balance of countervailing powers implies that certain power-holding interest groups maintain constraints which — apart from 'balancing' other particularistic interests — obviously prevent practical solutions which would be beneficial to the great majority of people. In this kind of situation any attempt to preserve and maintain the balance of power implies a stalemate which deprives the majority of people from significant benefits. Underneath the beautiful balance of power there is an imbalance as to how easily people can find access to the good things of life, and this imbalance cannot be changed as long as there is a stalemate in the so-called balance of countervailing powers.

The countervailing power argument thus begs the question. If it dominates the debate, it detracts attention from the need to study objectively the issues and the material contradictions implied by so-called balanced interests. It is most probable that wage-earners' funds will change the balance of power and threaten the kind of 'pluralism' we have today. But as long as the pluralism and countervailing power argument is not supplemented with a thorough empirical study of *what* it is that is 'threatened' by changing the 'balance', and as long as it neglects to carry out careful deductions and extrapolations of *what* will instead emerge in terms of material conditions and social relations as well as power, this kind of argument has no real substance.

Most of the remaining objections either lack substance or point to effects which have been anticipated by proponents of wage-earners' funds, and which can be rather easily neutralized.

It is said that wage-earners' funds threaten the market economy — as if the market economy were not a mixed blessing. In fact firms with wage-earners' funds will operate on competitive commodity markets where the demands of consumers furnish income and information to producers just the way they are supposed to do in the theory of markets. But stock markets and markets for financial capital generally have proved to operate in a manner which eliminates or reduces the competitive element of markets. To the extent that wage-earners' funds constitute a real threat against this aspect of the market economy, it is all to the good. Unless a distinction is made between commodity and capital markets, the whole debate about wage-earners' funds and the market economy becomes completely pointless.

There are several unresolved questions with regard to the relationships between wage-earners' funds and the capital market (SOU 1979:8, pp. 89—97). With a relatively large number of funds which pursue an active, professional and profitable investment policy, we would facilitate competition on the capital market and a reduction of capital concentration, at least temporarily. The US trade union system of pension funds operates in this way (Drucker, 1976). But at the same time such a large number of funds, geared mainly to profitable investments in production, would make it more difficult to realize the objective of local wage-earners' influence over production through capital ownership.

However, not only local influence but also effective national co-ordination of investments is made more difficult with a large number of competing capital funds. The LO—SAP Report attempts to cater for these various objectives of local and national influence, and a competitive capital market, by proposing a relatively large number of regional funds, two national funds with different composition, and a delegation of influence deriving from shares in wage-earners' funds to local unions. Whether or not this synthesis of local, regional and national interests, and of capital market and local union influence is the best possible one is difficult to say at present. But it is possible to say most definitely that those who object to wage-earners' funds because they believe that such funds will destroy the operation of market forces where such forces operate reasonably well as decentralized allocators of resources rather than as concentrators of capital, are simply wrong.

Another version of the unjustified allegation that wage-earners' funds threaten the market economy insists that such funds will create a giant monopoly. While competitive free enterprise — the shimmering ideal which is always juxtaposed against any alternative economic system — exhibits a very large number of owners of enterprises, a system of wage-earners' funds would have only *one single owner*, mainly labour, organized in a giant trade union structure. This argument, voiced by an economist of some international repute (Lindbeck, 1979, pp. 49f), is so embarrasingly crude that any thoughtful reader should be able to discern the trickery involved. With the same kind of trickery one might say that in private enterprise there is only *one single owner*, namely capital organized in giant conglomerates and in one powerful Confederation of Employers, whereas a fully fledged system of wage-earners' funds would have as many owners as there are workers and other shareholders represented at shareholders' meetings all over the country. By shifting the level of analysis in the middle of an argument you can prove anything.

The remaining objections in this rather sad parade of honest but simplistic normative analysis, confused political ideology and argumentative trickery deal with possible effects of wage-earners' funds on an intermediate organizational level, and on the level of single firms. These objections are less far-fetched, and more realistic than some of the previous objections, but do not seem to carry much weight.

A social democratic critic (Leijon, 1979) has maintained that wage-earners' funds may destroy the Swedish trade union principle of solidarity in wage policy. If this is true, it is certainly a very serious objection because one of the main reasons for wage-earners' funds advanced in the early 1970s by LO was that only a system of wage-earners' funds would make it possible to maintain such a policy of solidarity without 'excess profits' and without a further concentration of industrial wealth.

Leijon assumes that decentralized labour control over capital would tend to increase wage differentials between more and less successful companies, and at the same time to diminish the strength of LO in its attempts to counteract this tendency.

In fact this is a possibility which has been anticipated by proponents of wage-earners' funds, and effective measures against such a tendency have been suggested (Södersten, 1973, p. 485, and 1976, p. 207).

Both bourgeois and social democratic critics have furthermore suggested that the trade union movement itself might be torn apart with the introduction of wage-earners' funds, because unions then would be seated at both sides of the collective bargaining table — namely both as owners of industrial capital and as representatives of employees making demands for wage increases, improved working conditions, etc.

No doubt the structure and activities of the trade union movement must undergo major changes as a result of an introduction of wage-earners' funds. The kind of relationships between capital and labour which are natural under private enterprise would have to change when this system is superseded. Gunnar Nilsson, the chairman of LO, once drily remarked: 'Obviously we can't maintain private capitalism just in order to preserve present relationships between capital and labour.' (LO–Tidningen, 1976, no. 1).

However, a dual role of trade unions is not something new, nor is it something associated only with wage-earners' funds. Even within capitalism as we know it today, unions have a dual role reflecting the dual character of labour itself: under capitalism labour is at the same time a *'factor of production'* in the capitalist order, depending on the success of this order for its reproduction, and a *class* which is involved in a struggle, more or less limited as it may be, with capital.[5] In the past this dual role has often involved conflicts between national and local levels of union activity. But as wage-earners' funds become significant this dual role will probably take on a different and less antagonistic character than the conflict between capital and labour in contemporary capitalism.

In fact our previous argument concerning 'collective unity of command' would seem to require that conflicting incentives, interests and information are processed *within* one single collective actor who in a sense is involved in a 'conflict with itself', rather than by a division of functions and responsibilities between different actors operating at cross-purposes with each other. With this in mind we conclude that those who point a warning finger to the dangers of a dual role for unions, simply do not understand the benefits which follow from this new, non-antagonistic duality when the system approaches a collective labour unity of command within the enterprises involved.

There is one final objection which is often raised whenever collective ownership of capital, in one form or the other, is being evaluated. It is said that the creative and innovative impulse which is so necessary for industrial progress will dry up if private profit is not maintained as an incentive. Collective ownership through wage-earners' funds is supposed to be a danger because it supposedly eliminates this incentive.

There is little or no substance in this objection. It is derived from an extremely simplified and primitive theory of motivation, which is rejected by most psychologists and sociologists concerned with the study of invention and innovation (Noble, 1977, and Norman, 1969). Pecuniary incentives are among the least important in this context.

In fact it is easy to find examples of cases where the motive of profit-maximization has stopped the introduction of an innovation. In highly capital intensive industry the introduction of innovations which would substantially change and improve the product may require costly modifications or replacements of machinery. No profit-maximizing industry would introduce such changes unless they were assured, for instance through legislation, that their competitors would have to take on the same costs.

Another aspect of this motivational problem is the incentive structure of workers in profit-maximizing companies. According to the very economic theory maintained by those who emphasize the great significance of private profit as a motive, workers in profit-maximizing companies have only one option in maximizing *their* gains, namely to minimize their effort in relation to their pay (Södersten, 1973, p. 485). Piecework may to some extent increase the effort, but certainly not in a manner which encourages an innovative and creative use of the skills and experiences of workers. In Sweden where monthly salaries have recently replaced piece-rates in many sectors of industrial work, as a result of trade union pressures, any extra effort, innovative or otherwise, primarily increases the profit of the owners, not the gain of labour. And since innovations which increase productivity usually entail certain risks — if they succeed, the risk of workers being laid off, and if they fail, the risk of criticism — the most economically rational thing to do for workers is to become passive risk-minimizers. For the same reason workers in profit-maximizing enterprises tend to resist innovation introduced from above (Södersten, 1975, p. 28).

This destructive incentive structure among workers in profit-maximizing industries stands in stark contrast to the incentive structure in enterprises geared to maximize the gains of workers rather than of external owners of capital. In such enterprises every successful experiment, every increase in productivity, every improvement of technology increases the residual which workers control or share among each other (Södersten, 1975, p. 28).

This nutshell diagnosis, summarizing some of the differences between the incentive structures of enterprises maximizing (1) the profits of external capital or (2) the gains of labour, may not be conclusive. But at least it throws considerable doubt on the belief that the profit-motive of private capitalism is the only guarantee for innovation and creativity in industrial production.

What Kind of Innovations do we Need?

Unquestionably industrial production needs creativity and innovation. But in view of the contradictions and problems of mature capitalism empirically documented and theoretically analysed in Chapters 4–10 of this book, in view of the quandary in which we find ourselves about the feasibility and legitimacy of various political solutions to these problems, as illustrated in Chapter 11, and finally in view of the precarious and unsettled power relations between various actors on the stage which we illuminated in all the chapters of Part III, it is obvious that the innovations we need most of all must deal not with details of technology alone but with the structure of our economic and political systems.

Whatever we think of the details of proposals for wage-earners' funds and some of their effects, it is clear that these proposals which emanate from the labour movement address themselves in an innovative manner to these broader system-problems. In this chapter we have surveyed a number of objections against wage-earners' funds, and we have characterized at least some of the objections emanating from bourgeois politicians and economists, and from spokesmen of the business community, as ill-conceived, spiteful and propagandistic. Whether one shares my criticism of these particular objections or not, they are still not very innovative. They address themselves neither to our system-problems, nor to the innovative proposals submitted by the labour movement, but rather to a strawman of various alleged evils set up specifically as a target for propagandistic vilification.

But this image of polarization between structural innovators from the labour movement, whatever these innovations are worth, and the opposing forces of bourgeoisie and capital, whatever justification their resistance may have, is not the whole picture. There are cracks in the ideological facade of the bourgeoisie and the business community. To characterize this ideological facade as altogether reactionary and deceptively propagandistic would be incorrect. We have pointed out that Nils Åsling, leading Centre Party politician and Minister of Industrial Affairs in the 1976—8 bourgeois government, wrote rather respectfully about the labour movement and its demand for wage-earners' funds only a few months before the 1979 elections (see above, p. 221). In the election campaign itself this opening toward the labour movement was certainly closed. Such things happen in election campaigns. But the door can be opened again.

In the long run no bourgeois government in Sweden with a parliamentary majority of one can run the country without seriously considering proposals from the labour movement, even if the last two election campaigns and the interelection period 1976—9 gave proof of very little but aggressive manifestations of bourgeois self-sufficiency.

I have also pointed out that even publications of the business community have contained contributions which indicate a clear awareness of the problematic of capital ownership and power which provoked the labour movement to propose wage-earners' funds (see above, p. 275).

> If you wish to reduce the power of present owners there are two possibilities. You can retain the present legal linkage between ownership and power but transfer the rights of ownership to somebody else. The best known example of this method in Sweden is Meidner's proposal of wage-earners' funds.
>
> Another method is to dissolve the linkage between ownership and power. As far as the big companies are concerned this implies that you transfer the administrative and management rights of owners to some other group without therefore depriving the owners of their shares, and the economic rights associated with these shares. (Lidén, Lindencrona et al., 1979, p. 24).

With simple but ingenious logic Lindencrona has discovered, or rather rediscovered that there is a method other than wage-earners' funds to solve the problem involved. What he rediscovered is what Gunnar Adler-Karlsson has called functional socialism. Lindencrona certainly does not use the term 'functional socialism'; but with regard to his 'second method' he acknowledges his intellectual debt to Östen Undén, Professor of Civil Law and Minister of Foreign Affairs in a Social Democratic government (1945—62), who laid the conceptual foundations for Adler-Karlsson's notion of functional socialism (Lidén, Lindencrona et al., 1979, p. 25, note 5).

I have discussed functional socialism elsewhere in this book (see above, p. 61) and found it wanting in some respects. But here that is not the point. The point is that Gustav Lindencrona, a respected professor of financial law, in contrast to some other professors who have voiced objections against wage-earners' funds, has discussed these matters in an admirably intellectual fashion, in a book published by a study-organization linked closely to the business community. But that is not all. The last chapter of that book was written by a number of managing directors in a number of well-known Swedish enterprises, and they have taken Lindencrona's second method of 'functional socialism' quite seriously − even though they also avoided using that term − and seriously enough to propose a new and innovative structure for company boards and company management (Lidén, Lindencrona et al., 1979, pp. 104f).

It would carry us too far to discuss the innovative proposal of these managing directors − a proposal which seems to me quite comparable at least with the transitional stage of the Meidner plan. Again the point I wish to make here is that the business community does contain voices which articulate a serious concern with the problem of ownership and economic power − voices which are independent enough to propose solutions which meet many if not all the requirements stated by the labour movement. In a hopeful mood this could be considered a beginning of a 'managerial revolution' which makes it possible not only to dream of but also to hope realistically for solutions to some of our most urgent system-problems in collaboration between labour and management, and with owners of capital relegated to a position of secondary importance in terms of power.

But it is also a fact that the innovative impulse involved originated in the labour movement. This is not said simply to allocate merit where it belongs, historically speaking. Without the involvement of the labour movement our problems will remain unsettled. Basically these are the problems of what we have called the extended working class; and eventually the problems of this working class also become the problems of management, and of democratic politics.

No doubt we can expect nasty remarks from surviving new leftists about 'class collaboration', and about the reformist labour movement as a 'traitor' of the working class, at any time when a collaboration between labour and management is mentioned, as I have done above. But similar warnings have also been heard from the reformist trade union movement, as I have indicated earlier in my summary of an article by Anna Hedborg. But the trade union movement, in contrast to the new left, always voiced such warnings in an undogmatic fashion adjusted to the realities of actual relations of power between capital and labour. As Anna Hedborg − a voice from a new-style old left − indicated in her article, these power relations in Sweden have been and still are changing in favour of labour. This fact makes it possible to view collaboration between labour and management in a new and different light. How new?

A leading social democratic theoretician has pointed out to me that the proposals made by Lidén, Lindencrona and others in fact come very close to some suggestions made already in 1847 by one of the founding fathers of Marxism, Friedrich Engels (Hansson, 1976, p. 56). Engels suggested that capitalists could be bought off by transforming their shares into government bonds (Marx–Engels Werke 4, p. 373). This would assure them of their dividends at the same time as it would eliminate their economic power over the appointment of company boards. Government bonds do not entitle the owner to any such influence. Government bonds, in contrast to cash compensation to shareholders, cannot be used for investments in new capitalist enterprises, and thus counteract the trend toward concentration of capital. The benefits from government bond dividends can more easily be regulated through taxes.

I am not saying that Lidén and Lindencrona are going as far as Engels. They certainly express a wish to reduce the importance of the link between ownership of shareholding capital and economic power, and they seem concerned about capital concentration, but still they want to retain a limited influence for capital owners. In spite of this the basic principle they advocate is the same as that proposed by Friedrich Engels.

Once management is being extricated from the influence of shareholding capital owners in the manner suggested above, a collaboration between labour and management can no longer be described simply as a class collaboration between labour and capital. New social relations of production are then emerging.

21 Wage-earners' Funds and the Contradictions of Mature Capitalism

In the preface of this book I pointed out that we have no primary interest in evaluating whether or not proposals of the Swedish labour movement — such as wage-earners' funds — approximate some *idealized* model of socialism. Our main question is rather whether or not such proposals *address* themselves in a comprehensive and reasonably realistic fashion to *resolving the contradictions of mature capitalism*. In Part II these contradictions were empirically explored. Now we ask: Would wage-earners' funds address themselves to these contradictions, and contribute to their resolution? To what extent can wage-earners' funds reduce and eventually resolve the contradiction between labour and capital, the contradictions between forces and social relations of production, and the extended contradictions we have described, in Part II?

These questions will be answered in the following by systematically referring to the main rubrics about contradictions in Part II. In such a manner we can at least assess whether or not wage-earners' funds *address* themselves to those contradictions.

Wage-earners' Funds and the Contradiction between Capital and Labour

The accumulation of capital under the direct or indirect control of private capitalists is a fruit of unpaid surplus labour and, as Marx was fully aware, also a fruit of supply—demand relations setting the prices on commodity and factor markets. Labour only retains that part of their fruits of labour which is needed for its reproduction at a level determined by the successes of previous wage struggle, by socially accepted standards of living which also are a result of previous struggle, and by what organized labour currently can twist out of the hands of private capital given prevailing conditions on the factor and commodity markets.

It is this private appropriation and control of the fruits of labour, in its various forms, which constitutes the basic contradiction between labour and capital under capitalism. What would wage-earners' funds do to reduce or eliminate this contradiction?

The answer might seem quite self-evident. If large companies are required by law to issue shares, amounting to 20 per cent of yearly profits, to wage-earners' funds, this means that surplus appropriated by private capital is reappropriated by labour. By definition this implies a successive elimination of the contradiction between labour and capital, as labour increasingly reappropriates and takes control over an increasing portion of capital accumulated.

Even though this is a conclusion true by definition, some complications emerge when we move from the level of definition to the wider context of social relations of production, and to considering possible capitalist counter-moves.

Firstly, it is possible that the reappropriation of capital by labour mentioned above will imply an increasingly bureaucratic or technocratic union control over capital rather than a more democratic control with a high degree of workers' participation in union affairs (see our discussion of the 'vulnerabilities' of labour strength in Chapter 15). But from what we know about unions in Sweden, it cannot reasonably be said that the contradiction between capital and labour will become greater, even with a bureaucratically managed system of wage-earners' funds, than with ordinary private capitalism.

Secondly, it is quite possible that capitalists, in order to evade the effects of legislation on wage-earners' funds, restructure large companies by breaking them up into formally independent smaller companies which do not reach the threshold of 500 employees suggested as a starting-point for the issuing of wage-earners' shares in the LO—SAP report. For multinational corporations it is also possible to evade the obligation to issue wage-earners' shares by taking out all or most of their profits in branches abroad.

All this does not affect the logic of our conclusion, but restricts the area within which this logic can be applied. On the other hand such capitalist counter-moves can in their turn give rise to legislative counter-moves which eventually and definitely may re-establish and expand the area within which our logic holds. Therefore I do not consider this complication as undermining the validity of my argument about the successive reduction of the contradiction between labour and capital through wage-earners' funds, even though the political process involved certainly will become more complicated by the kind of counter-moves just indicated.

More serious is another complication which results from looking at the reduction of contradictions between capital and labour in isolation from other kinds of contradictions within capitalism. The successive reappropriation of capital by labour through wage-earners' funds, if pursued in a piecemeal fashion without other structural changes, would in the long run only replace private capitalism with a capitalism without private capitalists. The logic of capitalist production, with its tendency to produce unemployment and various negative externalities, could quite possibly continue to operate even though private capitalists are successively replaced by labour capitalists. The contradiction between labour and private capital would then only be replaced by a conflict between unemployed labour and labour in control of capital.

However, in political reality this serious complication is less likely to materialize in a society with a labour movement conscious and well organized not only in unions but also on the political level. Only if a profit-sharing scheme is organized entirely in the form of individualized rather than collective profit-sharing, can we definitely predict that the logic of capitalism will continue to operate as usual. Collective labour ownership of capital within the framework of a politically conscious and well organized movement is unlikely to restrict itself in a piecemeal fashion to just replacing private capital with labour capitalists. It would most likely also address itself to contradictions of capitalism other than the basic contradiction between labour and capital.

Wage-earners' Funds and the Contradiction between Forces and Relations of Production

In mature capitalism social relations of production remain private in character, whether corporate or personal interests are involved, while productive forces have become increasingly social or even international in character. In other words: there is a mismatch between forces and relations of production in mature capitalism. The question here is whether wage-earners' funds would imply a change of the relations of production, making them more social in character, so as to match the increasingly social character of productive forces.

An answer to this question must take into account not only the role of wage-earners' funds on the level of single enterprises but the interlocking of this level with what is done on higher regional, social and international levels of political action and control. By definition a socialization of the relations of production implies the involvement of broader social interests than those represented at the level of single enterprises.

However, in Chapter 11 we maintained that labour, even in the context of the single enterprise, has a broader and more socially relevant spectrum of interests than capitalists and their managers (pp. 113f). If labour is in control of capital in a single enterprise, labour is forced to embark on a process of multi-dimensional satisficing which takes this broader and more social spectrum of interests into account in a way which private capital cannot because of its primary and relatively exclusive interest in capital accumulation.

Therefore we conclude that the operation of wage-earners' funds, already at the level of single enterprises, would help to assure a production satisfying broader social interests than private capitalist production can do. In this sense relations of production in a system of wage-earners' funds would become more social in character even if we limit our analysis to the level of single enterprises. In situations of economic crisis collective labour operating within a system of wage-earners' funds would be unlikely to allow the destruction of capital and labour power by premature closing down of enterprises, by decreasing capital investments to a minimum, by the firing of workers, or by moving capital abroad. In such situations collective labour would be more likely to apply wage-restraint than under private capitalism, or may even temporarily reduce wages in the interests of simultaneously maintaining employment, profitability, competitive price levels, productivity and forward-looking investments. Stagflation caused by mark-up pricing and lack of investments would therefore be less likely in a system of wage-earners' funds.

Altogether this means that a fully fledged system of wage-earners' funds produces a smaller problem-load to be tackled by state-interventionist crisis-management. However, this does not mean that wage-earners' funds, operating at the level of single enterprises, can completely eliminate the contradictions between forces and relations of production under mature capitalism. If wage-earners' funds operate only on that level, that system might be considered as a form of decentralized democratic and collective capitalism which has succeeded in eliminating some problems of capitalism, while leaving other capitalist problems unresolved. They must then be attacked outside such a system, for instance by state interventions and planning.

With regard to socially needed investments which can be determined only on higher levels than the single enterprise, it is particularly important to reckon with that part of the LO—SAP proposal which suggests national and regional development funds financed by fees calculated on the basis of wages, salaries and other income (p. 263). While wage-earners' funds based on profit-sharing fail to increase collective savings, the national and regional development funds proposed can substantially increase savings for capital investment without at the same time increasing the value of private capital in a way which makes the contradiction between capital and labour more pronounced. Crises as a result of failing private investments or 'investment strikes' thus become less likely. An increasing value of capital through investments can be more easily accepted by labour if such investments contribute to the assets of labour rather than to private capital.

We have already mentioned the problem of unemployment. Even though an enterprise managed by collective labour is unlikely to fire members of the collectivity during periods of crisis, such enterprises are also unlikely to invite new working members in larger numbers in periods of economic expansion since that would reduce the relative gains of the existing labour collectivity (Vanek, 1971, pp. 25–9). When workers leave the enterprise because of old age or other reasons, they may not be replaced. The volume of production can still be maintained by increasing productivity. Therefore an economy based largely on wage-earners' funds would most likely fail to maintain, and even more to expand access to gainful work.

Some reservations must be added to this conclusion, however, because it is based on somewhat questionable assumptions regarding wages in labour-controlled enterprises within a wage-earners' fund system such as the one suggested by LO–SAP. If LO's principle of solidarity in wage policy (pp. 262 and 282f) is to be rigorously maintained even within a system of wage-earners' funds, then the significance of wage-incentives is somewhat reduced, and thereby also the incentive to limit the size of labour in order to maintain or increase one's wages. But even now LO's principle of solidarity is not always kept that rigorously. Some degree of wage drift is allowed in more successful enterprises. Therefore the logic of our argument on the size of the labour force in enterprises would hold to some extent even if LO's principle of solidarity is maintained in the current manner. Furthermore, there are other incentives of a more collective nature – the incentive of maintaining or increasing the solidity of one's enterprise and its wage-earners' funds – which operate in the same direction.

Therefore I conclude that an economy based on wage-earners' funds and labour-controlled enterprises may be unable to increase access to gainful work. Such demands can probably be effectively dealt with only by supplementary measures taken outside the sphere of labour-managed enterprises. The private capitalist sector of smaller enterprises which remains outside the wage-earner-fund system, state interventions and national and regional development funds encouraging the establishment of new enterprises, must take responsibility for creating new job opportunities.

However, a mixture of smaller private enterprises *and* larger enterprises run within a system of wage-earners' funds entails certain problems which are unavoidable within mixed transitional economies. If a smaller private enterprise, by virtue of its success, grows closer to the threshold of 500 employees suggested by LO—SAP as the entry-point to the system of wage-earners' funds, then the private incentive for growth may be reduced. Objectively speaking this contradiction may not be very serious because of the various precautions taken in the proposed Swedish system as to the length of the period of transition and its safeguarding of shareholders' interests etc., but psychologically incentives for growth may still be hurt.

In Yugoslavia where the threshold for its system of workers' self-management is as low as five employees, a number of ingenious measures have been invented to maintain incentives for small-scale enterprise, and to make the transition to a system of workers' self-management less threatening to a dynamic private small-scale entrepreneur. If he is not regularly elected by workers as manager of the enterprise when it comes to exceed five employees (which he is likely to be if he did a good overall job as an entrepreneur), then he is compensated for his investments and his interest. In the proposed Swedish system these transitional problems would be of a different nature because of both the higher threshold and the much slower transition.

State interventions outside a system of wage-earners' funds are required not only because of the problems of employment and transition just mentioned. There are also needs for state intervention *ex post*, and co-ordination and planning *ex ante* generated by the complex and interdependent nature of contemporary economies, and by the long-term social implications of present-day production and marketing. These and other broad-ranging social characteristics of the economy cannot be tackled by wage-earners' funds as such.

But, as we have indicated in Chapter 20, no proponent of wage-earners' funds claims that such funds alone, without supplementary political measures and democratic state interventions, can resolve all the problems of mature capitalism. However, because of the historical heritage of close collaboration between the union and political-party wings of the Swedish labour movement, we can expect a more fruitful and non-contradictory co-ordination between the democratic state and the industry when labour is in control of enterprises through their funds than when private capital is in control (Södersten, 1976, p. 205).

In this book we have not discussed in detail the more conventional state-socialist solutions to the contradictions between forces and relations in mature capitalism. Such solutions have been rejected offhand by us in a rather summary fashion, with reference to the experiences of Eastern European countries (p. 126f). Apart from being a way to save space for a more comprehensive discussion of solutions closer to home, this neglect of state socialism is also an expression of our political predilections which we have no reason to hide. Readers who look for a more thorough analysis of state socialism, we must refer to other books. For a survey and evaluation of arguments for and against central planning, see L. Udéhn, 1980.

Here, in concluding this section on the contradictions of forces and relations of production, I only wish to point out that state socialism resolves this contradiction not by reducing the concentration of capital into more decentralized forms of labour control over production but by socializing concentrated capital through state ownership. In blueprint form this certainly appears much more clear-cut and satisfactory as a solution to the contradictions of capitalism than a system of wage-earners' funds, particularly if the state is rooted in a stable and vital democratic tradition (which has not been the case in Eastern Europe). But as we have repeatedly indicated, blueprints may exclude crucial, unmanageable and restive aspects of reality. Therefore blueprints should not be evaluated in isolation from this reality, in the thin air of abstracted construction, but with due regard to the effect of other basic and extended contradictions such as those treated in Part II of this book, and other contradictions specific to centralized planning and administration. We now turn to the ability of wage-earners' funds to address and resolve those other contradictions.

Wage-earners' Funds and Market Self-destruction

In Chapter 6 we illuminated the tendency of competitive markets to self-destruct over time through the concentration and centralization of private capital resulting from the operation of market forces themselves. In state socialism this contradictory character of the competitive market is resolved by eliminating the market as a social reality, and by replacing it with presumably consistent central planning and regulation. However, central planning can certainly make use of the *theoretical model* of market forces even in the absence of competitive markets as a *social reality*, by simulating market processes in a computer in order to determine prices and an optimal allocation of resources (Lange, 1972). This has been tried by Gosplan, the central planning agency of the USSR. The great advantage of using market forces in the planning office rather than in social reality is that each run on the computer can be made to start from scratch without the iterative cumulative processes which in social reality tend to destroy competitive markets over time. In principle the central planning office can thus operate with perfect markets and perfect competition *ex ante* rather than *ex post* — a dreamworld for theoretical economists. The disadvantage of this method is obvious. The solutions arrived at in the central planning agency are the solutions of computers and planners. Even if these solutions are correct from the point of view of sound economic theory, and known empirical facts, they are not necessarily the solutions of hundreds, thousands and millions of economic actors at different levels of the economy. Therefore central planning requires a command economy in order to implement 'correct' economic solutions. But plan implementation and administration is fraught with as many failures and human as well as structural shortcomings as the social reality of self-destructing competitive markets — or even more so, as liberal economists used to maintain (Hirsch and Goldthorpe, 1978, p. 76). Be that as it may: here we will rather look at wage-earners' funds as a possible solution to the self-destructive tendencies of *real* markets, not theoretical ones.

The self-contradictory character of competitive markets is due to the fact that competitive success breeds further success both on commodity and capital markets — and cumulative failure for those who find it difficult to compete. The growth of size, the conglomerative, oligopolistic or monopolistic expansion of successful companies, and the destruction, or conglomerative, oligopolistic, or monopolistic absorption of weaker competitors is the mechanism involved. A system of wage-earners' funds where different enterprises operate on reasonably competitive commodity markets would seem to be able to maintain rather than to destroy these market forces for the following two reasons which have been mentioned in our previous discussion.

Firstly, success in a labour-controlled enterprise within the kind of wage-earners' fund system we envisage does not breed continuous growth in terms of size, and in terms of capital controlled by the given enterprise alone. As I pointed out in my references to analyses of the employment effects of labour-controlled enterprises, such enterprises may not respond to success by expanding the number of workers.

Thus enterprises will not grow much in size. The employment problem in society as a whole must be solved by creating new enterprises which in fact may contribute to increase rather than to decrease competition.

Secondly, financial success may certainly to some extent increase the solidity of labour-controlled enterprises; but by design greatly increasing capital funds in the system of wage-earners' funds envisaged cannot be used by single enterprises to purchase other enterprises. They will rather be channelled through regional and national funds to other parts of the economy for investments in new enterprises and to social investments democratically decided at those levels. A concentration and centralization of capital in private hands beyond democratic control is impossible — except of course in the remaining private sector where, however, such growth is counteracted once companies attain the critical size of, say, 500 employees — a threshold value which certainly can be adjusted downwards by political decision if private capitalists try to avoid this critical point by breaking up their companies into several smaller, seemingly independent units.

Thus a system of wage-earners' funds, supplemented with necessary regional and national political interventions, would seem to maintain and develop competition on commodity markets while preventing the market-destructive concentration and centralization of private capital.

Wage-earners' Funds and the Destruction of Incentive Structures

As we indicated in Chapter 6 the incentives which are the psychological mainsprings of the capitalist system tend to be destroyed firstly by the intermittent, tendential fall of the rate of profit. Its intermittent and far from universal character implies that this destruction of incentives is only partial, and less likely, for instance in concentrated multinational corporations minimally exposed to international competition and capable of mark-up pricing to attain target profits. But the tendency is widespread enough to have serious repercussions on incentives for investments in the capitalist order.

Incentives for work and for increasing private consumption also seem to approach a ceiling in mature capitalism, and to become less salient than other incentives related to needs for other qualities of life and work than those offered by capitalist consumer society (pp. 84f). The incentive structure of work in capitalist enterprises shapes the worker into a passive risk-minimizer rather than into an active and innovative producer (p. 284). A fully fledged system of wage-earners' funds which would involve a high degree of workers' self-management can be expected to change these failing incentive structures of private capitalism at several levels.

Firstly, we can expect the profit-elasticity of investments to be less within a system of wage-earners' funds than in private capitalism. When profit falls under private capitalism, shareholding and financial capital tends to move rather swiftly to more profitable locations at home or abroad. This is supposed to imply optimal resource allocation — yes, from the point of view of single shareholders and financial institutions, perhaps, but not necessarily from the point of view of society as a whole, and certainly not from the point of view of displaced workers. However, by design wage-earners' funds do not allow such 'optimal' movements of capital; and furthermore the workers in control of management in single enterprises within such a system usually have no option but to face squarely the challenge of temporarily falling profits, and to look for ways to invest whatever capital is available in forward-looking investments in preparation for the future. Alternatively they may remain passive and fail to invest, or even squander their resources by allowing themselves too high remunerations from work, thus playing havoc with their own enterprise and their own personal futures. But according to conventional theories of economic motivation this is at least less likely. Statistically speaking such outcomes would then be less frequent than the destruction of capital and demobilization or marginalization of labour which in private capitalism often is the result of so-called optimal allocation of resources.

Under private capitalism profit is necessary not only for the accumulation of capital, but also as a 'message', as information from the market. Without that information, investors fail to invest. The 'information costs' involved in attaining the significant profits which convey such messages, must be paid by workers through wage restraint, and by consumers subject to mark-up pricing.

In a system of wage-earners' funds profits will also to some extent be used as market information, but investment rates will probably not be as closely linked to information of such a temporary nature as to more long-term considerations of a broader spectrum of interests. Furthermore, the 'cost' of this information is a cost which contributes to, rather than detracts from, the long-term accumulation of labour assets; therefore it appears as a 'cost' to labour only in a short-term perspective.

Secondly, qualitative incentives competing with the quantitative incentives of consumer society can find more natural outlets in labour-controlled enterprises, by self-managed improvements in the quality of working-life and work environment, improvements which are difficult to attain in a system mainly geared to private accumulation of capital.

Thirdly, the destructive incentive structure of passive risk-minimization in work under private capitalism is less likely to dominate in labour-controlled enterprises (p. 284). Active and innovative workers will be more common, even if the system cannot guarantee that every worker exhibits such traits.

It should be noticed here that the motivational assumptions underlying these conclusions are rather conservative; indeed they are rather similar to assumptions made about incentives in conventional economic theory. The main difference is that the incentives and incentive structures of workers are considered more seriously and constructively by us than by mainstream economists who usually are more concerned with consumer, shareholder and investor incentives while considering workers only as a factor of production, as 'human capital' bought as a commodity on the labour market.

Wage-earners' Funds and Negative Externalities

I have already indicated that the incentive structure of labour-controlled enterprises is more likely to favour improvements of work environment than the incentive structure of private capitalism. But as regards the effects of such labour control with respect to more wide-ranging environmental effects outside the single enterprise, incentives may not be strong enough in labour-controlled enterprises, even though, as we remarked in Chapter 11 (p. 134), workers usually are more exposed to such outside environmental effects than are other categories of people. But here the regional and national levels of the wage-earners' fund system, because of the democratic accountability of regional and national bodies, will be pressed to take responsibility for tackling more broad-ranging environmental effects, particularly if the voting public is as concerned with environmental threats as they are today according to the survey data presented in Part III.

Wage-earners' Funds and the Contradictory Nature of the Capitalist Welfare State

As I have pointed out, a system of wage-earners' funds will generate less of a problem for the state than will our present system of private capitalism. The total volume and cost of state interventions will therefore probably decrease in the kind of wage-earners' system envisaged, other things being equal of course.

But a characterization of the volume and cost of state interventions is quantitative in character, not structural, and therefore does not allow conclusions on whether the contradictory nature of the capitalist welfare state will be reduced by a system of wage-earners' funds.

State interventions in mature welfare capitalism are contradictory because (i) some state interventions exhibit what we have called market-conformity (p. 114) and may in fact enhance capitalist growth, thus refining the private capitalist system; (ii) more recently other types of state interventions have implied severe violations of the rules of the market by expanding a costly production of non-commodified use-values, and by subsidies to 'sick' companies, thus counteracting the adjustment mechanisms of the market and rigidifying the structural aspects of economic crises (pp. 116f).

What we have said earlier about the incentive structures of the wage-earners' fund system would seem to indicate that enterprises in that kind of system are less likely to get 'sick', because of a lower profit-elasticity of future-oriented investments, and also more likely to be capable of 'self-care' in case of 'sickness', as a result of a higher solidity and higher commitment to continued production even at constant or temporarily lower levels of remuneration for work. If this conjecture is reasonably valid, it implies that there will be less need for state interventions of type (ii) while state interventions of type (i) will remain important — including the state determining crucial parameters for decentralized market forces along the lines suggested by socialist economists such as W. Brus (1972). The contradiction between these two types of state interventions will then be reduced.

Summary and Conclusions

On all counts, except for the contradictions generated by the internationalization of capital, wage-earners' funds supplemented with suitable political interventions at regional and national levels seem to contribute to addressing and reducing the contradictions of mature capitalism, judging from my arguments in this chapter. But my arguments could be faulty and biased because of both the fact that wage-earners' funds remain untested in practice and to preconceived political ideas about the virtues of such funds. How, we may ask, is it possible at all to evaluate scientifically the problem-solving capability of a problem-solution which remains a proposal, a blueprint which has not yet left the drawing board?

In answering such a question we must consider what is required to make arguments about untested proposals scientifically reasonable and credible.

First, let us discuss the least demanding of the tasks I have set myself in this chapter: to find out to what extent wage-earners' funds supplemented with appropriate political interventions *address* themselves to the contradictions of mature capitalism in a way which capitalism itself and state socialism do not. It should be noted here that I have deliberately avoided asking to what extent wage-earners' funds address themselves and help us to attain the ideologically formulated *goals* so often emphasized by proponents of wage-earners' funds. This is because arguments made in terms of goals and means often, if not always, tend to become simplified and distorted. Goals specified within the framework of some political ideology tend to be sought with means which are similarly tainted ideologically, with little concern for the complexity of underlying causal processes, and the possibility of side-effects which endanger the goal to be attained. The compelling virtue of ideals can make you forget disturbing aspects of reality, and entice you into easy convictions about the value of means which are said to help in realizing such ideals.

I have asked to what extent a properly supplemented system of wage-earners' funds addresses itself to the realities of contradictory capitalism rather than to the ideals expressed by proponents of wage-earners' funds. These realities have been theoretically and empirically explored in Part II of this book. There we stand on a reasonably firm empirical and theoretical ground. If you compare the headings of the chapters on capitalist contradictions in Part II with those aspects of wage-earners' funds which have been covered in Part IV, and more systematically sorted out in this chapter, you can see that the issues implied by the contradictions explored in Part II are addressed by the kind of system described in Part IV – except for the issues raised by the internationalization of capital. But this latter issue is not addressed by capitalism either.

The method of verification here involved is one of *critical inspection* of the *similarity of issues raised* by mature capitalism (as theoretically and empirically shown in Part II), and *issues addressed* by the system of wage-earners' funds outlined in Part IV. Only independent critical inspection and discussion by other analysts can reveal whether I have been critical enough in my inspection of the issues involved. For the time being, and for all practical purposes I think I have contributed to show that a system of wage-earners' funds, appropriately supplemented with political interventions on regional and national levels, indeed does address the contradictions of capitalism better than capitalism itself, or state socialism. State socialism, however, may to some extent be in a better position to ward off the effects of the internationalization of capital, at least under certain historical conditions.

More demanding is to prove that wage-earners' funds not only *address* the contradictions of capitalism but actually help to *reduce* them. Here two different kinds of argument are involved: (i) arguments about *structures*, their compatibility or contradiction, and about the removal and replacement of incompatible structures; (ii) arguments about *actors*, their incentives and economic motivation within the kind of structures proposed in a system of wage-earners' funds, as distinguished from a system of private capitalism.

Structures can be critically inspected for the options and constraints they contain, and their compatibility. In the near future methodologists may develop more formal techniques for examining structures than those employed in my own line of argument. Unfortunately, the predominance of so-called methodological individualism among contemporary sociologists, and the lack of interest in technicalities among Marxists, seem to have prevented the refinement of formal techniques for studying structures, structural options, constraints, contradictions and change — even though attempts in this direction are being made (see, for instance, G. Hernes, 1976). In the absence of such techniques for the kind of task I have set myself, I can only offer my arguments in this chapter as a target of critical analysis by technically-minded readers and commentators. For the time being I conclude that the kind of system of wage-earners' funds outlined here would indeed reduce the effect of mature capitalist structures which maintain the contradictions between capital and labour, which contradict the highly social character of contemporary productive forces, which imply the destruction of wholesome competition on commodity markets, which allow the production of negative externalities, which destroy incentives and call for far-reaching state interventions which introduce further contradictions in addition to those which justified state interventions in the first place.

With regard to actors, their incentives and economic motivation within the kind of structures here concerned, it has been impossible for us to study in practice how real actors act within a system of wage-earners' funds simply because no such system exists on the scale presupposed by the LO–SAP proposals. Given more time and space we could have studied a similar but in some aspects much more far-reaching system such as the Yugoslav system of workers' self-management on the basis of the rather scanty empirical evidence available. Instead I have applied the motivational assumptions used and tested by the kind of mainstream economists and econometricians who have raised objections against wage-earners' funds (see Chapter 20). By using their assumptions I have at least safeguarded my argument against accusations of using unconventional and untested assumptions about economic incentives. I have also on one point used the concept of elasticity, and the econometrically established fact that the elasticity of demand tends to be lower when substitutes for the given object of demand are less accessible. This is why the profit-elasticity of investments can be expected to be lower in a system of wage-earners' funds than in a system of private capitalism. By design a wage-earners' fund system leaves no exit at the enterprise level for substitute investments outside the given enterprise when there is a slack in profitability in this enterprise. The only alternative to exit is the improvement of production within the given enterprise. And on higher regional and national levels considerations of the market mechanism of exit will most likely be balanced by broader social considerations, because of the political nature of decisions at those levels.

If anything, our conclusions regarding the economic motivations of actors in a wage-earners' fund system are likely to be on the conservative side. If we add to our conventional assumptions about *individual* economic motivation some reasonable assumptions about effects of the *collective solidarity* likely to be fostered in labour-controlled enterprises, several of our conclusions would be further strengthened (Södersten, 1973).

Having established that a system of wage-earners' funds, supplemented with appropriate political interventions at regional and national levels, is capable of reducing the contradictions of mature capitalism, at least as far as we can judge, there remains a question which I have studiously avoided up till now in order not to ideologically inflame the discussion: Is the introduction of such a system of wage-earners' funds a step toward socialism?

Here I refer back to my discussion of how to define socialism in Chapter 1. There — also in order to avoid an idealistic approach tainted by ideological biases — I suggested that short-circuiting definitions of socialism in terms of control over the means of production should be avoided. Such definitions tend to be short-circuiting because they propose a problem-solution without carefully looking into the problems to be solved. Instead I suggested a more cumbersome and deductive definition of socialism in terms of the capability of such a system to overcome or reduce the various contradictions of mature capitalism. Given this kind of definition of socialism and the assumption that my tentative conclusions about wage-earners' funds in this chapter are correct, it follows analytically that a wage-earners' fund system such as the one here discussed is a real step on the road to socialism. But only a step inasmuch as the LO—SAP report envisages a remaining private sector for middle-sized and smaller enterprises. Linkages with the international capitalist order also are a constraint on moving quickly in a socialist direction, apart from whatever political constraints of a domestic nature may exist. Furthermore, as we will point out in the final chapter, the introduction of wage-earners' funds involves problems dealing with the design of industrial technology, with existing differences of decision-making competence, and a new social morality, which must be resolved.

In discussions with some colleagues about an earlier version of this manuscript I have met a very perceptive and interesting objection against my way of arriving at the conclusion that wage-earners' funds constitute a step toward socialism. My studied avoidance of the question whether wage-earners' funds is a step toward socialism until the very end of this book, and the fact that the very first chapter contains a definition of socialism which makes my conclusion about wage-earners' funds analytically true, has been characterized as a trick to deceive and divert the attention of those who consider wage-earners' funds to be only another refinement of capitalism. I have stacked my cards from the very beginning in order to obtain the outcome I wanted, and failed to reveal openly my ideological prejudices, it has been maintained.

In a sense there is an element of truth in these allegations. But this manner of analytic work is also a characteristic of a lot of scientifically established and now widely accepted theoretical construction. A certain theoretical conclusion may be envisaged in a vague and tentative way at the beginning of the analytic process already, and definitions and assumptions are then arranged to make it possible to construct a coherent and logical argument to arrive at the conclusion anticipated. But because theoretical construction is only one component of scientific work, empirical corroboration being the other equally important component, there is always the risk that the whole beautiful and coherent theoretical structure thus constructed falls into pieces when confronted with empirical facts on some of its more sensitive spots — unless the structure can be 'saved' by more or less arbitrary auxiliary assumptions.

In cases where strong ideological convictions are involved, this manner of work, involving theoretical construction as well as empirical corroboration, pursued without 'openly revealing' one's ideological preconceptions, does have some advantages. It helps, at least temporarily, to deideologize the problems involved and allows a more thorough, less short-circuiting line of argument and empirical study. In the present case, for instance, an extensive exploration of various contradictions of the capitalist order, and of the relevance of wage-earners' funds for reducing or resolving such contradictions has been called for — an exploration which would not have been necessitated by simple ideological formulas concerning possession and control of the means of production or on the aims of wage-earners' funds. Unanticipated aspects of the problem may thus be discovered which might have remained unnoticed if an openly revealed ideological preference had been introduced at an early point; such preferences often give rise to defensive postures which restrict your attention.

The fact that my conclusion about the socialist character of wage-earners' funds is analytically true, given my premises, does not mean that it is true by definition and thus an empty tautology. The conclusion requires not only the definition of socialism I have suggested, but also an assumption that my points about wage-earners' funds and the contradictions of capitalism are factually, not analytically, true. It is the combination of these factual assumptions and my definition of socialism which logically leads to the conclusion I have drawn. The conclusion can be challenged by questioning not only the appropriateness of my definition of socialism and/or the truth of my factual assumptions about wage-earners' funds and the contradictions of capitalism, but also by contesting my assertions about these contradictions in Part II. To me the least important among these premises is my definition of socialism. If someone convinces me that what I have called socialism in fact comes closer to what in generally acceptable usage is some other kind of 'ism', then I would not hesitate to conclude that wage-earners' funds is a step on the road to that 'ism'. If the other premises were effectively challenged, then I would be in trouble necessitating a reassessment and revision of my assertions on capitalism and/or of the proposals for wage-earners' funds. But that is the kind of trouble which makes truly intellectual work challenging and worthwhile.

On this point it might be of some interest to make a few remarks about a certain latitude of interpretation allowed by my manner of defining socialism in terms of the reduction and resolution of the contradictions of private capitalism. One of these contradictions is the self-destruction of market mechanisms through the concentration and centralization of private capital. In this chapter I have asserted that a properly supplemented system of wage-earners' funds would reduce this contradiction and help to maintain a reasonably competitive commodity market. With such a system you take a step toward a kind of *market socialism* without the concentration and centralization of private capital which destroys market forces in the long run.

But there are socialists who do not accept the operation of market forces at all. Why reject their criticism of the market without further discussion? My only reason has been negative: the centrally planned command economy which is the only known socialist alternative to market socialism does not convince me as being better. This does not mean that I find a socialist critique of market socialism completely unjustified. Here one could also refer to Kenneth Arrow's (1951) well-known finding that it is impossible to logically arrive at a welfare function by aggregating votes. This is as true for 'votes' cast through purchases on a market as for votes cast in political elections. The competitive market favours the production of cheap goods in mass demand even if the intensity of the need for such goods is rather low, while disfavouring the production of goods which satisfy more intense and basic needs, if such needs are less swiftly manifested in the form of mass demand. This is a further contradiction inherent in the structure of competitive markets in addition to the self-destructive character of such markets under private capitalism. But the risks for a concentration and abuse of power which are implied by a centrally planned command economy seem to me to be worse than the Arrow type of contradiction which certainly will remain in competitive commodity markets even under market socialism.

The Arrow type of contradiction is logically impossible to resolve as long as decisions on the direction of commodity production are based on aggregate consumer decisions. However, I can alternatively envisage a decentralized, more disaggregated economy based on 'voice' instead of a highly aggregated market economy of 'exit' — to use Albert Hirschman's (1970) well-known distinction. But a vision is one thing, and the realization of an economy based on 'voice' is another. To my knowledge, no one — not even Albert Hirschman himself — has ever thought of the concept 'economy based on voice', much less practised it on a large scale.

A rather uneconomic feature of an economy based on voice would be the rather high communication costs involved. For consumers to voice their demands with regard to specific commodities by communicating these demands directly to the producer would take considerable time or require the employment of a large number of Ralph Naders, while the act of exit from the market for a specific product is an instantaneous act costing virtually nothing. However, the development of electronic devices — a mixed blessing in many connections — may in the future reduce the communication costs of 'voice' considerably. Here there are many exciting challenges for inventors and innovators in the combined fields of applied electronics and consumer activities.

While such inventors and innovators are at work, we return to the less far-fetched innovation of wage-earners' funds and market socialism. I will here finally make a few remarks about the relevance of a system of wage-earners' funds for other mature capitalist countries than Sweden. Even though my discussion originally took off from the Swedish LO—SAP proposal, this chapter has addressed itself to an evaluation of such a proposal in a much broader theoretical context which would seem to allow a generalization of our conclusions to other mature capitalist countries as well. However, we have then only taken into account the structural universals of this matter, not the historical specificities which may affect the relevance of various details of the LO—SAP report for other countries. If this book is able to stimulate analytic studies or discussions of such questions in countries other than Sweden it will have attained one of its purposes. Sweden is not alone in the Western world to face serious contradictions of mature capitalism.

Producers' co-operatives will certainly be considered in such further discussion. They are sometimes proposed as a better and more truly 'socialist' alternative to collective labour profit-sharing schemes. However, even where industrial producers' co-operatives come into being, not through labour takeovers of bankrupt private companies, but as genuinely new undertakings, their importance is at present marginal. The real problem of mature capitalism is the concentration and centralization of capital in giant companies or conglomerates. They cannot so easily be taken over by labour in the form of producers' co-operatives. This statement in no way downgrades the significance of such experiments as, for instance, the Mondragon co-operatives which in a comprehensive manner include the functions of a whole region, from production, research and development, and banking, to education and culture. In areas unencumbered by current big business this could very well be a pattern for the future, deserving full support from the labour movement.

22 Beyond Wage-earners' Funds and Economic Democracy

Obviously the introduction of some kind of wage-earners' funds and the beginning of economic democracy cannot be the last step on the road to socialism in capitalist countries. What is there beyond? In order to look ahead with realism and foresight it is often useful first to look backwards on past history. Let us therefore once more, and for the last time, place current proposals for wage-earners' funds and economic democracy in a historical perspective.

The first task which the reformist labour movement set for itself at the beginning of this century was not to introduce socialism but to *remove poverty*, not only through wage struggle but also by political means. This was seen as requiring the introduction of *political democracy*, that is general and equal rights to vote in free elections, and all the other well-known rights of assembly and organization, freedom of speech, etc. which are associated with political democracy. We find that the labour movement in this early phase of its history collaborated closely with liberals.

Often the term liberal democracy is used as an equivalent of political democracy, the term preferred by most Swedish political scientists. Marxists often speak of bourgeois democracy in this context. But the terms liberal and bourgeois democracy fail to do justice to the fact that the working class in many countries were pre-eminent in the struggle for general and equal voting rights in frèe elections. A bourgeoisie had existed for more than one hundred years, and so had liberals; but democracy still did not emerge at that time in most European countries. In many countries it was only when the labour movement had gained strength and started their struggle for democracy that general and equal voting rights in free elections were finally introduced.[1]

Once political democracy was achieved (1921 in Sweden), and workable labour majorities were attained — in Sweden this occurred in the mid-1930s — the main question was how poverty could be fought most effectively with the means at hand. The strategy of the Swedish labour movement during this second stage was to promote *stable economic growth within the framework of the capitalist order* in order to provide a larger national cake to be shared more equitably both through *unionized wage struggle* and *welfare state redistributions*. Again, this was not a socialist policy in a strict sense, but a social—liberal policy of capitalist growth, market-conforming state interventions to make the economy less sensitive to business cycles, and welfare state redistribution of wealth. The social democrats could pursue this social—liberal policy of 'social reforms without socialism'² much more consistently than the Liberal Party probably ever could have done because of their liberal hang-ups about the state, and their non-existing relationships with the trade union movement.

Radical socialists from Sweden and elsewhere — some of them without any record of successful political or union struggle to improve the material conditions of the working class — have over the years criticized the Swedish Social Democratic Party for its lack of socialist policies, and its acceptance and even promotion of capitalist growth. But in my view the Swedish Social Democrats have little reason to be ashamed even from a socialist point of view. If socialism is based on a dialectical historical—materialist conception of history rather than on abstract, non-dialectical and perhaps elitist socialist ideals, it is obvious that it is of great advantage from a socialist point of view to allow the productive forces to develop as far as possible within the capitalist order, and to allow the contradictions of this order to unfold so as to make them sufficiently visible to mobilize a system-transcending struggle — or in other words to allow the material conditions required for the creation of new higher social relations of production to mature in the womb of the old capitalist society. In fact the multi-stage social democratic strategy — a strategy which was already formulated in the 1930s — comes much closer to the original Marxian formulation of historical materialism than the road to socialism followed by the countries which today call themselves socialist.

Of course I am not saying that the Russian October Revolution was wrong, or that the Chinese or Yugoslav revolutions were wrong, or that Marxism—Leninism is completely without interest simply because they failed to conform with the original formulations by Marx. History is history, and Marx himself had a keen sense for the fact that the history of socialism could unfold in a manner quite different from what he himself originally envisaged. What I am saying is that socialist or communist denigrations of the social democratic strategy as non-socialist cannot be justified by references to Marx. It may seem rather academic to make this point. But it is not. A frank and fruitful discussion among communists, socialists and social democrats is impossible unless these basic misunderstandings have been removed.

Social democrats in Sweden agree that the second stage of the reformist labour movement has come to an end now that the postwar period of sustained economic growth has ground to a halt. It is no longer sufficient to struggle to remove remaining poverty by promoting the creation and redistribution of wealth within the framework of a capitalist mode of production. The reasons for this statement have been clarified and empirically documented in Part II of this book. Now the main task is not to *promote the growth of wealth* but to *control wealth* which has become highly concentrated and centralized and which tends to behave in a manner which threatens productive investments, employment levels and the quality of working life as well as the quality of use of leisure time.

Proposals for wage-earners' funds, regional and national development funds and similar proposals are aimed primarily at controlling wealth by transferring it to new categories of owners, namely to collective labour or social ownership, or by cutting the links between capitalist ownership of wealth and the exercise of economic power in the various ways suggested in Part IV of this book. This is the third stage of reformist labour-movement strategy, the stage of *economic democracy*. But controlling wealth for what purpose?

While the achievement and exercise of political power through political democracy — the main strategies of the first two historical stages of the reformist labour movement — had a very concrete and precise goal in sight, namely to remove poverty through policies of stable economic growth and redistribution, we cannot pin-point an equally clear purpose of the third stage of economic democracy — except the aim of control over capital itself. That is why we need to ask: what comes beyond wage-earners' funds and economic democracy? For what purpose will they be used? For further economic growth and for further increases in levels of private consumption only?

Partly we have answered these questions already — but only partly. Theoretically we have proved the reasonability of assuming that workers as collective actors have a broader, more socially relevant and adequate repertory of incentives, and thus more capability for 'multi-dimensional satisficing' than private capital owners who are interested mainly in capital accumulation and expansion of profitable consumer markets. In Chapters 7 and 14 we have presented data proving that fully employed workers in Sweden give less priority to an increase of private consumption than to social investments aimed at improving the quality of working life, environment and leisure time.

But favourable incentive structures of collective labour may not automatically bring about the results we expect on the basis of theoretical and empirical generalizations such as those mentioned above. The 'art of street crossing' — to refer once more to the parable explicated in Chapter 19 — does not come about automatically without some training, and such training would also have to include the acquisition of ideas about the direction in which you want to move. Similarly quite different results of labour 'multi-dimensional satisficing' can be expected as a result of the levels of training and the goals involved. As a prelude to such training a debate is needed with regard to goals and styles of labour-controlled management. Alternative conceptions of labour-controlled management style, content and aims are needed to provide multi-dimensional satisficing with a sufficiently broad understanding of the options available, and the criteria of choice. What is after all *satisfying* enough in multi-dimensional satisficing? What will in practice be the priorities defined within the broader range of satisfactions in a system managed under the control of wage-earners' funds?

In one sense some of these questions are not for us to answer. They must be answered by those directly involved in production, labour-controlled management and also in central democratic investment planning. But these are certainly questions for us to *ask*, if not to answer. These are questions about various alternative long-term aims of an economic system based on wage-earners' funds or similar arrangements.

It could of course be maintained that economic democracy, just like political democracy, is a matter of the *structure and method* of decision-making only, not a matter of the *content* of decision-making. Liberal interpreters of political democracy in particular have emphasized that it would be wrong to include specifications of the content of democratic politics in the definition of political democracy. Such definitions should only specify the methods for resolving political differences, and the formal structures required to assure the application of such methods. Democratic socialists, while agreeing about the necessity of specifying these political structures and methods, have often emphasized the need to specify at least some aspects of the *substance* of democratic politics as well.[3] In order to maintain the legitimacy and workability of political democracy it is a prerequisite that poverty and excessive inequality are removed.

Whether to make this prerequisite part of the definition of the political democracy or not, is a matter which we do not have to settle here. It is sufficient to state that the legitimacy and workability of political democracy would seem to depend on some prerequisites such as the removal of excessive inequalities, even if this is considered an empirical rather than a definitional statement.

Similarly it could be maintained that *economic* democracy, once its basic methods and structures have been introduced, depends for its legitimacy and workability on certain preconditions such as the reduction not mainly of poverty but of work alienation and excessive differentials in decision-making competence. If these goals fail to be realized by a system of wage-earners' funds, or even by full workers' self-management, such a system is not likely to survive for long.

But because work alienation and differentials of decision-making competence are bound to be rather widespread when wage-earners' funds are introduced, as a heritage from the capitalist mode of production just like poverty was a heritage from pre-democratic times, a primary goal of economic democracy would be the struggle to remove work alienation and differences of competence.

Among other things the realization of such primary goals would seem to require a change of technology to make it more humane.[4] It requires a close enough connection between the 'life projects' of workers and their work situation. Not only efficient work with a minimum of work alienation is needed, but also an integration of life and work, that is a production designed to satisfy basic human needs at all the levels of the Maslowian hierarchy, and not only the immediate needs of productivity, income and employment.

Technological change of this nature, and changing relationships between life and work are topics large enough to require studies of their own. These are the kinds of studies which should be pursued beyond the present discussion of wage-earners' funds. Without realistic solutions to these problems, often against the constraints set by the relatively long terms of service of present day industrial hardware, we will not have travelled far on the road to democratic socialism, even if we have taken the first steps.

Similarly a reduction of differentials of decision-making competence requires organizational innovations which go much beyond the mere formality of replacing private capital with collective labour control on the local level, and of introducing democratic control of economic parameters on the national level. This new form of economic power must be filled with a new content mobilizing the potentials and the motivations of all working men and women. One aspect of this 'new content' is a new social morality which articulates and resolves the dilemmas of broadly shared human predicaments in transitional and post-capitalist societies.

Social morality in capitalist society, with all its pluralist variety, revolves around appeals for *individual* refinement, gratification, achievement or betterment. The morality of present-day 'youth culture' with its narcissistic focus on pleasure and enjoyment in more or less commercialized forms also focuses on *individual* values. A social morality based on considerations of country and society is often looked upon with suspicion, and for very different reasons. The businessman is suspicious of such appeals unless they can earn him a profit in projects for national reconstruction or national defence. He defends 'individualism' against the 'creeping socialism' of government interventions which claim to represent the interests of society as a whole. The true liberal is understandably sceptical about appeals to broader social interests in view of the repression and cruelty committed in the name of country and state all through the history of mankind. Marxists disavow any appeals to broader social interests in capitalist societies because of the contradictory nature of such societies and instead appeal to working class morality. Marxists can acknowledge the need for a new social morality focusing on broad social issues and dilemmas only as part of a struggle for new social relations of production. But because these dilemmas are already visible today, it is not impossible to draw the outlines of such a new morality now.

Take a concrete issue such as nuclear power. Apart from its economic and technological aspects it poses a moral dilemma, a choice between alternative energy-producing technologies which have far-reaching and very different structural implications. Producing energy in plants based on oil (which will not last for very long) or coal (which will last much longer) will produce a pollution of carcinogenic substances resulting in certain premature death of a relatively large number of persons over time. Civilian nuclear power would seem to be much cleaner. To the best of our knowledge it has not killed many individuals over the past twenty years. But *if* a big reactor accident takes place — and the well-known Three Mile Island accident at Harrisburg was very close to such a big accident — then a very large number of people will be killed or fatally affected instantaneously, in one blow, disrupting existing social networks and with social implications extending far beyond the location of the nuclear reactor involved. In contrast to such an accident the deaths of people exposed to carcinogenic pollution from oil and coal are spread out in time, and are experienced by those involved as private tragedies which cannot, in each individual case, be traced back with certainty to the effects of pollution.

How do we make a choice between an energy alternative producing the slow and successive but certain private death of, say, X number of people over, say, a fifty-year period, and another alternative implying a much smaller probability of a much larger accident involving more or less immediate death and fatal damage to X people in one blow, disrupting whole communities, and creating fear and apprehension in whole societies?

Individualistic social morality has no answers to such questions. The question here is not whether the two alternatives just mentioned are realistic in every detail. In fact it can be maintained that the nuclear energy alternative will be unable to provide all the energy needed, and therefore must be supplemented with oil and coal-produced energy. The two alternatives are thus not that clear-cut. It is also obvious from our research in Part III that the extended working class, at least, views the threat of pollution not simply as a piecemeal, private threat but as a systemic, structural threat. But our question should still be sufficient to indicate the character of moral choice in an advanced industrial society, whether capitalist or transitional or socialist for that matter, namely the fact that we are threatened not only as private citizens but collectively with respect to our lives, our social relations and networks, our trust in the structure of social arrangements, as a result of the increasingly social character of our productive forces, and their possibly far-reaching future consequences. Therefore a new social morality must go beyond the private individualistic concerns which are predominant in bourgeois society, and also beyond the short-sighted focus which we have allowed ourselves so far.

But how is it possible to prevent the transformation of such a new social morality into some kind of authoritarian ideology in the superstructure of a hierarchically organized society? Obviously this will not be prevented by having even the best moral philosophers formulate a non-authoritarian version of this new social morality. It can be prevented only by a broadly based democratic political struggle against authoritarian applications of hierarchy. As part of that struggle we have the struggle against alienation and differentials of decision-making competence mentioned above.

But once the effectiveness of that struggle is assured, moral philosophers still have something to contribute. As far as I can see a central concept in such moral philosophy must be the concept of *predicament* defined at the intersection of objective structures and individual needs and values, or at the intersection of the realms of necessity and freedom, as we have suggested in Chapter 12.

We need neither prophets of doom nor facile optimism. We live in an exciting period of history surrounded by obvious dangers and perhaps somewhat less obvious challenges and possibilities. The clarification and realization of these possibilities, and a reduction of these dangers, is a momentous task requiring the concerted efforts of labour movements, 'managerial revolutions', concerned citizens, social scientists, innovative technologists and moral philosophers.

Appendix I

Table A.I.1: **Main classes and strata by more detailed breakdowns in branches of the economy (percentages)**

	Industrial workers	Service workers	Middle strata	Total
Workers in industrial production	100	—	—	37
Storage, transport and sales workers	—	21	—	8
Workers in the service sector	—	11	—	4
Workers in reproduction: schools, hospitals etc.	—	15	—	6
Technicians in industrial production, supervisors	—	9	43	14
Office clerks	—	26	17	14
White-collar employees in sales, banks etc.	—	10	11	7
White-collar employees in 'reproduction'	—	4	27	8
White-collar employees in service sector	—	4	2	2
	100	100	100	100
N=	462	489	293	1244

Source: Our own sample survey in Stockholm's and Kopparberg's provinces; see Appendix II.
Note: Managers are not included in this table.

Table A.I.2: Perception of the importance of some threats against people like oneself by social class (percentages)

	Industrial workers	Service workers	Middle strata	Managers	Total
CAPITALISM					
No threat	27	32	52	80	36
Some threat	39	42	32	16	38
Big threat	34	26	16	4	26
SOCIALISM					
No threat	59	46	43	17	49
Some threat	26	36	34	42	32
Big threat	15	18	22	41	19
THE STATE					
No threat	40	26	34	32	34
Some threat	33	37	34	32	34
Big threat	27	37	32	36	32
N=	430	451	279	25	1185

Source: Our own sample survey; see Appendix II.
Note: The fact that total N in this and the following table is lower than in Table A.I.1 is due to non-response or don't-know replies.

Table A.I.3: Combination of perceptions of threats from capitalism and socialism (percentages)

	Industrial workers	Service workers	Middle strata	Managers	Total
Capitalism greater threat than socialism	53	42	26	8	41
Capitalism and socialism equal threats	32	36	41	20	36
Socialism greater threat than capitalism	15	22	33	72	23
	100	100	100	100	100
N=	417	439	279	24	1159

Source: Our own sample survey; see Appendix II.

Table A.1.4: 'Greatest threats' as obtained by the method of ranking, by social class

	Industrial Workers	Service workers	Middle strata	Total
Environmental pollution	40	48	45	46
Unemployment	35	27	23	27
Nuclear power	6	10	11	9
Capitalism	8	2	9	6
Inflation	8	5	4	5
Other threats	2	9	6	5
N=	52	60	47	164*

*A small number of managers were also included in this total
Source: Our own sample survey; see Appendix II.
Note: Instead of allowing respondents to rate one threat at a time, the question producing these findings required the ranking of all the threats in one single operation. In this way we obtained a finer discrimination among the 'great threats'. Unfortunately, the ranking question was not used to supplement the rating question in the total sample, but only in a smaller, random subsample (see Appendix II).

Table A.1.5: Percentage voting for the main parties in parliamentary elections in Sweden since 1944

	Communist Party	Social Democrats	Centre Party	Liberal Party	Conservative Party
1944	10.3	46.7	13.6	12.9	15.9
1948	6.3	46.1	12.4	22.8	12.3
1952	4.3	46.1	10.7	24.4	14.4
1956	5.0	44.6	9.4	23.8	17.1
1958	3.4	46.2	12.7	18.2	19.5
1960	4.5	47.8	13.6	17.5	16.5
1964	5.2	47.3	13.2	17.0	13.7
1968	3.0	50.1	15.7	14.3	12.9
1970	4.8	45.3	19.9	16.2	11.5
1973	5.3	43.6	25.1	9.4	14.3
1976	4.8	42.7	24.1	11.1	15.6
1979	5.6	43.2	18.1	10.6	20.3

Source: SOS Allmanna Valen 1979. Del 1.

Appendix II

Methods of Sampling and Statistical Analysis

The empirical data presented in Part III of this book have been collected through questionnaires and interviews with employees, managing directors and board members in a sample of firms in Stockholm and Kopparberg provinces.

As a first step in this sample the National Central Bureau of Statistics randomly selected a number of working places with at least ten employees each in these two provinces. Information about the number of working places, sampling probabilities for different strata of working places, etc. are presented in Table A.II.1.

The firms involved were contacted by letter and telephone, if necessary, and with their help we acquired lists of employees. Samples of employees were drawn from these lists. In this second stage sampling probabilities were calculated in such a manner that non-response in the first stage was compensated. Table A.II.1 contains information about non-response and sampling probabilities for this second stage. In March 1976 this sample of employees received our questionnaire which was answered and returned by 64.8 per cent, that is 1294 respondents.

There was considerable non-response in both stages of this two-stage sampling procedure. We have carried out an analysis of non-response and its effects for the second stage. Our main method of analysis has been to cross-tabulate time of return of the questionnaire (without reminder, after the first, second, third or fourth reminder) and some crucial variables included in our survey (see Cornfield, 1942).

In addition we have compared the distribution of answers to some questions in our survey with answers to the same questions used in other surveys with a national coverage. These comparisons were made not in order to assess sampling bias in our more limited samples from Stockholm and Kopparberg provinces, but rather in order to establish to what extent results from these two provinces could be assumed to be roughly representative of the country as a whole.

Table A.II.1: Two-stage sample characteristics (PSUs → SSUs)

PSUs = Primary Sampling Units: firms
SSUs = Secondary Sampling Units: employees

No. of employees per firm		No. of firms (PSUs)	Sampling fractions of PSUs intended %	No. of lists of employees obtained	Fraction of lists obtained %	Sampling fractions of SSUs from lists %	No. of questionnaires dispatched	Response fractions of SSUs obtained %
Stockholm's province	10–19	2,927	0.5	9	0.30	66.6	101	52.4
	20–49	1,902	1.0	10	0.53	36.4	113	53.9
	50–99	681	2.0	3	0.44	45.4	96	59.3
	100–199	319	5.0	9	3.20	6.2	108	60.4
	200–499	204	5.0	7	2.94	5.8	149	63.7
	500–	100	10.0	5	5.00	4.0	428	55.6
Kopparberg's province	10–19	483	5.0	13	2.40	82.6	202	62.8
	20–49	308	5.0	7	2.33	85.8	207	57.0
	50–99	101	10.0	4	3.20	60.0	160	68.8
	100–199	49	20.0	6	12.00	16.6	149	71.1
	200–499	22	50.0	7	27.20	6.4	136	64.7
	500–	12	50.0	3	25.00	8.0	286	61.5

Notes: Larger firms were over-represented by design in our sample.

In calculating the obtained response fractions of SSUs we have not eliminated those employees who no longer were part of the population of employees at the time of our survey (recent pensioners, employees who had left their jobs etc.). The actually obtained sampling fractions of employees (SSUs) are thus in actual fact somewhat higher than indicated in this table, and non-response somewhat lower.

*Figure A.II.1 Percentage estimates for a number of crucial variables at different
levels of cumulative completeness of the sample*

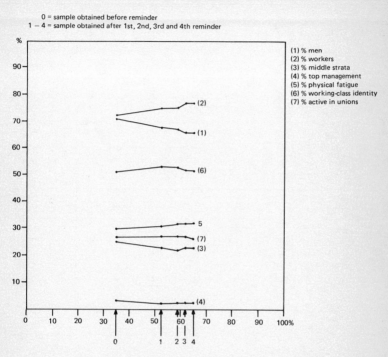

0 = sample obtained before reminder
1 — 4 = sample obtained after 1st, 2nd, 3rd and 4th reminder

(1) % men
(2) % workers
(3) % middle strata
(4) % top management
(5) % physical fatigue
(6) % working-class identity
(7) % active in unions

Figure A.II.1 would seem to indicate that non-response has had
rather little influence on our findings. On the whole late respondents to
our questionnaire do not contribute to change our sample estimates
greatly on significant survey variables. There are some exceptions to
this general impression, however. Women had a tendency to reply somewhat later to our questionnaire than did men, and we can therefore
assume that women are somewhat under-represented in our actual
sample. Because a smaller number in the working class answered our
questionnaire without any reminder, we can also assume that workers
may be somewhat under-represented among those responding to our
questionnaire. However, because most of our analysis has focused on
distributions where these various classes and strata are controlled for
we do not expect this particular bias to have influenced our findings
to any greater extent. With regard to more attitudinal kinds of questions
such as the ones on class identification and feeling of physical fatigue
after work we find little or no differences in the distribution of answers

to this question among early and late respondents to our questionnaire. This also holds for level of union activity. In Table A.II.1 we find a somewhat higher incidence of non-response among employees in Kopparberg province than in Stockholm province. This regional difference can probably be accounted for by the difference we have already found with regard to non-response between the working class and higher strata; Kopparberg province has a larger share of working class members than Stockholm province.

Table A.II.2 which compares the response distributions for a number of questions on work environment in our surveys and in a nationwide level of living study carried out by the National Central Bureau of Statistics would seem to indicate that our sample from Stockholm and Kopparberg provinces manifest response distributions closely similar to those obtained in national sample surveys.

Table A.II.2: Percentages of affirmative replies to a number of questions in our survey and corresponding percentages in a nationwide representative survey (ULF) using the same questions

| | *Percentages of Affirmative Answers* | |
	Our Survey	*ULF Survey**
Is your work hectic?	58	57
Is your work monotonous?	21	19
Is your work mentally straining?	36	33
Do you have much influence over the planning of your work?**	33	39

*Source: *Levnadsförhållanden. Rapport No. 2,* Sysselsättning och arbetsplatsförhållanden 1974, Stockholm: LiberFörlag 1976.

**The questions used in the two surveys are not completely identical in this case.

A random sub-sample of 200 individuals was later drawn from among those who had responded to our questionnaire, and 182 of these could be interviewed personally in February 1977, that is nearly a year after our questionnaires had been collected. The National Central Bureau of Statistics was responsible for carrying out the interviews. In this book we have utilized these follow-up interviews to a very limited extent, for instance in Table A.I.3.

As a basis for our study of managing directors and company board members we consulted the archives of the Swedish Patent and Registration Office and took the names of all managing directors and board members in those firms which had placed lists of employees at our disposal. In March 1977 *all* these managing directors and company board members received a questionnaire which also contained some questions identical to those answered by employees. This was thus intended to be a total survey, not a sample survey. Answers were returned by 74 per cent of all those who received our questionnaires. However, if we look more closely at those company board members who had been appointed by local unions, answers were received only by 62 per cent, due mainly to the fact that the archives of the Swedish Patent and Registration Office were not always updated with regard to this category of board members.

Finally, it should be emphasized that our statistical analysis of the data collected has been focused mainly on simple cross-tabulations to establish the distribution of relevant variables among various categories in our samples. More complex multivariate analyses have not been carried out simply because our research questions have been of a descriptive rather than a causal nature. Our main purpose has been to assess various dimensions of strength of the working class, and various strata rather than to explain the causes of such variations.

Notes

Part I
Chapter 1

1. Sten Johansson, a leading Swedish sociologist and a social democrat, in his book *När är tiden mogen?* (1974) discusses whether time is ripe for socialism in Sweden. He thinks it is and points out some directions of desirable socialist reform in Sweden today.

2. On the basis of a cross-national analysis of sixty-four countries Wilensky (1975) has found that variations in welfare expenditures can be better explained by level of economic development than by type of political regime, official ideology or popular sentiments about equality. He concludes that economic growth and its demographic and bureaucratic outcomes are the root cause of the general emergence and development of the welfare state — regardless of whether the regimes are 'socialist' or 'capitalist', 'collectivist' or 'individualist', etc. (p. viii). However, at an advanced stage of affluence we may find that countries matched for per capita income differ sharply in their politics of welfare due to degree of centralization of government, the organization of the working-class, etc.

Wilensky's study has been criticized mainly on three grounds. Firstly, his *research design*, in its overly ambitious attempt to establish universal relationships by including as many as sixty-four countries in the analysis, has made it at the same time necessary and most difficult or impossible to control for the very large number of variables which may influence the results. To compare analytically a smaller number of countries more similar in economic and systemic terms, but different with regard to, say, their political orientations and type of government, could have been more fruitful. Secondly, it has been pointed out that Wilensky's *independent political variables* were badly chosen; it would have been better to assess the effect of labour party cabinet influence, and the longevity of such influence. Thirdly, the *relevance and validity* of Wilensky's choice of indicators for his *dependent variable* of welfare state expenditures has been questioned. As a measure of the egalitarian implications of welfare expenditures the ILO definition of such expenditures in relationship to GNP which Wilensky has applied is quite deficient, as Walter Korpi has pointed out (1979, p. 5). See also Korpi and Shalev (1979), John D. Stephens (1979), Francis G. Castles (1978), Charles Hewitt (1977) and Lars Björn (1976).

3. For the views of a socialist active in the Democratic Party, see Michael Harrington (1979).

4. In the 1960 US election campaign President Eisenhower, in an attempt to warn the electorate against the 'welfare policies' suggested by J. F. Kennedy, referred to the high suicide rate and other signs of warning in a 'fairly friendly European country' experimenting with socialism and welfare. This reference was obviously to Sweden. In March 1976 *Fortune* magazine, for instance, published an article 'How Electrolux cleans up in socialist Sweden'. The interviews with

Swedish managers contained in that article made it perfectly clear that these managers had found their collaboration with Sweden's 'socialist government' quite fruitful from a business point of view. Apart from the fact that this demonstrates that the social democratic government emphasized capitalist economic growth with welfare redistributions of the national product in the 'second stage' of social democratic development (see Chapter 21 in this book), it also illuminates the tendency of the US establishment to label any far-reaching welfare expenditures undertaken by a social democratic labour government as 'socialist', a label which I do not accept. The policies of the social democrats in their forty-four years of governmental power were essentially social—liberal — that is a use of state interventions within the context of a so-called mixed economy. On the other hand the 'social—liberalism' of the social democrats could be pressed much more consistently and energetically than the bourgeois social—liberals would have dared undertake, given their ideological hang-ups regarding the role of the state (see Chapter 2).

5. At the time of finishing this manuscript a cross-national study by John D. Stephens (1979) was published which answers many if not all of our questions concerning the predicaments and prospects of democratic socialism in a comparative perspective, particularly about Sweden. Relevant comparative studies with a somewhat more limited focus have just been published by Korpi and Shalev (1979 and 1980). In the spring of 1980 Erik Olin Wright is initiating a comparative empirical study of the class structures of USA, Sweden, Italy, England and Finland with a particular focus on the 'contradictory class locations' discussed in our Chapter 13.

6. According to a well-known Swedish encyclopedia *socialization* (= *socialisering*, in Swedish) implies a large-scale transfer of private property to societal ownership or control. One of the earlier editors of this encyclopedia, Tage Erlander, was responsible for this formulation. Much later he became Prime Minister in a social democratic government. This notwithstanding it would be inaccurate to state — as Thorbjörn Fälldin (Centre Party leader, and present Prime Minister) did in the election campaign of 1976 — that the social democratic interpretation of socialism is equivalent with socialization. Swedish social democrats have always maintained that socialization in the sense of a nationalization of the means of production is only one of several alternative avenues toward socialism.

7. In response to completely unfounded bourgeois allegations regarding the risks of a Soviet-type socialism, if social democrats were allowed to continue their political rule in Sweden, the social democrats half-heartedly introduced the notion of 'blue-and-yellow socialism' *(blågul socialism)* in the election campaign of 1976, referring to the colours of the Swedish flag. Advertising agencies illustrated this with images of good and friendly life in beautiful natural settings; socialism was said to imply human concern and security *(trygghet)*, claims which could be made by any political party.

8. In a paper on 'Enterprises, Markets and States' presented at the XIth World Congress of Political Science in Moscow, August 1979, Göran Therborn, an internationally known Marxist and sociologist, suggested that the state should be seen not as an actor 'in its own right' but as a 'terrain' on which capital and labour appear as actors through their respective organizations. Just as the metaphors of 'arena' or 'stage' the metaphor of 'terrain' would seem to have some limitations. In some contexts the state may also appear as an actor mandated by other actors, and operating under the structural options and constraints which are constituted not only by the given mode of production but also by the residual tasks of the state in that context. The 'terrain' of the state has its own structural options and constraints and is surrounded by the 'terrains' of enterprises and markets; and actors representing capital, labour and state appear on all of these 'terrains'. A closer look would reveal not only actor—actor interactions but also

actor—structure interactions in all these 'terrains'. For a more thorough theoretical analysis of this whole complex we would need the kind of multi-level structure—actor model suggested by Gudmund Hernes (1976) for the study of 'Structural Change in Social Processes', including 'dialectical' change (p. 532 ff). At an earlier point in our project it was my intention to apply this kind of model, but it turned out to extend our theoretical analysis far beyond the aim of the present study which is a theoretically guided descriptive assessment of the strength of capital and labour in dealing with the contradictions of mature capitalism.

9. A rather typical example of this dogmatic use of ideological formulas in distinguishing true and false socialists is found in a paper by Sune Sunesson (1976) on state ideology and trade unions in Sweden. His main tool of ideological criticism is the derogatory term 'Lasallean'. Having classified Swedish social democracy and trade unions as Lasallean, he seems to have no need for any further analysis of the concrete historical predicaments of the reformist Swedish labour movement at different points in time. The lessons learned from critical incidents such as the General Strike in 1909 and the prolonged Metal Workers' Strike in 1945 are not even mentioned in Sunesson's paper. Sunesson's approach could be contrasted with the approach of Anna Hedborg (1976) in a paper which we will summarize in Chapter 19 of this book.

Another example, taken from another ideological context, can be found in Peter F. Drucker's recent book *The Unseen Revolution. How Pension-Fund Socialism came to America* (1976, p. 1ff).

> If 'socialism' is defined as 'ownership of the means of production by the workers' — and this is both the orthodox and the only rigorous definition — then the United States is the first truly 'socialist' country. Through their pension-funds, employees of American business own at least 25 per cent of its equity capital, which is more than enough for control. . . . In terms of socialist theory, the employees of America are the only true 'owners' of the means of production. Through their pension-funds they are the only true 'capitalists' around, owning, controlling, and directing the country's capital funds'. The 'means of production', that is the American economy — again with agriculture the only important exception — is being run for the benefit of the country's employees.

Drucker carefully avoids any questions about what it means, in fact, to 'control', 'direct' and 'benefit'. Indeed he points out that no one seems to have heard of this 'socialist' pension scheme in the United States, and that 'not one in a thousand seems to realize that through this pension plan he actually owns American business' (p. 40). It remains a riddle how anyone can use a scheme of which he is ignorant, as a tool of active control and direction. The best one can say about the ideological asides of Drucker's book is that they are thought-provoking.

10. Karl R. Popper's criticism of holistic utopianism and 'wholesale' social engineering (1969) comes to mind at this point. Popper argues that wholesale in contrast to piecemeal social engineering tends to be repressive and undemocratic. This argument neglects that a societal order such as capitalism, even when combined with a liberal democracy of piecemeal reforms, can develop and retain structurally repressive traits. However, Popper seems to admit the possibility of stepwise piecemeal reforms guided by holistic rather than more limited considerations of societal problems. Ernst Wigforss, a social democratic theoretician and former Minister of Finance in Sweden, has discussed this possibility with reference to what he calls 'provisional utopias' (1962, pp. 82-131).

11. For an illuminating discussion of two notions of contradiction in *Capital* by Marx, see Maurice Godelier (1972a, pp. 77-86 and 179-86). The second of these notions — the increasing contradiction between forces and social relations of

production — implies that mature capitalism generates a number of human and societal problems and costs. This view is sometimes challenged by pointing to the existence of similar problems in so-called socialist countries in Eastern Europe. All 'advanced industrial societies' are said to have similar problems, whether they are capitalist or socialist. This challenge can be met with any of the three following types of argument: (i) Eastern Europe is not socialist but state-capitalist. (ii) Eastern Europe certainly has problems, but those which are similar to the problems of capitalism are much less pronounced or of a different character — for instance unemployment and inflation — a statement which can be empirically tested. Other problems are not at all similar to capitalist problems, but are generated in 'transitional formations between capitalism and communism' located in a somewhat hostile and highly competitive capitalist world order. (iii) Socialism is an ideal type which *by definition* implies the resolution of the basic problems of capitalism. If this ideal is not approximated anywhere in the world it cannot be used in comparative studies of existing societies but only as a guide for political theory and praxis aimed at abolishing the contradictions and problems of capitalism on the road to socialism. The last approach is illustrated in the present chapter.

12. See for instance I. Avakumović (1964), W. S. Vuchinich (1969), B. Horvat (1969) and B. Denitch (1980). For a collection of papers on workers' self-management in Yugoslavia, see Obradović and Dunn (1978).

Chapter 2

1. A pioneering and fundamental document in the history of Swedish Social Liberalism is Bertil Ohlin's pamphlet (1936) *A Free or Directed Economy*. A more academic treatment of related problems is found in Erik Lundberg (1958).

2. Terms such as 'scientific' socialism and 'real' Marxism would seem to flourish particularly in settings where Marxism and socialism have assumed the character of absolute authority, and thus have become much more than guidelines for the scientific exploration and revolutionary transformation of capitalist societies. For an authoritative source of this type, see O. Kuusinen et al., *Fundamentals of Marxism—Leninism* (1964) But also outside the Soviet orbit we do find interpretations of Marxism as a positivist science unveiling 'objective laws' of history. For a Marxist critique of such interpretations, see Lucio Colletti (1972, pp.229—36), particularly his reference to the fact that Marx viewed the 'objective laws' of the capitalist order as a 'false objectivity' which can be turned upside down.

Chapter 3

1. Thus historical materialism alone, as originally formulated by Karl Marx, cannot explain fully the emergence of socialist regimes in countries like the Soviet Union, China, Vietnam, Cuba, etc. Marxism—Leninism addresses itself to the problems raised by the 'unorthodox' emergence of socialism in these countries.

2. This statement of course refers to Marx's well-known dictum that 'No social order ever disappears before all the productive forces for which there is room in it have been developed; and new higher relations of production never appear before the material conditions of their existence have matured in the womb of the old society.' (Marx, 1971b, p. 6). Martin Nicolaus (1972, pp. 306—33), on the basis of a close reading of the *Grundrisse*, sheds more light on the problems here involved. See particularly his concluding statements (p. 333).

3. Karl Marx (1971b): 'From forms of development of the forces of production, these relations turn into their fetters. Then comes the period of social revolution.' For an enlightening account of how Marx and Engels viewed the 'revolutionaries', and the problems of 'reform versus revolution' in nineteenth century Europe, see Sven-Ove Hansson (1976).

4. This observation did not hold in the earlier phases of social democratic rule – perhaps because the Social Democratic Party at that time did not yet appear as fully integrated with the political establishment held responsible for the economic situation. Nor did it hold after the defeat of the Social Democratic Party in the 1976 elections, in the middle of a long recession. In fact, social democrats at that time received majority support in public opinion polls. It would thus appear that social democratic popularity has been partly a function of an interaction between business cycles and the establishment position. When social democrats were not in government, and before they became fully integrated in the political establishment even though they were in government positions, recessions increased the support for the Social Democratic Party; in periods of recession when social democrats were fully integrated in government positions, however, this reduced the popularity of the social democrats. For a longitudinal empirical study demonstrating the effects of crisis symptoms such as unemployment, inflation and changes in real income on the popularity of the Social Democratic Party, in or out of government, see Lars Jonung and Eskil Wadensjö (1979).

5. Obviously the simultaneous appearance of peaks of business cycles, and a strong electoral support for the social democrats in government are not sufficient conditions for embarking on the road to socialism. The political and union branches of the labour movement must also feel the urgency of a socialist reconstruction of society, and sufficiently strong pressures in this direction from their constituencies. In a reformist labour movement like the Swedish one such a convergence of circumstances is most likely if social democrats occupy government positions in a temporary upswing of the economy *after* a relatively protracted recession which has helped to make the contradictions of mature capitalism more visible to the general public as well as to politicians and trade union leaders. Furthermore, it is necessary that the business community be relatively divided and weakened as a result of that recent crisis and the systemic inconsistencies it revealed. One of the main purposes of this book is to assess the extent to which a country such as Sweden is approaching a situation with such characteristics.

6. Leif Lewin in his book *Planhushållningsdebatten* (1966) has provided a detailed summary and explication of political themes vindicated, and policies advocated in the Swedish debate about social and economic planning from the 1920s and up to the 1960s. I disagree with Lewin's use of the term 'socialism' (see also Dahlkvist, 1975), but as a source book documenting an important period of Swedish politics, his book is most useful. See also Nils Elvander's study on the politics of taxation in Sweden from 1945–70 (1972), and his paper, in English, on 'Scandinavian Social Democracy: its Strength and Weakness' (1979, particularly pp. 19–35), even though I have some reservations about his evaluation of more recent ideological developments within the Swedish Social Democratic Party.

7. In fact the slogan 'social reforms without socialism' is an old slogan of the Swedish Liberal Party, *Folkpartiet*, which again in the 1976 campaign became a popular slogan directed against the social democratic government – in spite of the fact that the social democrats in government had a very long tradition of exactly 'social reforms without socialism'.

Part II

The more theoretical sections in Part II have been written by Ulf Himmelstrand who also has condensed, edited and translated a number of more extensive working papers in Swedish written by Lars Lundberg. Lars Lundberg is thus responsible for some of the commentary and most of the documentation and empirical materials assembled for Chapters 5, 6, 7 and 9. In Chapter 10 the section on state subsidies to industry is based on a monograph by Lars Lundberg (1979) which is being published in its entirety, together with materials from parts of this project, in Swedish.

Chapter 4

1. In this context it would take us too far astray to discuss the theoretical short-comings of empirical studies reporting a lack of correlation between objective and subjective indicators. Suffice it to say that a convincing and scientifically meaningful demonstration of the absence or existence of relationships between objective and subjective indicators must take off from a theoretically penetrating analysis of *what* objective circumstances affect *what* aspects of subjective consciousness, and from a choice of objective and subjective empirical indicators guided by such a theoretical analysis. Too often studies such as the one by Erik Allardt mentioned in the main text which claim to demonstrate a lack of relationship between objective and subjective indicators take off from an arbitrary assembly of whatever objective indicators are available such as level of education, income, housing, occupation, etc., correlating them with various subjective indicators of satisfaction, adjustment, alienation and the like. The theoretical question is never asked why and how the objective indicators chosen would have such and such a relationship with subjective indicators, or whether objective and subjective indicators of a different character might have been more theoretically appropriate for a study of relationships between objective and subjective realms of human life. For a discussion of relevant theoretical questions in this context see Ulf Himmelstrand (1976).

Our criticism of Erik Allardt's conclusions on the relationships between subjective and objective indicators does certainly not rule out our high appreciation for other aspects of his comparative study of objective and subjective welfare and happiness dimensions in the Nordic countries. For a full account, unfortunately only in Swedish, of this comparative study, see Erik Allardt (1975).

2. The book edited by Coser and Rosenberg is a good example because it is a very good text. In the first edition their selections from Marx concerned class, division of labour and 'class cohesion in conflict', — 'cohesion' being a favoured social psychological term in the 1950s. The structural context of class conflict was left largely unilluminated because of the truncated nature of the quotations. In later editions of this reader, however, some excellent excerpts on Marx's notion of alienation have been added, and also a page on the contradictions between forces and relations of production, but with the misleading comment that ideas, according to Marx, 'were but epiphenomenal reflections' of the modes of production (Coser and Rosenberg, 3rd edn., 1969, p. 664). Other textbooks in sociological theory, like the one written by Nicolas S. Timasheff (1964, rev. edn., pp. 46ff) depicted Marx as a simplistic economic determinist just as Sorokin did in his *Contemporary Sociological Theories* (1928). It would certainly be worth making a more thorough study of the changes in how US sociology textbooks have presented Marx during the last fifty years. A breakthrough for a more analytic and fair representation of Marx in common US textbooks in sociology was probably achieved with Irving M. Zeitlin, *Ideology and the Development of Sociological Theory* (1968).

3. See Karl Marx, *Capital*, Vol. 1, 1976, Parts III and IV. Surplus value is still a most controversial notion in Marxian economic theory. It is because this notion

is founded on the labour theory of value that it is controversial. (For a critical assessment of Marxian thinking on this point, see G. N. Halm, 1968, Chapter 11. For a more sympathetic view, see three papers by Leif Johansen, Alfredo Medio and H. J. Sherman in Hunt and Schwartz (eds.), pp. 295–364).

However, there are some elements of the concept of surplus value which survive even if the limited range of the labour theory of value is acknowledged. If the price paid for labour (including also the 'crystallized labour' embodied in the tools and machines actually used in labour) were not lower than the price obtained for the total product of labour, then the owner of means of production and labour power would have no profit to accumulate, no surplus to consume or reinvest. Then there would be no capitalism. That is pretty self-evident. It is when we move from what is self-evident, and proceed to discuss how to *explain* and determine the value of that portion of labour which is required for social reproduction of labour power, and the value of machine depreciation and the surplus value appropriated by capitalists, it is then that Marxist and non-Marxist economists get into trouble with each other. Mainstream economists, accustomed as they are to think of value in terms of prices set by supply and demand relationships, may find it difficult to follow Marx when he measures value only in terms of the number of working hours needed to produce a commodity or to reproduce labour power. Intellectually honest Marxists, on the other hand, are usually willing to admit that demand and supply relationships, and pricing are important in that context, and point out that Marx treated such mechanisms in the latter volumes of *Capital*. At the same time they emphasize, however, that the labour theory of value, even though quite useless in running a central bank or in collective bargaining, still fulfils an important intellectual task in clarifying the meaning of the capital relationship, and of capitalism and its evolution (see several articles in Horrowitz (ed.), 1968).

Fortunately our book does not consist of detailed advice to central banks or to collective bargainers. Our aim is to intellectually and empirically clarify the conditions and predicaments of mature welfare capitalism. But if the common Marxian definitions of surplus value still confuse our readers, we offer them a somewhat denatured but still presumably Marxist definition suggested by Paul Baran, the well-known Marxist economist: Surplus value consists of 'the entire difference between aggregate net output and the real income of labour' (Baran, 1957, Chapter 2, note 1). None of the terms of this definition derive from the labour theory of value.

4. The most succinct summary of historical materialism can be found in *A Contribution to the Critique of Political Economy* by Marx himself (1971b). For an enlightening and systematic if not completely uncontroversial explication, see Oscar Lange (1963, Chapter 2). See also W. Shaw (1978) whom we have quoted in several contexts, and J. McMurtry (1978). For a critical assessment of historical materialism from what is claimed to be a Marxist standpoint, see Cutler, Hindess, Hirst and Hussain (1977, Chapter 5). Tom Bottomore's *Marxist Sociology* (1975) covers the Austro-Marxist contributions, and part of the current debate. Göran Therborn (1976) has placed historical materialism in its historical and theoretical context – see particularly Chapters 6 and 7.

5. At the time when Ralf Dahrendorf published his much quoted book on *Class and Class Conflict in Industrial Society* (1959) he was often characterized by US sociologists as 'neo-Marxist', a label which today seems quite misleading. The ignorance about Marxism revealed by such labels can be illustrated also by the fact that Talcott Parsons, in reviewing S. M. Lipset's *Political Man* (1960) could describe it as an example of a non-dogmatic *Marxist* approach! (See Lipset's introduction to the *Anchor* paperback edition of *Political Man*, 1963, pp xx).

For an attempt to analytically and empirically refute Dahrendorf's theory of class conflict, see Joseph Lopreato (1966 and 1967).

6. In response to criticism Godelier has later amended this statement, admitting that it was inadequate to some extent. He concedes that the antagonistic contradiction between productive forces and capitalist relations of production, to the extent that it is 'the direct consequence of limits immanent to the capitalist relations of production, is also in a certain sense *present from the beginning* of the system; it exists in a latent state at the beginning of the system. But it exists *as such*, that is, as a contradiction that is actively antagonistic, only after the appearance of large-scale industry' (1972b, p. 255). By replacing the words 'was not manifest', instead of the expression 'it did not exist' in Godelier's original formulation, as quoted in our main text, one could do justice to the spirit of his later amendment.

7. Even in Marx's own account of the emergence of early capitalism (in Part VIII of *Capital*, Vol. 1), it is far from obvious how the new productive forces of manufacture could unfold *within* feudalism. A crucial factor in this development was the expansion of urban commerce — cheap purchase and expensive sales — and later the re-investment of the profit in manufacture (Elster, 1973). In the agricultural sector dominated by the feudal mode of production, Perry Anderson (1974) has described the final phase of feudalism in England as a *crisis* of productive forces due to various factors of scarcity rather than as a development of such forces fettered by feudal relations of production. For a discussion of some of these processes of transition from feudalism to capitalism, see R. Hilton (ed.), (1976,) and W. Shaw (1978), pp. 133-49

8. Sometimes the metaphor of 'fettered' forces of production is used to characterize economic recessions or crises when productive forces are not being utilized to their full capacities, but are partly idle. If this interpretation were correct, every recession would offer 'time for social revolution'. Our interpretation is more restrictive and implies that one can speak of 'fettered' forces of production only when a *new* technology or *new* forms of work organiza-tion appear on the design tables and call for new and less privatized relations of production, but are forcefully resisted wherever they appear by existing private capitalist social relations of production (see p. 137).

One unavoidable objection against this rather restricted interpretation of the notion of 'fettered' forces of production is that it fails to do justice to Marx's own usage of this term which is less consistent and precise. Even though this term appears repeatedly in contexts where Marx diagnoses the contradictions of mature capitalism on the verge of 'social revolution', the term does appear occasionally also in other contexts. However, our task is not to 'do justice' to Marx — we leave that to the Marxologists — but to make use of his theoretical framework in a way which seems to us logical and fruitful. We find some support for our usage in William Shaw's careful scrutiny of various interpretations of this notion (1978, Chapter 3, particularly pp. 89ff and 98-103). Shaw is certainly aware of the fact that Marx hardly was bound to a totally consistent and precise usage, but: 'Nonetheless, the concepts are fairly stable and may be plotted with a reasonable degree of accuracy' (p. 150).

Chapter 5

1. There is a close connection between the agricultural policy of Sweden and its foreign policy: non-alignment in peace, and neutrality in war. One of the conditions required to make this foreign policy credible is to maintain a reasonable self-sufficiency in Swedish agricultural production, in spite of the fact that it would be more economical to import some agricultural products rather than to produce them in Sweden itself. However, the increasing capital and fertilizer intensity of Swedish agriculture would seem to make it increasingly

vulnerable to war-time blockades because much of the fertilizers and components of agricultural capital goods must be imported.

2. The Wallenberg 'empire' in fact has been strengthened in the course of the current economic crisis. For an up-to-date and very thorough presentation of the Wallenberg group of companies, and its international structure in terms of share-holding, ownership, control and number of employees, see *Veckans Affärer* — a Swedish *Business Week*-type of journal — no. 45, December 1978, pp. 15–34.

3. The 'school' of Milton Friedman, the well-known University of Chicago economist, is not one of these which have doubts.

4. Another area where it might be possible to study critical incidents illustrating transgressions of the boundaries of self-defined business responsibility is the editing of internal company news bulletins. These are usually financed by the company but edited to make them appear as a service to company employees. Workers and unions may have representatives on the editorial board. Could such a bulletin publish materials questioning details or the broad outline of company policy? What kind of company, if any, would be willing to take responsibility for a bulletin with such an open editorial policy? What issues become involved in critical incidents at this boundary line of responsibility. These are some of the questions which could be raised in a study of critical incidents in such a context.

5. One of the main reasons mentioned by Gunnar Adler-Karlsson against the nationalization of enterprises is the fact that compensation to private owners would be enormously expensive, and place very substantial and concentrated amounts of money in the hands of capitalists. The political costs of political controversies about nationalizations would certainly not be balanced by benefits in terms of greatly decreasing capital concentration and capitalist control over financial resources, according to Gunnar Adler Karlsson (1967a).

6 The functionalist approach to property also involves other complications relating to the relative weight and convertibility of the various functions which constitute property. Adler-Karlsson is aware of these complications, but does not provide satisfactory solutions to them (1967b, p. 102, note 19; unfortunately the English translation of Adler-Karlsson's book does not include the footnote section in the Swedish original). The problems involved cannot be solved within functionalist theory itself but requires deduction from other kinds of theories, structural and economic. For instance, it could be maintained, on the basis of such theories, that an exclusive or near-exclusive right of capitalists to make decisions on the use of financial capital and existing capital assets in production, and to procure or dispose of capital on capital markets, is the most central and crucial function of all those associated with private property rights. The execution of other functions are largely or totally dependent on the way in which capital is used (cf. our discussion on p. 231f). But if we attribute a greater weight, among various functions of private property, to the right and practice of control over financial, capital and other capital assets, the question still remains how to combine our observations of this central and highly weighted function with our observations of other less heavily weighted functions of private property. The arbitrary multiplicative weighting of functions, as distributed among actors with different percentages of functional control, suggested by Adler-Karlsson, is simple enough but has no scientific basis. Instead of his quasi-quantitative solution we would suggest a more qualitative type of analysis of 'attribute spaces' along the lines suggested by Lazarsfeld and Barton (1951), resulting perhaps in a taxonomy of rank-ordered, partially ordered, or unordered sub-types of social relations of production within the main type of capitalism. This is a challenging intellectual task which as yet remains to be accomplished. But it requires a detailed treatment of its own, and thus falls outside the scope of this book.

Chapter 6

1. Even though the assertion we have made on the self-destructive character of market forces would seem generally true, there are exceptions in cases where the benefits of scale are negligible or completely absent. For instance, there are certain types of service production which require 'intimacy' or a dispersion of small-scale units, and where the overhead costs of large-scale administrative co-ordination of such smaller units adds nothing to their productivity and profitability.
2. See Altvater, Hoffman and Semmler (1979), Chapters 9 and 10.

Chapter 7

1. A survey conducted by The Swedish Shareholders Association lends support to this assertion. A significant majority (87 per cent) of the respondents stated that they buy shares with the intention of keeping them for five years or more. Only 7 per cent of the shareholders seem to view the purchase of shares as a speculative investment, by stating their intention to sell their shares within two years or less (Aktiespararen, 1977:4).

Chapter 8

1. There is a rich literature on various kinds of social and political cleavages of a non-economic nature. Much of it has been summarized in Lipset and Rokkan, *Party Systems and Voter Alignments* (1967).
2. Apologetic leftists used to add another explanation of the multiplication of left-wing fractions: CIA infiltrators. There are some hints in Marchetti and Marks (1974, pp. 165 and 251), and in P. Agee (1974) about CIA manoeuvres to inflate the image of a communist threat, and to sow dissent in communist parties but this is scarcely sufficient to document CIA as a *major* cause of left-wing splinter movements.

Chapter 9

1. For a short explanation of the concept 'external effects' which includes so-called negative externalities, see for example Herfondahl and Kneese (1974, pp. 50-3).
2. In 1972 OECD adopted the so-called 'The Pollutor Pays Principle' which recommends member governments to let the producers carry the costs for pollution reduction. As instruments for this internalization of environment costs, OECD has suggested not only charges — that is prices for pollution — but also product and process standards and prohibition (OECD, 1975, pp. 11-17). In Sweden the method of allocating charges or prices to industrial pollution has been recommended by Erik Dahmén (1968).
3. According to a Swedish Government Commission Report on SO_2 emissions (not yet published at the time of writing) such emissions are much more widespread in Eastern than in Western Europe, whether these emissions are measured per units of GNP or per capita. It has been suggested to us that this can be explained largely by the fact that Eastern European countries must rely extensively on low-grade and sulphor-rich domestic coal deposits (brown coal) not only for industrial use but also for house heating.

According to an article by A. J. Tipisev, a Soviet expert, in *Pulp and Paper*

Canada (8, August 1977, pp. T171-4) the main thrust of environmental protection in the Soviet Union is water pollution prevention.

4. According to Swedish Official Statistics on traffic accidents (SOS 1978: Vägtrafikolyckor med personskada, table 11, here supplemented with the latest figures for 1978) the number of fatal accidents involving drivers and/or passengers culminated in 1971 (669 killed). Thereafter there is a significant downward trend in spite of the increasing number of motor-cars, with the lowest of fatalities (600 killed) in 1978. A corresponding trend is found for the number of seriously injured drivers and passengers, whereas the trend for light injuries is less clear.

5. We are here concerned not only with the well-known increasing social costs of relief work, unemployment insurance and other similar measures, but with the less known effects of unemployment on the health and life of unemployed. According to a study made at the Institute for Psychiatric Demography at the Psychiatric Hospital in Risskov, near Århus, Denmark, unemployment leads to a tripling of suicide and fatal accidents. It was found that the risk of a violent death was greater if one had been unemployed for longer than six months over a five-year period (see Olsen and Lajer, 1979). Psychological effects of unemployment have been explored in Edith Ovesen (1978). A classical study of this type is the one by Zawadski and Lazarsfeld (1935). It is rather amazing that studies from the 1930s and the 1970s document the existence of the same kinds of effects of unemployment, even though at different levels, in spite of the much greater access to unemployment insurance and other types of social welfare in the 1970s.

6. These statistics on sheltered work have been taken from Berglind and Rundblad (1975), p. 120.

7. Deaths by drug addiction in the Stockholm area alone have increased significantly in the last few years (25 known cases in 1975, 46 in 1976, 49 in 1977 and 60 in 1978). The median age of the victims was between 25 and 27 years. These figures are taken from unpublished reports obtained from the National Board of Health and Welfare (Socialstyrelsen). The real figures are probably higher, but this does not affect the trend.

8. In a book with the telling title *Democracy without Power,* Kronlund, Carlsson, Jensen and Sundström-Frisk (1973) have described the situation in the LKAB mines after the 1969 wildcat strike. Of particular interest in this context is their report on falling accident rates 1968-71 as a result of a change from piece rate to monthly salaries (pp. 66-72).

9. I am grateful to Stig Arne Nohrstedt for some as yet unpublished findings from his study (1977).

10. However, in such cases where the costs of state interventions are covered mainly by various kinds of taxes, and wage restraints on domestic private consumption, production may still find outlets on new export markets, if they are available. But on the other hand an increasing dependency on international markets makes us more dependent on fluctuations in the international economy; and on that arena single state interventions have little or no taxing or controlling power. By bringing about a reallocation of economic activities to arenas beyond the control of the single state, state interventions paid through constraints on private consumption could contribute to make the whole system of state interventions less and less efficient, and more and more difficult to finance.

But the state may also try to 'fill in' with more public consumption of industrial products in periods when private consumption is held back, in order not to make the economy too dependent on international markets. To balance the costs of such public consumption against the use of domestic industrial resources is easier than to control the behaviour of international markets. In fact it can be maintained that production and productivity in the private sector to a large extent have been stimulated by this kind of expansion of the public sector (Gustafsson, 1977, p. 12). However, so far we have a limited knowledge of the relative importance of the stimulating versus the curtailing effects of the public sector on the private.

Chapter 10

1. Lenin's work on the State and Revolution (1964) is an obvious point of departure for most contemporary Marxist treatises of the 'capitalist state'. But the departures are manifold, and go in different directions. See for instance R. Miliband (1969) and N. Poulantzas (1973). For a discussion of the contrasting approaches of these two authors, see E. Laclau (1977, Chapter 2), and Esping-Andersen, Friedland and Wright (1976). See also G. Therborn (1977 and 1978) and his partial self-reappraisal (1979). For other allegedly more 'heretic' Marxist approaches, see J. Habermas (1973), C. Offe (1972) and A. Wolfe (1977). With the advent of 'Eurocommunism' the Marxist approach to the capitalist state has found new applications (Carillo,1977). For a non-Marxist treatment of 'the modern state', see G. Poggi (1978).

However, the unsurpassed non-Marxist treatise in this field would seem to be John Kenneth Galbraith's volume on *The New Industrial State* (1967, particularly Chapters 26-28), and the sequel *Economics and the Public Purpose* (1973). Even though Galbraith's terminology differs from that found in Marxist treatises on the same topic, and even though his conclusions rest on experience, observation and insight rather than on derivations from some kind of theory about 'the logic of capital', his conclusions are in many respects similar to those of Marxist scholars. The state has become an instrument of the industrial system; the 'technostructure' at the same time requires close collaboration with the state, and the 'myth of separation' of the public and the private, in order to minimize government interference with the private spending of public money (1967, p. 314).

2. At the Department of Economic History, University of Uppsala, Professor Bo Gustafsson has initiated a number of research projects, based on historical and comparative data, to explore the causes of the expanding public sector in capitalist countries. The first comprehensive report to appear from this project is Anders Forssman (1979), *A Theory on the State and Public Expenditures* (in Swidish, with an English summary). A pioneering work in this field was Gunnar Myrdal (1960), *Beyond the Welfare State*.

3. The most influential publication documenting the economic policy of the Swedish labour movement during this postwar period was *Samordnad näringspolitik* (Co-ordinated Economic Policy), published in 1961 by LO, the Swedish Federation of Trade Unions. However, the basic elements of this approach were accepted by LO already at the 1951 LO-Congress. A first attempt to implement this approach was made by the Social Democratic Government during the 1955-7 recession. For an excellent English summary of this approach, see a paper by Andrew Martin (1978).

4. We are not saying that economic efficiency and growth is a sufficient or even a necessary source of political legitimacy. But no doubt economic efficiency wherever it appears contributes in some measure to political legitimacy; and where such legitimacy has few other sources, a decreasing economic efficiency may further undermine whatever legitimacy there is. See S. M. Lipset (1960, Chapter 3) and G. Poggi (1978, pp. 132f).

5. For a thorough and broad-ranging criticism of Karl Popper's methodology, see I. Johansson (1975).

Chapter 11

1. For a more thorough discussion, and an attempt to empirically operationalize

the concept of capitalist systemic power, see Chapter 16. Basically this concept is based on the assumption that the power of capitalists is *impersonal;* it derives not from their personal characteristics or personal influence as defined in networks of social and political relationships but from the fact that capitalists are the pinnacle of a system based on impersonal laws of capital accumulation and market processes which cannot be resisted without seriously disturbing the performance of the system. Therefore the systemic power of the capitalist class as such can be ascertained as a variable only by empirically establishing the *penetration* of this system into the web of society, its *autonomy* in relationship to that society, etc. The systemic power of individual capitalists, similarly, can be studied in terms of the penetration and autonomy of their ownership of capital in relationship to the overall shareholding structure of the given capitalist economy, but with due regard to the penetration of this economy into the web of society as a whole. Thus, a capitalist with supreme ownership over a major portion of the capitalist sector of the economy may wield less systemic power than a capitalist with a smaller proportion of capitalist ownership power, if the capitalist economy in the latter case has penetrated society more completely than in the former.

Part III

Göran Ahrne wrote the Swedish manuscript underlying Chapters 13, 14 and the final section of Chapter 15, and Leif Lundberg the Swedish manuscript underlying Chapters 17 and 18. They were also responsible for collecting and analysing the empirical data for these chapters. Ulf Himmelstrand wrote Chapter 12, most of Chapter 15 and Chapter 16. Furthermore, he condensed, translated and supplemented Ahrne's and Lundberg's Swedish manuscripts.

Chapter 12

1. Alain Touraine (1980) has pointed out that 'the dissidents who oppose Communist regimes no longer reason in terms of class struggle even when they say they are Marxists but in terms of the Rights of Man, as opposed to the absolute State'. This is understandable, but in countries where these rights are more fully secured it is still justified to focus attention mainly on class divisions and class struggle.
2. This interview was published in a popular weekly magazine, *Vecko Journalen.*

Chapter 13

1. The sample has been described in more detail in Appendix II, pp. 319f. Our data analysis was based on responses from 1294 employees. The two provinces selected for our sample — Stockholm and Kopparberg provinces — cannot, of course, be assumed to represent Sweden as a whole. On the other hand we have been able to show that questions used in both national samples and in our sample render approximately the same response distributions in our sample as in national samples (see Appendix II, Table A. II.2).
2. While Korpi's data on metal workers from 1967 indicated a curvilinear relationship between age and a belief in the utility of unions — with the youngest and the oldest believing most strongly in them — our data show a linear relationship: the percentage considering unions a good support in improving the position of labour increases steadily from 63 per cent among industrial workers

below 25 years of age to 84 per cent in the oldest age brackets of industrial workers (above 55 years). The same tendency can be found among service workers, even though on a somewhat lower level, the corresponding percentages being 53 to 78 per cent. Our data indicate that 25 years of age was a significant line of demarcation with regard to the incidence of union membership and activity among industrial workers in 1976. Among industrial workers less than 25 years of age, 26 per cent remained unorganized, whereas in all other age brackets the percentage of unorganized was only 8 per cent or less. The same tendency can be found among service workers, but with larger percentages of unorganized across all age levels: about 40 per cent unorganized among service workers less than 25 years old, and 19 per cent or less being unorganized in older age brackets.

Chapter 14

1. Mainly responsible for the common misconception that Marx formulated a 'law of increasing misery' among workers under capitalism are J. Schumpeter (1974) and K. Popper (1945). However, a Marxist economic historian such as Kusczynski (1968, Chapters 2 and 3) has also maintained that Marx predicted such absolute 'immiserization'. A most careful and detailed criticism of such images of Marx as a prophet of doom rather than as a scientific analyst of capitalism has been carried out by Mats Dahlqvist (1978, pp. 378-403 and 611-42). See also J. McMurtry (1978, pp. 62, 78 and 170) and W. Shaw (1978, pp. 87f).
2. Allen H. Barton and R. Wayne Parsons (1977) have pointed out a number of statistical pitfalls in using correlation methods in measuring variations in 'consistency' in the belief structures of various groups or strata. Results from such correlational studies may be substantively misleading because correlation coefficients are affected not only by the structuring of beliefs but also by the heterogeneity of the groups or strata compared with regard to their belief structures. 'The use of the correlation coefficient to compare populations as to the degree of constraint, structure, or predictability of attitudes thus depends on the two populations being equally heterogeneous in attitudes.' (Barton and Parsons, 1977, pp. 163f). Because our combination of factor analysis and class analysis is based on correlation matrices of responses from different social classes, these methodological warnings are relevant also in our particular case. Therefore we have compared the standard deviations for responses to all our threat questions in the social classes involved in our comparison. For most of these threat questions the standard deviations are virtually identical in the social classes involved in our study; in a few cases they differ, but not significantly. The different factorial structures emerging in our analysis would thus seem to be affected only by the structuring of beliefs and not by variations in the degree of heterogeneity of the social classes involved.
3. This critical argument was suggested by Jan Lindhagen in discussions about an earlier version of this chapter.
4. In a special election issue of the socialist magazine *Zenit* (5, 1976, pp. 4-45) there is a careful analysis of class and electoral bases of Swedish political parties.
5. In December 1975 an electoral reform was passed which gave voting rights in local elections to immigrants with foreign citizenship but resident in Sweden for at least three years. Social democrats have also been pushing the idea that immigrants with foreign citizenship should be given voting rights in national elections once they have been resident in Sweden for, say, three years, but so far no parliamentary action has been taken on this idea. Swedish citizenship can normally be awarded to non-Scandinavian immigrants after five years of Swedish residence.

Chapter 15

1. In the 1976 elections about 43 per cent of all students voted for bourgeois parties, and 40 per cent for labour parties. Of these 40 per cent the main communist party (VPK) obtained 8 per cent which is the highest percentage of communist voters in any stratum or other social category reported in election surveys. Only 5 per cent of workers voted communist (O. Petersson, 1978, Table 2.1, p. 13).

2. This assumption is based on the outcomes of immigrant voting in the 1976 Swedish local and regional elections. See T. Hammar (1977).

3. Olof Petersson, the author of the official report on the 1976 elections (1978) and of numerous articles on earlier election results.

4. For an up-to-date analysis of the development of the electoral basis of political parties in Sweden, see Rune Åberg (1979). In our own analysis we have in particular taken the following trends into account:

Firstly, the proportion of housewives in the electorate is decreasing; a greatly increasing proportion of married women are becoming gainfully employed (Korpi, 1978, p. 280), particularly in lower white-collar service jobs, as we have shown earlier. As a result they can be expected to vote for labour parties more frequently than housewives. This is also the case; in fact female service workers vote labour more commonly than male service workers (Korpi, 1978, p. 274).

Secondly, young people now enter the electorate already at the age of eighteen; the voting age was lowered in 1975. This means that the youngest voting cohorts become included in the electorate before their class positions have fully crystallized. It has been argued that this gives the bourgeois parties some advantage among young voters. At eighteen quite a number of young people today have had a very limited experience of working life, but a rather extended experience of the latently 'bourgeois' influence of school, and of Americanized mass culture and entertainment, it has been maintained. However, empirical data speak rather convincingly in the opposite direction. In the growing so-called 'non-manual' categories, younger voters proved to vote labour (social democratic and communist) more frequently than older non-manual workers already in the 1970 election (Korpi, 1978, p. 279). In the 1976 election when social democrats lost their government position this tendency was still discernible (Petersson, 1978, p. 19).

Since age-level is closely correlated with level of education, as a result of an expansion of higher levels of education to young people from all classes and strata, it is worthwhile here to control for the influence of education. When this is done it becomes even more obvious that the labour parties are receiving a greater number of votes from young voters (Petersson, 1978, p. 35). At higher levels of education this is particularly due to the large communist vote among young people; but the social democrats did not do badly either. The bourgeois trend suspected among younger voters as a result of their increasing education is thus counteracted by the fact that an increasingly large proportion of the higher educated have a working class background which has a significant impact on their voting behaviour (Petersson, 1978, p. 36).

Thirdly, however, the labour parties seem to have been losing some votes within the traditional working class itself, particularly in the strata located between the industrial working class, and what we have called service workers — namely in storage, transport, sales, etc. This has been attributed to the great geographical mobility of the labour force during the postwar years, and particularly to the influx of workers with a petty bourgeois or farming background into some urban working class occupations (*Zenit*, 1976, p. 18). Harold Swedner and Nader Fatahi (1978) have demonstrated quite high levels of political alienation and disenchantment in urban areas where there has been this kind of influx. Workers with this kind of background have tended either not to vote at all, or to vote for the Centre Party rather than for the labour parties (cf. also *Zenit*, 1976, and Petersson, 1978, p. 28f). However, the proletarian-ization of small-farmers and the petty bourgeoisie is probably coming to an end, and therefore the Centre Party cannot be expected to reap much further electoral benefits from this category of workers.

Finally, with regard to immigrant workers from abroad, the past wave of immigration now seems to have receded and quite a number of immigrants might choose to apply for Swedish citizenship within the next couple of years. They can then be added to the potential electoral base of the labour parties. (Widgren, 1978, pp. 4 and 12).

Analyses such as these lead to the conclusion that the potential electoral base of the labour parties is far from decreasing, but will remain rather constant or even increase in size (Korpi, 1978, p. 322f). Of course such overall estimates of electoral bases by their very nature must remain rather crude, derived as they are from an evaluation of the effects of contradictory processes such as the increasing number of married women in employment, the increasing number of non-voting foreign immigrants in the labour force, geographical mobility, the decreasing number of industrial workers, the increasing number of deskilled white-collar jobs, etc. Statistically speaking it is difficult, but not impossible, to evaluate such joint effects of contradictory processes.

5. Because of constitutional technicalities which cannot be discussed here, the Social Democratic Party did not find it feasible to press for new elections immediately to take advantage of the demise of the three-party bourgeois cabinet. The Social Democratic Party leadership, against many warnings from its cadres, decided to allow the Speaker of the Parliament to continue his attempts to seat a new bourgeois cabinet — this time a minority cabinet based on the Liberal Party alone. If the Social Democrats in Parliament had voted against this new Liberal minority cabinet, events may have developed in some alternative directions. Either a Social Democratic minority cabinet may have been formed — but this would have required support or abstention from at least some bourgeois parliamentarians — and the minority Social Democratic cabinet would then have announced an immediate election which it most probably would have won in view of its strong support in public opinion polls at that time. However, it was rather unlikely that the bourgeois parties would support the formation of such a minority Social Democratic cabinet, by voting for such a cabinet or by abstaining; and therefore the most likely alternative to the minority Liberal cabinet actually formed would have been a re-composed three-party bourgeois government. If such a re-composed three-party bourgeois government had been formed in October 1978 this would of course have maintained the basis of Labour Party mobilization which we are discussing right now, namely the visibility of weaknesses in the common bourgeois front. But for various reasons the Social Democrats abstained in the vote for or against the formation of a Liberal minority cabinet which thus could obtain the necessary parliamentary majority.

6. After two months with the Liberal Party leader figuring conspicuously as Prime Minister in television interviews and newscasts, the Liberal Party increased its support in public opinion polls by about 3 per cent in November 1978, while the Social Democrats lost their absolute majority while retaining a majority together with the small Communist Party. The fact that the Social Democrats continued to lose some of their strong previous public support in the period up to the election in September 1979 when public opinion polls predicted a very close race indeed between the bourgeois and socialist blocks, would seem to support the hypothesis that weaknesses of the bourgeois front accounted for a significant portion of the public support obtained by the Social Democratic Party in the period before October 1978. At least in the early phases of the minority liberal

cabinet of October 1978 the electorate seems to have formed a rather favourable image of the new minority Liberal cabinet as being much more determined and unified than the previous three-party bourgeois cabinet. This image was probably more important than any particular Liberal stand on various political issues. Because of the minority position of the new Liberal cabinet political issues were somewhat garbled and largely concealed under a parliamentary discussion of various questions of procedure and tactical voting. However, it is quite possible that this lack of a clearly articulated Liberal stand on important political issues contributed in the long run to the decreasing support for the Liberal Party in the last six months before the elections in September 1979. With hindsight it would seem possible to say that the Liberal Party in the 1979 election campaign, by relying too much on the image of the party leader and the prestige of his position as Prime Minister, failed to articulate its own views on important issues of considerable interest to potential Liberal voters.

7. The watering down of labour legislation initiated under the previous Social Democratic government could be illustrated by the Act on Workers' Co-determination (MBL). More details on this piece of legislation are provided in Chapter 17. In 1976 it was obvious that MBL and Company Law were contradictory on several points. The Social Democrats suggested legislation implying that Company Law should yield and MBL take precedence in cases where these two pieces of legislation might clash. As a result of the defeat of Social Democrats in the 1976 elections no such legislation was passed. Those parts of MBL which presuppose collective agreements on workers' co-determination between labour and capital have been obstructed by SAF, the Swedish Employers' Confederation, in protracted collective bargaining which in the fall of 1979 still had not resulted in any collective agreement satisfactory to trade unions. In the press, TV and radio a large number of interviews with workers and trade union officials have made it perfectly clear that now there is a widespread disenchantment with MBL among workers. Without a more far-reaching control over capital itself, MBL seems to have increased the length and frequency of meetings between unions and management only, and not the co-determination which was intended.

8. This was indicated by several expert commentators in press and radio, and particularly by Olof Petersson. He could support his interpretation by referring to data from several earlier elections where party affiliations did change, and where the 'election wind' blew in a certain direction without any corresponding change in the attitudes of voters, as revealed in representative panel studies as well as repeated sample surveys.

9. The ultimate labour weapon to deal with management intransigence is the strike. Is it possible to use this weapon successfully in a socialist system of workers' self-management to deal with a widening gap between union experts and rank-and-file workers? The answer seems to be conditionally affirmaive, judging from the Yugoslav experience. A former Yugoslav union man, Neca Jovanov, defended a doctoral thesis in 1975 at the University of Ljubljana on *Workers' Strikes in the Socialist Federal Republic of Yugoslavia from 1958 to 1969*. He is now a professor at the University of Belgrade. Jovanov's book would seem to look quite objectively at strikes in Yugoslavia. The following kinds of headings indicate that strikes are not considered by the author as something unnatural which must be suppressed: 'Satisfying of Direct Workers Demands' — 'Removal of Direct Reasons Causing Strikes' — 'Removing of Real Reasons Causing Strikes' (p. 171) — 'Positive Social Consequences of Strikes' (p. 173). A rather detailed summary of Jovanov's analysis and empirical findings has been published in the English language in J. Obradović and W. Dunn (eds) (1978), pp. 339—73.

Chapter 16

1. Hans Zetterberg (1978) has suggested the fitting notion of the 'permit state' to take account of the fact that the state in Sweden in many crucial areas has tried to avoid detailed regulations, and instead introduced certain general prohibitions which, however, can be lifted after applications for concessions from the state, concessions which are awarded under certain conditions, but once awarded allow companies or other subjects to pursue their interests without further regulation.

2. In Sweden the main legal instrument for disciplining labour is the Labour Court with parity representation of labour, capital and the state. The main sanctions available are fines which, however, have remained constant for a long time in spite of inflation. Bourgeois members of Parliament have suggested an increase in these fines, but so far this has not been accepted by Parliament. Another sanction, hotly disputed by labour activists but accepted by the leadership of central union organizations, is the right of management to fire workers who repeatedly have been involved in organizing wildcat strikes. Union leaders have defended their stand on this issue by pointing out that the conditions under which this rule can be applied are so restricted that, in practice, it could not be used except in very few extreme cases.

3. Among lower level white-collar employees about 24 per cent voted for the Centre Party and 20 per cent for the Liberal Party in the 1976 elections. For middle level white-collar employees the figures were 20 and 20 per cent respectively. But the Centre Party also attracted the votes of 17 per cent of industrial workers, and 22 per cent of other workers (O. Petersson, 1978, Table 2.1, p. 13).

Chapter 17

1. For a theoretical and empirical social—psychological treatment of the conditions under which we can expect discrepancies between attitudes verbalized in more general and in more specific terms, see U. Himmelstrand (1960a and 1960b). See also two now almost forgotten books by Thurman Arnold on *The Symbols of Government* (1935) and *The Folklore of Capitalism* (1937).

2. Even though the questionnaire offered our respondents the opportunity to allocate 'influence scores' to *the state* on this point, as well as to various aspects of *capital* and *labour,* only a negligible number of such scores were in fact allocated to the state in the areas covered by our question — on average less than 1 per cent.

3. Changes in legislation for the benefit of the weaker part in an agreement or contract is a tacit principle in Swedish legislation, according to legal experts we have consulted, but this is rarely stated explicitly in legal acts.

4. Direct state interventions in conflicts between employers and employees were considered in a few instances during the 1940s and 1950s, but they were never realized. In 1947 the Parliament introduced a piece of legislation which gave the state the right to take over the police which at that time was municipal. This made it possible to introduce an official duty to serve for the police officers who then were prepared to go on strike. In 1951 the Parliament similarly proposed a compulsory solution of a conflict at municipal hospitals. But these pieces of legislation never had to be enacted; it seems that the very threat of state intervention was sufficient to resolve the conflicts involved. At one occasion, however, the state has actively intervened in a wage conflict through legislation. This was in the early 1970s when two union organizations — SACO and SR — who organize academically trained civil servants in public administration had gone on strike

against the state and municipalities in order to strengthen their positions in wage negotiations. The state and municipalities responded with lockouts. In that situation the Parliament passed a law which prolonged the collective agreements in force before the strike.

Part IV
Chapter 19

1. This disillusionment was founded on the argument that the proposed national and regional development funds only would contribute collective savings of labour to capital accumulation within the existing order. Labour would thus help to pay for further capitalist development rather than to take successive control over capital, as suggested in Meidner's original profit-sharing proposal. Only the future will reveal whether the Social Democratic Party leadership has shelved Meidner's proposal, or similar designs, for good or only temporarily. Temporarily, I believe. However, already now it is obvious that the national and regional development funds proposed not only would contribute collective savings to capital investments, but also affect the distribution of decision-making power over investments between labour and capital, to the advantage of labour, and in a much shorter time than it would take to make wage-earners' funds of the Meidner type sufficiently powerful (see pp. 267f). However, this shift of power would take place on a much higher level of economic decision-making than single enterprises, whereas the Meidner proposal would secure more power for labour also on the enterprise level.
2. The following brief account of profit-sharing and collective-saving schemes in some other countries is based entirely on information contained in the first report from the Government Commission investigating problems and proposals for wage-earners' funds (SOU 1979:8, pp. 15-47).

Chapter 20

1. To provide a reasonably complete list of references to books and articles written about wage-earners' funds in Sweden since 1975 would require several pages. The basic text was written by Rudolf Meidner and his collaborators, and is also available in English translation (1978). A large number of articles on wage-earners' funds can be found in *LO-Tidningen* and in the social democratic journal *Tiden*. A journal of the Swedish Association of Economists, *Ekonomisk Debatt*, devoted a special issue to the matter (1976, no. 1), and so did the Communist Party journal *Socialistisk Debatt* (1977, no. 5) which also contained an excellent invited article by a social democrat, Sven-Ove Hansson. The business community initiated a counter-proposal based on a voluntary individual profit-sharing scheme (Waldenström et al., 1976). The best known piece of polemic against wage-earners' funds has been written by a professor of economics, Assar Lindbeck (1979), a crude and analytically surprisingly poor attack which, however, cannot quite measure up to the level of propagandistic distortion and vilification manifested in a pamphlet by Dan Norling (1977) published by SAF, the Swedish Employers' Confederation. Within the business community the analytically most competent and innovative attempt to illuminate the underlying problems of economic power and decision-making is, in my view, by Lars Lidén, Gustav Lindencrona and others (1979). Erik Åsard (1978) gives background on union policy and strategy.
2. The LO-SAP Report also suggested that the yields from wage-earners' shares be deducted not only from the taxable profits of enterprises, but also from the fees to be paid to the regional development funds. At the same time as this implies an

increasing solidity of business firms — but a solidity increasingly controlled by labour rather than by capital — it also implies decreasing tax revenues for the state which, in case of need, must be compensated for by other taxes. Finally, a legal guarantee is suggested which would prevent the abolition of divided payments to the disadvantage of private minority shareholder interests.

3. My guess about the lack of enthusiasm for centralistic socialism among social democratic proponents of 'citizen funds' or the like, and their tendency to think in normative terms about economic democracy, is simply based on my personal knowledge of those concerned.

4. This contradictory bourgeois stand — silently accepting the undemocratic nature of economic decision-making in capitalist enterprises while labelling a system of wage-earners' funds as undemocratic — appears in a particularly sharp profile when expressed by leading spokesmen of the Centre Party. On top of the contradiction just mentioned, Centre Party spokesmen have superimposed another logical inconsistency. In spite of the fact that the Centre Party vocally rallies around an ideology of 'decentralization' and 'small is beautiful', their spokesmen have favoured a democratization of the economy through a more active democratic control over the investment policies of the giant and centralized General Pension Funds rather than through the more decentralized democratic control possible within a system of wage-earners' funds. To attribute these inconsistencies to ignorance and a limited capacity for logical thinking among the bourgeois politicians involved would seem somewhat more far-fetched than to attribute them to the propagandistic requirements of party-political battles. However, as we have pointed out in Chapter 16, a Centre Party spokesman such as Nils Åsling, Minister of Industry in the first and the third bourgeois government in recent years, has also attempted to keep a door open to labour movement proposals for wage-earners' funds within the framework of what he calls a 'synthesis'. Illogical as this 'synthesis' would seem, it may still turn out to provide a suitable bridgehead for future Centre Party collaboration with the Social Democrats, if the present bourgeois government collapses. In unstable multi-party politics it is sometimes considered a good tactic to keep all options wide open.

5. Gunnar Olofsson (1979, pp. 96f) has drawn my attention to Mario Tronti's (1974) analysis of this dual character of labour. Labour is both *part* of capital, in the form of variable capital, and *opposed* to capital in class struggle. From this theoretical vantage point Mario Tronti draws conclusions very different from our own. In a very undialectical and unhistorical fashion he completely rejects not only all trade unionist and social democratic but also all communist organizations as instruments of the ideology and interests of capital. Marxist theory is perverted into a tool for categorical labelling of friends and foes rather than being used to specify the historically and structurally given options and constraints of socialist praxis.

Chapter 22

1. Göran Therborn, in a seminal paper on 'The Rule of Capital and the Rise of Democracy' (1977) points out the shortcomings of both Marxist and non-Marxist analyses of the rise of democracy. Among Marxists the dismissal of bourgeois democracy by Lenin has 'more often stimulated barren functionalist speculation about the role of democracy under capitalism than inspired serious research on the historical development and operation of capitalist democracy' (Therborn, 1977, p. 4 note 5). He points out that 'bourgeois democracy' no longer can be dismissed by Marxists as a 'mere sham' after the experience of Fascism in the 1930s and 1940s. Democracy now must be seen as an 'important popular

conquest, which lays the basis for further advance' (Therborn, 1977, p. 5). In his essay Göran Therborn has carried out a study of the historical emergence of 'bourgeois democracy' in seventeen countries of the OECD. He concludes that democracy never was handed down from above, and emphasizes 'the enormous role of the labour movement' in the process of democratization (Therborn, 1977, p. 23). 'However, although the labour movement was the only consistent democratic force on the arena, it was nowhere strong enough to achieve bourgeois democracy on its own, without the aid of victorious foreign armies, domestic allies more powerful than itself, or splits in the ranks of the enemy' (Therborn, 1977, p. 24). In many countries mobilization for national liberation and military defeats in foreign wars contributed greatly to the development of bourgeois democracy, and in this part of the mobilization process the urban intelligentsia, the petty bourgeoisie and farmers often played a decisive role beside the pressures from the labour movement.

For a more limited study — focusing only on the Nordic countries — see Stein Kuhnle (1975).

2. See note 7 in Chapter 3.

3. Giovanni Sartori (1965), in his well-known exposition of democratic theory, after 464 pages of articulate and eloquent passages on the meaning of democracy, methods of defining democracy, and the relations of democracy to other political ideals and realities made the following remarks on p. 465: 'To someone who accused him of taking sides, the placid Abbot Galiani once replied drily, and irritably: "Je ne suis pour rien. Je suis pour qu'on ne déraisonne" — I am in favor of nothing. I am against people talking nonsense. If I may borrow from Galiani, I am for liberal democracy because I am against incompetence and cheaters.'

As I understand this passage, Sartori is for democracy not because he himself, or democracy for that matter, is for liberalism or socialism or any other political ideal, but because democracy is a system or a procedure which makes it possible for any such political ideals to find a politically relevant expression with a minimum of cheating and incompetence. The virtues of democracy are not a result of whatever virtues may be inherent in the political *substance* of its decisions, but only of the merits of *methods* and *procedures* which allow competent decision-making to take place in response to aggregates of freely expressed inclinations of every member of a mass electorate. See also Schumpeter (1974, Ch. 22).

This notion of democracy comes very close to definitions put forward by Herbert Tingsten (1945) and Alf Ross (1948) except that these authors were more formal in their definitions, and introduced them earlier in their expositions. But even a Swedish Marxist such as Göran Therborn has accepted this way of defining democracy (1977, p. 4). Even though Therborn, like other Marxists, maintains that democracy, in *effect,* favours a reproduction of the capitalist mode of production, he is unwilling, unlike other Marxists, to make this effect part of the *definition* of 'bourgeois democracy'.

However, in the late 1950s and early 1960s we had in Sweden a debate between Herbert Tingsten, professor of political science, and Ernst Wigforss, social democratic theoretician and long-time Minister of Finance, about the extent to which definitions of democracy could and should be cleansed completely from any reference to the substance and values of politics. Wigforss (1959, pp. 113f and 1962, pp. 49-61) maintained that such puristic definitions of democracy were misleading. According to him the overarching ideology of democracy is not completely neutral with regard to the several political ideologies of conservatism, liberalism, socialism, etc. which appear on the stage of democratic politics. The principles of democracy, if taken serious and not restricted only to stipulating the technicalities of democratic method, demand the expansion of these principles from the political to the economic sphere. Wigforss could have added that the political method of democracy as practised and understood in so-called liberal democracies always presupposes that political decisions be limited to a public sphere excluding crucial economic decisions of the business community. In this sense liberal proponents of the more limited formal definitions of democracy tacitly do exactly what they say should not be done; by democracy they understand a specific delimitation of the *content* of democratic decisions, and not only a substantively neutral political method.

4. Sven-Ove Hansson, in an excellent article on the long-term goals of socialism beyond the socialization of ownership to the means of production, has made a number of crucial observations about the needs for technological change in that long-term perspective:

> Our present technology of production and our whole style of life has been generated by, and bears the imprint of capitalist competition. Therefore, the main part of our efforts to eliminate the destructive effects of capitalism will remain even after we have replaced the external forms of capitalism, its specific pattern of ownership, with other forms. This will be a gigantic task for generations of political and union activists. For this reason it would be fatal for the labour movement if it relaxed its present role as a critic of society and became a conservative administrator of a socialist system. Such a system would certainly retain a number of deficiencies from capitalist society calling for a continued radical and critical movement with an ideology aiming not only at the administration but at a profound transformation of society.

Hansson points out that our present technology is designed to operate within the framework of hierarchical command-structures, and implies a detailed division of labour conducive mainly to efficiency in capital accumulation rather than to the preservation and development of the human dignity of workers. A take-over of ownership over the means of production will not change overnight the kind of technology developed under capitalism:

> For anyone who spends forty hours a week with attaching lids to bottles of detergent, the fact that she participates in one or two hours of meetings per week in her capacity as co-owner of the enterprise does certainly not imply a sufficient improvement in her life situation when in fact she spends the remaining 38 or 39 hours with putting lids on bottles.

In order to better integrate the two roles as worker and owner what is needed is not necessarily a less advanced technology but a different and perhaps as advanced technology which it will take time to design. The earlier we start working on such new designs even before economic democracy has been fully instituted, the better will these new democratic forms operate from the very beginning of a new socialist era.

See also André Gorz, editor, (1976, pp. 159-89) and D. Noble (1977).

References

Note: The letters Å, Ä and Ö used in Swedish references will be found in this order at the end of the alphabet.

Abelson, R. P. (1959), 'Modes of Resolution of Belief Dilemmas', *Journal of Conflict Resolution,* Vol. 3, 1959, pp. 343-52.

Abrahamsson, B. and Bröström, A. (1980), *The Right of Labour,* London SAGE Publications (forthcoming).

Adler-Karlsson, G. (1967a), *Functional Socialism,* Stockholm: Prisma.

Adler-Karlsson, G. (1967b), *Funktionssocialism,* Stockholm: Prisma.

Agee, P. (1974), *Inside the Company: CIA Diary,* Harmondsworth: Penguin Books.

Ahrne, G. (1976). *Den gyllene kedjan. Studier i arbete och konsumtion,* Stockholm: Prisma.

Ahrne, G. (1977), 'Vad betyder klassindelningen?' Projektet Samhällsförändring i Sverige, Sociologiska institutionen, Uppsala.

Ahrne, G. (1978a), 'Om klass, arbete och medvetande i Sverige mot slutet av 70-talet', in *Sociologisk Forskning,* no. 4, 1978.

Ahrne, G. (1978b), 'Krisförväntningar och mättnad', Uppsala, Sociologiska institutionen, manuscript.

Allardt, E. (1975), *Att ha, att älska, att vara: om välfärd i Norden* Lund: Argos.

Allardt, E. (1976), 'Dimensions of Welfare in a Comparative Scandinavian Study', *ACTA SOCIOLOGICA,* Vol. 19, 1976.

Althusser, L. (1971), 'Ideology and Ideological State Apparatuses', in *Lenin and Philosophy and Other Essays,* New York: Monthly Review Press.

Altvater, E. (1973), 'Notes on Some Problems of State Interventionism', in *Kapitalistate,* Vol. I, no. 1, 1973.

Altvater, E., Hoffman, J. and Semmler, W. (1979), *Vom Wirtschaftswunder zur Wirtschaftskrise.* Ökonomie und Politik in der Bundesrepublik, Berlin: Verlag Olle and Walter.

Amin, S. (1974), 'Accumulation and Development: A Theoretical Model', in *Review of African Political Economy,* no. 1, 1974.

Anderson, P. (1974), *Passages from Antiquity to Feudalism,* London: New Left Books.

Argyris, C. (1972), *The Applicability of Organizational Sociology,* Cambridge: Cambridge University Press.

Arnold, T. (1935), *The Symbols of Government,* New Haven: Yale University Press.

Arnold T. (1937), *The Folklore of Capitalism,* New Haven: Yale University Press.

Arrow, K. (1951), *Social Choice and Individual Values,* New York: John Wiley and Sons.

Avakumović, I. (1964), *History of the Communist Party of Yuguslavia.* Aberdeen: Aberdeen University Press.

Bachrach, P. and Barratz, M. S. (1970), *Power and Poverty, Theory and Practice,* London: Oxford University Press.

Bain, J. S. (1966), *International Differences in Industrial Structure. Eight Nations in the 1950s*, New Haven/London: Yale University Press.

Baran, P. (1957), *The Political Economy of Growth*, New York: Monthly Review Press.

Barton, A. H. and Parsons, R. W. (1977), 'Measuring Belief System Structure', *Public Opinion Quarterly*, Vol. 41, 1977, pp. 159-80.

Beckholmen, K. (1979), *Torpet Göteborg:* Eriksbergs Verkstadsklubb.

Bell, D. (1976), *The Cultural Contradictions of Capitalism*, New York: Basic Books.

Bentzel, R. (1953), *Inkomstfördelningen i Sverige*, Uppsala: Almqvist and Wiksell.

Berglind, H. (1979), 'Förtidspension eller arbete. En studie av utveckling och regionala variationer', in *SOU 1977:88*, Stockholm: Liber Förlag.

Berglind, H. and Rundblad, B. (1975), *Arbetsmarknaden i Sverige: ett sociologiskt perspektiv*. Stockholm: Esselte Studium.

Berntson, L. (1974), *Politiska partier och sociala klasser*, Staffanstorp: Cavefors.

Björkman, M. and Fleming, D. (1974), 'Stamokap kontra Stinkap kontra Althusser-skolan', in *Häften för Kritiska Studier*, no. 5, 1974.

Björkman, T. (1978), 'De Lönsamma arbetsmiljöerna', in *Sociologisk Forskning* no. 2, pp. 11-30.

Björn L. (1976), *Labour Parties and the Redistribution of Income in Capitalist Democracies*, Ann Arbor, Mich.: University Microfilms International (Ph.D thesis from the University of North Carolina at Chapel Hill).

Blau, P. (1964), *Exchange and Power in Social Life*, New York: John Wiley and Sons.

Boston Consulting Group (1978), *En ram för svensk industripolitik*, Stockholm: Liber.

Bottomore, T. (1975), *Marxist Sociology*, London: Macmillan.

Bowles, S. and Gintis, H. (1979), 'The Crisis of Capital and the Crisis of Liberal Democracy: The Case of the United States'. Paper presented to the *Round Table on the Subkective Forces of Socialism*, Cavtat, Yugoslavia, September 1979.

Braverman, H. (1974), *Labor and Monopoly Capital*, New York: Monthly Review Press.

Brus, W. (1972), *The Market in a Socialist Economy*, London: Routledge and Kegan Paul.

Burns, T. and Buckley, W. (eds.) (1976), *Power and Control, Social Structures and their Transformation*, London: Sage Studies in International Sociology.

Carillo, S. (1977), *Eurocommunism and the State*, London: Lawrence and Wishart.

Castles, F. G. (1978), *Social Democratic Image of Society. Study of the Action and Origins of Scandinavian Social Democracy in Comparative Perspective*. London: Routledge and Kegan Paul.

Chandler, Jr., A. D. (1977), *The Visible Hand*, Cambridge, Mass.: The Belknap Press of Harvard University Press.

Chenery, H. et al. (1974), *Redistribution with Growth*, London: Oxford University Press.

Colletti, L. (1972), *From Rousseau to Lenin. Studies in Ideology and Society*, London: New Left Books.

Cornfield, J. (1942), 'On Certain Biases in Samples of Human Populations', *Journal of American Statistical Association*, Vol. 37, pp. 63-8.

Coser, L. A. (1956), *The Functions of Social Conflict*, Glencoe, Ill.: The Free Press.

Coser, L. A. and Rosenberg, B. (eds.) (1957), *Sociological Theory: A Book of Readings*, 1st edn., New York: Macmillan.

Coser, L. A. and Rosenberg, B. (eds.) (1969), *Sociological Theory: A Book of Readings*, 3rd edn., New York: Macmillan.

Crozier, M. J., Huntington, S. P. and Watanuki, J. (1975), *The Crisis of Democracy. Report on the Governability of Democracies to the Trilateral Commission*, New York: New York University Press.

Cutler, A., Hindess, N., Hirst, P. and Hussain, A. (1977), *Marx's Capital and Capitalism Today*, Vol. 1, London: Routledge and Kegan Paul.

Dahl, R. (1957), 'The Concepts of Power', *Behavioral Science*, Vol. 2, 1957, pp. 201-15.

Dahlberg, L. and Grenninger, C. M. (1974), *Arbetsmiljö: yrkesskador, vårdkostnader*, Stockholm: Sveriges Kommunaltjänstemannaförbund.

Dahlqvist, M. (1975), *Staten, socialdemokratin och socialismen*, Stockholm: Verdandidebatt/Prisma.

Dahlqvist, M. (1978), *Att studera Kapitalet. Första boken*, Staffanstorp: Cavefors.

Dahlström, E. (1954), *Tjänstemän, näringslivet och samhället*, Stockholm: Studieförbundet Näringsliv och Samhälle, Norstedts.

Dahlström, E., et al. (1971), *LKAB och demokratin*, Stockholm: Wahlström and Widstrand.

Dahmén, E. (1968), *Sätt pris på miljön*, Stockholm: SNS.

Dahrendorf, R. (1959), *Class and Class Conflict in an Industrial Society*, London: Routledge and Kegan Paul.

Denitch, B. (1980), 'Spontaneity and Organization: Revolutionary Party and Modernization' in U. Himmelstrand (ed.) *Spontaneity and Planning in Social Development*, London: SAGE Publishers.

Drucker, P. (1976), *The Unseen Revolution, How Pension Fund Socialism came to America*, New York: Harper and Row.

Ekeh P. (1974), *Social Exchange Theory. The Two Traditions*, London: Heinemann.

Elster, J. (1973), *Nytt perspektiv på økonomisk historie*, Oslo: Pax Forlag.

Elvander, N. (1972), *Svensk skattepolitik 1945-1970*, Stockholm: Rabén and Sjögren.

Elvander, N. (1979), *Scandinavian Social Democracy: its Strength and Weakness*, Stockholm: Almqvist and Wiksell International.

Engwall, L. (1973), *Models of Industrial Structure*, Lexington, Mass.: Lexington Books.

Esping-Andersen, G., Friedland, R. and Wright, E. O. (1976), 'Modes of Class Struggle and the Capitalist State', in *Kapitalistate* no. 4-5, 1976, pp. 186-220.

Forssman, A. (1979), *En teori om staten och de offentliga utgifterna*, Uppsala Universitet 1979: Diss.

Fredriksson, C. and Lindmark, L. (1976), *Nationella och lokala produktionssystem.* Umeå: Strudier i företagsekonomi, 22.

Frydén E. (1977), 'Den ekonomiska diktaturen i demokratin Sveridge', in *Social välfärd genom marknadsekonomi*, Stockholm: Svenska Arbetsgivareföreningen.

Företagen 1974, *Sveriges Officiella Statistik*, Stockholm: SCB/Liber.

Företagen 1975, *Sveriges Officiella Statistik*, Stockholm: SCB/ Liber.

Gabel, J. (1975), *False Consciousness. An Essay on Reification*, Oxford: Basil Blackwell.

Galbraith, J. K. (1967), *The New Industrial State*, London: Hamish Hamilton.

Galtung, J. (1966), 'International Relations and International Conflicts: A Sociological Approach', *Transactions of the Sixth World Congress of Sociology*, Geneva: International Sociological Association.

Gardell, B. (1976), *Arbetsinnehåll och livskvalitet*, Stockholm: Prisma.

Giddens, A. (1973), *The Class Structure of the Advanced Societies*, London: Hutchinson University Library.

Gillman, J. M. (1969), *Das Gesetz des tendenziellen Falls der Profitrate*, Frankfurt: E V A.

Godelier, M. (1972a), *Rationality and Irrationality in Economics*, New York:

Monthly Review Press.

Godelier, M. (1972b), 'Dialectical Logic and the Analysis of Structures: A Reply to Lucien Sève', in *International Journal of Sociology*, Vol. II, no. 2-3, summer–fall 1972.

Gorz, A. (1964), *Stratégie ouvrière et néo-capitalisme*, Paris: Edition du Seuil.

Gorz, A. (ed.) (1976), *The Division of Labour*, Hassock: Harvester Press.

Gorz, A. (1978), 'Introduction' in *Le Nouvel Observateur*, 4 December 1978.

Greenspan, A. (1977), 'Investment Risk: The New Dimension of Policy', in *The Economist*, 6 August 1977.

Gustafsson, B. (ed.) (1977), *Den offentliga sektorns expansion. Teorioch metodproblem*, Uppsala Studies in Economic History 16, Stockholm: Almqvist and Wiksell International.

Gustafsson, B. (1978), 'Kapitalismens kris – och vägen framåt', in *Socionomen* no. 17, 1978.

Habermas, J. (1973), *Legitimationsprobleme im Spätkapitalismus*, Frankfurt am Main: Suhrkamp.

Halm, G. N. (1968), *Economic Systems. A Comparative Analysis*, New York: Holt, Rinehart and Winston.

Hammar, T. (1977), 'The First Immigration Election'. Abbreviated version of a preliminary report (Report no. 4), Stockholm: Commission on Immigration Research.

Hansson, S. O. (1976), 'Socialismens långsiktiga målsättningar: vad kommer efter ägandefrågan?', in *Tiden* no. 6 1976.

Harrington, M. (1979), 'Social Retreat and Economic Stagnation', *Dissent*, Spring 1979, pp. 131-4.

Harrod, R. (1958), 'The Possibility of Economic Satiety – Use of Economic Growth for Improving the Quality of Education and Leisure', in *Problems of United States Economic Development*, I. pp. 207-13, New York: Committee for Economic Development.

Hedborg, A. (1976), 'Makten är odelbar', *Tiden*, no. 4, 1976, pp. 217-25.

Hedman, L. (1978), *Svenskarna och u-hjälpen*, Uppsala: Acta Universitatis Upsaliensis. Studia Sociologica Upsaliensia 14.

Herfondahl, O. C. and Kneese, A. V. (1974), *Economic Theory of Natural Resources*, Colombus, Ohio: Charles E. Merrill.

Hermansson, C. H. (1971), *Monopol och storfinans – de 15 familjerna*, Stockholm: Rabén and Sjögren.

Hernes, G. (1976), 'Structural Change in Social Processes', *American Journal of Sociology*, November 1976.

Hewitt, C. (1977), 'The Effect of Political Democracy and Social Democracy on Equality in Industrial Societies: A Cross-National Comparison', *American Sociological Review*, Vol. 42, 1977, pp. 450-64.

Hilferding, R. (1973), *Das Finanzkapital*, Bd I-II, Frankfurt am Main: Europäische Verlagsanstalt.

Hilton, R. (ed.) (1976), *The Transition from Feudalism to Capitalism*, London: New Left Books.

Himmelstrand, U. (1960a), *Social Pressures, Attitudes and Democratic Processes*, Uppsala: Almqvist and Wiksell.

Himmelstrand, U. (1960b), 'Verbal Attitudes and Behaviour: A Paradigm for the Study of Message Transmission and Transformation', *Public Opinion Quarterly*, Vol. 24.

Himmelstrand, U. and Lindhagen, J. (1970), 'The Rejected Status-Seeker in Mass Politics: Fact and Fiction' in *ACTA SOCIOLOGICA*, Vol. 17 pp. 213-36.

Himmelstrand, U. (1973), 'Tribalism, Regionalism, Nationalism, and Secession in Nigeria', Chapter 15 in Eisenstadt, S. N. and Rokkan, S. (eds.) *Building States and Nations, Volume II*, Beverly Hills: SAGE Publications.

Himmelstrand, U. (1976), 'Human Predicaments at the Intersection of Objective and Subjective Realms', paper presented to the *IPSA World Congress* in Edinburgh, 16—21 August 1976.

Himmelstrand, U. (1978), 'Aktionsforschung und angewandte Sozialwissenschaft', Chapter 3 in Moser, H. and Ornauer, H. (eds.), *Internationale Aspekte der Aktionsforschung*, München, Kösel-Verlag.

Hirsch, F. (1977), *Social Limits to Growth*, London: Routledge and Kegan Paul.

Hirsch, F. and Goldthorpe, J. H. (1978), *The Political Economy of Inflation*, London: Martin Robertson.

Hirschman, A. (1970), *Exit, Voice and Loyalty*, Cambridge, Mass.: Harvard University Press.

Homans, G. (1961), *Social Behaviour: its Elementary Forms*, New York: Harcourt, Brace and World.

Horvat, B. (1969), *An Essay on Yugoslav Society*, White Plains: International Arts and Sciences Press.

Horvat, B. (1977), 'Between East and West while Opting for Socialism: Comparative Social Organization'. Paper presented to the *Symposium on The Small Welfare State between Domestic Pressures and International Dependency*, Uppsala, 1977. (manuscript)

Horrowitz, D. (ed.) (1968), *Marx and Modern Economics*, New York: Monthly Review Press.

Hunt, E. K. and Schwartz, J. G. (eds.) (1972), *A Critique of Economic Theory. Selected Readings*, Harmondsworth: Penguin.

Hurd, R. (1978), 'The Myth of the Unemployment—Inflation Trade-off' in M. G. Raskin, (ed.), *The Federal Budget and Social Reconstruction*, Washington, D.C.: Institute of Policy Studies.

Ingelhardt, R. (1971), 'The Silent Revolution in Europe: Intergenerational Change in Post-Industrial Societies', *American Political Science Review*, Vol. 65, 1971, pp. 991-1017.

Israel, J. (1978), 'Swedish Socialism and Big Business' in *ACTA SOCIOLOGICA*, Vol. 21, no. 4, 1978, pp. 341-53.

Johansson, I. (1975), *A Critique of Karl Popper's Methodology*, Stockholm: Scandinavian University Books, Esselte Studium.

Johansson, S. (1974), *När är tiden mogen?* Stockholm: Tiden.

Johansson, S. (1976), 'Det tredje skedets politiska problematik', in *Tiden*, no. 7, 1976, pp. 342-53.

Jolin, C. (1974), *Sverige nästa*, Malmö: Bernces förlag.

Jonsson, B. (1978), 'Some Notes on Counter-Cultural and Societal Change'. Paper presented at the *9th World Congress of Sociology*, August 1978, Uppsala.

Jonung, L. and Wadensjö, E. (1979), 'The Effect of Unemployment, Inflation and Real Income Growth on Government Popularity in Sweden', *Scandinavian Journal of Economics*, no. 2, 1979, pp. 341-53.

Jovanov, N. (1975), *Workers' Strikes in the Socialist Federal Republic of Yugoslavia from 1958-1969*. Doctoral Dissertation in Slovenian, Ljubljana.

Kapp, K. W. (1978), *The Social Costs of Business Enterprise*, Nottingham: Spokesman.

Karasek Jr. R. A. (1976), *The Impact of the Work Environment on Life Outside the Job*. Doctoral Thesis: Massachusetts Institute of Technology.

Korpi, W. (1972), *Varför strejkar arbetarna?*, Stockholm: Tiden.

Korpi, W. (1977), 'Vad hotar arbetarrörelsen?' in *Tiden, no. 3*, 1977.

Korpi, W. (1978), *The Working Class in Welfare Capitalism*, London: Routledge and Kegan Paul.

Korpi, W. (1979), 'Välfärdsstatens variationer: forskningsproblem om socialpolitska strategier i de kapitalistiska demokratierna', *Sociologisk Forskning,* Vol. XVI, no. 1, pp. 3-28.

Korpi, W. and Shalev, M. (1979) 'Strikes, industrial relations and class conflict in capitalist societies', in *British Journal of Sociology,* Vol. XXX, no. 2, June 1979.

Korpi, W. and Shalev, M. (1980), 'Strikes, Power and Politics in the Western Nations, 1900–1976', *Political Power and Social Theory,* Vol. 1, 1979, pp. 301-334.

Kronlund, J., Carlsson, J., Jenson, I. and Sundström-Frisk, C. (1973), *Demokrati utan makt, LKAB efter strijken,* Lund: Prisma.

Kuhnle, S. (1975), *Patterns of Social and Political Mobilization: A Historical Analysis of the Nordic Countries,* London: SAGE Publications (Contemporary Political Sociology Series No. 06-005, Vol. 1).

Kusczynski, J. (1968) *Die Geschichte der Lage der Arbeiter unter dem Kapitalismus,* Berlin, DDR: Akademie-Verlag.

Kuusinen, O. et al. (1964), *Fundamentals of Marxism–Leninism. Manual.* (2nd rev. edn.), Moscow: Progress Publishers.

Laclau, E. (1977), *Politics and Ideology in Marxist Theory,* London: New Left Books.

Lagerlöf, Elisabeth (1975), 'Accident Research – Theories and Methods', in *Ambio,* Vol. 4, no. 1, 1975.

Lane, R. (1977), 'Legitimation of market and state in a market society'. Paper submitted to the *Conference on Legitimation and Delegitimation of Regimes.* New York: City University of New York.

Lange, O. (1963), *Political Economy, Vol. I: General Problems,* New York: Macmillan.

Lange, O. (1972), 'The Computer and the Market' in Nove, A. and Nuti, D. M. (eds.), *Socialist Economics,* Harmondsworth: Penguin Books.

Larsson, K. A. (1973), 'Den svenska ekonomins internationella beroende', in *Häften för Kritiska Studier,* no. 8, 1973.

Lazarsfeld, P. F. and Barton A. H. (1951), 'Qualitative Measurement in the Social Sciences: Classification, Typologies and Indices', in Lerner, D. and Lasswell, H. D. (eds.), *The Policy Sciences,* Stanford: Stanford University Press.

Leijon, A. (1979), *Solidarisk lönepolitik eller löntagarfonder? Den svenska modellens sammanbrott,* Stockholm: Tema Nova.

Lenin, V. (1964), *Collected Works. Volume 25,* Moscow: Progress Publishers.

Lenski, G. E. (1954), 'Status-Crystallization: A Non-Vertical Dimension of Social Status', *American Sociological Review,* Vol. 19, 1954, pp. 405-13.

Lewin, L. (1966), *Planhushållningsdebatten,* Stockholm: Almqvist and Wiksell.

Lidén, L., Lindencrona, G. et al. (1979), *Agarmakt på avskrivning?* Stockholm: SNS.

Lijphart, A. (1977), *Democracy in Plural Societies. A Comparative Exploration,* New Haven: Yale University Press.

Liljeström, R. (1976), Roller i omvandling, Stockholm: SOU 1976:71.

Lindbeck, A. (1979), *Fondfrågan,* Stockholm: Alba.

Lindhagen, J. (1976), 'Åren vi förlorade', in *Tiden,* no. 10, 1976.

Lindhagen, J. (1977), 'Men å andra sidan', in *Tiden,* no. 8, 1977.

Lindhagen, J. and Nilsson, M. (1971), *Hotet mot arbetarrörelsen,* Stockholm: Tiden.

Lindholm, R. and Norstedt, J.-P. (1977), *Volvo-rapporten,* Stockholm: SAF.

Lindqvist, S. (1974), *Jordens gryning, Jord och makt i Sydamerika, del 2* Stockholm: Bonniers.

Lipset, S. M. (1960), *Political Man,* New York: Doubleday and Co.

Lipset, S. M. (1963), *Political Man* (Anchor Books Edition), New York: Doubleday and Co.

Lipset, S. M. and Rokkan, S. (eds.) (1967), *Party Systems and Voter Alignments,* London: Collier-MacMillan.

Lopreato, J. (1966), 'Il Conflitto di Classe in Italia', *Tempi Moderni,* Vol. 26, pp. 43-86.

Lopreato, J. (1967), 'Class Conflict and Images of Society', *The Journal of Conflict Resolution,* Vol. 11, 1967, pp. 291-3.

Lundberg, E. (1958), *Konjunkturer och ekonomisk politik,* Stockholm: Konjunkturinstitutet and SNS.

Lundberg, L. (1979), *Subventionerna till industrin,* Uppsala University, Department of Sociology.

Lundh, L. G. (1973), 'Ägande och kontroll under senkapitalismen' in *Häften för Kritiska Studier,* no. 8, 1973.

LO–SAP (1978) *Löntagarfonder och kapitalbildning – förslag från LO–SAPs arbetsgrupp,* Stockholm: LO–SAP.

Löner, Priser, Skatter, Rapport till LO-kongressen 1976. Stockholm: Prisma.

Mage, S. H. (1963), *The 'Law of the Falling Tendency of the Rate of Profit'. Its Place in the Marxian Theoretic System and Relevance to the US Economy.* Ph.D. thesis, Columbia University.

Mallet, S. (1975), *The New Working Class,* Nottingham: Spokesman Books.

Mandel, E. (1968), *Marxist Economic Theory,* Vols. 1–2, London: Merlin Press.

Mandel, E. (1975), *Late Capitalism,* London: New Left Books.

Mandel, E. (1977), 'Late Capitalism, State Power and the Transition to Socialism in Western Europe'. Paper presented to the *Symposium on The Small Welfare State between Domestic Pressures and International Dependency,* Uppsala, 1977. (Manuscript).

Marchetti, V. and Marks, J. D. (1974), *The CIA and the Cult of Intelligence,* New York: Alfred A. Knopf.

Martin, A. (1978), 'The Dynamics of Change in a Keynesian Political Economy: The Swedish Case and its Implications', *British Political Yearbook,* Vol. 4.

Marx-Engels Werke, Vol. 4, Berlin (DDR): Dietz Verlag.

Marx, K. (1971a), *Capital. Volume III,* Moscow: Progress Publishers.

Marx, K. (1971b), 'A Contribution to the Critique of Political Economy', in Freedman, R. (ed.), *Marx on Economics,* Harmondsworth: Penguin.

Marx, K. (1976), *Capital, Vol. I.* Harmondsworth: Penguin.

Mayntz, R. and Scharpf, F. W. (1975), *Policy-making in the German Federal Bureaucracy,* Amsterdam: Elsevier.

McMurtry, J. (1978), *The Structure of Marx's World-View,* Princeton: Princeton Unversity Press.

Meidner, R. et al. (1976) *Kollektiv kaptalbildning genom löntagarfonder.* Rapport till LO-kongressen 1976, Stockholm: Prisma.

Meidner. R. (1978), *Employee Investment Funds. An Approach to Collective Capital Formation,* London: Allen and Unwin.

Merton, R. K. (1957), *Social Theory and Social Structure* (revised and enlarged edition), Glencoe, Ill.: The Free Press.

Miliband, R. (1969), *The State in Capitalist Society,* New York: Basic Books.

Myrdal, G. (1960), *Beyond the Welfare State,* New Haven: Yale University Press.

Nicolaus, M. (1972), 'The Unknown Marx', in Blackburn, R. (ed.), *Ideology in Social Science. Readings in Critical Social Theory,* London: Fontana/Collins.

Nicolin, C. (1977), 'Inledningsanförande', *SAF-kongressen sammanfattad,* Stockholm: SAF.

Nilsson, T. (1977), 'Arbetsdelning och klassindelning' in *Sociologisk Forskning,* nos. 2–3, 1977.

Nisbet, R. A. (1966), *The Sociological Tradition,* New York: Basic Books.

Noble, D. (1977), *America by Design,* New York: Alfred A. Knopf.

References 353

Nohrstedt, S. A. (1977), 'Bakgrunden till skogsarbetarstrejken 1975', in *Arkiv*, nos. 11–12, 1977.

Norling, D. (1977), *Fritt näringsliv eller fondsocialism*, Stockholm: Svenska Arbetsgivareföreningen.

Norman, R. (1969), *Variation och omorientering. En studie av innovationsförmåga*, Stockholm: SIAR-S-21 (mimeo).

OECD (1975), *The Polluter Pays Principle. Definitions, Analysis, Implementation*, Brussels: OECD.

Obradović, J. and Dunn, W., (eds), (1978), *Workers' Self-Management and Organizational Power*, Pittsburgh: University of Pittsburgh International Center for International Studies.

O'Connor, J. (1973), *The Fiscal Crisis of the State*, New York: St. Martin's Press.

Offe, C. (1972), *Strukturprobleme des Kapitalistischen Staats*, Frankfurt am Main: Suhrkamp.

Ohlin, B. (1936), *Fri eller dirigerad ekonomi?* Göteborg: Folkpartiets ungdomsförbund.

Ohlström, B. (1977), *Vilda strejker inom LO-området 1974 och 1975*, Stockholm: LO:s utredningsavdelning.

Olofsson, G. (1979), *Mellan Klass och Stat*, Lund: Arkivs avhandlingsserie.

Olsen, J. and Lajer, M. (1979), 'Violent Death and Unemployment in Two Trade Unions in Denmark', *Social Psychiatry*, Vol. 14, 1979, pp. 139-45.

Olson Jr., Mancur (1969) 'The Relationship between Economics and other Social Sciences', in S. M. Lipset (ed.), *Politics and the Social Sciences*, New York: Oxford University Press.

Olsson, H. (1978), 'Produktivt och improduktivt arbete', in *Häften för Kritiska Studier*, no. 2, 1978.

Ovesen, Edith (1978), *Arbetslöshetens psykiska följdverkningar*, Stockholm: Rabén and Sjögren.

Parkin, F. (1971), *Class Inequality and Political Order*, London: MacGibbon and Kee.

Petersson, O. (1978), 'The 1976 Election: New Trends in the Swedish Electorate', *Scandinavian Political Studies*, Vol. I – New Series – nos. 2–3, pp. 109–210.

Petersson, O. (1978), *Valundersölmomgar, Rapport 2. Väljarna och valet 1976*, Stockholm: Liber Förlag/Allmänna Förlaget/SCB.

Poggi, G. (1978), *The Development of the Modern State*, London: Hutchinson.

Popper, K. R. (1945), *The Open Society and its Enemies. 2: Hegel and Marx*, London: Routledge and Kegan Paul.

Popper, K. R. (1963), *Conjectures and Refutations*, London: Routledge and Kegan Paul.

Popper, K. R. (1969), *The Poverty of Historicism*, London: Routledge and Kegan Paul.

Poulantzas, N. (1973), *Political Power and Social Classes*, London: New Left Books.

Poulantzas, N. (1975), *Classes in Contemporary Capitalism*, London: New Left Preliminär Nationalbudget (1980), Stockholm: Konkunkturinstitutet och Ekonomidepartementet.

Pryor, F. L. (1972), 'An International Comparison of Concentration Ratios', in *The Review of Economics and Statistics*, Vol. LIV, 1972, pp. 130-40.

Raskin, M. G. (ed.) (1978), *The Federal Budget and Social Reconstruction*, Washington, D.C.: Institute for Policy Studies.

Rokkan, S. (1970), *Citizen, Elections, Parties*, New York: McKay.

Ronge, V. (1978), 'Offentlig politik. Mellan statsteori och empirisk politisk forskning', in *Häften för Kritiska Studier*, no. 5, 1978.

Rose, A. (ed.) (1962), *Human Behavior and Social Processes. An Interactionist Approach*, Boston: Houghton Mifflin Co.

354   Beyond Welfare Capitalism

Ross, A. (1948), *Varför demokrati?*, Stockholm: Tiden.

Runciman, W. G. (1966), *Relative Deprivation and Social Justice*, London: Routledge and Kegan Paul.

Rydén, B. (1971), *Fusioner i svensk industri*, Stockholm: Industrins Utrednings-institut.

SAP (1975), *Programme of the Swedish Social Democratic Party* (adopted by the 1975 Party Congress), Borås: published by the Social Democratic Party of Sweden (SAP).

Sartori, G. (1965), *Democratic Theory*, New York: Frederick A. Praeger.

Sartre, J. P. (1963) *Search for a Method*, New York: Alfred A. Knopf.

Sarv, H. (1973), *Logistik. En referensram för integrerade materialflöden*, Stockholm: Sveriges Mekanförbund.

Scase, R. (1972), ' "Industrial Man": A Reassessment with English and Swedish Data', *British Journal of Sociology*, Vol. 23, 1972, pp. 204-20.

Scase, R. (1974a), 'Relative Deprivation: A Comparison of English and Swedish Manual Workers', in Wedderburn, D. (ed.), *Poverty, Inequality and Class Structure*, Cambridge: Cambridge University Press.

Scase, R. (1974b), 'Conception of the Class Structure and Political Ideology: Some Observations on Attitudes in England and Sweden', in *The Social Analysis of Class Structure*, London: Tavistock Publications.

Scase, R. (1977), *Social Democracy in Capitalist Society*, London: Croom Helm.

Schumpeter, J. A. (1974), *Capitalism, Socialism and Democracy*, London: Unwin University Books.

Seeman, M. H. (1967), 'Powerlessness and Knowledge: A Comparative Study of Alienation and Learning', in *Sociometry*, no. 2, 1967.

Segerstedt, T. and Lundqvist, A. (1955), *Människan i industrisamhället. Del II. Fritidsliv — samhällsliv*, Stockholm: Studieförbundet Näringsliv och Samhälle, Norstedts.

Shaw, W. H. (1978), *Marx's Theory of History*, London: Hutchinson University Library.

SIND PM (1975:4), *Underleverantörsproblematiken*, Stockholm: Statens Industriverk.

Simon, H. A. (1968), *Administrative Behaviour*, 2nd edn., New York: MacMillan/The Free Press.

Sorokin, P. (1928), *Contemporary Sociological Theories*, New York: Harper and Brothers.

Soydan, H. (1975), *Social Structure and Subjective Culture. A Macrosociological Inquiry into an Atlas of Affective Meanings*. Doctoral thesis at Uppsala University, 1975.

Stajner, R. (1979), *Krisen. De samtida krisernas anatomi och en kristeori för kapitalismens neoimperialistika stadium*, Lund: Arbetarkultur.

Stephens, J. D. (1979), *The Transition from Capitalism to Socialism*, London: Macmillan Press.

Stevenson, P. (1974), 'Monopoly Capital and Inequalities in Swedish Society', in *The Insurgent Sociologist*, 1974, pp. 44-58.

Sunesson, S. (1976), 'State Ideology and Trade Unions in Sweden', in *Kapitalistate*, nos. 4-5, 1976, pp. 271-84.

Swedner, H. and Fatahi, N. (1978), 'Överger väljarna SAP — eller SAP väljarna?' in *Tiden*, no. 8, 1978.

Söderpalm, S. A. (1976), *Direktörsklubben. Storindustrin i svensk politik under 1930- och 40-talen*, Stockholm: Zenit/Rabén and Sjögren.

Södersten, B. (1973), 'Arbetarstyrd ekonomi', *Ekonomisk Debatt*, no. 8, 1973, pp. 479-90.

Södersten, B. (1975), 'Mer om arbetarstyrd ekonomi', *Ekonomisk Debatt*, no. 1, 1975, pp. 24-35.

Södersten, B. (1976), 'Den sanna pluralismen. Teser om löntagarstyre' in *Tiden*, no. 4, 1976, pp. 197-209.

TCO (1978), *Löntagarkapital genom fonder — ett principförslag*. (Report to the 1979 TCO Congress) Stockholm: TCO.

The Swedish Council for Environmental Information and the National Swedish Environment Protection Board (1979), *The Environment and its Management in Sweden*, Solna.

Therborn, G. (1972), 'Om klasserna i Sverige 1930-1970', in *Zenit* no. 2, 1972.

Therborn, G. (1976), *Science, Class and Society*, London: New Left Books.

Therborn, G. (1977), 'The Rule of Capital and the Rise of Democracy', *New Left Review*, no. 103, 1977, pp. 3-41.

Therborn, G. (1978), *What Does the Ruling Class Do When it Rules?*, London: New Left Books.

Therborn, G. (1979), 'Enterprises, Markets and States. A First, Modest Contribution to a General Theory of Capitalist Politics'. Paper presented at the *IPSA World Congress*, 12—18 August, 1978.

Timasheff, N. (1964), *Sociological Theory — Its Nature and Growth*, New York: Random House.

Tingsten, H. (1937), *Political Behavior*, Westminster: King and Son.

Tingsten, H. (1945), *Demokratins problem*, Stockholm: Norstedts förlag.

Tingsten, H. (1967), *Den svenska socialdemokratins idéutveckling, 1-2*, Stockholm: Aldus/Bonniers.

Tipisev, A. J. (1977), 'Environmental Protection in Soviet Pulp and Paper Industry', *Pulp and Paper Canada*, Vol. 78, 1977, pp. T171-T174.

Touraine, A. (1979), *Le Voix et le Regard*, Paris: Edition Seuil.

Touraine, A. (1980), Manuscript, to be published in *Political Psychology* in 1980.

af Trolle, U. (1978), *Strategi för en my välfärd*, Stockholm: Liber.

Tronti, M. (1974), *Arbeiter und Kapital*, Frankfurt am Main: Verlag Neue Kritik.

Turner, R. (1956), 'Role-Taking, Role Standpoint, and Reference Group Behavior', *American Journal of Sociology*, 1956, pp. 316-28.

Udéhn, L. (1980), 'Central Planning: Postscript to a Debate', in Himmelstrand, U. (ed.) *Spontaneity and Planning in Social Development*, London: SAGE publications (forthcoming).

Vanek, Jaroslav (1971), *The Participatory Economy. An Evolutionary Hypothesis and a Strategy for Development*, Ithaca: Cornell University Press.

Vem *äger Sverige?* Fakta om makt och ägande ur Koncentrationsutredningen, Stockholm: Prisma.

Vuchinich W. S. (1969), *Contemporary Yugoslavia. Twenty Years of Socialist Experiment*, Berkeley: University of California Press.

Watchel, H. and Adelsheim, P. (1978), 'Inflation and Unemployment: or Which came first, the Chicken or . . . ' in Raskin, M. G. (ed.), *The Federal Budget and Social Reconstruction* (1978), Washington D.C.: Institute for Policy Studies.

Waldenström, E. et al. (1976), *Företagsvinster, kapitalförsörjning, löntagarfonder*, Stockholm: Sveriges Industriförbund och SAF.

Wallentin, H. (1978), *Svenska folkets historia*, Stockholm: Prisma.

Weber, M. (1948), *From Max Weber* (ed. by H. H. Gerth and C. Wright Mills), London: Routledge and Kegan Paul.

Wibe, S. (1976), 'Monopol kch monopolkapitalism?' in *Häften för Kritiska Studier*, Nos. 7-8, 1976.

Wibe, S. (1978), 'Efterfråge- eller profitkris: en jämförande analys av krisen på 30-talet och idag', in *Zenit*, no. 1, 1978.

Widgren, J. (1978), *Report to OECD (SOPEMI) on Immigration to Sweden in 1977 and the first half of 1978*, Stockholm: Commission on Immigration Research, Ministry of Labour.

Wigforss, E. (1959), *Kan dödläget brytas? Dagspolitik och utopi,* Stockholm: Tidens förlag.

Wigforss, E. (1962), *Frihet och Gemenskap,* Stockholm: Tiden.

Wiking-Faria, P. (1976). 'Statens subventionspolitik' in *Häften för Kritiska Studier,* nos. 7–8, 1976.

Wilensky, H. (1975), *The Welfare State and Equality,* Berkeley: University of California Press.

Wilensky, H. (1976), *The 'New Corporatism', Centralization and the Welfare State,* Beverly Hills: SAGE Publications.

Wolfe, A. (1977), *The Limits of Legitimacy, Political Contradictions of Contemporary Capitalism,* New York: The Free Press.

Wood, R. C. (1961), *1400 Governments: the Political Economy of the New York Metropolitan Region,* New York: Harvard University Press.

Wright, E. O. (1976), 'Class Boundaries in Advanced Capitalist Societies', in *New Left Review,* no. 98.

Wright, E. O. (1978), *Class, Crisis and State,* London: New Left Books.

Wrong, D. (1961), 'The Oversocialized Conception of Man in Sociology', *American Sociological Review,* Vol. 26. 1961, pp. 183-93.

Zawadski, B. and Lazarsfeld, P. (1935), 'The Psychological Consequences of Unemployment', *Journal of Social Psychology,* Vol. 6, 1935, pp. 224-51.

Zeitlin, I. (1968), *Ideology and the Development of Sociological Theory,* New Jersey: Prentice Hall.

Zetterberg, H. and Busch, K. (1975), 'Allmänhetens prioritering av offentlig och privat konsumtion', in Tarschys, D. m fl: *Offentlig sektor i tillväxt,* Stockholm: SNS.

Zetterberg, H. (1978), 'The Swedish Election 1976'. Paper presented to the WAPOR-session held in conjunction with the *9th World Congress of Sociology* in Uppsala, 14-19 August 1978.

Åberg R. (1979), 'Social Mobility and Class Structuration, in *ACTA SOCIOLOGICA* 1979 no. 3, pp. 247-73.

Åsard, E. (1978), *LO och löntagarfondsfrågan: En studie i facklig politik och strategi,* Stockholm: Raben and Sjögren (Doctoral dissertation with English summary).

Åsling, N. G. (1979). *Industrins kris och förnyelse. Näringspolitiken inför 80-talet,* Stockholm: LT:s Förlag.

Öhman, B. (1970), 'Arbetsmarknadspolitikens utveckling 1948–69', in *Meddelanden från Utredningsbyrån 1970:* 17, Stockholm: AMS.

Östlind, A. (1975), *Arbetsmarknadspolitik och löneutjömning ären 1964-1974.* Stockholm: Riksdagens revisorers kansli.

Newspapers, Journals and Magazines

Aktiespararen, 1977:4

Dagens Nyheter, 25 February 1979.

Ekonomisk Debatt No. 1, 1976, 'Issue on Ownership and Power in Business'.

LO—Tidningen, No. 1, 1976.

Socialistisk Debatt, no. 5, 1977.

Veckans Affärer, no. 26, 1977.

Veckans Affärer, no. 45, 14 December 1978.

Zenit, no. 5, 1976.

Official Publications and Statistics

Ds Ju 1979:1, *Vägar till ökad välfärd* (Bjurel-rapporten), Stockholm: Justitie-departementet/Liber-Allmänna Förlaget.

Government Bill 1976/77 (1976), Stockholm: Riksdagstryck.

Government Bill 1977/78 (1977), Stockholm: Riksdagstryck.

SCB (1978), *Arbetsmarknadsstatistisk årsbok 1977*, Stockholm: Statistiska Centralbyrån/Liber-Allmänna Förlaget.

SCB/RFS (1977), *Yrkesskador 1974*, Stockholm: Riksförsäkringsverket/Liber-Allmänna Förlaget.

SOS (1978), *Vägtrafikolyckor med personskada*, Stockholm: Statistiska Central-byrån.

SOS (1979), *Allmänna Valen 1979.* Del. 1. Stockholm: Liber/Allmänna förlaget.

SOU 1966:69, *Trafikutveckling och trafikinventeringar* (by S. Godlund), Stockholm: Liber Förlag.

SOU 1968:5, *Industrins struktur och konkurrensförhällanden.* Koncentration-sutredningen 3, Stockholm: Liber Förlag.

SOU 1968:7, *Ägande och inflytande inom det privata näringslivet.* Koncentra-tionsutredningen 5, Stockholm: Liber Förlag.

SOU 1968:60, *Arbetsmarknadsverket och arbetsmarknadspolitik 1*, Stockholm: Liber Förlag.

SOU 1976:4, *Internationella konventioner inom arbetarskyddet*, Stockholm: Liber Förlag.

SOU 1976:71, *Roller i omvandling* (by Rita Liljeström, Gillan Liljeström-Svensson, Gunilla Fürst-Mellström), Stockholm: Liber Förlag.

SOU 1979:8, *Löntagarna och kapitaltillväxten, 1. Löntagarfonder — backgrund och problemanalys*, Stockholm: Liber Förlag.

SOU 1979:9, *Löntagarna och kapitaltillväxten, 2*, Stockholm: Liber Förlag.

Index

Note: The letters Å, Ä and Ö used in Swedish references will be found at the end of the alphabet.

Abelson, R. P., 226, 346
Abrahamsson, B., 278, 346
accidents, 104-6, 108, 334
actors, analogy of, 141-5, 148-52, 302-3
Acts of Parliament, Swedish *see* legislation
Adelsheim, P., 46, 78-80, 355
Adler-Karlsson, G., 61-2, 64, 286, 332
affluent society, Sweden as, 168-79
aggregation, statistical, 142
Ahlmark, P., 220
Ahrne, G., 84, 148, 157, 168, 176, 336, 346
Agee, P., 333, 346
agriculture, 52, 94, 331
Allardt, E., 36, 169, 329, 346
Althusser, L., 8, 346
Altvater, E., 8, 131, 333, 346
Amin, S., 77, 346
Anderson, P., 331, 346
Argyris, C., 83, 346
arms race, 170
Arnold, T., 341, 346
Arrow, K., 306
Austria, 4
automation, 46, 67; *see also* mechanization
autonomy, capitalist, 211-16

Babbage, C., 65
Bachrach, P., 210, 346
Bain, J. S. 55-6, 347
Bank of Sweden, 248
Baran, P., 347
bargaining, collective, 18, 165, 224, 259, 271

Barratz, M. S., 210, 346
Barre, Monsieur, 219
Barton, A. H., 332, 337, 347, 351
basic contradictions, 43-50
Beckholmen, K., 135, 347
Belgium, 47, 56-7, 62, 75
Bell, D., 122, 347
benefits *see* welfare benefits
Bentzel, R., 45, 347
Berglind, H., 101, 347
Berntson, L., 89, 347
Björkman, M., 347
Björkman, Torsten, 8-9, 64, 67
Björn, L., 324, 347
Blau, P., 142, 347
Board Representation for Employees Act, 224
Boston Consulting Group, 114, 347
Bottomore, T., 330, 347
bourgeois society, 144-5; *see also* capitalist
Bowles, S., 131, 347
Braverman, H., 65, 155, 157, 347
Brazil, 75
Broström, A., 278, 346
Brus, W., 136, 347
Buckley, W., 210, 347
bureaucracy, 127, 163, 201, 274, 279
Burns, T., 210, 347
Busch, K., 168, 356

Canada, 47, 56-7, 86, 88
capital/ism/ist
    accumulation of, 65-8, 289; autonomy of, 211-16; centralization of 15; changes in, 69-88 ; and commodification, 40-43; control

of, 41-3; defined, 41-3; early,
331; influence of, 229-39, 245-
51; and issue formation, 35-7; and
labour, 40-46, 224-44, 289-91;
labour as, 65-6; late, 206; power
of, 7-8, 23, 210-23; production
relations in, 46-68; property relations in, 60-64; social penetration
of, 211-16; and state, 224-44;
strength of, 26-7, 152-4. 210-23,
251-3; as threat, 170, 173, 226,
317; and wage-earners' funds,
289-307; work relations in, 64-8;
see also contradictions; market;
mature capitalism; pollution;
production; unemployment
Carillo, S., 335, 347
Carlsson, J., 334, 351
cartels, 72-3; *see also* multinational
firms
Castles, F.G., 324, 347
Centralist Organization of Salaried
Employees (TCO), 182-4, 204,
219-20, 223, 267-8, 282
centralization
of capital, 15; of industry, 48,
53-8, 71-2
Centre Party of Sweden, 194, 200-
202, 204, 218-23, 286, 341,
343
Chandler, A. D. Jr, 71
changes
in enterprises, 246-8; in incentive
patterns of capitalism, 83-8; in
market structures of capitalism,
69-82
Chenery, H., 214, 347
Chile, 123-4
China, 3, 94
CIA infiltration, 333
cities, 14, 173
class
analysis, 149-52; attitudes,
316-17; in Britain, 169, 180, 325;
collaboration, 287; predicaments,
147-8; and progressive liberalism,
19; struggle, 29-30, 38, 122,
149-52, 167; and training, 158-9,
161; unity, lack of, 8; *see also*

social consciousness; working
class
Co-determination at Work Act
(MBL), 197, 228-9, 237, 340
collective labour, 43-5
collective solidarity, 303
collectivity, 293
Colletti, L., 327, 347
commerce, growth of, 52
commodification of labour and
capital, 40-43
communism, 170
Communist Party of Sweden (VPK),
188, 192-4. 203, 273-6, 318,
338
competence, judgemental, 134-5
competitive markets, 53, 69-82; *see
also* markets
computerization, 206; *see also*
mechanization
concentration of industry, 53-8
71-3; *see also* centralization
conglomerates *see* concentration
consciousness
false, 151; social, 167-86, 208-9
Conservative Party of Sweden, 194,
202, 204, 218, 223, 318
consumption, 45, 81, 83-4, 96, 134
contradictions
basic, 43-50; between capital and
labour, 44-6, 289-91; between
forces and relations of
production, 13, 39, 46-50, 291-5;
of capitalism, 13, 36-7, 40-50,
84, 89-138, 261, 289-300;
extended, 43-50, 89-92; of interventionist state, 110-29; of
mature capitalism, 289-307; and
Marx, 13, 37-50, 326, 331
control, significance of, 41-3
Cornfield, J., 319, 347
correlates of working-class consciousness, 182-5
Coser, L. A., 37, 150, 329, 347
cost, labour as, 77
crisis, management of, 25-6
crisis-generation, 58, 81-2
Crozier, M. J., 113, 125, 348
culture, political, 35-7

Cutler, A., 49, 330, 348

Dahl, R., 210-11, 348
Dahlberg, L., 104, 106, 348
Dahlqvist, M., 39, 45, 337, 348
Dahlström, E., 62, 180, 348
Dahmén, E., 333, 346
Dahrendorf, R., 41-2, 143, 150, 330
348
data problems, 4
decentralization, 221, 280, 282
decision-making, 68, 332
defeatism, 245
demobilization, electoral, 190
democracy, economic, 198-9,
311-12;
'excesses' of, 125; political, 274,
308-10; social, 6-10; see also
Swedish Social Democrats
democracy, industrial see wage-
earners' funds; worker participation
Denmark, 75, 269-70
destruction
of incentive structures, 297-9;
of market, 295-7
development funds, 292-3
differential rewards, 38
differentials
decision-making, 312;
labour, 65-6
diseases, occupational, 104-6, 108
dispersal of industry, 13-14
distribution, 53
distribution of property, 42
distrust in capital, 218
division of labour, 52, 65, 258
Drucker, P. F., 281, 326, 348
drug addiction, 103, 334
duality of labour, 343

Eastern Europe, 94-5, 127, 136, 279-
80, 295
economic democracy, 198-9, 311-12
economic dependency, 51-8
economy, politicization of, 123-6
education, 134-5
Eisenhower, Dwight D., 324
Ekeh, P., 142, 348
elections, Swedish

1976, 18, 112, 153, 199-201,
223, 239, 318, 328; *1979*, 199,
202, 221, 223, 261, 264, 318,
339; *1982*, 264, 338, 341;
pressure to win, 9
electoral
bases of political parties, 187-90;
demobilization, 190;
mobilization, 196-209; reform,
337-9
Elster, J., 331, 348
Elvander, N., 328, 348
embourgeoisement, 8, 147, 168, 175,
187-209
employers see management; Swedish
Employers Confederation
employment, 134, 230-2, 243; see
also industry; labour; unemployment
Employment-promoting Measures
Act, 243
Employment Security Act, 197,
227-9
energy see nuclear energy
Engels, F., 4, 288
England, 4; see also Great Britain
enjoyment, infrastuctures of, 84
enrichment, job, 67
environment, 17, 19, 93-7, 106-7,
209, 225-6, 241-4, 333; see
also safety; work environment
Erlander, T., 325
Esping-Andersen, G., 6, 8-10, 14.
335, 348
Eurocommunism, 4, 335; see also
Communist Party
exchange, social, 142
'exit', 306
exports, Swedish, 5, 29, 217, 334;
under-developed countries, 77
extended contradictions of capitalism, 43-50, 89-92
external disturbances, 67
externalities
and interdependence, 59-60;
negative, 93-109, 134, 299, 333

Fälldin, T., 220, 222, 325
false consciousness, 151

Fatahi, N., 338
'fettered' forms of production, 331
financial solidity, 216
Finland, 75, 325
fiscal crisis, 120
Fleming, D., 8-9, 347
forces of production, 51-8
foreign investment, 74-5
Forssman, A., 335, 348
France, 4
    industry in, 56-7; nationalization
    in, 62-3; politics of, 191; profit
    in, 86, 269-70; Swedish invest-
    ment in, 75; unemployment in,
    119, 218
Frederiksson, C., 53, 348
Friedland, R., 6, 335, 348
Friedman, M, 123, 332
Frydén, E., 63, 348
functional socialism, 286-7
funds, restructuration, 198; see also
    wage-earners' funds
future
    images of, 245-53; social
    democracy in, 16; of Sweden,
    121; of working-class power,
    203-9

Gabel, J., 151, 348
Galbraith, J. K. 71, 335, 348
Galiani, Abbot, 344
Galtung, J., 150, 348
Gardell, B., 106, 348
Gemeinschaft, working-class, 179-81,
    191
Germany, Federal Republic of
    (West), 4, 25, 129, 131
    industry in, 57; nationalization in,
    62-3; profits in, 88, 269-70;
    Swedish investment in, 75;
    unemployment in, 47, 218
Germany, Democratic Republic
    (East), 86
Giddens, A., 23-4. 156. 161, 180-81.
    348
Gillman, J. M., 46, 348
Gintis, H., 131, 347
GNP *see* gross national product
Godelier, M., 13, 44, 46, 326, 331,

348-9
'golden chain', 167-8
Goldthorpe, J. H., 296, 350
Gorz, A., 168, 206, 345, 349
Great Britain, 4
    class in, 169, 180, 325; industry
    in, 56-7; and investments, 74-5;
    nationalization in, 62; politics in,
    191; profit in, 86, 88; unemploy-
    ment in, 47, 218
Greenspan, A., 217, 349
Grenninger, C. M., 104, 106, 348
gross national product, Swedish, 5,
    52, 216-17, 268
growth, economic, 45
Gustafsson, B., 111-12, 135, 335-6,
    349

Habermas, J., 119-20, 122, 335, 349
Halm, G., 330, 349
Hammar, T., 338, 349
Hansson, S. O., 137, 288, 328, 342,
    345, 349
Harrington, M., 324, 349
Harrisburg nuclear reactor, 202, 313
Harrod, R., 84, 349
Hedborg, A., 269-71, 287, 326, 349
Hedman, L., 169, 173, 181, 349
Herfondahl, O. C., 333, 349
Hermansson, C. H., 55, 349
Hernes, G., 302, 326, 349
Hewitt, C., 324, 349
Hilferding, R., 55, 349
Hill, P., 88
Hilton, R., 331, 349
Himmelstrand, U., 144, 150, 193,
    328, 336, 341, 349
Hindess, N., 49, 330, 348
Hirsch, F., 84, 296
Hirschman, A., 16, 306
Hirst, P., 49, 330, 348
historical materialism, analysed, 37-9
Hoffman, J., 131, 333, 346
Homans, G., 142, 350
Horrowitz, D., 330, 350
Horvat, B., 136, 350
human predicaments, 35-7
Huntington, S. P., 113, 125, 348
Hurd, R., 80, 350

Hussain, A., 49, 330, 348

ideological community, 143
ideological strength of capital, 153,
    210-18, 234-9
ideology of wage-earners' funds, 301
identity, working-class, 180-82
illness benefit, 18
immigrants, 151, 337, 339
incentives, 69-86, 141-2, 260-61,
    284, 297-300
India, 75
indicators of character of social
    relations of production, 51-68
individualism, 20n, 303, 313-14
individualization, 168
Industrial Policy Bill (Sweden), 220
Industrial Safety Act (Sweden), 197,
    227
industry
    centralization of, 48, 53-8, 71-2;
    dispersal of, 13-14; employment
    in, 155-6, 160-61, 174-86 *passim*;
    interdependence of, 51-8; nation-
    alization of, 5-6, 62-3, 119, 211,
    332; ownership of, 61-4; and
    politics, 18, 26-31; problems of,
    17-18; size of units, 54-6, 86, 291,
    294; social costs of, 93-109; and
    social vulnerability, 56-8; societal,
    12-13, 17-18, 48-9; *see also*
    investment; labour; nationaliz-
    tion; production; workers;
    working-class
inflation, 173, 225, 249; *see also*
    stagflation
influence of capital and labour in
    enterprises, 229-39
infrastructures of enjoyment, 84
Ingelhart, R., 36
innovations needed, 285-8
inputs, industrial, 12
instrumentalist approach to capital-
    ism, 6-10
insurance, unemployment, 115
integration, industrial, 55
interactionism, symbolic, 142
interdependence, economic, 51-8
interests, common, 169
international competition, 74-5

intervention *see* state
inversion effect, 217
investment, 5, 86-8, 263, 292, 303
    companies, 55, 63, 73; decisions
    of, 230-31, 241, 243; Swedish,
    abroad, 74-5, 217-18
issue formation in capitalist societies,
    35-7
Italy, 4, 47
    class in, 325; industry in, 56-7;
    nationalization in, 62; profit in,
    86; unemployment in, 218

Japan, 47, 56-7, 86, 88
Jensen, I., 334, 351
Johansen, L., 330
Johansson, I., 335, 350
Johansson, Sten, 324
Jolin, C., 6, 350
Jonung, L., 328, 350
Jovanov, N., 340
judgemental competence, 134-5

Kapp, K. W., 93-4
Kennedy, J. F., 324
Kneese, A. V., 333, 349
Korpi, W
    on metal workers, 336; on strikes
    and politics, 26, 112, 200, 277,
    324, 351; on working-class, 154,
    156, 163-6, 168, 179, 190, 280
    350
Kronlund, J., 334, 351
Kuhnle, S., 344, 351
Kusczynski, 337
Kuusinen, O., 327, 351

labour
    duality of, 343; and capital,
    40-46, 224-44, 289-91; as capital,
    65-6; collective, 43-5; commodi-
    fication of, 40-43; as cost, 77;
    division of, 52, 65, 258; exploita-
    tion of, 19; influence of, 228-39,
    245-51; interdependence of, 52-6;
    and law, 226-9; mobility of, 14;
    and management, 226-9; process,
    39; and state, 224-44; strength of,
    26-7, 112, 152-66, 205-6; surplus

value of, 38, 41, 330; types of, 157-8; *see also* unemployment; work; working-class
Labour Party (Swedish), 187-209, 218, 233, 339
Laclau, E., 335, 351
Lagerlöf, E., 104, 351
Lajer, M., 334, 353
Lane, R., 120, 223, 351
Lange, O., 296, 330, 351
Larsson, K., 74, 76, 351
Lasallean democracy, 326
late capitalism, 206
Latin America, 217
law, labour and management, 226-9
Lazarsfeld, P. F., 332, 334, 351, 354
legislation, Swedish, 197-7, 224, 227-9, 243, 290, 340-41
legitimation, 120-22
Leijon, A., 282, 351
Lenin, 335, 343
Lenski, G. E., 150, 351
Lewin, L., 328, 351
Liberal Party (Swedish), 193-4, 204, 218-20, 223, 309, 318, 328, 339-41
liberalism, 17-22
Lidén, L., 275, 286-8, 342, 351
Lijpardt, A., 150, 351
Liljestrom, R., 106, 351
Lindbeck, A., 136, 282, 342, 351
Lindencrona, G., 275, 286-8, 342, 351
Lindhagen, J., 190-91, 193, 201, 337, 351
Lindholm, R., 53, 351
Lindmark, L., 53, 348
Lindqvist, S., 217, 351
Lipset, S. M., 7, 113, 330, 333, 335, 351-2
living standard, 45, 134, 170
LO *see* Swedish Confederation of Trade Unions
lontagarfonder, 198; *see also* wage-earners' funds
Lopreato, J., 330, 352
LO–SAP Report, 263-8, 275-7, 281, 290-94, 302, 304, 307, 342, 352

Lundberg, E., 116, 327, 336, 352
Lundberg, Lars, 329, 352
Lunden, O., 286
Lundh, L. G., 55, 73, 352
Lundquist, A., 175, 177-80

McMurtry, J., 330, 337, 352
macro-micro relations, 141-3
Mage, S. H., 46, 352
Mallet, S., 157, 352
management, 174-6, 226-9, 259, 261, 287; *see also* labour
Mandel, E., 8, 29, 31, 113-14, 156, 161, 206, 352
Marchetti, V., 333, 352
marginalist theory, 141-2
marginalization of older workers, 17
market
  competitive, 53, 69-82; conformity, 115; defined, 143; economy, 40-41, 123-4; forces, 222, 306; self-destruction of, 53, 69-82, 295-7; self-regulating, 120; simulation, 296; structures, changes in, 69-82
mark-up pricing, 78-80
Marks, J. D., 333, 352
Martin, A., 335, 352
Marx, Karl/Marxism
  on analysis of society, 25, 309, 313, 352; on bourgeois democracy, 308-9; and capitalism, 3-10, 44-50, 64-6, 73, 78, 89, 137; on class, 38, 149, 167; and contradictions, 13, 37-50, 326, 331; and crisis element, 58; and revolution, 328; and Shaw, 64-6; and social consciousness, 167; and social context, 76-7; and socialist transformation, 131, 135, 309, 313, 327; on state, 7-10; and Swedish Social Democracy, 24-5; Weber and, 42
mature capitalism, 3, 83-5, 131, 289-307; *see also* capitalism
Mayntz, R., 114, 352
MBL *see* Workers Co-Determination
mechanization, 170, 173, 206; *see also* automation; technology

media, mass, 6
Medio, A., 330
Meidner, R., 62, 65, 198, 216, 262-6. 273, 286, 342, 352
mergers, industrial, 53-6, 73
Merton, R., 148, 352
meta-power *see* systemic power
micro-macro relations, 141-3
middle strata, 161, 174-8 *passim*
Miliband, R., 7, 335, 352
militancy, 18, 245
mixed economy, 112-15, 294
mobility, labour, 14
mobilization, electoral, 190-209
monarchy, 61
monopolization, 23, 69, 72-3, 79
morality, social, 313-14
motivation, 284
multinational firms, 170, 241, 243, 290; *see also* cartels
Myrdal, G., 335, 352

National Pension Insurance Fund, 221
nationalization of industry, 5-6, 62-3, 119, 211, 332
negative externalities, 93-109, 134, 299, 333
negative view of state, 238-9
neo-colonialism, 77
'neo-Marxism,' 41
Netherlands, 47
    investment by, 74; industry in, 57; nationalization in, 62; profits in, 86, 269-70
Nicolaus, M., 327, 352
Nicolin, C., 120-21, 125, 238-9, 352
Nilsson, Gunnar, 283
Nilsson, T., 157, 161, 190, 352
Nisbet, R., 38, 352
Noble, D., 46, 284, 352
Nohrstedt, S. A., 334, 353
Norling, D., 136, 342, 353
Norman, R., 284, 353
Norstedt, J., 53, 351
nuclear power, 170, 173, 200-202, 220, 313-14
numerical strength
    of capital, 153; of working-class, 155-8, 205

O'Connor, J., 119-20, 217
Ohlin, B., 277, 327, 353
Ohlström, B., 163, 353
oil prices, 80, 97
oligopoly, market as, 71-2, 79
Olofsson, G., 343
Olsen, J., 334, 353
Olson Jr., Mancur, 142, 353
Olsson, H., 156, 161, 353
OPEC countries, 80
opinion polls, 194
organizational strength
    of capital, 153; of working-class, 162-6. 207-8
Ovesen, E., 334, 353
Offe, C., 119, 122, 124, 335, 353
organization of working-class, 21, 28, 155-209
ownership of industry, 61-4

Palme, O., 194, 218
Parking, F., 169
Parsons, R. W., 337, 347
Parsons, Talcott, 330
part-time work, 160, 162
'participation', 269; *see also* worker participation
passivity, worker, 297-9
penetration, social, of capitalism, 211-16
pensions, 100-101, 277, 336: *see also* retirement
Petersson, O., 122, 195, 201, 338-40, 353
Pinochet, 123-4
pluralism, 6-8, 274, 277
Poggi, G., 110, 335, 353
political culture, 35-7
political democracy, 274, 308-10
political nature of questions on work, 239-44
political parties, 18, 26, 187-209; *see also* Communist, Conservative; Labour; Liberal: politics: Swedish Social Democrats
political strength, 153, 187-218
political will, 196
politicization of economy, 123-6
politics, 166, 186
    and industry, 18, 26-31; and

unions, 197-8, 204, 223; see also
  political parties
pollution, 19, 93-7, 106-7, 225-6,
  241-4, 333
Popper, K., 123, 129, 326, 337, 353
population explosion, 170
'porosity', of working day, 66
Poulantzas, N., 8, 156, 161, 335, 353
power
  capitalist, 7-8, 23, 210-23; and
  class struggle, 149-52; vulnerability of, 211
predicaments, 35-7, 145-9; see also
  quandary
price leadership, 80
prices, 78-81, 241
private enterprise see capital
private production of negative externalities, 93-106
privatization of social consciousness,
  200
problems
  of capitalism, 11-16, 185; of
  industry, 17-18
problem-solution, definitions of, 11
producer, man as, 144
production
  contradictions in, 13, 39, 46-50,
  291-5; control over, 10; forces of,
  51-8; private, of negative externalities, 93-106; relations, 13, 39,
  46-68, 291; see also industry;
  investment
profit, 298, 303
  controlled, 79-80;
  and crises, 81-2; decisions on,
  230, 234; falling, 46, 85;
  86-8; sharing, 220, 222, 264-72
profitability, 18, 133
progressive liberalism, 19
proletarianization, 206
property see capital
property relations, capitalist, 60-64
Pryor, F. L., 56, 353
pyramid of companies, 55

quandary of mature capitalism,
  126-9; see also predicaments
'quarrels', political, 195

questions on work, political nature
  of, 239-44

recession, 216-17
rehabilitation, vocational, 99-100
relations of production, 13, 39,
  46-68, 291
relationships in enterprise, 224-53
representation see worker
  participation
repression, 123-4
responsibility, business, 58-60
retirement, 100-101; see also
  pensions
revolution, social, 49, 328; see also
  socialist transformation
robotization, 46, 206; see also
  mechanization
Rokkan, S., 7, 150, 333, 352-3
Ronge, V., 124, 353
Rose, A., 142, 353
Rosenberg, B., 37, 329, 347
Ross, A., 344, 353
routinization of work, 157
Runciman, G., 148, 353
Rydén, B., 54-6, 354

SACO, 183-4, 341
SAF see Swedish Employers Confederation
SAP see Swedish Social Democrats
safety, industrial, 197, 227, 233; see
  also work environment
salary see wages
samples of firms, 319-23
Sartori, G., 344, 354
Sarv, H., 52, 354
satisficing, 133-4, 137
saving, 263, 268-72
Scase, R., 169, 180, 354
Scharpf, F. W., 114, 352
Schumpeter, J., 337, 354
scientific socialism, 22
Seeman, M., 135, 354
Segerstedt, T., 175, 177-80, 354
segregated work, 66
self-destruction, market, 53, 69-82,
  295-7
self-regulating market, 120

Semmler, W., 131, 333, 346
separation of labour and capital,
     40-43
service workers, 161-2, 165, 174-86
     passim
Shalev, M., 112, 324-5, 351
shareholders, 230-34, 266, 274, 333;
     see also wage-earners' funds
Shaw, W. H., 37, 49, 60, 64-6,
     330-31, 337, 354
sheltered work, 99-100, 102
Sherman, H. J., 330
Simon, H., 133, 354
simulation, market, 296
size of industrial units, 54-6, 86, 291,
     294
Smith, A., 65, 71
social characters and private
     production of negative
     externalities, 93-106
social consciousness, working-class,
     167-86, 208-9
social costs of industry, 93-109
social democracy, 6-10; *see also*
     Swedish Social Democrats
social exchange theory, 142
social liberalism, 17-22
social morality, 313-14
social penetration of capital, 211-16
social relations of production, 51-68,
     291
social structure and predicaments,
     141-9
social subordination, 157-8
social vulnerability, 56-8
socialism
     anti-, 201; 'creeping', 111;
     definition of, 5-16 *passim*; image
     of, 209, 324-5; rise of, 308-9;
     scientific, 22; 'so-called', 93-7;
     and social liberalism, compared,
     17-22; as threat, 170, 173, 317;
     as wage-earners' funds, 304-7;
     see also Swedish Social Democrats
social transformation *see*
     transformation
socialization (nationalization), 5-6,
     325
socialization

of losses, 248; mechanisms of,
     124; over-, 143-4; of
     reproduction, 53
societal nature of industry, 12-13,
     17-18, 48-9
society *see* affluent; capitalism;
     socialism
sociology, contradiction in, 37-40
Söderpalm, S. A., 239, 354
Södersten, B., 279, 283-5, 295, 303,
     354
Sorokin, P., 37, 329, 354
Soviet Union, 3, 6, 15, 94
Soydan, 151
Spain, 4
speculation, 85; *see also* investment
stage analogy *see* actors
stagflation, 46, 78-80, 114, 216-17;
     see also inflation
Štajner, R., 253, 354
STAMOCAP, 8
state
     and capital, 224-44; function, 5;
     interventionist, 7-8, 19, 110-29,
     230, 241, 243, 248, 279, 294,
     300, 317; and labour, 224-44;
     negative view of, 238-9; as threat,
     170, 173, 225-6; *see also*
     nationalization
statistics, cross-national, 4
Stephens, J. D., 324-5, 354
Stevenson, P., 22, 354
STINCAP, 8
stock companies, 41
street-crossing, art of, 258-61
strength
     of capital, 26-7, 152-4, 210-23,
     251-3; of labour, 26-7, 50, 112,
     152-66, 187-209; political, 153,
     187-218
strikes, 19, 26, 163, 326, 334
structural threat awareness, 183-4;
     see also threats
structural-functionalists, 142-3
structuralist approach to capitalism,
     6-10
structures
     arguments about, 302; market,
     changes in, 69-82; social, 141-9

struggle *see* class
strukturfonder, 198
sub-contracting, 53
subordination, social, 157-8
subsidies, state, 116-19
suffrage, universal, 198
Sundqvist, S., 125
Sundström-Frisk, C., 334, 351
Sunesson, S., 326, 354
surplus value, 38, 41, 330
Sverige, V., 63, 72
Sweden
    Bank of, 248; economic inter-
    dependence in, 51-6; exports, 5,
    29, 217, 334; living standards, 45;
    ownership of industry in, 61-4;
    relationships in industry, 224-53;
    sample firms in, 319-23; socialist
    transformation in, 3, 23-31,
    135-8; *see also* gross national
    product; political parties; Swedish
    Social Democrats; unemploy-
    ment; unions; working-class
Swedish Confederation of Trade
        Unions (LO)
    membership of, 182-4; and
    politics, 204, 219-20, 223, 335
    power of, 197; SAF, 228; and
    wage-earners' funds, 136, 262-3,
    270-71, 282-3; and wage policy,
    293
Swedish Employers Confederation
        (SAF)
    and industry, 238-9, 243; and
    politics, 197, 219, 238-9;
    power of, 282; and salaries, 18;
    split in, 250; and unions, 224,
    227-8, 340
Swedish Social Democrats
    described, 4-10; 308-10; electoral
    defeat, 239, 261. 328; and
    Liberals, 339-40; programme of,
    263; and socialist transformation,
    23-31; support for, 318, 328; and
    working class, 187-209; *see also*
    elections; politics
Swedner, H., 338
Switzerland, 57
symbolic interactionism, 142
systemic power of capital, 133-4,

153-4, 211-19, 260, 336

taxes, 249, 328
TCO *see* Centralist Organization of
    Salaried Employees
technology, 345; *see also*
    mechanization
Thatcher, M., 219
theatre analogy *see* actors
Therborn, G., 39, 142-3, 156, 176,
    325, 330, 343-4, 355
Third World, 74, 77
threats, perception of, 169-76, 183-4,
    209, 224-6, 274, 317
Timasheff, N. S., 329, 355
time and motion studies, 66
Tingsten, H., 24, 113, 344, 355
Tipisev, A. J., 333, 355
tjunsteman, 161
Touraine, A., 143-4, 150, 336, 355
trade cycles, 69, 78
trade unions *see* unions
traffic accidents, 334
training and class, 158-9, 161
transformation, socialist, 3, 23-31,
    131, 135-8, 309, 313, 327
transportation, 52, 97
Trilateral Commission, 113, 119,
    125, 132
af Trolle, U., 78, 86, 112-13, 125,
    151-2, 217, 355
Tronti, M., 343, 355
trust, 218
Turner, R., 144, 355

Udehn, L., 296, 355
Undén, Ö., 61
underconsumption, 81
underdeveloped countries, 74, 77
unemployment
    in capitalist countries, 46-7,
    218-19; and collectivity, 293;
    effects of, 98-104, 334; insurance,
    115; and mechanization, 206; and
    negative externalities, 107-8; and
    prices, 79, 81; and systemic
    power, 218-19; as threat, 170,
    173, 209; in USA, 14, 47, 218;
    youth, 103, 106

unions
  bureaucracy in, 274; and class,
    183-4; development of, 40, 43-5;
    discipline in, 341; influence on
    enterprises, 224-5, 230-9, 245-51;
    and legislation, 197-8; militancy, 18;
    and politics, 197-8, 204, 223;
    strength of, 162-6; in USA, 281;
    and wage policy, 222; and worker
    age, 336-7; and worker participa-
    tion, 135-6, 204, 270-71, 287;
    see also Centralist Organization
    of Salaried Employees; Swedish
    Confederation of Trade Unions
United Kingdom, 4; *see also* Great
    Britain
United States
  class in, 325; industry in, 55-6;
    and investment, 74-5; market
    forces in, 222; and Marx, 329;
    and politics, 191; prices in, 79;
    and profit, 86, 88; socialism in,
    326; and Sweden, 324-5;
    unemployment in, 14, 47, 218;
    unions in, 281; urban problems
    in, 14; *see also* Boston Consulting
    Group
unity of command, 259-60
unity, class, lack of, 8
urban problems, 14, 173
USSR, 296
utility, marginal, 141-2
utopians, 128-9

vacations, 18
value, surplus, 41, 330
Vietnam, 3
viljenriktning, 196
'voice', 306
VPK *see* Communist Party
vulnerability of power, 211
vulnerability, social, 56-8

Wachtel, H., 46, 78-80, 355
Wadensjo, E., 328, 350
wage
    drift, 293; increased, 18, 83-4;
    influence of, 241-3; low, 65, 81;
    policy, 222, 264, 274, 282,
    292-3; restraint, 134, 262;
    struggle, 149-50
wage-earners' funds, 136, 207,
    230-3, 257-72
    objections to, 273-88; and
    contradictions of mature capital-
    ism, 289-307
Waldenstrom, E., 342, 355
wants, concept of, 142
Watanuki, J., 113, 125, 348
weakness, subjective sources of,
    245-53
Weber, M., 42, 142, 355
welfare benefits, 18, 115, 122, 324-5
welfare capitalism, quandary of,
    126-9, 198-9, 299-300
white-collar workers, 11, 157-61,
    172-86 *passim*, 206, 220
Wibe, S., 46, 54, 72-3, 81-2, 86, 355
Wildgren, J., 338, 355
Wigforss, E., 61, 270, 326, 344, 355
Wiking-Faria, P., 119, 355
Wilensky, H., 4, 324, 355-6
will, political, 196
Wolfe, A., 335, 356
women, 160, 162, 188, 321, 338
Wood, R. C., 111, 356
work
    accidents at, 104-6, 108, 334;
    attitudes to, 168-9; disease at,
    104-6; environment, 27, 84,
    159-62, 170, 173, 183-4, 197,
    227, 230-31, 233, 322; part-time,
    160, 162; questions on, 239-44;
    relations, 64-8; routinization of,
    157; segregated, 66; sheltered,
    99-100, 102; *see also* labour
workers
    age, 336-7, participation of,
    134-7, 196-7, 204, 224; passivity
    of, 297-9; service, 161-2, 165,
    174-86 *passim*; *see also* industry;
    labour; management; middle
    strata; wage-earners' funds
Workers Co-determination Act
    (MBL), 207
working-class, 151
    extended, 158-86; *Gemeinschaft*,
    179-82, 191; organization of, 21,

28. 155-209; social consciousness
of, 167-86, 208-9; strength of,
26-7, 30, 112, 152-66, 187-209;
see also class; unions
Wright, E. O., 6, 82, 115, 156-7, 162,
181, 325, 335, 348, 356
Wrong, D., 143, 356

youth unemployment, 103, 106
Yugoslavia, 14-15, 57, 294, 327, 340

Zawadski, B., 334, 356
Zeitlin, I., 329, 356
Zenith, 338-9
Zetterberg, H., 168, 341, 356

Åberg, R., 338, 356
Åsard, E., 342, 356
Åsling, N., 220-23, 286, 343, 356

Öhman, B., 101-2, 356
Östlind, A., 99, 101-2, 356